Social Foundations of Judaism

EDITORS

Calvin Goldscheider

Brown University

Jacob Neusner

The Institute for Advanced Study
Brown University

Wipf & Stock
PUBLISHERS
Eugene, Oregon

Wipf and Stock Publishers
199 W 8th Ave, Suite 3
Eugene, OR 97401

Social Foundations of Judaism
By Goldscheider, Calvin and Neusner, Jacob

ISBN: 1-59244-943-3
Publication date 10/14/2004
Previously published by Prentice-Hall, Inc., 1990

For Ben Halpern, Brandeis University

The intellectual father of contemporary
social science in Jewish studies

Contents

PART II
THE AGE OF DIVERSITY: JUDAISMS AND MODERNIZATION, 1789–

PART III

Toward the Twenty-first Century: Contemporary Judaisms in America and in the State of Israel

Preface

Religion is something that people do together to accomplish shared goals. Hence religion is a social fact, and the artifacts of religion—texts, drawings, dances, and music, for example—form components of a shared, therefore a social, system. We address the social foundations of religion because religion encompasses a shared world-view, explains a shared way of life, identifies the social entity of those who realize the way of life and live by the world-view. Accordingly, religion forms the integrating power that makes a single statement out of a society's culture, family structure, social order, philosophy, politics, and economics, a single cogent statement formed as much out of the individual's life cycle as through the communal calendar that distinguishes one season from another and marks a day as holy. The stakes in studying the social foundations of religion are high. This is an anthology, formed of a single case, about the relationship between religion and society, between ideas and attitudes that people hold and the social world that they form together and in which they live.

This anthology presents examples of how, in the case of Judaism, religion relates to society; that is, how the various Judaisms that Jews have brought into being have described, analyzed, and interpreted the social world in which, in their minds and imaginations, they lived. We mean to illustrate the ways in which a religion, exemplified by a Judaism, conceives humanity to organize itself, the structures of society and the divisions of the social order, the tasks of the group and the responsibilities of the family and the individual within the larger group.

These social issues find resolution in a religion's theory of the whole and of the parts within the whole. Accordingly, it is that theory of the whole which focuses our attention and demands our sustained inquiry, if we propose to explain to ourselves the social order of civilization. And, prior to our own day and now too except only in some limited circumstances, it was and is religion which has presented that theory of the whole. If we want to grasp all together and all at once an account of all the world, the group within the world, the family within the group, the individual within the family—that theory which has situated everything and everyone in its proper place—we turn to religion.

This anthology attempts to bring together in one volume research drawn from both the humanities and the social sciences in the study of Judaism and in the study of Judaisms in various contexts over time. The first editor is a sociologist; the second, a historian of religion. We have found productive and stimulating the ongoing conversation between our respective disciplines as we have carried on that conversation, and we see in the union of the social study of religion and the religious study of religion a promising approach to what we conceive to be a protean force in human affairs. If this textbook anthology serves its purpose, then the study of the social foundations of religion will address other important religious traditions and other interesting societies, leading to the comparative study of religion and society that presently is somewhat inaccessible and not well documented.

Our selections cover the classical and modern periods in the history of Jews and Judaism. We have gathered illustrations from a wide range of publications, focusing on the content and contexts of Judaism. In the first section, we introduce the major theoretical themes in the study of Judaism in classical and modern times. We discuss what the content of Judaism is and how Judaisms are studied in context.

Our first group of selections focuses on the formative age of Judaism (500 B.C. to A.D. 640), starting with the Judaisms of the Pentateuch and the Mishnah. That is the age in which the main lines of Judaism that predominated, the Judaism set forth in the Mishnah and developed in the Talmuds and later writings in a long, continuous age of unfolding, took shape. We then turn to the unfolding history of that same Judaism in classical times (640 to 1789), presenting selections that review mysticism and the interplay of economics and Judaism in medieval Judaism. In these papers we ask for examples of how the interplay between religious conviction and social context is laid out. The papers by Ivan Marcus and Raphael Mahler present diverse conceptions, one focused upon ideas, the other on the interplay between social class and economic interest, a non-Marxist and a rigorously Marxist approach, respectively.

Part Two deals with the diversity of Judaisms in the transformation of the Jews from the late eighteenth century to the present. We begin with an overview of the Judaic reformation in the context of political and social changes within European modernization. We also offer several illustrations of new Judaisms forming in America, Reform Judaism, and Zionism in Europe. Our interest is in tracing the unfolding of religious systems in the setting of social and political change.

Our final group of selections moves us toward the twenty-first century in the United States and in the state of Israel, the two places in which the most Jews live and in which the religious worlds of Judaism (or, as we prefer, "Judaisms") unfold. We have included selections on the emergence of new forms of religious denominations among Jews in America as well as their new civil religion. Ethnic forms of Jewish expression and synagogue social life are reviewed. In all of these aspects we pursue the same question concerning how religion derives from but also imposes its shape upon the social order.

Several selections are included on Judaisms in Israel, including the social foundations of Israeli Judaism, the development of Conservative and Reform Judaism in the state of Israel, and the emerging forms of Zionist Judaism. Together these selections reflect some of the most important research on Judaisms in context as they have emerged over the centuries.

CALVIN GOLDSCHEIDER

JACOB NEUSNER

Acknowledgments

The editors acknowledge with thanks the thoughtful comments provided by William Scott Green, University of Rochester, and John F. Wilson, Princeton University. We also gratefully acknowledge permission to reprint the following copyrighted materials:

Chapter One
RELIGION AND SOCIETY IN THE FORMATION OF THE JUDAISM OF THE PENTATEUCH

Jacob Neusner, *Self-Fulfilling Prophecy: Exile and Return in the History of Judaism* (Boston, 1987: Beacon Press). © 1987 by Jacob Neusner. Reprinted by permission of Beacon Press.

Chapter Two
RELIGION AND SOCIETY IN THE LAW OF THE MISHNAH

Jacob Neusner, *Major Trends in Formative Judaism. Third Series. The Three Stages in the Formation of Judaism* (Chicago, 1985: Scholars Press for Brown Judaic Studies), pp. 37–68. © 1985 Brown University. Reprinted by permission.

Chapter Three
THE SOCIAL FOUNDATIONS OF MEDIEVAL MYSTICISM IN JUDAISM

Ivan Marcus, *Piety and Society. The Jewish Pietists of Medieval Germany* (Leiden, Netherlands, 1981: E.J. Brill), pp. 1–2, 11–17, 59–65, 71–75. © 1981 by E.J. Brill. Reprinted by permission of the publisher and author.

Chapter Four
RELIGION AND ECONOMICS IN MEDIEVAL JUDAISM

Jacob Katz, *Tradition and Crisis: Jewish Society at the End of the Middle Ages* (New York, 1961: The Free Press) pp. 64–75. © 1961 by The Free Press. Reprinted with permission of The Free Press, a division of MacMillan, Inc.

Chapter Five
A MARXIST VIEW OF HASSIDISM

Raphael Mahler, *A History of Modern Jewry, 1780–1815* (New York, 1971: Schocken Books), pp. 430–439, 446–454. © 1971 by Raphael Mahler. Reprinted by permission of Pantheon Books, a division of Random House, Inc.

Chapter Six
THE JUDAIC REFORMATION AS A SOCIOPOLITICAL PROCESS

Calvin Goldscheider and Alan Zuckerman, *The Transformation of the Jews* (Chicago, 1984: University of Chicago Press), pp. 63–75. © 1984 The University of Chicago. Reprinted by permission of The University of Chicago. All rights reserved.

Chapter Seven
THE RISE AND RECEPTION OF ZIONISM IN THE NINETEENTH CENTURY

Ben Halpern, *The Idea of the Jewish State*, 2nd ed. (Cambridge, Mass., 1969: Harvard University Press), pp. 55–68, 69–71, 72–78, 81–84. © 1969 by The President and Fellows of Harvard College. Reprinted by permission of Harvard University Press.

Chapter Eight
JUDAISM IN AMERICA: THE SOCIAL CRISIS OF FREEDOM

Jacob Neusner, *Israel in America. A Too-Comfortable Exile?* (Boston, 1985: Beacon Press), pp. 1–44. © 1985 by Beacon Press. Reprinted by permission of Beacon Press.

Chapter Nine
RELIGION AND ETHNICITY IN THE AMERICAN JEWISH COMMUNITY

Marshall Sklare, "Religion and Ethnicity in the American Jewish Community: Changing Aspects of Reform, Conservative and Orthodox Judaism," in Jacob Katz (ed.), *The Role of Religion in Modern Jewish History,* (Cambridge, Mass., 1975: Association of Jewish Studies), pp. 147–59. © 1975 by Association of Jewish Studies. Reprinted by permission of Association of Jewish Studies.

Chapter Ten
CIVIL RELIGION AND THE MODERN JEWISH CHALLENGE

Jonathan Woocher, "Civil Religion and the Modern Jewish Challenge," in Jonathan Woocher, *Sacred Survival: The Civil Religion of American Jews* (Bloomington, In., 1986: Indiana University Press), pp. 1–21. © 1986 by Indiana University Press. Reprinted by permission of Indiana University Press.

Chapter Eleven
THE SYNAGOGUE IN AMERICA

Samuel Heilman, "Synagogue Life as a House of Study," in Samuel Heilman, *Synagogue Life: A Study of Symbolic Interaction* (Chicago, 1976: The University of Chicago Press), pp. 221–51. © 1976 by The University of Chicago. Reprinted by permission of The University of Chicago.

Chapter Twelve
ETHNICITY, AMERICAN JUDAISM, AND JEWISH COHESION

Calvin Goldscheider, "Ethnicity and Religion in American Judaism" in C. Goldscheider, *Jewish Continuity and Change* (Bloomington, In., 1986: Indiana University Press), pp. 151–171, 181–184. © 1986 by Indiana University Press. Reprinted by permission of Indiana University Press.

Chapter Thirteen
THE SOCIAL FOUNDATIONS OF ISRAELI JUDAISM

Shlomo Deshen, "Israeli Judaism," *International Journal of Middle Eastern Studies,* Volume 9 (1978), pp. 141–69. © 1978 by Cambridge University Press. Reprinted by permission.

Chapter Fourteen
REFORM AND CONSERVATIVE JUDAISM IN ISRAEL

Ephraim Tabory, "Reform and Conservative Judaism in Israel: A Social and Religious Profile," *American Jewish Year Book,* 1983 (New York & Philadelphia, 1982: American Jewish Committee and Jewish Publication Society of America), pp. 41–61. © 1982 by American Jewish Committee and the Jewish Publication Society of America. Reprinted by permission.

Chapter Fifteen
FROM RELIGIOUS ZIONISM TO ZIONIST RELIGION

Gideon Aran, "From Religious Zionism to Zionist Religion: The Roots of Gush Emunim," in *Studies in Contemporary Jewry*, 1986, 2: 116–143. © 1986 by Indiana University Press.

Introduction

The Social Foundations of Judaism in Classical and Modern Times

From Content to Context

RELIGION AND CIVILIZATION

Religion is important because the story of civilization is written by religion, which so forms attitudes and viewpoints as to move nations, societies, and communities to act in one way as opposed to another. What people believe God wants of them, approves or disapproves, rewards or punishes, tells them how to live and what to do together. Whether the consequent deeds are private and individual or public and social, Heaven's dictates inform and enthuse humanity in society. Because, moreover, the social world forms the matrix for the individual and family, it is the power of religion to define and inform society that matters in framing the story of civilization. Society endures, social continuities defining the range of choice for individual and family alike. Accordingly, if we propose to describe religion, to analyze its traits and effects, and to interpret its character as a formative force in civilization, we ask about the social world framed and formed by religion. At stake in the answer is the understanding of how humanity forms society, creates culture, sustains civilization. That understanding comes to us when we grasp the way religion informs society, frames the possibilities of culture, and defines what it means to live in civilization.

The whole, then, has held together, and now holds together, in a great many societies by reason of the social imagination of religion. We need hardly point to the power of religion in the social order of whole nations, East and West alike, or to the capacity of religion to destroy the social order in countries as disparate as Ireland and Iran. Religion as a social force comprises an act of shared imagination concerning the social world. Seen as a formative and definitive structure, religion encompasses three components and holds all three together: ethos, ethics, and ethnos. That is to say, religion is made up of the mentality, the world-view—above all, the world-defining view—that religion sets forth to link Heaven to Earth and holds all together and all at once, in proper balance, proportion, and composition, all things that live or have ever lived in the here and now of the social world we know. True, that forms no small claim for religion, but it is a claim well substantiated in the history of religion and in the contemporary sociology and politics of religion too. Accordingly, to make sense of civilization as humanity has known it for the brief moment in which humanity has formed the consciousness to want to know itself, religion takes center stage. Its sense of things, its explanations, its modes of sorting things out and placing all things into perspective—these acts of imagination define and dictate the traits of those social worlds that have endured over time.

In trying to make sense of civilization we propose to ask ourselves how religion forms and informs social worlds. But the answer comes from the study of psychology, history, philosophy, sociology, and anthropology, the principal intellectual tools at our disposal in the study of religion, as well as from the study of religion as a world-defining force and fact. The social scientific and humanistic orientations to the study of religion treat the subject matter of religion as an independent variable. The question of civilization as now framed requires answers from the facts of society but also from the fantasies of humanity imagining, thinking, wondering. Out of the results of both the social order and the imaginative life come the attitudes and viewpoints that impart shape and structure to the social life. Because people believe things, they do things, define their lives and give them up, for instance. True, we may describe a society by appeal to diverse indicative traits. But if we hope to make sense of that society and explain what holds it together, imparts purpose and cogency to the whole, gives to the parts that symmetry and balance, composition and order, that makes society social and enduring, we must interrelate the facts of sociology and the fantasies of faith.

In the intersection of the social world and the realm of imagination we find the (to the outsider) nonsense that (to the engaged person) makes sense of the this and the that of everyday social life. We claim that religion stands in conjunction with, not over or separate from, the social world that appeals to religion. Religion sets forth the account and explanation for how things are and ought to be: what God wants. Explaining the parts and making them whole and coherent, religion then stands for the power of imagination to account for reality. And, as everyone knows, the inner eye shapes vision, and imagination dictates how history is made and how people make their lives.

The Study of Religion

Wanting to know how and why the story of civilization is written by religion, we naturally find our way to the study of religion. And what, in religion, we want to investigate is the power of religion to form attitudes and viewpoints so as to move nations and societies to act as they do—however that is. But when we take up the systematic study of religion, we find ourselves bound by the limitations of the sorts of evidence to which, over time and in the present, we gain access. The evidence concerns not religion but religions. Religion, after all, does not exist in abstract form except in the imagination of the academic scholar of religion. Religion in the world exists only as religions, one by one. We then propose to generalize about religion out of the data of religions. And religions moreover testify to their qualities not in generalities but in concrete kinds of evidence. Religions speak through diverse media, for diverse purposes, to diverse issues. Religions in the here and now come to concrete expression in many ways. To study one religion or a set of religions, we require knowledge of philosophy; to investigate another, we need to know the possibilities of the theater; a third will require us to know about visual arts; a fourth, about music; a fifth, about dance; a sixth, about storytelling. As many as there are religions, so many are the modes of paramount expression, hence the types of evidence, that demand analysis. This anthology collects articles on a single religious world, Judaism, in only a few of its religious systems, Judaisms. The articles are meant to exemplify the broader issues at hand and to provide stimuli for thinking about diverse religions, makers of varied worlds. Judaisms provide examples, and, within the long history of Judaisms, we have chosen only a few instances of the interplay between content and context in setting forth cases of the social foundations of Judaism in classical and modern times.

The System of Judaism

Before proceeding, let us now offer definitions for terms that have already made their appearance. In all that follows, two usages predominate: first "system," then "religious" or "Judaic" system. By "system," we refer to three things that are one, ethos, ethics, and ethnos

1. Ethos: a world-view, which by reference to the intersection of the supernatural and the natural worlds accounts for how things are and puts them together into a cogent and harmonious picture.
2. Ethics: a way of life, which expresses in concrete actions the world-view and which is explained by that world-view.
3. Ethnos: a social group, for which the world-view accounts, which is defined in concrete terms by the way of life, and therefore which gives expression in the everyday world to the world-view and is defined as an entity by that way of life.

A religious system is one that appeals to God as the principal power. A Judaic system is a religious system—ethos, ethics, ethnos—that identifies the Hebrew Scriptures or "Old Testament" as the principal component of its canon and appeals to those writings for authority. A Judaism, then, comprises not merely a theory—a book or a set of ideas or ideology or theology—distinct from social reality. A Judaism is an explanation for the group (*an* "Israel") that gives social form to the system and an account of the distinctive way of life of that group. A Judaism—that is, a Judaic system—derives from and focuses upon a social entity, a group of Jews who (in their minds, at least) constitute not *an* Israel but *Israel*. How Judaisms relate to the social circumstances of Jews, then, forms the problem of this anthology.

What makes the study of the interplay of context and content interesting is the quest for the points of interrelationship and connection. A religious system holds together on its own and at the same time holds in cogent balance the society that understands itself by appeal to that system. But how to find a way of holding together the three components of a religious system—ethos, ethics, ethnos? What serves is a hypothesis that reads these components as elements of an answer to a question. If we can propose a single encompassing statement that constitutes the system's recurrent message and judgment, then we can claim to formulate a theory of the answer to the question of cogency and coherence, both for the system and for the society that the system represents. From that knowledge we can make a good guess at the question to which the answer responds. So, in studying the interplay of religion and society we aim to formulate indirectly and by inference a theory on the description of the system—ethos, ethics, social entity—and the analysis of that system—urgent question, compelling answer.

Religion is often adduced as an explanation of why a social system sustains itself. We see the issue of why a system originates and survives, if it does, or fails, if it does, by itself as not pertinent to the analysis of a system. A system on its own is like a language. A language forms an example of language if it produces communication through rules of syntax and verbal arrangement. That paradigm serves full well however many people speak the language, or however long the language serves. Two people who understand each other form a language community, even, or especially, if no one else understands them. So too by definition religions address the living, constitute societies, frame and compose cultures. For however long, at whatever moment in historic time, a religious system always grows up in the perpetual present, an artifact of its day, whether today or a long-ago time. The only appropriate tense for a religious system is the present. A religious system always *is*, whatever it was, whatever it will be. Why so? Because its traits address a condition of humanity in society, a circumstance of an hour—however brief or protracted the hour and the circumstance.

When we ask that a religious composition speak to a society with a message of the *is* and the *ought* and with a meaning for the everyday, we focus on the power of that system to hold the whole together: the society the system addresses, the individuals who compose the society, the ordinary lives they lead, in ascending order of consequence. And that system then forms a whole and well-composed structure. The structure stands somewhere, and, indeed, the place where it stands will secure for the system either an extended or an ephemeral span of life. But the system, for however long it lasts, serves. And that focus on the external present justifies our interest in analyzing why a system works (the urgent agenda of issues it successfully solves for those for whom it solves those problems) when it does, and why it ceases to work (loses self-evidence, is bereft of its "Israel," for example) when it no longer functions. The phrase, the *history* of a *system*, presents us with an oxymoron. Systems endure in that eternal present that they create. They evoke precedent, but they do not have a history. A system relates to context but, as we have stressed, exists in an enduring moment (which, to be sure, changes all the time). We capture the system in a moment, the worm consumes it an hour later. That is the way of mortality, whether for us one by one, in all mortality, or for the works of humanity in society. But systemic analysis and interpretation requires us to ask questions of history and comparison, not merely description of structure and cogency. So in this exercise we undertake first description (that is, the text), then analysis (that is, the context), and finally, interpretation (that is, the matrix), in which a system has its being. That explains one of the basic methods of this anthology. We present successive examples of systems, past and present, as these illustrate the question we have taken as primary: the interplay of systems and circumstances. By this we mean the discovery of how an urgent question finds its self-evidently valid answer and generates a Judaism. We do not give a continuous history of Judaism in the Jew's society, but examples of Judaisms in societies of Jews.

The Ecology of a Judaism

What is at stake in this reading of religion, in the case of a Judaism, as the statement of a society's fundamental system? The answer to that question brings us to the ecology of a Judaism. What we propose to exemplify is how to investigate, through the case of a Judaism, what we call the ecology of religion—that is, the interplay between a religious system and the social world that gives to that system its shape and meaning. When we understand a religious system in the context of the social order, we grasp whatever in this world we are likely to understand about religion in the shaping of the civilization of humanity. And no other generative force in civilization has exceeded in power and effect the formative force of religion. Accordingly, in this method we have meant to exemplify in a very particular setting the larger problem of how to relate the content of a religion to its context, social culture to religious conviction, above all, social change (which is public and general) to symbol change (which is particular and invariably distinctive to its setting). The study of the ecology of religion is, therefore, whether and how religion forms an independent variable in the shaping of civilization.

We draw upon a metaphor from the natural and social sciences for the study of religion. Our inquiry concerns whether, in the analysis of the interrelated components of civilization, religion constitutes a singular constituent of the whole. Ecology is a branch of science concerned with the interrelationships of organisms and their environments. By "ecology of" we mean the study of the interrelationship between a particular religious way of viewing the world and living life, and the historical, cultural, social, economic, and especially political situation of the people who view the world and live life in accord with the teachings of their religion. That Jews have formed ongoing groups, existing over time in various places, and hence describing, analyzing, and interpreting in context a Judaism, does not conclude the work of studying the ecology of Judaism as exemplar of the ecology of religion. An ongoing social entity, after all, yields more than a single system, but the ecology of the social entity in its indicative traits requires attention not only for its change but also for its enduring qualities.

But what can we say of the ecology of not a Judaism but of Judaism, now meaning *all* Judaisms? We see two fundamental traits to that ecology, one social and political, the other religious and fundamentally autonomous, of the material realities of society altogether. In so stating, we lay down our claim that religion constitutes an independent variable in the study of society and culture.

The former fact of the ecosystem encompassing all Judaisms—the politics that will affect all Judaisms—is readily identified. There are some facts that affect all Jews and that will define the realities addressed by any "Israel," that is to say, the social entity formed of any group of Jews. We point not to what is "essentially Jewish," terms that bear no clear meaning to us, but only to what is, as a matter of social reality, a fact of existence for all Jews. The Jewish people form a very small group, spread over many countries. One fact of their natural environment is that they form a distinct group in diverse societies and have been so over time.

A second is that they constitute solely a community of fate and, for many, of faith, in that they have few shared social or cultural traits.

A third is that they do not form a single political entity.

A fourth is that they look back upon a very long and in some way exceptionally painful history.

A world-view suited to the Jews' social ecology must make sense of their unimportance and explain their importance. It must define an ethos that will sustain and not only explain the continuing life of the group and persuade people that their forming a distinct and distinctive community is important and worth carrying on. The interplay between the political, social, and historical life of the Jews and their conceptions of themselves in this world and the next—that is, their world-view, contained in their canon, their way of life, explained by the teleology of the system, and the symbolic structure that encompasses the two and stands for the whole all at once and all together—these define the focus for the inquiry into the political side of the ecology of the religion at hand, that is, the ecology of Judaism.

The Religious Component of All Judaisms

What about the religious component of the ecology of Judaism? If we claim that when we study religion, we deal with what is among the most important forces in the formation of the life of civilization, we have also to ask about the religious component of the enduring ecology of the social entity. What we want to know about religion, as exemplified by the ecology of Judaism, therefore, is how religion forms an uncontingent force in society and politics and what is the nature of the religious system *per se*. In asking about the political and social problem addressed by matters of belief, we do not treat religion as merely instrumental, that is, as a way of saying something else altogether. The fundamental allegation of our method is that religion stands at the center of the world of humanity in society.

In part, we claim that when we study the ecology of religion, we study written evidence about how through religious systems—ethos, ethics, ethnos—humanity in society responded to challenge and change, mediated between the received tradition of politics and social life and the crisis of the age and circumstance. Religion is not trivial, not private, not individual, not simply a matter of the heart. Religion is public, political, social, economic. The religious component of the ecosystem in which a Judaism finds its place derives from the fundamental and generative religious structure to which all Judaisms have conformed, a religious structure that persists and applies ubiquitously because, under diverse circumstances, that deep structure shaping all Judaisms precipitates a crisis and also resolves that crisis.

Every Judaism finds its indicative trait as a Judaism in its appeal to a single scripture, the Pentateuch in particular. That is not to suggest there is an "essential" Judaism that occurs everywhere and that defines what we mean by (a, or any) Judaism; it is to claim that there is a recapitulated paradigm, a pattern that every Judaism turns out to recapitulate. And the reason, so we maintain, is that the social world of every group of Jews sets forth a set of facts that require explanation and interpretation. Not only so, but every group of Jews appeals to a common Scripture, one that creates a set of explanations and interpretations known in advance, so to speak; these constitute that paradigm. The paradigm then works because it imposes upon social facts a received pattern, a set of expectations and anticipations. That pattern, we shall propose, involves the creation of resentment and also the remission of resentment, and every Judaism recapitulates a single pattern of resentment and remission.

For reasons that pertain to its very structuring of the consciousness of all Israels in relationship to their diverse circumstances, the Pentateuch forms the other ecosystem for a Judaism. Accordingly, we have now to take account of the ongoing, inherited realities that frame any given Judaic system and that invariably for all Judaisms define the setting for the systemic authorship that produces the writings. A religious system—for example, a Judaism seen as a subset of Judaism—takes a place within a larger set of affined religious systems. In the present context, *a* Judaism can be shown to relate to prior Judaisms, all Judaisms forming a diachronic fact, one framed by matters of attitude and conviction, as much as (for a given moment) a synchronic fact. True enough, there is not now, and never has been, a single Judaism. There have been only Judaisms, each with its distinctive system and new beginning, all resorting to available antecedents and claiming they are precedents, but in fact none with a history prior to its birth. Each system begins on its own, in response to a circumstance that strikes people as urgent and a question they find ineluctable. But all Judaisms not only address a single social-ecological system, that of the Jews.

The Pentateuch, the Five Books of Moses, framed out of inherited materials, sets forth certain attitudes and viewpoints that would define for all Judaisms to follow a single structure of experience and expectation. And that structure stood independent of the social and political facts of any given group of Jews to whom, and for whom, a Judaism was meant to speak. Accordingly, while we identify one ecosystem of the religion, Judaism, as social and political, the other, in our view, must be classified as religious: the religious ecosystem for a religion, a Judaism. All Judaisms have addressed resentments in their respective "Israels," and these resentments are precipitated by the Pentateuchal theory of its "Israel," that is, the social entity of the Pentateuchal Judaism, and the concomitant world-view and way of life of that same system. All Judaisms have not only dealt with, but also have resolved, those resentments. All Judaisms in one way or another sorted out whatever social experience their "Israels" proposed to explain by appeal to the tension of exile and the remission of return, and Judaisms in general appeal to the fixed paradigm of Israel's exile and return. That singular and indicative appeal formed an ecological fact for all Judaisms, as much as the Jews' minority status and utopian situation defined issues to be addressed by any Judaism.

Exile and Return in Judaism

To repeat, we propose not an essentialist but a recapitulative definition, and that brings us to the experience that is imposed by the paradigm. In the selections that follow, we see a variety of recapitulations of the paradigm, in the formative history of Judaism in Part One, in the formation of a civil religion of Holocaust and Redemption ("exile" and "return" in cosmic dimensions) in Part Two and in the replay of the paradigm through Zionism and the state of Israel in Part Three. But the original reading of the Jews' existence as exile and return derives from the Pentateuch, which was composed as we now have them (out of earlier materials, to be sure) in the aftermath of the destruction of the Temple in 586 B.C. and in response to the exile to Babylonia. The experience selected and addressed by the authorship of the document is that of exile and restoration. The framing of events into the pattern at hand represents an act of powerful imagination and interpretation. It is an experience that is invented, because no one person or group both went into "exile" and also "returned home." Diverse experiences have been sorted out, various persons have been chosen, and the whole has been worked into a system by those who selected history out of happenings and models out of masses of persons. Since no Jews after 586 B.C. actually experienced what in the aggregate Scripture says happened, the materials within Scripture were "selected." Since Scripture does not record a particular person's experience, it is not autobiographical; writing for society at large the personal insight of a singular figure is also not an account of a whole nation's story. Many Jews in the Judea of 586 B.C. never left. And, as is well known, a great many of those who ended up in Babylonia stayed there. Only a minority went back to Jerusalem. Consequently, the story of exile and return to Zion encompasses what happened to only a select number of families, who identified themselves as part of the family of Abraham, Isaac, and Jacob, and their genealogy as the history of Israel. Those families that stayed and those that never came back would have told as normative and paradigmatic a different tale altogether had they written the Torah.

The experiences of the few that formed the paradigm for Israel beyond the restoration taught as normative lessons that in fact generated profound alienation.

Let us state with emphasis the lessons people claimed to learn out of the events they had chosen for their history: *the life of the group is uncertain, subject to conditions and stipulations.* Nothing is set and given, all things a gift: land and life itself. But what actually did happen in that uncertain world—exile but then restoration—marked the group as special, different, select. There were other ways of seeing things, and the Pentateuchal picture was no more compelling than any other. Those Jews who did not go into exile, and those who did not "come home," had no reason to take the view of matters that characterized the authorship of Scripture. The life of the group need not have appeared more uncertain, more subject to contingency and stipulation, than the life of any other group. The land did not require the vision that imparted to it the enchantment, the personality, that, in Scripture, it received: "The land will vomit you out as it did those who were here before you." And the adventitious circumstance of Iranian imperial policy—a political happenstance—did not have to be recast into return. So nothing in the system of Scripture—exile for reason, return as redemption—followed necessarily and logically. Everything was invented: interpreted.

The uncertainty of the life of the group in the century or so from the destruction of the First Temple of Jerusalem by the Babylonians to the building of the Second Temple of Jerusalem by the Jews, with Persian permission and sponsorship returned from exile, formed the paradigm. With the promulgation of the "Torah of Moses" under the sponsorship of Ezra, the Persians' viceroy, at ca. 450 B.C., all future Israels would then refer to that formative experience as it had been set down and preserved as the norm for Israel in the mythic terms of that "original" Israel. The Israel was not of Genesis and Sinai and the end of the moment of entry into the promised land, but the "Israel" of the families that recorded as the rule and the norm the story of both the exile and the return. In that minority genealogy, that story of exile and return, alienation and remission, imposed on the received stories of pre-exilic Israel and adumbrated time and again in the Five Books of Moses and addressed by the framers of that document in their work over all, we find that paradigmatic statement in which every Judaism, from then to now, found its structure and deep syntax of social existence, the grammar of its intelligible message.

In theological terms, that experience rehearsed the conditional moral existence of sin and punishment, suffering and atonement and reconciliation, and, in social terms, the uncertain and always conditional national destiny of disintegration and renewal of the group. That moment captured within the Five Books of Moses—that is to say, the judgment of the generation of the return to Zion, led by Ezra, about its extraordinary experience of exile and return—would inform the attitude and viewpoint of all the Judaisms and all the Israels beyond. Accordingly, we identify as a fact of the diachronic ecology of all Judaisms that generative and definitive moment precisely as all Judaisms have done, that is, by looking into that same Scripture. All Judaisms identify the Torah or the Five Books of Moses as the written-down statement of God's will for Israel, the Jewish people (which, as a matter of fact, every Judaism also identifies as its own social group). We suppose that on the surface, we should specify that formative and definitive moment, recapitulated by all Judaisms, with the story of Creation down to Abraham and the beginning of his family, the children of Abraham, Isaac and Jacob. Or perhaps we are advised to make our way to Sinai and hold that that original point of definition descends from Heaven. But allowing ourselves merely to retell the story deprives us of the required insight. Recapitulating the story of the religion does not help us understand the religion. Identifying the point of origin of the story, by contrast, does. For the story tells not what happened on the occasion to which the story refers (the creation of the world, for instance) but how (long afterward and for their own reasons) people want to portray themselves. The tale therefore recapitulates that resentment, that obsessive and troubling point of origin, that the group wishes to explain, transcend, transform.

Every Judaism found as its task the recapitulation of the original Judaism: exile and return, resentment of circumstance and reconciliation with the human condition of a given "Israel." Each made its own distinctive statement of the generative and critical resentment contained within that questioning of the given, that deep understanding of the uncertain character of the existence of the group in its normal location and under circumstances of permanence that (so far as the Judaic group understood things) characterized the life of every other group but Israel. What for everyone else (so it seemed to the Judaisms addressed to the Israels through time) was a given, for Israel was a gift. What all the nations knew as how things *must* be Israel understood as how things *might not be:* exile and loss, alienation and resentment, but, instead of annihilation, renewal, restoration, reconciliation, and (in theological language) redemption. That pattern, permanently inscribed in the Torah of God to Moses at Sinai, would define for all Israels over all time that matter of resentment demanding recapitulation: leaving home, coming home. What is that one systemic trait that marks all Judaisms and sets them apart from all other religious systems, viewed jointly and severally? The religious ecology of Judaisms is dictated by that perpetual asking of the question Who are we? That trait of self-consciousness, that incapacity to accept the group as a given and its data—way of life, world-view, constituting the world of an Israel, a Jewish people, in the here and now—is the one thing that draws together Judaisms from beginning to end. Jews' persistent passion for self-definition characterizes all of the Judaisms they have made for themselves. What others take as the given, the Jews perceive as the received, the special, the extraordinary. And that perception of the remarkable character of what to other groups is the absolute datum of all being requires explanation.

Since the formative pattern imposed that perpetual, self-conscious uncertainty, treating the life of the group as conditional and discontinuous, Jews have asked themselves who they are and invented Judaisms to answer that question. Accordingly, no circumstances have permitted Jews to take for granted their existence as a group. Looking back on Scripture and its message, Jews have ordinarily treated as special, subject to conditions and therefore uncertain, what (in their view) other groups enjoyed as unconditional and simply given. Why the paradigm renewed itself is clear: This particular view of matters generated expectations that could not be met and hence created resentment—and then provided comfort and hope that made possible coping with that resentment. Specifically, each Judaism retells in its own way and with its distinctive emphases the tale of the Torah, the story of a non-people that becomes a people, that has what it gets only on condition, and that can lose it all by virtue of its own sin. It is a terrifying, unsettling story for a social group to tell of itself, because it imposes acute self-consciousness and chronic insecurity upon what should be the level plane and firm foundation of society. That is, the collection of diverse materials joined into a single tale on the occasion of the original exile and restoration because of the repetition in age succeeding age also precipitates the recapitulation of the interior experience of exile and restoration—always because of sin and atonement.

Hence, the power of religion to form an independent variable, alongside politics, economics, and the facts of social organization and structure, derives from its capacity (in the case at hand) to form a permanent paradigm and to perpetuate a single attitude and experience. And how was and is this done? Promising what could not be delivered, then providing solace for the consequent disappointment, the system at hand precipitated in age succeeding age the very conditions necessary for its own replication. Precipitating resentment and then remitting the consequent anguish, religion itself forms a self-perpetuating fact of the ecology of religion. Religion is not only a category of the life of society, politics, economics. An irreducible fact of humanity, there is a dimension of the social power of religion that is uniquely religious.

From Judaism to Judaisms

While the permanent paradigm that perpetuates a single experience shaped Judaism as a religion, the social scientific approach focuses on Judaisms in context. Following the long and distinguished tradition of Weber, Marx, and Durkheim, social scientists place the study of variation and change in Judaism in the context of the comparative and historical analysis of Jews and their communities. This orientation goes beyond the description of historical patterns by testing propositions about historical processes; rather than focusing solely on country or community case studies, it emphasizes systematic cross-national comparisons of Judaisms. Multiple comparisons of Judaisms and non-Judaisms, over time and in different societies, are the basis for understanding Judaisms in their contexts. And through systematic comparisons, it becomes possible to analyze the translation of the Judaism of "exile and return" into the Judaisms of the societies.

What do we examine when we study Judaisms? Four major dimensions of religion are encompassed within the social scientific investigation of Judaisms: (1) the religious behavior, beliefs, and values of Jews; (2) the religious institutions of the Jews; (3) the linkages between Judaism and other aspects of social life—family, economy, polity, and culture; and (4) particular religious ideologies and religious social movements. Within each of these areas of investigation, social scientists emphasize historical and cross-national comparisons and comparisons between Jews and others. We treat the extent of change in Jewish religious values as part of those processes that require explanation, investigating empirically their role in shaping Judaism and Jewish life, without assuming their centrality on theoretical grounds. The social scientific study of Judaism, therefore, treats the religion of the Jew as a complex set of variables, not as a constant.

In the areas of behavior, beliefs, and values, the focus is on changes in the patterns of religious observances and religious ritual, variations in what Jews do religiously, what they believe and their attitudes toward Judaism and ritual observance, and the importance of religious observances and activities for them and their communities. Of central importance are changes and variations in religious values, ideologies, and the ideals expressed by an elite, whether and how these ideals and values are transmitted to the Jewish community. The methodological emphasis on systematic comparisons between the religions of Jews and of non-Jews, using theoretical frameworks common to both and applying general models to the study of Judaisms, allows us to identify that which is particular to Judaism in a specific context and that which is a more generalizable feature of the religion of groups under similar conditions. Most importantly, comparisons facilitate the analysis of how the content of Judaism, exile and return, is translated into the Judaisms of particular contexts. Each Judaism reinterprets the core themes of exile and return, in its form and in its idiom, in response to contexts that are social, economic, and political as well as cultural and ideological.

By necessity, comparisons are made in historical and cross-national community studies. Social science questions relate to how the religion of the Jews is related to other institutional, cultural, political, economic, and social patterns of Jews and to the broader societies of which they are a part; and how these linkages are different for Jews and others. As such, the analysis of Judaism focuses on the ways religion changes over time and varies with different social, economic, political, and cultural contexts; it includes, as well, how new institutions—religious and secular—emerge in different settings as responses to religious change.

Because the social scientific study of Judaism deals with the life of Jews and the institutions of the Jewish community, comparisons between the religions of Jews and non-Jews require as well comparisons of the social-community contexts of Jews and others. A key research issue concerns how the changing configurations of religion and religious institutions are related to the changing cohesion of the Jewish community, over time and among the societies in which Jews live. Do changes in religious observances result in the declines in the extent to which economic and family networks are Jewish? Does the shift in religious ideology lead to changes in the stability of Jewish families? Are religious ideological changes associated with shifts in occupational concentration, migration, and educational attainment? Do religious values influence the political and cultural expressions of Jews? In what ways is Judaism central or marginal to the lives of Jews and the institutions of their communities? In short, the social scientific study of Judaism attempts to examine systematically (*i.e.*, theoretically, methodologically, and empirically) the changing determinants and consequences of Judaism (in its multidimensional forms and expressions) for the lives of Jews and the structure of their communities. Analytically, research on these questions necessitates multiple comparisons over time, cross-culturally and cross-societally, among Jews and between

Jews and non-Jews. These are the ways the social scientist treats religion as a set of variables.

The goal is to use the social scientific mode to ask new questions about Judaism in context, to reshape our understanding of changes in the expressions and institutions of Judaism, comparatively and historically. We thus have to move beyond a description of the internal workings of religious institutions and the expressed ideals of a religious elite for understanding the Judaisms of contemporary societies. Two major limitations characterize an emphasis on studying the internal workings of religious institutions and concentrating on the religious elite: the error of assuming a cross-cultural commonality of one Judaism (*i.e.,* that context does not matter for content) and the error of assuming the disintegrative forces of change (*i.e.,* that the newly formed contents are weaker than, not only different from, earlier forms). Let us explain. Studying the internal structure of Jewish institutions and focusing solely on the elite, we center analytic attention solely on the Jews and assume that there are cross-cultural religious commonalities among Jews and that Jewish values are monolithic. Religious uniformity and continuity are assertions, rather than the objects of systematic study. The core paradigm of Judaism, of exile and return, does not assume the ways in which the paradigm of Judaism is worked out is identical for all the Judaisms. Indeed, our argument is that each Judaism works out the paradigm of the Judaism of exile and return in its context and in its mode, moving the content of Judaism into the context of each Judaism. Thus, the social scientific study of Judaism always involves the study of the new formulations of the Judaic system in context and is not primarily the study of the more conspicuous forms of variation and change in the religious movements of Judaism (Hasidism and Reform Judaism, for example).

The focus on the internal structure of the institutions of Judaism and on the values expressed as norms by the religious elite results in the interpretation of change in the context of religious decline. It is often implicitly assumed or asserted as a "given" of analysis that the forces of modernization have had a negative impact on Judaism and traditional values because these are what most manifestly have changed. It has always been the case that the values of the religious elite, always in their specific contexts, have changed, and the religious institutions of one context have been altered to fit into a new context. It would be untenable in the social science mode to assume that change and variation were unusual or exceptional. Change and variation in Judaism have been integral parts of the variety of communities, societies, and cultures of the Jewish experience. Judaisms have emerged to interpret and reinterpret the Judaic paradigm of exile and return in the multiplicity of forms generated by the experiences of the Jewish context. In this sense, it is a limiting assumption to treat change as distintegration and crisis without allowing for the possibility that change might also represent opportunity and challenge.

Thus, for example, a classic work in the social history of the Jews begins by describing "traditional society" as one "based upon a common body of knowledge and values handed down from the past." It is further asserted that the traditional society "accurately describes the whole of world Jewry, at least from the talmudic era (200 C.E.) up to the age of European Emancipation (during the first half of the nineteenth century), and it applies to some part of Jewish society even in more recent times."[1] The analysis further assumes that there is an "underlying national unity of the Jewish people in the lands of their dispersion." "This unity," it is asserted, "is an indisputable fact."[2] It is not surprising that the focus of that social history is on Judaic values and ideals, assuming that they will reveal the reality of Judaism and Jewish life; the internal structure of the community and its religious institutions are examined, trusting that they will convey the religiosity of the community. There are no systematic comparisons among Jewish communities given the "fact" of underlying unity. It follows from these premises that change is described as "crisis" and transformation as "disintegration."

In contrast, the thrust of our argument is that social scientific study of Judaism focuses on general theoretical frameworks, methodological strategies, and empirical evidence about Judaisms in comparative and historical perspectives. These general theories about social change and ethnic continuity, about the general sociology of religion and of culture, are applied to the study of Judaism in context, to the analysis of Jews and their communities. While there are specific features of Judaism that relate to the Judaism of Scriptures, reinventing core themes of Judaism in new contexts, the sociology of Judaism focuses precisely on those new contexts to study how each Judaism is shaped and reshaped as a Judaism. Each new form of Judaism requires analysis; each needs to be identified and studied systematically. Each new Judaism responds to context and shapes it.

The general assertion or assumption that Jewish culture is a constant over time and place treats cultural variation as the description of the exotic or radically different form of ritual or religious observance. In anthropological work this often involves comparing "Eastern" (*e.g.*, Yemenite, Morrocan) Jewish cultures with a "Western" ashkenasic model and is the prelude to dealing with the changes generated by migration to new places where older cultural forms are disrupted and new forms of cultural blends are emerging.

Judaism in the Context of Culture

We do not in any way deny the need to study Judaism in the context of culture, nor do we denigrate the importance of values in the lives of Jews and in the expressions of their Judaism. We also do not deny that values play a role in the perpetuation of group continuity and in the manifestation of Judaism. Rather, we argue for the following social science principles:

1. Treat the role of religious values as part of structural as well as cultural contexts.
2. Question explanations that focus solely on culture and test with evidence the often unstated assumption that values are the major determinants of social and religious change.

[1] J. Katz, *Tradition and Crisis: Jewish Society at the End of the Middle Ages.* New York: Schocken Books, 1961, p. 3.

[2] Ibid., p. 7.

3. Demonstrate whether and how religious ideologies are the major factors shaping the ways in which people express their commitments to community.
4. Examine whether declines in some forms of religious or cultural expression by necessity implies the disintegration of all forms of religious expression.
5. Challenge the notion that the ideals of Judaism are the only basis for measuring the current behavioral expressions of Judaism (or even the behavioral expressions of past generations).
6. Investigate whether religious change implies a decline in religion and under what conditions alternatives to one form of religious expression weakens the social fabric of the community.
7. Assume that Judaism in particular contexts is relative and changing, testing always whether the ideals of the elite reflect the behavior of the people, and whether norms and behavior are identical.

These are fundamental premises of social science but are often rejected by those who study Judaism when they assume the "uniqueness" of the Jewish people, the "continuity" of Judaism from the past to the diverse communities of the present, without specifying what is content and what is context, and assuming always that there is a "decline" of Judaism and hence of the Jewish people in the context of modern, open, pluralistic societies.

While it is clear that specific features of Judaism may influence the shape of Jewish communities and the responses of Jews to the communities in which they live, it is also clear that these specific features operate in a social structural context, requiring an analysis of social situations in order to disentangle how and where these factors are important, what they determine, and how they work. To argue that the "Jewish condition" is mainly or solely determined by abstract religious values and Jewish culture or by non-Jews (*e.g.*, anti-Semitism) is to misread the complexities of Judaism in context and to ignore the social, economic, political, and cultural variation among Jewish communities; it is to fail to specify the conditions under which the core themes of all Judaisms are shaped by the particular contexts of each Judaism.

Transformation and Judaism

Sociology, in particular, and the social sciences, more generally, provide a perspective that is fundamental not only for the study of Judaism and Jewry but also for understanding human society in all of its manifestations, one that can be applied to all societies at all points in time. Some have applied them to the study of the Biblical period; others have used social scientific theories to map out issues of the Mishna and the Talmud and to study Jews, their communities and cultures, at distant times and places. The application of social scientific perspectives to study contemporary manifestations of Judaisms need not be—indeed, cannot be—ahistorical. A central sociological question, perhaps the master theme, in the social scientific study of contemporary Judaisms is the impact of the transformation or "modernization" of society on the religion of the Jews. We have noted earlier the multidimensionality of Judaism and discussed the various elements involved in studying Judaism in behavioral, institutional, and communal terms. Here we need to clarify issues associated with transformation and modernization as master contexts translating Judaism into Judaisms. We focus on transformation in the social scientific, not the historical, sense. Thus, our question of transformation and Judaism is not addressed to when "modern" society begins, a question of the periodization of history but rather: How do the processes of modernization, secularization, and transformation unfold, and, in turn, how these processes relate to changes in the lives of people, in the institutions of society, in the structure of social relations, and the generational transmission of Jewish values and culture?[3] How do these transformations alter Judaism to form new systems of Judaisms?

What, then, are the major analytic themes in the social scientific study of Judaism in the context of the transformation of Jews and their communities? The master theme of contemporary social science is the analysis of the transformation of societies and the variety of groups within them as a result of modernization. Industrialization, urbanization, political and social mobilization, and cultural change and secularization are among the major elements. The key processes involve structural differentiation and the expansion of political and economic opportunities. New structures and values, new institutions, new ways of behaving and thinking, new jobs, residences, political movements, cultures, and ideologies, as well as new sources of conflict, competition, and inequality, have emerged in the modern era. Our master question then becomes: What has been the impact of these transformations on the Jews, generally, and on their religious systems, specifically? How has the modernization of the societies in which Jews lived affected their Judaism? Are the consequences of modernization for the transformation of the Jewish community and Judaism similar to the consequences for others in terms of direction, extent, and pace of change? How have Jews, their leaders and elites, religious and secular, their organizations and institutions, responded to the sweep of modernization? With the dissolution of the older bases of cohesion, what new types of communal bonds, associational ties, and cultural forms link Jews to one another? In turn, what are the relationships of new forms of communal cohesion and religious transformations? What are the bases of solidarity, in the Durkheimian sense, among Jews and their communities as they were transformed by modernization? And, in turn, how does Judaism transformed relate to these changes? Since it is not tenable to assume that Judaism will not respond to the dramatic changes transforming traditional to modern society, the question becomes, How do the Judaisms of modern society shape and reshape the themes of exile and return of Judaism?

These questions focus our attention on broad changes over time and their effects on Jews and their communities. They are directed to the broader issue of how modernization has transformed Judaism into Judaisms. History has a central place in sociological analyses of Jews; not the 4,000-year history of Jews everywhere, but historical processes associated with the transformation of Jews in modern societies. We are concerned about those particular processes associated

[3]L. Kochan, "The Methodology of Modern Jewish History," *Journal of Jewish Studies* 36 (1985), pp. 185–94.

with modernization, not about all historical change. So our focus is not on an abstract and oversimplified notion of historical events and sequences but on the processes associated with the modernization of societies, communities, families, and individuals. In our context, we want to link these to the transformation of Judaism in all its dimensions.

Our questions, therefore, involve, first and foremost, a focus on historical change of a particular sociological kind and analytic type. They also require a second type of comparison in addition to changes over time—variation across communities within and between countries. The objective of cross-community and historical comparisons is not to isolate the exotic and unique; rather it is to frame analytic questions (why these religious changes and not others; why particular religious changes occur in community X and not in community Y; why at time B and not time A; why for some Jews and not for others in the same society at the same time) and provide a comparative basis for testing theories and hypotheses with empirical evidence. So the first analytic issue is to place the study of Judaism and Jews in the framework of theories of transformation and change.

Judaism and the Role of Others

A second analytic strategy is to incorporate the systematic comparison of Jews and others as an integral part of our research agenda. We can focus solely on the Jews and their communities, analyzing their patterns over time and in various communities. We can learn much from such "internal" group comparisons, but these alone are insufficient to address analytic themes in the social sciences. Ideally, we would want to compare systematically the religions of Jews and the many groups of non-Jews over time and in various societies. Such comparisons provide the basis for evaluating the structural and cultural sources of Jewish distinctiveness and assessing whether differences between Jews and non-Jews are temporary and transitory or whether they are embedded in the social structure. Comparisons between the religions of non-Jews and Jews are essential in identifying how the particular manifestations of Judaism are shaped by contexts.

It is clearly not appropriate analytically to compare Jews with non-Jews without taking into account and disentangling differential structural *and* cultural patterns. Thus, for example, comparing the development of religious institutions and religious ideologies among Jews in Germany in the nineteenth century with all Germans, without taking into account the specific jobs, urban location, and education of the Jews, would be misleading. Such a crude comparison would reveal differences between Jews and non-Jews, reflecting in large part social class and rural–urban residential differences but not necessarily specific factors associated with Jewishness or Judaism, the place of Jews in German society or their "culture." On the one hand, to know that differences between Jews and non-Jews in nineteenth-century Germany are primarily the consequence of socioeconomic and demographic differences shapes a series of specific analytic questions regarding the determinants and consequences of the particular socioeconomic and demographic characteristics of German Jewry. On the other hand, in neutralizing the socioeconomic and demographic effects, we are able to focus on other powerful structural and cultural factors. But to simply attribute crude differences between Jews and non-Jews to "culture" and "values' particular to Jews without studying non-Jews directly and without taking into account the social, political, demographic, and economic contexts of our comparisons results in a series of distortions in our understanding of social change among Jews in Europe and America over the past century. Only through systematic comparison do we begin to understand how and why the core themes of Judaism are translated into the particular forms of Judaic expressions.

In the analysis of religious reform in nineteenth-century Western Europe, in the comparisons between the religious transformations of Judaism and other religions in Europe during the nineteenth century and America in the twentieth century, and in the comparisons of religious and political transformations in various countries, including the state of Israel, analysis has revealed consistently the value of comparisons, yielding new insights derived from comparative analysis.[4] For example, comparative analysis allows us to interpret why some aspects of Reform Judaism emerged in Germany and not in France and points to the underlying similarity of diffusion processes of political ideologies in Russia and religious ideologies in Germany in the nineteenth century.[5] Furthermore, we are able to disentangle the relative importance of changes in religious ideology and economic, demographic, and political factors to account for the differential spread of religious reform throughout Germany. The comparative similarities in the levels of synagogue attendance, to take another example, among Jews in the state of Israel and in the United States suggested general processes of secularization in two very different Jewish communities in distinct sociocultural contexts. These and related analytic findings emerge when multiple comparisons—historical, cross-community, and with non-Jew—are the bases for the systematic social scientific analysis of Judaism. Without comparisons, we are left with description, not analysis, and no basis for testing theories and hypotheses.

But why focus on the Jews? Are there analytic considerations, beyond issues of self-interest and ethnocentrism, that justify our investigation of the Jews? If not, general sociologists will learn from our sociology of the Jews, and we will address only one another. The Jews form a useful subject for research because they are a small group, well documented, with a long history; they also exhibit enormous diversity. This diversity allows for the introduction of various factors in explaining facts, and where and when religious belief or practice forms one of those factors, there are sufficient variables for testing the importance of the religious factor. Because of their role in diverse political and economic entities, it proves fruitful analytically to address questions about the processes of transformation to the Jewish group rather than to total societies. A more reasonable, manageable unit of analysis than a total heterogeneous society, the Jews prove accessible and important.

[4]For examples, see the discussion in C. Goldscheider and A. Zuckerman, *The Transformation of the Jews*. Chicago: University of Chicago Press. 1984.

[5]See the selection in this anthology Chapter Six.

Moreover, comparative analysis is facilitated by the central role Jews have played in places of earlier and later modernization within Europe and in the new nations of America and Israel. The comparative study of Jews thus provides an analytic handle for understanding general processes of western development just as it does for understanding the role of religions in society. The location of Jews in various societies makes it efficient to examine changes across societies comparatively while focusing on the community level. There is significant internal variation when the total society is used as the unit of analysis, to the extent that crucial patterns are oftened neutralized by countervailing processes; cross-societal comparisons only compound these analytic difficulties. And while the Jews occupy a unique position in Western societies, insights derived from a sociological analysis of the Jews are generalizable to others when the focus is on analytic issues within comparative and historical perspectives.

Issues of modernization apply to Jews and their communities as they apply to total societies and to other ethnic and minority groups. The examination of the transformation of the Jews yields insight as well into critical theories associated with the social, political, economic, and cultural integration of minority, ethnic, and religious groups in the processes associated with modernization, including social differentiation, communal cohesion, intergroup relations, and the structural and cultural dimensions of assimilation. Important aspects of the core theories of ethnicity in pluralistic societies can be systematically tested within the framework of the sociology of the Jews.[6] There are, in addition, particular Jewish issues of modernization that are of importance in exploring modern Jewish society. These include the specifics of Judaism, anti-Semtisim, and the internal structure and organization of the Jewish community.

Specific Features of Judaism in Context

In the modernization of the Jews, Judaism was transformed. The normative and communal centrality of Judaism declined. As the older order changed, so did the institutions legitimizing that order. As religion changed, it was redefined, and new forms of communal identification emerged. How these changes evolve, what becomes the bases of the new forms of legitimacy and consensus, and how cultural and value consensus emerge are key issues. The responses of religious movements and ideologies to the challenges of modern secular society and how they relate to other social–religious movements require clarification. The transformation from religious centrality to communal ethnic diversity poses the fundamental concern for Jewish continuity and discontinuity at the community and individual levels. Clearly, religiosity (or religiousness) is not only or primarily an issue of personal commitment to specifically religious institution or ideologies. It is social and communal. These broader contexts are often lost when the sociologies of Judaisms are discussed solely in the context of their formal ideologies and organizational

[6]See, for example, C. Goldscheider, *Jewish Continuity and Change*. Bloomington, IN: Indiana University Press, 1986, p. 1ff.

patterns and not in terms of the social definitions of membership and identification, family and generation patterns. The "Jewish *verstehende*" requires a sociological *verstehende* grounded in the rich sociological tradition of Weber, Marx, and Durkheim, among others.

A second particular feature in the analysis of modern Jewish society relates specifically to anti-Semitism and ethnic–religious discrimination in general. How important are attitudes, policies, and ideologies of governments and of non-Jews in understanding the transformation of Judaism? How does political anti-Semitism relate to various ideologies and governments? How does anti-Semitism in its political and attitudinal forms relate to conflict, competition, and inequality within societies? How is anti-Semitism affected by the presence of other minorities in the society? How are political and attitudinal dimensions of anti-Semitism related to one another and to the general attitudes and values of non-Jews and Jews? How do these dimensions relate to the size and structure of the Jewish community? These questions are particular to Jews, in ways that are perhaps different from the way they are for religious, ethnic, and racial minorities in general. There cannot be a comprehensive sociology of Judaism without taking into consideration the political, social, and attitudinal context of the non-Jewish "other." But again, social structural and cultural contexts are critical for understanding the "other" and in evaluating the relative importance of "others" in determining variation and change among Jews. How modern forms of anti-Semitism—and its most extreme form, the Holocaust—reshaped the Judaism of exile and return and generated new forms of Judaism in the post-Nazi era is of critical importance.

The changing internal structure of the Jewish community, its variation across societies, and the relationship of Jews to religious institutions and organizations that are the formal network of the community is the final area of specific analytic concern. Clearly the organization of the Jewish community is transformed in the process of modernization. How and why the formal structure changes and what the role of ideological factors is in shaping those changes are major questions. How these institutional changes are linked to, determine, and are the consequence of changes in the social structure of the Jewish community are critical issues. How does the organizational structure of the Jewish community link to the formal organizational and institutional structure of the general community and the formal institutional structure of its religious organizations? In short, the sources of growth, expansion, and competition among organizations and the emergence of new institutions need to be analyzed in the broader contexts of organizational theory and other institutional developments occurring in society. As organizations and institutions change, so do elites; as the centrality of religion declines, so does the authority and power of the rabbis; as religion takes on new forms and new secular and religious organizations are shaped, new organizational elites emerge with new sources of power and new bases of resources. The linkages between religious and secular organizational developments within the Jewish community and the changing relationships between ethnic and religious dimensions of Jewish identity and identification are prime theoretical and empirical areas of inquiry.

These are complex issues that relate to Jews specifically and to changes in the place of Jews in modern society. In large part, these issues revolve around the forces shaping why particular changes occur among Jews and how Jews respond relative to non-Jews. But we ask questions not only about the determinants of changes among Jews but also about the consequences of these changes for Jewish continuity. More particularly, we focus on the implications of the transformation of the Jewish community for the relative cohesion of the Jewish community. We analyze the relative cohesion of communities under different conditions; we should not infer the *implications* of change from the changing characteristics of the Jewish community. Thus, for example, the increasing secularization of Judaism, in terms of the reduction in traditional religious ritual observances and ritual practices, has been documented in almost every study of modern Jewish communities. Often, the inference has been made that patterns of secularization have negative consequences for the cohesion of the Jewish community; from the point of view of the community, therefore, secularization is treated as one indicator of the decline of the Jewish community in modern society. That is the case only when we confuse Judaism with Jewishness and equate the religion of the Jews with the strength of the Jewish community. These dimensions were more interchangeable in the past, when religion was more central in the lives of Jews and connected in integral ways to social, economic, family, cultural, and political aspects of Jewish communities. In modern pluralistic societies, the two questions have to be untangled: (1) How are changes in religion linked to other processes of transformation? and (2) What are the implications of the new emerging Judaisms for the cohesion of the community? Only if the cohesion of the Jewish community is defined by the religiosity of the Jewish community, then, by definition, would a change in religiosity imply a decrease in Jewish cohesion. The more profound question is phrased differently: How do the new forms of Judaism in modern society link to the nature of Jewish cohesion? And, in turn, how have the new Judaisms translated the Judaism of exile and return in the new contexts of modernity?

Emphasis on the religious behavior and on the characteristics of Jews and their communities needs to be separated from an analysis of values and attitudes, if only to see how behavior and values are related. The study of elites, norms, ideologies, and ideas is important but should not be viewed as substitutes for analyzing the behavior of the masses and the characteristics of their communities. The elite, by definition, is not a cross-section of the community. To study the elite, comparatively and historically, is a most engaging area of investigation, but it is not the same as studying the Jewish community. Norms, values, and ideas are not synonymous with behavior. Values, ideologies, and culture need to be studied as phenomena to be explained no less than as sources of explanation. Indeed, there is a critical need to test the relative importance of structural and cultural explanations of social processes, no less among Jews than as part of the general sociological analyses of groups. Elite ideas are but one of many determinants of mass behavior; they are rarely the only determinants of the behavior even of elites.

We need to ask theoretical questions to guide our empirical inquiries and identify new areas of comparative research among contemporary Jews and their communities. It is a grand intellectual challenge and a complex scholarly agenda to place the sociological study of the Jews and Judaism in the broader context of the societies of which they are a part, to examine the unique and the general, to test theories and hypotheses, to investigate the general social, economic, cultural, political patterns of the Jews and their communities, and to see connections among communities, comparing Jews and others systematically and over time. It is the agenda of the social sciences in general. It is doubly difficult when the focus is on Jews and their communities because of the need to investigate one group among many and to link their analysis with those of other groups, other Jews, and societal patterns in general. The permutations are extensive. Nevertheless, and perhaps because of it, it is an intellectual challenge of the highest order and worth pursuing. When the social scientific study of Jews is connected to the humanistic orientation to religion, each perspective generates new maps to discover new linkages by raising new questions.

The systematic study of Judaism is linked to the study of the Jews and their communities. To understand these links, we need to place the analysis of the Jews in the perspectives not only of the social sciences but of the humanities. By specifying those theoretical and methodological linkages, we put the issues of social science in systematic order. Then can we begin to connect these to the study of religion in general and Judaism in particular within the humanities. Combining social science and humanistic perspectives is thus the first step toward the ongoing search for grand integrative theories. As an initial initiative in what we conceive as an inviting and illuminating inquiry, we offer this anthology of articles written both by the two editors and by many others.

PART I The Formative and the Classical Ages of Judaism: 500 B.C. to A.D. 640, 640 to 1789

Chapter 1

Religion and Society in the Formation of the Judaism of the Pentateuch

Jacob Neusner

While commonplace wisdom holds that society shapes religion, the history of Judaism also shows that religion shapes society. It does so by setting forth a view of matters that is wholly a fabrication, a reconstruction of events out of whole cloth and an interpretation of those reconstituted events; this fictive conception then is adopted by generations as an account of who as a social entity they are and what as a "holy society," e.g., as an "Israel," they should do. The case in point derives from the Pentateuch, which created, then fostered, a theory of Jews' social life that perpetuated itself for generations to come. Specifically, Jewish societies were shaped for millennia by the conception that Jews were in exile and were to return home. The original reading of the Jews' existence as exile and return derives from the Pentateuch, the Five Books of Moses, which were composed as we now have them (out of earlier materials, to be sure) in the aftermath of the destruction of the Temple in 586 B.C. and in response to the exile to Babylonia. The experience selected and addressed by the authorship of the document is that of exile and restoration.

But that framing of events into the pattern at hand represents an act of powerful imagination and interpretation. It is an experience that is invented, because no one person or group both went into "exile" and also "returned home." Diverse experiences have been sorted out, various persons have been chosen, and the whole has been worked into a system by those who selected history out of happenings, and models out of masses of persons. I say "selected," because no

Jews after 586 actually experienced what in the aggregate Scripture says happened. None both went into exile and then came back to Jerusalem. So, to begin with, Scripture does not record a particular person's experience. More to the point, if it is not autobiographical, writing for society at large the personal insight of a singular figure, it also is not an account of a whole nation's story. The reason is that the original exile encompassed mainly the political classes of Jerusalem and some useful populations alongside. Many Jews in the Judea of 586 never left. And, as is well known, a great many of those who ended up in Babylonia stayed there. Only a minority went back to Jerusalem. Consequently, the story of exile and return to Zion encompasses what happened to only a few families, who identified themselves as the family of Abraham, Isaac, and Jacob, and their genealogy as the history of Israel. Those families that stayed and those that never came back had they written the Torah would have told as normative and paradigmatic a different tale altogether.

That experience of the few that formed the paradigm for Israel beyond the restoration taught as normative lessons of alienation. Let me state with emphasis the lessons people claimed to learn out of the events they had chosen for their history: *the life of the group is uncertain, subject to conditions and stipulations. Nothing is set and given, all things a gift: land and life itself. But what actually did happen in that uncertain world—exile but then restoration—marked the group as special, different, select.*

There were other ways of seeing things, and the pentateuchal picture was from the viewpoint of the actualities of society and politics no more compelling than any other. Those Jews who did not go into exile, and those who did not "come home," had no reason to take the view of matters that characterized the authorship of Scripture. The life of the group need not have appeared more uncertain, more subject to contingency and stipulation, than the life of any other group. The land did not require the vision that imparted to it the enchantment, the personality, that, in Scripture, it received: "The land will vomit you out as it did those who were here before you." And the adventitious circumstance of Iranian imperial policy—a political happenstance—did not have to be recast into return. So nothing in the system of Scripture—exile for reason, return as redemption—followed necessarily and logically. Everything was invented, interpreted, that is to say, through the medium of religious conviction.

That experience of the uncertainty of the life of the group in the century or so from the destruction of the First Temple of Jerusalem by the Babylonians in 586 to the building of the Second Temple of Jerusalem by the Jews, with Persian permission and sponsorship returned from exile, formed the paradigm. With the promulgation of the "Torah of Moses" under the sponsorship of Ezra, the Persians' viceroy, at ca. 450 B.C., all future Israels would then refer to that formative experience as it had been set down and preserved as the norm for Israel in the mythic terms of that "original" Israel, the Israel not of Genesis and Sinai and the end at the moment of entry into the promised land, but the "Israel" of the families that recorded as the rule and the norm the story of both the exile and the return. In that minority genealogy, that story of exile and return, alienation and remission, imposed on the received stories of pre-exilic Israel and adumbrated time and again in the Five Books of Moses and addressed by the framers of that document in their work over all, we find that paradigmatic statement in which every Judaism, from then to now, found its structure and deep syntax of social existence, the grammar of its intelligible message.

What generalizations emerge out of the social history of Judaism as a fabrication? The first is that no Judaism recapitulates any other, and none stands in a linear and incremental relationship with any prior one. The second is that all Judaisms recapitulate that single paradigmatic experience of the Torah of "Moses," the authorship that reflected on the meaning of the events of 586–450 selected for the composition of history and therefore interpretation. That experience (in theological terms) rehearsed the conditional moral existence of sin and punishment, suffering and atonement and reconciliation, and (in social terms) the uncertain and always conditional national destiny of disintegration and renewal of the group. That moment captured within the Five Books of Moses, that is to say, the judgment of the generation of the return to Zion, led by Ezra, about its extraordinary experience of exile and return would inform the attitude and viewpoint of all the Israels beyond. What has been said now requires that we review the opening propositions of the preface.

In the case of Judaism, therefore, religion imparts *its* pattern upon the social world and polity. The social world recapitulates religion; religion does not recapitulate the given of society, economy, politics, let alone of an emotional reality that is wholly personal. Because of the paradigmatic power of a single generative experience, which constitutes the exegetical fulcrum for all theories of religion, in the case of Judaism (and I should imagine other religions of its classification) religion shapes the world, not the world, religion. Specifically, it is the Jews' religion, Judaism, that has formed their world and framed their realities, and not the world of politics, culture, society, that has made their religion.

The theory proposed here, therefore, points to a particular selection and interpretation of events of a distinctive sort, the character of which imposes its singular shape upon all Judaisms that followed it, then to now. These events are understood to stand for exile, identified with everything people find wrong with their life, and return, marking what people hope will happen to set matters right. The future would see a recurrent pattern, deriving from the first. Each Judaism identifies what is wrong with the present and promises to make things tolerable now and perfect in the indeterminate future. A Judaism therefore stands for a situation to escape, overcome, survive. The repeated pattern of finding the world out of kilter ("exile") but then making it possible to live for the interim in that sort of world, that generative paradigm, perpetuates profound resentment: why here? why us? why now? And, to the contrary (and this is the resentment) why not always, everywhere, and forever? So a Judaic religious system recapitulates a particular resentment. In this way each Judaism relates to other Judaisms, religious systems. Each one in its own way, on its own, will address and go over that same pattern, all addressing the same original experience. That is why a sequence of happenings, identified as important history and therefore a paradigmatic event, then, is recapitulated in age succeeding age, whether by one Judaism in competition with another or by one Judaism after another. But, as a matter of systemic fact, no Judaism recapitulates any other, though each goes over the same paradigmatic experience.

Before proceeding to the next stage in the argument, I owe the reader the recognition that the usage, *a Judaism*, or *Judaisms*, violates accepted language rules. When people use the word, Judaism, they use it only in the singular, and they assume they refer to a single religion, or religious tradition, extending (if not from creation) from Sinai to the present. Instead, I refer not only to *a* Judaism, but, more commonly, to a Judaic *system*. That is to say, I define in categories not broadly understood the genus of which I speak, a religion, as well as the species of that genus, a Judaism. Specifically I understand by a religious system three things, ethos, ethics, ethnos, that are one:

1. an ethos is a world-view, which by reference to the intersection of the supernatural and the natural worlds accounts for how things are and puts them together into a cogent and harmonious picture;
2. an ethics stands for a way of life, which expresses in concrete actions the world-view and which is explained by the world-view;
3. and an ethnos refers to a social entity, e.g., a group, for which the world-view accounts, which is defined in concrete terms by the way of life, and therefore which gives expression in the everyday world to the world-view and is defined as an entity by that way of life.

A Judaic system then comprises not merely a theory—a book—distinct from social reality but an explanation for the group (again: "Israel") that gives social form to the system and an account of the distinctive way of life of that group. A Judaism is not a book, and no social group took shape because people read a book and agreed that God had revealed what the book said they should do. Let me state with emphasis: a Judaic system derives from and focuses upon a social entity, a group of Jews who (in their minds at least) constitute not an Israel but Israel.

I imagine that a Judaic system could treat as not essential a variety of rules for the everyday life. In modern times that indifference to rule-making for this morning's breakfast proves characteristic of Judaisms. Or it may fail to articulate elements of a world-view to answer a range of questions others deem fundamental. Contemporary Judaisms do not treat as urgent philosophical questions found absorbing by earlier system-builders. But no Judaic system can omit a clear picture of the meaning and sense of the category, Israel. Without an *Israel*, a social entity in fact and not only in doctrine, we have not a system but a book. And a book is not a Judaism, it is only a book.

We ask how we may know one Judaism from some other. When we identify Judaisms in one period after another, we begin by trying to locate, in the larger group of Jews, those social entities that see themselves and are seen by others as distinct and bounded, and that further present to themselves a clear account of who they are and what they do and why they do what they do: the rules and their explanations, their Judaism. This reading of the social foundations of Judaisms rests on the simple premise that religion always is social, and therefore also political, a matter of what people do together, not just what they believe in the privacy of their hearts. And a Judaism for its part addresses a social group, an Israel, with the claim that that group is not merely an Israel but Israel, Israel *in nuce,* Israel in its ideal form, Israel's saving remnant, the State of Israel, the natural next step in the linear, continuous history ("progress") of Israel, everything, anything—but always Israel. So a Judaism, or a Judaic system, constitutes a clear and precise account of a social group, the way of life and world-view of a group of Jews, however defined.

The theory denies there is now, or ever was, a single Judaism, because there is no linear and incremental history of one continuous Judaism, beginning, middle, end. There has never been Judaism, only Judaisms. But there is a single paradigmatic and definitive human experience, which each Judaism reworks in its own circumstance and context. In a broader sense, therefore, the present field-theory of the relationship of society and religion in a particular religious tradition that comprises a variety of expressions may be summarized in the propositions that generalize on the case of Judaisms:

1. No religious system (without a given set of related religions) recapitulates any other.
2. But all religious systems (within a given set) recapitulate resentment. A single persistent experience for generation after generation captures what, for a particular group, stands for the whole of the human condition: everything all at once, all together, the misery and the magnificence of life.

What I have said requires the immediate specification of that single paradigmatic experience to which all Judaisms, everywhere and under all conditions, refer. As a matter of simple fact, we may identify that generative and definitive moment precisely as all Judaisms have done, that is, by looking into that same Scripture. All Judaisms identify the Torah or the Five Books of Moses as the written-down statement of God's will for Israel, the Jewish people (which, as a matter of fact, every Judaism also identifies as its own social group). I suppose that on the surface, we should specify that formative and definitive moment, recapitulated by all Judaisms, with the story of Creation down to Abraham and the beginning of his family, the children of Abraham, Isaac and Jacob. Or perhaps we are advised to make our way to Sinai and hold that that original point of definition descends from heaven. But allowing ourselves merely to retell the story deprives us of the required insight. Recapitulating the story of the religion does not help us understand the religion. Identifying the point of origin of the story, by contrast, does. For the story tells not what happened on the occasion to which the story refers (the creation of the world, for instance) but how (long afterward and for their own reasons) people want to portray themselves. The tale therefore recapitulates that resentment, that obsessive and troubling point of origin, that the group wishes to explain, transcend, transform.

To be an Israel—the social component of a Judaism—from then to now has meant to ask what it means to be Israel. The original pattern meant that an Israel would be a social group the existence of which had been called into question and affirmed—and therefore always would be called into question, and remained perpetually to be affirmed. Every Judaism then would find as its task the recapitulation of the original Judaism. That is to say, each made its own distinctive statement of the generative and critical resentment contained within that questioning of the given, that deep understanding of the uncertain character of the existence of the group in its normal location and under circumstances of permanence that (so far as the Judaic group understood things) characterized the life of every other group but Israel. What for everyone else (so it seemed to the Judaisms addressed to the Israels through time) was a given for Israel was a gift. What all the nations knew as how things *must* be Israel understood as how things *might not be:* exile and loss, alienation and resentment, but, instead of annihilation, renewal, restoration, reconciliation, and (in theological language) redemption. So that paradigmatic experience, the one beginning in 586 and ending in ca. 450, written down in that written Torah of Moses, made its mark. That pattern, permanently inscribed in the Torah of God to Moses at Sinai, would define for all Israels over all time that matter of resentment demanding recapitulation: leaving home, coming home.

To understand the collectivity of these histories of Judaisms as they appear all at once—the genus of which, all together, they comprise the species—we should imagine a people that tells its story through dance, as do many peoples of Africa, or through ornately carved works of art, as do many peoples of Polynesia and Melanesia. Taking up our position at the edge of the village, we should see jump-dancers of East Africa, each group leaping in its intricate patterns. To us they all appear to jump alike. But to them each set of dancers establishes its own rhythm. Now if—to continue the analogy—we grasp what is happening, we realize that the dancers' sets each forms its own dance, that is to say, its own story of who it is. Our eye sees the whole, and, untutored, perceives only the generality. But the educated eye discerns the distinct patterns of steps and movements and grasps the distinctions that make important differences. And that eye grasps that it is no village at all, but a meeting of many villages. So too the ignorant vision understands Maori art as a sequence of abstract patterns, but *te Maori* read the story of their twenty-four peoples, their original canoes, each told in its pattern, through its narrative of art. In the Auckland museum we see that assembly that forms of the whole *te Maori*, but the Maori know better than that.

Jews preserve the many-times-told stories of their groups not through dance nor through art. They make up Judaisms, each for its occasion, and then those to whom *a* Judaism is Judaism uncover that continuity and connection between their Judaism and Judaism—whatever then serves for that occasion. Words not dance, words not wood-working—these form the signs and signals of the story. And the words, read in context, form sentences, paragraphs—messages, Judaisms, each with its full and complete account of the world and what it means, the way of life and how one lives, it, in an Israel, a Jewish people. That is not to suggest the dances are not once dance: in East Africa they jump, in West Africa they swirl, and that is a difference that distinguishes the one from the other, that is, all dancers on the one side of Africa from all dancers on the other. What is that one systemic trait that marks all Judaisms and sets them apart from all the dances of the dancers and all the carvings of the carvers? It is (as my statement of the field-theory makes clear) that perpetual asking of the question other social groups (in Jews' eyes) seem to have answered for themselves for all time: who are we? That trait of self-consciousness, that incapacity to accept the group as a given and its data—way of life, world-view, constituing the world of an Israel, a Jewish people, in the here and now—is the one thing that draws together Judaisms from beginning to end. Jews' persistent passion for self-definition characterizes all of the Judaisms they have made for themselves. The jump-rhythms of all the jumpers, the swirls of all the swirling lines, the incisions of the wood carvers and the tattoos on all the faces—these for the Jews find their counterpart in Jews' obsessive self-consciousness about their group. What others take as the given the Jews perceive as the received, the special, the extraordinary. And that perception of the remarkable character of what to other groups is the absolute datum of all being requires explanation.

That wonderment about who "we" are and what "we" mean together presents a puzzle, since, after so long a trek through history, why Jews should not yet have found their final answer hardly is clear. True, for many the answer lies in the distant past, and explanation derives from the story of what has happened. But that is a self-evident evasion, for history answers no questions that we have not, to begin with, identified as questions answered by history, that is, by sequences of events: first this, then that, therefore....But just as in logic, an argument based on the reasoning, because one thing came before the other, therefore one thing caused the other (in logic, the fallacy of *post hoc, ergo propter hoc,* because something happened after something else, it happened on account of that something else), is self-evidently false, so too in ordinary affairs, the connectedness of events rests not on temporal sequence, unless to begin with we have concluded that event X stands behind and has therefore caused event Y. But that is a naked mistake in the simplest logic.

If, therefore, a mere narrative of history is meant these days to serve the purpose of explanation, it is because of an evasion, on the one side, and a deep misunderstanding of the character of Judaisms on the other. The evasion represents the easier side to perceive: people find it easier to recite than to explain. That is why they play out the conventions of show-and-tell and let the answers come from they know not where: self-evidence, mostly. The incomprehension of Judaisms derives from accepting as fact the claim of a Judaism to constitute Judaism: as it was in the beginning, as it is, and on through time. The linear and incremental story of Judaism that today serves—beginning from Abraham, ending with this morning's events in Jerusalem or Jewish Providence—constitutes a profound theological judgment. It does not record how things really were. For no Judaism—Judaic system made up of a world-view, a way of life, and a particular group of Jews, an Israel, whose collective life is explained by the one and patterned by the other—stands in a linear and incremental relationship with any other. Indeed, none relates to any other at all, except in making selections from a common treasury of historical detritus. But the selections from the rubbish heap of history—the holy books, the customs and ceremonies (so to speak)—always follow the inner logic of a system, which, after the fact, makes its choices, pronounces its canon.

Still, every Judaic system takes as urgent a set of questions deemed ineluctable and demanding answers. And, in one way or another, those questions have persisted as the center of system after system. They turn on the identity of the group; they rest on the premise that the group's existence represents choice and not a given of nature or necessity. That obsessive self-awareness, a characteristic trait, masks a deeper experience that evidently defines for one generation after another and for one group of Jews after another that ineluctable question that, collectively, the group must answer. Why, among the settled peoples of time, the Jews, along with the Chinese and the Armenians among the oldest peoples of continuous historical existence on the face of the earth, should not have determined for themselves answers to the question of self-identification, is for us to find out. But to begin with, we recognize that the question is not a given, that other groups satisfactorily account for themselves and go on to other questions, and that the critical tension in the life of Jews' groups deriving from perplexity about the fundamental datum of group existence presents a surprise and a puzzle.

Let me now spell out this theory accounting for the character and definition of all of the diverse Judaisms that have taken shape since the destruction of the first Temple of Jerusalem in 586 and the return to Zion, building of the second Temple of Jerusalem, and writing down of the Torah, a process complete in 450 B.C. Since the formative pattern imposed that perpetual, self-conscious uncertainty, treating the life of the group as conditional and discontinuous, Jews have asked themselves who they are and invented Judaisms to answer that question. Accordingly, on account of the definitive paradigm affecting their group-life in various contexts, no circumstances have permitted Jews to take for granted their existence as a group. Looking back on Scripture and its message, Jews have ordinarily treated as special, subject to conditions and therefore uncertain, what (in their view) other groups enjoyed as unconditional and simply given. Why the paradigm renewed itself is clear: this particular view of matters generated expectations that could not be met, hence created resentment—and then provided comfort and hope that made possible coping with that resentment. To state my thesis with appropriate emphasis: *Promising what could not be delivered, then providing solace for the consequent disappointment, the system at hand precipitated in age succeeding age the very conditions necessary for its own replication. Successive Judaisms, each one by itself, recapitulated that paradigmatic resentment.*

To conclude: in Scripture we deal with a composite of materials, each with its own viewpoint and traits of mind. It was only after the destruction of the First Temple of Jerusalem in 586 B.C. that the Torah, that is, the Five Books of Moses, came into being, a pastiche of received stories, some old, some new, all revised for the purposes of the final authorship. It was in the aftermath of the destruction of that temple and the later restoration of the exile to the land that that authorship wrote the origins of Israel, the Jewish people. In light of Israel's ultimate destiny, which the authorship took to be the loss and restoration of the land, the origins of the people in its land took on their cogent meaning. Israel then began with its acquisition of the land, through Abraham, and attained its identity as a people through the promise of the land, in the covenant of Sinai, and the entry into the land, under Joshua. Israel's history then formed the story of how, because of its conduct on the land, Israel lost its land, first in the north, then in the south—and that despite the prophets' persistent warnings. From the exile in Babylonia, the authorship of the Torah recast Israel's history into the story of the conditional existence of the people, their existence measured in their possession of the land upon the stipulation of God's favor. Everything depended on carrying out a contract: do this, get that, do not do this, do not get that—and nothing formed a given, beyond all stipulation. The task of that authorship demanded the interpretation of the condition of the present, and their message in response to the uncertainty of Israel's life beyond exile and restoration underlined that uncertainty of that life. Had the Temple not been destroyed in 586, or had some other generative and paradigmatic experience imposed its mark upon all the Israelite systems to follow, the strands of the pentateuchal mosaic, read each on its own, would have been so composed as all together to provide examples of that other paradigm. That is for instance a pattern that would have identified that world created by an Israel that had never left home in exile but then returned to its land, that is, that had never confronted extinction and survival. What a Judaism might have been had Israel been spared the fantasy of being shaped by obsession with exile and return, alienation and reconciliation no one knows.

All we do know is what that small number of Israelite families, who remembered the exile, survived in Babylonia, and then, toward the end of the sixth and fifth centuries B.C., returned to Zion, imagined. I have already underlined the fact that the vast majority of the nation did not undergo the experiences of exile and return. One part never left, the other never came back. That fact shows us the true character of the Judaism that would predominate: it began by making a selection of facts to be deemed consequential, hence historical, and by ignoring, in the making of that selection, the experiences of others who had a quite different perception of what had happened—and, for all we know, a different appreciation of the message. The fact that the ones who came back, and, by definition, many who were taken away, were priests made all the difference, as the books of Ezra and Nehemiah indicate. For to the priests what mattered in 586 was the destruction of the Temple, and what made a difference "three generations later" was the restoration of Zion and the rebuilding of the Temple. To them the cult was the key, the Temple the nexus between heaven and earth.

The nation—as seen by the priests, as defined by the priests—restored to its land may be compared to a person healed from a life-threatening illness—or to a poet all the time. To such as these, nothing loses its astonishing quality. Once recovered, to a now-well person, nothing ever can look the same as it did before. Life cannot be taken for granted, as a given. Life becomes a gift, each day an unanticipated surprise. Everything then demands explanation, but uncertainty reigns. The comparison fails, to be sure, when we realize that while the consciousness of life as a gift of grace changes things for the survivor alone, the return to Zion, cast as it was into the encompassing language of the Five Books of Moses, imposed upon the entire nation's imagination and inner consciousness the unsettling encounter with annihilation avoided, extinction postponed, life renewed—

temple restored as portrayed in the Priestly authors' Leviticus and Numbers. To explain the power of the priests' tale, we need hardly invoke the conception of a shared national consciousness, a collective myth of nationhood subject to condition and stipulation, forever threatened with desolation, always requiring renewal. For the Torah, the Pentateuch, taught that one lesson of the human condition of Israel, the Jewish people, every Sabbath everywhere to everybody. So to Israel the Torah imparted the picture of society subject to judgment. And it was the priests' judgment in particular that prevailed. All Judaisms to come would in some way or other find in the priests' paradigm the model to which either to conform or object. The priests' Torah, the Pentateuch in its final statement, constituted the first Judaism and defined the paradigm of all that were to follow.

Chapter 2

Religion and Society in the Law of the Mishnah

Jacob Neusner

Apart from the scriptural law codes, in antiquity no single system of law governed all Jews everywhere. So we cannot describe "Jewish law" as one encompassing system, any more than Jews formed a single coherent society. We can discuss different systems of law, as these governed different groups of Jews. The Scripture's several codes of course made their impact on the diverse systems of law that governed various groups of Jews, or Jewish communities in various places. But that impact never proved uniform. In consequence, in no way may we speak of "Jewish law," meaning a single legal code or even a common set of encompassing rules everywhere held authoritative by Jewry. The relationship between the legal system of one distinct group of Jews to that governing some other proves various. Here we deal with one such system alone, and that is the legal system of the Mishnah, seen in its context, which is the life of some Jews in the Land of Israel in the later first and second centuries of the Common Era, that is to say, from some time just before the destruction of the second temple by the Romans in 70 through the Romans' defeat of the Jews led by Bar Kokhba in 132–135 and on for approximately three generations thereafter, ca. 200.

The Mishnah is an encompassing law code brought to closure in ca. 200 C.E. under the sponsorship of Judah the Patriarch, ethnic ruler of the Jewish communities of the Land of Israel ("Palestine"). Laid forth in six divisions, the laws of the Mishnah take up the sanctity of the land and its use in accord with God's law ("Seeds" or agriculture), the differentiation and passage of sacred time and its impact upon the cult and the village ("Appointed Times"), the sacred aspects of the relationship between woman and man ("Women" or family law), civil law ("Damages"), the conduct of the cult in appropriate regularity and order ("Holy Things"), and the protection of food prepared under the rules of cultic taboos from contamination ("Purities"). The laws of the document throughout lay stress upon the sanctification of Israel's life in the natural world through conformity to the rules governing the supernatural world. So the Mishnah's *halakhah* presents a very particular construction, one proposing to form Israel into a holy community in accord with God's holy law, revealed in the Torah given to Moses at Mount Sinai.

Much of the law of the Mishnah derives from the age before its final closure. In the Mishnah we see how a group of jurisprudents drew together a rich heritage of legal and moral traditions and facts and made of them a single system and can relate their points of stress and emphasis to the circumstances in which they did their work. The authors of the Mishnah in using available, sometimes very ancient, materials, reshaped whatever came into their hands. The document upon close reading proves systematic and orderly, purposive and well composed. It is no mere scrapbook of legal facts, arranged for purposes of reference. It is a document in which the critical problematic at the center always exercises influence over the peripheral facts, dictating how they are chosen, arranged, utilized. So even though some facts in the document prove very old indeed, on that basis we understand no more than we did before we knew that some facts come from ancient times. True *halakhah* as the Mishnah presents law derives from diverse sources, from remote antiquity onward. But the *halakhah* as it emerges whole and complete in the Mishnah, in particular, that is, the system, the structure, the proportions and composition, the topical program and the logical and syllogistic whole—these derive from the imagination and wit of the final two generations, in the second century C.E., of the authors of the Mishnah.

The *halakhah*, or law, of the Mishnah developed in response to the issues confronting the successive framers of the document. The *halakhah* of the Mishnah takes shape in a twofold process. Once a theme is introduced early in the history of law, it will be taken up and refined later on. Also, in the second and third stages in the formation of the Mishnah, many new themes with their problems will emerge. These then are without precedent in the antecedent thematic heritage. The common foundations for the whole always are Scripture, of course, so that I may present a simple architectural simile. The *halakhah* of the Mishnah is like a completed construction of scaffolding. The foundation is a single plane, the Scriptures. The top platform also is a single plane, the Mishnah itself. But the infrastructure is differentiated. Underneath one part of the upper platform will be several lower platforms, so that the supporting poles and pillars reach down to intervening platforms; only the bottom platform rests upon pillars set in the foundation. Yet another part of the upper platform rests upon pillars and poles stretching straight down to the foundation, without intervening platforms at all. So viewed from above, the uppermost platform of the scaffolding forms a single, uniform, and even plane. That is the Mishnah as we have it, six Divisions, sixty-three tractates, five hundred thirty-one chapters. But viewed from the side, that is, from the perspective of analysis, there is much differentiation, so that, from one side, the upper platform rises from a second, intermediate one, and, in places, from even a third, lowest one. And yet some of the pillars reach directly down to the bedrock foundations.

What is new in the period beyond the wars, that is, in the completed statement of the Mishnah of ca. 140–200, is that part of the ultimate plane—the Mishnah as a whole—which in fact rests upon the foundations not of antecedent thought but of Scripture alone. What is basic in the period before 70 C.E. is the formation of that part of the Mishnah which sustains yet a second and even a third layer of platform construction. What emerges between the two wars, of course, will both form a plane with what comes before, that platform at the second level, and yet will also lay foundations for a level above itself. But this intermediate platform also will come to an end, yielding that space filled only by the pillars stretching from Scripture on upward to the ultimate plane of the Mishnah's completed and whole system. So let me now describe what I believe to be the state of the law as a whole before 70.

The basic substrate of conceptions of the Mishnah as we know it originated before 70 in its Division of Purities. The striking fact is that the Sixth Division is the only one that yields a complete and whole statement of a topic dating from before the wars. Its principal parts are (1) what imparts uncleanness; (2) which kinds of objects and substances may be unclean; and (3) how these objects or substances may regain the status of cleanness. Joined to episodic rulings elsewhere, the principal parts of the Sixth Division speak, in particular, of cleanness of meals, food and drink, pots and pans. It then would appear that the ideas ultimately expressed in the Mishnah began among people who had a special interest in observing cultic cleanness, as dictated by the Priestly Code. There can be no doubt, moreover, that the context for such cleanness is the home, not solely the Temple, about which Leviticus speaks. The issues of the law leave no doubt on that score. Since priests ate heave offering at home, and did so in a state of cultic cleanness, it was a small step to apply the same taboos to food which was not a consecrated gift to the priests.

What is said through the keeping of these laws is that the food eaten at home, not deriving from the altar and its provision for the priesthood of meat not burned up in the fire, was as holy as the meal offerings, meat offerings, and drink offerings, consecrated by being set aside for the altar and then, in due course, partly given to the priests and partly tossed on the altar and burned up. If food not consecrated for the altar, not protected in a state of cleanness (in the case of wheat), or carefully inspected for blemishes (in the case of beasts), and not eaten by priests in the Temple, was deemed subject to the same purity-restrictions as food consecrated for the altar, this carried implications about the character of that food, those who were to eat it, and the conditions in which it was grown and eaten. First, all food, not only that for the altar, was to be protected in a state of Levitical cleanness, thus holiness, that is, separateness. Second, the place in the Land in which the food was grown and kept was to be kept cultically clean, holy, just like the Temple. Third, the people, Israel, who were to eat that food were holy, just like the priesthood, in rank behind the Temple's chief caste. Fourth, the act of eating food anywhere in the Holy Land was analogous to the act of eating food in the Temple, by the altar.

All of these obvious inferences point to a profound conviction about the Land, people, produce, condition, and context of nourishment. The setting was holy. The actors were holy. And what, specifically, they did which had to be protected in holiness was eating. For when they ate their food at home, they ate it the way priests did in the Temple. And the way priests ate their food in the Temple, that is, the cultic rules and conditions observed in that setting, was like the way God ate his food in the Temple. That is to say, God's food and locus of nourishment were to be protected from the same sources of danger and contamination, preserved in the same exalted condition of sanctification. So by acting, that is, eating like God, Israel became like God: a pure and perfect incarnation, on earth in the Land which was holy, of the model of heaven. Eating food was the critical act and occasion, just as the priestly authors of Leviticus and Numbers had maintained when they made laws governing slaughtering beasts and burning up their flesh, baking pancakes and cookies with and without olive oil and burning them on the altar, pressing grapes and making wine and pouring it out onto the altar. The nourishment of the Land—meat, grain, oil, and wine—was set before God and burned ("offered up") in conditions of perfect cultic antisepsis.

In context this antisepsis provided protection against things deemed the opposite of nourishment, the quintessence of death: corpse matter, people who looked like corpses (Lev. 13), dead creeping things, blood when not flowing in the veins of the living, such as menstrual blood (Lev. 15), other sorts of flux (semen in men, nonmenstrual blood in women) which yield not life but then its opposite, so death. What these excrescences have in common, of course, is that they are ambivalent. Why? Because they may be one thing or the other. Blood in the living is the soul; blood not in the living is the soul of contamination. The corpse was once a living person, like God; the person with skin like a corpse's and who looks dead was once a person who looked alive; the flux of the zab (Lev. 15) comes from the flaccid penis which under the right circumstances, that is, properly erect, produces semen and makes life. What is at the margin between life and death and can go either way is what is the source of uncleanness. But that is insufficient. For the opposite, in the priestly code, of unclean is not only clean, but also holy. The antonym is not to be missed: death or life, unclean or holy.

So the cult is the point of struggle between the forces of life and nourishment and the forces of death and extinction: meat, grain, oil, and wine, against corpse matter, dead creeping things, blood in the wrong setting, semen in the wrong context, and the like. Then, on the occasions when meat was eaten, mainly, at the time of festivals or other moments at which sin offerings and peace offerings were made, people who wished to live ate their meat, and at all times ate the staples of wine, oil, and bread, in a state of life and so generated life. They kept their food and themselves away from the state of death as much as possible. And this heightened reality pertained at home, as much as in the Temple, where most rarely went on ordinary days. The Temple was the font of life, the bulwark against death.

Once the meal became a focus of attention, the other two categories of the law which yield principles or laws deriving from the period before the wars present precisely the same sorts of rules. Laws on growing and preparing food will attract attention as soon as people wish to speak, to begin with, about how meals are to be eaten. That accounts for the obviously lively interest in the biblical taboos of agriculture. Since, further, meals are acts of society, they call together a group. Outside of the family, the natural unit, such a group will be special and cultic. If a group is going to get together, it will be on a Sabbath or festival, not on a workday. So laws governing the making of meals on those appointed times will inevitably receive attention. Nor is it surprising that, insofar as there are any rules pertinent to the cult, they will involve those aspects of the cult which apply also outside of the cult, that is, how a beast is slaughtered, rules governing the disposition of animals of a special status (e.g., firstborn), and the like.

What sort of a social entity appears to appeal to the kinds of rules I have identified? That the rules for meals pertain not to isolated families but to a larger group is strongly suggested by the other area which evidently was subjected to sustained attention before the wars, laws governing who may marry whom. The context in which the sayings assigned to the authorities before the wars are shaped is the life of a small group of people, defining its life apart from the larger Israelite society while maintaining itself wholly within that society. Three points of ordinary life formed the focus for concrete, social differentiation: food, sex, and marriage. What people ate, how they conducted their sexual lives, and whom they married or to whom they gave their children in marriage would define the social parameters of their group. These facts indicate who was kept within the bounds, and who was excluded and systematically maintained at a distance. For these are the things—the only things—subject to the independent control of the small group. The people behind the laws, after all, could not tell other people than their associates what to eat or whom to marry. But they could make their own decisions on these important, but humble, matters. By making those decisions in one way and not in some other, they moreover could keep outsiders at a distance and those who to begin with adhered to the group within bounds. Without political control, they could not govern the transfer of property or other matters of public interest. But without political power, they could and did govern the transfer of their women. It was in that intimate aspect of life that they firmly established the outer boundary of their collective existence. The very existence of the group and the concrete expression of its life, therefore, comes under discussion in the transfer of women. It therefore seems no accident at all that those strata of Mishnaic law which appear to go back to the period before the wars, well before 70, deal specifically with the special laws of marriage (in Yebamot), distinctive rule on when sexual relations may and may not take place (in Niddah), and the laws covering the definition of sources of uncleanness and the attainment of cleanness, with specific reference to domestic meals (in certain parts of Ohalot, Zabim, Kelim, and Miqvaot). Nor is it surprising that for the conduct of the cult and the sacrificial system, about which the group may have had its own doctrines but over which it neither exercised control nor even aspired to, there appears to be no systemic content or development whatsoever.

Once the group takes shape around some distinctive, public issue or doctrine, as in odd taboos about eating, it also must take up the modes of social differentiation which will ensure the group's continued existence. For the group, once it comes into being, has to aspire to define and shape the ordinary lives of its adherents and to form a community expressive of its larger world view. The foundations of an enduring community will then be laid down through rules governing what food may be eaten, under what circumstances, and with what sort of people; whom one may marry and what families may be joined in marriage; and how sexual relationships are timed.

The Mishnah's *halakhah* between the Wars of 66–70 and 132–135 marks a transition in the unfolding of the Mishnaic law and system. The law moved out of its narrow, sectarian framework. But it did not yet attain the full definition, serviceable—in theory and conception at least—for the governance of a whole society and the formation of a government for the nation as a whole, which would be realized in the aftermath of the wars. The marks of the former state remained. But those of the later character of the Mishnaic system began to make their appearance. Still, the systemic fulfillment of the law would be some time in coming. For the system as a whole in its ultimate shape would totally reframe the inherited vision. In the end the Mishnah's final framers would accomplish what was not done before or between the wars: make provision for the ordinary condition of Israelite men and women, living everyday lives under their own government. The laws suitable for a sect would remain, to be joined by others which, in the aggregate, would wholly revise the character of the whole. The shift after the Bar Kokhba War would be from a perspective formed upon the Temple mount to a vision framed within the plane of Israel, from a cultic to a communal conception, and from a center at the locative pivot of the altar, to a system resting upon the utopian character of the nation as a whole.

When we take up the changes in this transitional period, we notice, first of all, continuity with the immediate past. What was taking place after 70 is encapsulated in the expansion, along predictable and familiar lines, of the laws of uncleanness, so to these we turn first. If the destruction of Jerusalem and the Temple in 70 marks a watershed in the history of Judaism, the development of the system of uncleanness does not indicate it. The destruction of the Temple in no way interrupted the unfolding of those laws, consideration of which is well attested to when the Temple was standing and the cult was maintained. Development is continuous in a second aspect as well. We find that, in addition to carrying forward antecedent themes and supplying secondary and even tertiary conceptions, the authorities between the wars develop new areas and motifs of legislation. These turn out to be both wholly consonant with the familiar ones, and, while fresh, generated by logical tensions in what had gone before. If, therefore, the destruction of the Temple raised in some minds the question of whether the system of cleanness at home would collapse along with the cult, the rules and system before us in no way suggest so. To be sure, the destruction of the Temple does mark a new phase in the growth of the law. What now happens is an evidently rapid extension of the range of legislation, on the one side, and provision of specific and concrete rules for what matters of purity were apt to have been taken for granted but not given definition before 70, on the other. So the crisis of 70 in the system of uncleanness gives new impetus to movement along lines laid forth long before.

An essentially new topic for intense analysis was Holy Things. At issue now is the formation, between the wars, of laws governing the cult. The principal statement of this new system is as follows: the Temple is holy. Its priests therefore are indispensable. But the governance of the Temple now is to be in accord with Torah, and it is the sage who knows Torah and therefore applies it. Since a literal reading of Scripture prevented anyone's maintaining that someone apart from the priest could be like a priest and do the things priests do, it was the next best thing to impose the pretense that priests must obey laymen in the conduct even of the priestly liturgies and services. This is a natural step in the development of the law. A second paramount trait of the version of the system between the wars is its rationalization of those uncontrolled powers inherent in the sacred cult as laid forth by Leviticus. The lessons of Nadab and Abihu and numerous other accounts of the cult's or altar's intrinsic mana (inclusive of the herem) are quietly set aside. The altar sanctifies only what is appropriate to it, not whatever comes into contact with its power. In that principle, the sacred is forced to conform to simple conceptions of logic and sense, its power uncontrollably to strike out dramatically reduced. This same rationality extends to the definition of the effective range of intention. If one intends to do improperly what is not in any event done at all, one's intention is null. Third, attention is paid to defining the sorts of offerings required in various situations of sin or guilt. Here too the message is not to be missed. Sin still is to be expiated, when circumstances permit, through the sacrificial system. Nothing has changed. There is no surrogate for sacrifice, an exceedingly important affirmation of the cult's continuing validity among people burdened with sin and aching for a mode of atonement. Finally, we observe that the established habit of thinking about gifts to be paid to the priest accounts for the choices of topics on fees paid to maintain the cult. All pertain to priestly gifts analogous to tithes and heave offerings. Tithe of cattle is an important subject, and the rules of firstlings and other gifts to the priests are subject to considerable development. The upshot is that the principal concerns of the Division of Holy Things are defined by the end of the age between the wars.

The Division of Damages, dealing with civil law and government, contains virtually nothing assigned to authorities before the wars. Scribes in Temple times served as judges and courts within the Temple government, holding positions in such system of administration of the Israelite part of Palestine as the Romans left within Jewish control. The Division of Damages is remarkably reticent on what after the destruction they might have contributed out of the heritage of their earlier traditions and established practices. Materials of this period yield little evidence of access to any tradition prior to 70, except (predictably) for Scripture. When people at this time did take up topics relevant to the larger system of Damages, they directed their attention to the exegesis of Scriptures and produced results which clarify what Moses laid down, or which carry forward problems or topics suggested by the Torah. That is not evidence that thinkers of this period had access (or wished to gain access) to any source of information other than that one, long since available to the country as a whole, provided by Moses. It follows that, insofar as any materials at all relevant to the later Mishnaic system of Damages did come forth between the wars, the work appears to have begun from scratch. And not much work can have been done to begin with. There is no evidence of sustained and systematic thought about the topics assembled in the Division of Damages. We find some effort devoted to the exegesis of Scriptures relevant to the Division. But whether or not those particular passages were selected because of a large-scale inquiry into the requirements of civil law and government, or because of an overriding interest in a given set of Scriptures provoked by some other set of questions entirely, we cannot say.

The net result of the stage in the law's unfolding demarcated by the two wars is that history—the world-shattering events of the day—is kept at a distance from the center of life. The system of sustaining life shaped essentially within an ahistorical view of reality goes forward in its own path, a way above history. Yet the facts of history are otherwise. The people as a whole can hardly be said to have accepted the ahistorical ontology framed by the sages and in part expressed by the systems of Purities, Agriculture, and Holy Things. The people followed the path of Bar Kokhba and took the road to war once more. When the three generations had passed after the destruction and the historical occasion for restoration through historical—political and military—action came to fulfillment, the great war of 132 to 135 broke forth. A view of being in which people were seen to be moving toward some point within time, the fulfillment and the end of history as it was known, clearly shaped the consciousness of Israel after 70 just as had been the case in the decades before 70. So if to the sages of our legal system, history and the end of history were essentially beside the point and pivot, the construction of a world of cyclical eternities being the purpose and center, and the conduct of humble things like eating and drinking the paramount and decisive focus of the sacred, others saw things differently. To those who hoped and therefore fought, Israel's life had other meanings entirely.

The Second War proved still more calamitous than the First. In 70 the Temple was lost; in 135, even access to the city. In 70 the people, though suffering grievous losses, endured more or less intact. In 135 the land of Judah—surely the holiest part of the holy Land—evidently lost the bulk of its Jewish population. Temple, Land, people—all were gone in the forms in which they had been known. In the generation following the calamity of Bar Kokhba, what would be the effect upon the formation of the system of halakhah of the Mishnah? It is to that question that we now turn. The Mishnah's *halakhah* after the Wars shows us the system as a whole. For the *halakhah* reached its full and complete statement, as the Mishnah would present it, after the Bar Kokhba War. Over the next sixty years, from ca. 140 to ca. 200, the system as a whole took shape. To describe the completed halakhah, we survey the six divisions and their tractates and the main points covered in each.

The Division of Agriculture treats two topics, first, producing crops in accord with the Scriptural rules on the subject, second, paying the required offerings and tithes to the priests, Levites, and poor. The principal point of the Division is that the Land is holy, because God has a claim both on it and upon what it produces. God's claim must be honored by setting aside a portion of the produce for those for whom God has designated it. God's ownership must be acknowledged by observing the rules God has laid down for use of the Land. In sum, the Division is divided along these liens; (1) Rules for producing crops in a state of holiness—tractates Kilayim, Shebiit, Orlah; (2) Rules for disposing of crops in accord with the rules of holiness—tractates Peah, Demai, Terumot, Maaserot, Maaser Sheni, Hallah, Bikkurim, Berakhot.

The Mishnaic Division of Appointed Times forms a system in which the advent of a holy day, like the Sabbath of creation, sanctifies the life of the Israelite village through imposing on the village rules on the model of those of the Temple. The purpose of the system, therefore, is to bring into alignment the moment of sanctification of the village and the life of the home with the moment of sanctification of the Temple on those same occasions of appointed times. The underlying and generative theory of the system is that the village is the mirror image of the Temple. If things are done in one way in the Temple, they will be done in the opposite way in the village. Together the village and the Temple on the occasion of the holy day therefore form a single continuum, a completed creation, thus awaiting sanctification.

The village is made like the Temple in that on appointed times one may not freely cross the lines distinguishing the village from the rest of the world, just as one may not freely cross the lines distinguishing the Temple from the world. But the village is a mirror image of the Temple. The boundary lines prevent free entry into the Temple, so they restrict free egress from the village. On the holy day what one may do in the Temple is precisely what one may not do in the village. So the advent of the holy day affects the village by bringing it into sacred symmetry in such ways as to effect a system of opposites; each is holy, in a way precisely the opposite of the other. Because of the underlying conception of perfection attained through the union of opposites, the village is not represented as conforming to the model of the cult, but of constituting its antithesis.

The world thus regains perfection when on the holy day heaven and earth are united, the whole completed and done: the heaven, the earth, and all their hosts. This moment of perfection renders the events of ordinary time, of "history," essentially irrelevant. For what really matters in time is that moment in which sacred time intervenes and effects the perfection formed of the union of heaven and earth, of Temple, in the model of the former, and Israel, its complement. It is not a return to a perfect time but a recovery of perfect being, a fulfillment of creation, which explains the essentially ahistorical character of the Mishnah's Division on Appointed Times. Sanctification constitutes an ontological category and is effected by the creator.

This explains why the Division in its rich detail is composed of two quite distinct sets of materials. First, it addresses what one does in the sacred space of the Temple on the occasion of sacred time, as distinct from what one does in that same sacred space on ordinary, undifferentiated days, which is a subject worked out in Holy Things. Second, the Division defines how for the occasion of the holy day one creates a corresponding space in one's own circumstance, and what one does, within that space, during sacred time. The issue of the Temple and cult on the special occasion of festivals is treated in tractates Pesahim, Sheqalim, Yoma, Sukkah, and Hagigah. Three further tractates, Rosh Hashshanah, Taanit, and Megillah, are necessary to complete the discussion. The matter of the rigid definition of the outlines in the village, of a sacred space, delineated by the limits within which one may move on the sabbath and festival, and of the specification of those things which one may move on the Sabbath and festival, and of the specification of those things which one may not do within that space in sacred time, is in Shabbat, Erubin, Besah, and Moed Qatan. While the twelve tractates of the Division appear to fall into two distinct groups, joined merely by a common theme, in fact they relate through a shared, generative metaphor. It is, as I said, the comparison, in the context of sacred time, of the spatial life of the Temple to the spatial life of the village, with activities and restrictions to be specified for each, upon the common occasion of the Sabbath or festival. The Mishnah's purpose therefore is to correlate the sanctity of the Temple, as defined by the holy day, with the restrictions of space and of action which make the life of the village different and holy, as defined by the holy day.

The Mishnaic system of Women defines the position of women in the social economy of Israel's supernatural and natural reality. That position acquires definition wholly in relationship to men, who impart form to the Israelite social economy. It is effected through both supernatural and natural, this-worldly action. What man and women do on earth provokes a response in heaven, and the correspondences are perfect. So the position of women is defined and secured both in heaven and here on earth, and that position is always and invariably relative to that of men. The principal interest for the Mishnah is the point at which a woman becomes, and ceases to be, holy to a particular man, that is, enters and leaves the marital union. These transfers of women are the dangerous and disorderly points in the relationship of woman to man, therefore, as I said, to society as well. Five of the seven tractates of the Division of Women are devoted to the formation and dissolution of the marital bond. Of them, three treat what is done by man here on earth, that is, formation of a marital bond through betrothal and marriage contract and dissolution through divorce and its consequences: Qiddushin, Ketubot, and Gittin. One of them is devoted to what is done by woman here on earth: Sotah. And Yebamot, greatest of the seven in size and in formal and substantive brilliance, deals with the corresponding heavenly intervention into the formation and end of a marriage: the effect of death upon both forming the marital bond and dissolving it through death. The other two tractates, Nedarim and Nazir, draw into one the two realms of reality, heaven and earth, as they work out the effects of vows, perhaps because vows taken by women and subject to the confirmation or abrogation of the father or husband make a deep impact upon the marital life of the woman who has taken them. So, in sum, the Division and its system delineate the natural and supernatural character of the woman's role in the social economy framed by man: the beginning, end, and middle of the relationship.

The Mishnaic system of Women thus focuses upon the two crucial stages in the transfer of women and of property from one domain to another, the leaving of the father's house in the formation of a marriage, and the return to the father's house at its dissolution through divorce or the husband's death. There is yet a third point of interest, though, as is clear, it is much less important than these first two stages: the duration of the marriage. Finally, included within the Division and at a few points relevant to women in particular are rules of vows and of the special vow to be a Nazir. The former is included because, in the Scriptural treatment of the theme, the rights of the father or husband to annul the vows of a daughter or wife form the central problematic. The latter is included for no very clear reason except that it is a species of which the vow is the genus.

There is in the Division of Women a clearly defined and neatly conceived system of laws, not about women in general, but concerning what is important about women to the framers of the Mishnah. This is the transfer of woman and property associated with that same transfer from one domain, the father's, to another, the husband's, and back. The whole constitutes a significant part of the Mishnah's encompassing system of sanctification, for the reason that heaven confirms what men do on earth. A correctly prepared writ of divorce on earth changes the status of the woman to whom it is given, so that in heaven she is available for sanctification to some other man, while, without that same writ, in heaven's view, should she go to some other man, she would be liable to be put to death. The earthly deed and the heavenly perspective correlate. That is indeed very much part of larger system, which says the same thing over and over again.

The Division of Damages comprises two subsystems, which fit together in a logical way. One part presents rules for the normal conduct of civil society. These cover commerce, trade, real estate, and other matters of everyday intercourse, as well as mishaps, such as damages by chattels and persons, fraud, overcharge, interest, and the like, in that same context of everyday social life. The other part describes the institutions governing the normal conduct of civil society, that is, courts of administration, and the penalties at the disposal of the government for the enforcement of the law. The two subjects form a single tight and systematic dissertation on the nature of Israelite society and its economic, social, and political relationships, as the Mishnah envisages them. The main point of the first of the two parts of the Division is expressed in the sustained unfolding of the three Babas, Baba Qamma, Baba Mesia, and Baba Batra. It is that the task of society is to maintain perfect stasis, to preserve the prevailing situation, and to secure the stability of all relationships. To this end, in the interchanges of buying and selling, giving and taking, borrowing and lending, it is important that there be an essential equality of interchange. No party in the end should have more than what he had at the outset, and none should be the victim of a sizable shift in fortune and circumstance. All parties' rights to, and in, this stable and unchanging economy of society are to be preserved. When the condition of a person is violated, so far as possible the law will secure the restoration of the antecedent status.

The goal of the system of civil law is the recovery of the prevailing order and balance, the preservation of the established wholeness of the social economy. This idea is powerfully expressed in the organization of the three Babas, which treat first abnormal and then normal transactions. The framers deal with damages done by chattels and by human beings, thefts and other sorts of malfeasance against the property of others. The Babas in both aspects pay closest attention to how the property and person of the injured party so far as possible are restored to their prior condition, that is, a state of normality. So attention to torts focuses upon penalties paid by the malefactor to the victim, rather than upon penalties inflicted by the court on the malefactor for what he has done. When speaking of damages, the Mishnah thus takes as its principal concern the restoration of the fortune of victims of assault or robbery. Then the framer stake up the complementary and corresponding set of topics, the regulation of normal transactions. When we rapidly survey the kinds of transactions of special interest, we see from the topics selected for discussion what we have already uncovered in the deepest structure of organization and articulation of the basic theme.

The other half of this same unit of three tractates presents laws governing normal and routine transactions, many of them of the same sort as those dealt with in the first half. Bailments, for example, occur in both wings of the triple tractate, first, bailments subjected to misappropriation, or accusation thereof, by the bailiff, then, bailments transacted under normal circumstances. Under the rubric of routine transactions are those of workers and householders, that is, the purchase and sale of labor; rentals and bailments; real estate transactions; and inheritances and estates. Of the lot, the one involving real estate transactions is the most fully articulated and covers the widest range of problems and topics. The Babas all together thus provide a complete account of the orderly governance of balanced transactions and unchanging civil relationships within Israelite society under ordinary conditions.

The character and interests of the Division of Damages present probative evidence of the larger program of the philosophers of the Mishnah. Their intention is to create nothing less than a full-scale Israelite government, subject to the administration of sages. This government is fully supplied with a constitution and bylaws (Sanhedrin, Makkot). It makes provision for a court system and procedures (Shebuot, Sanhedrin, Makkot), as well as a full set of laws governing civil society (Babe Qamma, Baba Mesia, Baba Batra) and criminal justice (Sanhedrin, Makkot). This government, moreover, mediates between its own community and the outside ("pagan") world. Through its system of laws it expresses its judgment of the others and at the same time defines, protects, and defends its own society and social frontiers (Abodah Zarah). It even makes provision for procedures of remission, to expiate its own errors (Horayot).

The plan for the government involves a clear-cut philosophy of society, a philosophy which defines the purpose of the government and ensures that its task is not merely to perpetuate its own power. What the Israelite government, within the Mishnaic fantasy, is supposed to do is to preserve that state of perfection which, within the same fantasy, the society to begin everywhere attains and expresses.

This is in at least five aspects. First of all, one of the ongoing principles of the law, expressed in one tractate after another, is that people are to follow and maintain the prevailing practice of their locale. Second, the purpose of civil penalties, as we have noted, is to restore the injured party to his prior condition, so far as this is possible, rather than merely to penalize the aggressor. Third, there is the conception of true value, meaning that a given object has an intrinsic worth, which, in the course of a transaction, must be paid. In this way the seller does not leave the transaction any richer than when he entered it, or the buyer any poorer (parallel to penalties for damages). Fourth, there can be no usury, a biblical prohibition adopted and vastly enriched in the Mishnaic thought, for money ("coins") is what it is. Any pretense that it has become more than what it was violates, in its way, the conception of true value. Fifth, when real estate is divided, it must be done with full attention to the rights of all concerned, so that, once more, one party does not gain at the expense of the other. In these and many other aspects the law expresses its obsession with the perfect stasis of Israelite society. Its paramount purpose is in preserving and ensuring that that perfection of the division of this world is kept inviolate or restored to its true status when violated.

The Division of Holy Things presents a system of sacrifice and sanctuary: Matters concerning the praxis of the altar and maintenance of the sanctuary. The praxis of the altar, specifically, involves sacrifice and things set aside for sacrifice and so deemed consecrated. The topic covers these among the eleven tractates of the present Division: Zebahim and part of Hullin, Menahot, Temurah, Keritot, part of Meilah, Tamid, and Qinnim. The maintenance of the sanctuary (inclusive of the personnel) in dealt with in Bekhorot, Arakhin, part of Meilah, Middot, and part of Hullin. Viewed from a distance, therefore, the Mishnah's tractates divide themselves up into the following groups (in parentheses are tractates containing relevant materials): (1) Rules for the altar and the praxis of the cult—Zebahim Menahot, Hullin, Keritot, Tamid, Qinnim (Bekhorot, Meilah); (2) Rules for the altar and the animals set aside for the cult—Arakhin, Temurah, Meilah (Bekhorot); and (3) Rules for the altar and support of the Temple staff and buildings—Bekhorot, Middot (Hullin, Arakhin, Meilah, Tamid). In a word, this Division speaks of the sacrificial cult and the sanctuary in which the cult is conducted. The law pays special attention to the matter of the status of the property of the altar and of the sanctuary, both materials to be utilized in the actual sacrificial rites, and property the value of which supports the cult and sanctuary in general. Both are deemed to be sanctified, that is: qodoshim, "holy things."

Viewed as a whole, the Division of Purities treats the interplay of persons, food, and liquids. Dry inanimate objects or food are not susceptible to uncleanness. What is wet is susceptible. So liquids activate the system. What is unclean, moreover, emerges from uncleanness through the operation of liquids, specifically, through immersion in fit water of requisite volume and in natural condition. Liquids thus deactivate the system. Thus, water in its natural condition is what concludes the process by removing uncleanness. Water in its unnatural condition, that is, deliberately affected by human agency, is what imparts susceptibility to uncleanness to begin with. The uncleanness of persons, furthermore, is signified by body liquids or flux in the case of the menstruating woman (Niddah) and the zab (Zabim). Corpse uncleanness is conceived to be a kind of effluent, a viscous gas, which flows like liquid. Utensils for their part receive uncleanness when they form receptacles able to contain liquid. In sum, we have a system in which the invisible flow of fluidlike substances or powers serve to put food, drink, and receptacles into the status of uncleanness and to remove those things from that status. Whether or not we call the system "metaphysical," it certainly has no material base but is conditioned upon highly abstract notions. Thus in material terms, the effect of liquid is upon food, drink, utensils, and man. The consequence has to do with who may eat and drink what food and liquid, and what food and drink may be consumed in which pots and pans. These loci are specified by tractates on utensils (Kelim) and on food and drink (Tohorot and Uqsin).

The human being is ambivalent. Persons fall in the middle, between sources and loci of uncleanness, because they are both. They serve as sources of uncleanness. They also become unclean. The *zab*, the menstruating woman, the woman after childbirth, the tebul yom, and the person afflicted with *nega*—all are sources of uncleanness. But being unclean, they fall within the system's loci, its program of consequences. So they make other things unclean and are subject to penalties because they are unclean. Unambiguous sources of uncleanness never also constitute loci affected by uncleanness. They always are unclean and never can become clean: the corpse, the dead creeping thing, and things like them. Inanimate sources of uncleanness and inanimate objects are affected by uncleanness. Systemically unique, man and liquids have the capacity to inaugurate the processes of uncleanness (as sources) and also are subject to those same processes (as objects of uncleanness). The Division of Purities, which presents the basically simple system just now described, is not only the oldest in the Mishnah. It also is the largest and contains by far the most complex laws and ideas.

The final task is to relate the system as a whole to the world beyond. When we identify the generative issues of the system, the urgent questions to which the writing supplies self-evidently valid answers, we see the connection between system and circumstance. Let us begin with the considerations of class and economic interest. How are these sorted out? The critical issue in economic life is in two parts. First, Israel, as tenant on God's holy land, maintains the property in the ways God requires, keeping the rules which mark the Land and its crops as holy. Next, the hour at which the sanctification of the Land comes to form a critical mass, namely, in the ripened crops, is the moment ponderous with danger and heightened holiness. Israel's will so affect the crops as to mark a part of them as holy, the rest of them as available for common use. The human will is determinative in the process of sanctification. Second, what happens in the Land at certain times, at "appointed times," marks off spaces of the Land as holy in yet another way. The center of the Land and the focus of its sanctification is the Temple. There the produce of the Land is received and given back to God, the one who created and sanctified the land. At these unusual moments of sanctification, the inhabitants of the Land in their social being in villages enter a state of spatial sanctification. That is to say, the village boundaries mark off holy space. This is expressed in two ways.

First, the Temple itself observes and expresses the special, recurring holy time. Second, the villages of the Land are brought into alignment with the Temple, forming a complement and completion to the Temple's sacred being. The advent of the appointed times precipitates a spatial reordering of the Land, so that the boundaries of the sacred are matched and mirrored in village and in Temple. At the heightened holiness marked by these moments of appointed times, therefore, the occasion for an effective sanctification is worked out. Like the harvest, the advent of an appointed time such as a pilgrim festival is also a sacred season and is made to express that regular, orderly, and predictable sort of sanctification for Israel which the system as a whole seeks.

The counterpart of the Divisions of Agriculture and Appointed Times are Holy Things and Purities, dealing with the everyday and the ordinary, as against the special moments of harvest, on the one side, and special time or season, on the other. The Temple, the locus of sanctification, is conducted in a wholly routine and trustworthy, punctilious manner (Holy Things). The one thing which may unsettle matters is the intention and will of the human actor. This is subjected to carefully prescribed limitations and remedies. The Division of Holy Things generates its companion, the one on cultic cleanness, Purities. A system of cleanness, taking into account what imparts uncleanness and how this is done, what is subject to uncleanness, and how that state is overcome—that system is fully expressed, once more, in response to the participation of the human will. Without the wish and act of a human being, the system does not function. It is inert. Sources of uncleanness, which come naturally and not by volition, and modes of purification, which work naturally and not by human intervention, remain inert until human will has imparted susceptibility to uncleanness, that is, introduced into the system food and drink, bed, pot, chair, and pan, which to begin with form the focus of the system. The movement from sanctification to uncleanness takes place when human will and work precipitate it.

Now to the central issue: the generative and urgent question, the compelling and self-evidently valid answer. What are these, and how do they relate to the world beyond? The *halakhic* system presented by the Mishnah consists of a coherent logic and topic, a cogent world view and comprehensive way of living. It is a world view which speaks of transcendent things, a way of life in response to the supernatural meaning of what is done, a heightened and deepened perception of the sanctification of Israel in deed and in deliberation. Sanctification means two things, first, distinguishing Israel in all its dimensions from the world in all its ways; second, establishing the stability, order, regularity, predictability, and reliability of Israel at moments and in contexts of danger. Danger means instability, disorder, irregularity, uncertainty, and betrayal. Each topic of the system as a whole takes up a critical and indispensable moment or context of social being. Through what is said in regard to each of the Mishnah's principal topics, what the *halakhic* system as a whole wishes to declare is fully expressed. Yet if the parts severally and jointly give the message of the whole, the whole cannot exist without all of the parts, so well joined and carefully crafted are they all. The system as a whole responds to the crisis of chaos with a message of order: an order within, conceived as the right classification of all parts in a single, cogent conception of ethos, ethics, and ethnos: holy way of life, realizing the ideal of sanctification, for holy Israel. In response to the destruction of the holy temple and loss of the holy city, the end of the cult and the priesthood as instruments of sanctification, the system focused upon the people and the land as the well-ordered realization of that same sanctity that the priesthood and the temple had represented: from the priesthood to the holy people, from the temple to the holy land—these formed the answer to the question posed with ferocious urgency by the catastrophes of the age.

Chapter 3

The Social Foundations of Medieval Mysticism in Judaism

Ivan Marcus

In the last twelfth century, the Jewish communities of the Rhineland witnessed the emergence of an innovative Jewish pietistic circle, characterized by its own leadership and distinctive religious outlook. For almost a hundred years, the Jewish Pietists of medieval Germany constituted a small elite of religious thinkers who, along with their followers, developed and sought to carry out novel responses to a variety of social and religious problems. In particular, the writings of three principal figures have been preserved: R. Samuel b. Qalonimos, known as "the Pietist, the Holy, and the Prophet" [*he-hasid, ha-qadosh, ve-ha-navi*] (fl. mid-twelfth century); his younger son, R. Judah, known as "the Pietist" [*he-hasid*] (d. 1217); and Judah's relative and main disciple, R. Eleazar b. Judah of Worms who called himself "the Insignificant" [*ha-qatan*] (d. *ca.* 1230).

The German-Jewish Pietists constitute a case study of religious revival and adjustment, the first in medieval European Jewish history. Our concern here is to reexamine the Qalonimides and their followers as a religious sub-culture in pre-modern Jewish history and to understand the Pietist authors' goals and how they sought to reinterpret Judaism to achieve them. In the course of reconsidering the historical meaning of their pietistic works, such as *Sefer Hasidim*, it becomes clear that Samuel, Judah and Eleazar not only agreed with one another that the ideal Jew or *hasid* must pursue a personal goal of otherworldly salvation in a peculiar way, but they also differed about the social implications of their shared vision.

The three Qalonimides shared a pietistic vision grounded in a radical theory about the compound and infinitely demanding divine will, partly revealed, partly encoded in Scripture, and which was designed to provide the Pietist with a personal eschatology. This demanding program for the Pietist's salvation includes but extends beyond the rabbinic obligations of Jewish law.

Divinely arranged opportunities for otherworldly reward motivate all aspects of pietism: God concealed the complete divine will so that the Pietist who searches for and discovers it may earn a reward; God continuously makes the world into a series of trials and obstacles to make it difficult for the Pietist to fulfill the complete will, again, in order to provide the Pietist with increased opportunities to withstand the trials and thereby earn reward. The ascetic quality of German Hasidism is based on the central role played in their thinking by the divine scales of judgment: the Pietists continuously weigh this worldly inward enjoyment [*hana'ah*] and try to reduce it so as not to diminish otherworldly reward. The locus of obedience is not primarily external behavior, which is the main criterion by which Jewish and Gentile courts reward or punish, but the degree of the Pietist's inward zeal or sinful motivation. For it is the "heart" which is central, again, because thereby a limitless dimension is opened for a potentially infinite amount of reward. As Y. N. Simhoni noted, the Qalonimides formulated their pietistic ideal not merely as a practical application of ideas derived from others but as an expression of a theory of the religious life which they themselves created. At the center of that theory is the conception of the complex divine will which they usually called, as Haym Soloveitchik has pointed out, "the will of the Creator" [*rezon ha-bore*].

The German-Jewish Pietists' personal eschatology is a particular expression of the quest in Judaism for religious perfection and is "pietistic" in the specific sense of being based not on premises derived from mysticism or religious philosophy or a theory of Jewish law, but on a new understanding of the divine will. Pietism, as used here, refers to an interpretation of Judaism which holds that God's will consists of more than what was explicitly revealed in Scripture (Written Torah), more than the rabbinically derived expanded meanings which form the basis of rabbinic law (Oral Torah). Infinite in scope, the larger will consists of a third dimension encoded in Scripture but which is obligatory for the Pietist. Complementing the idea of God's larger will is the infinite obligation which the Pietist assumes of searching for and discovering it. The Pietist in medieval Germany must "forever be resourceful in fearing God" ["le- olam yehe adam arum be-yir ah"], that is, be engaged continuously in a search for the hidden will by striving to discover new prohibitions and make new proscriptive safeguards [*seyagim, gedarim*] around the forbidden. In so doing, the Pietist shows his true fear of God, which is understood as being afraid that one not love Him selflessly, sacrificially, totally.

But the process of this search, the Qalonimides teach, requires that the Pietist undergo a divinely arranged series of continuous trials, expressed in the power of the evil impulse [*yezer ha-ra'*] a rabbinic formulation for the passions and drives in oneself which God strengthens in order to test the would-be Pietist and provide opportunities for him to resist them and earn greater otherworldly reward. The soteriological basis of German Hasidism also is a reinterpretation of the rabbinic maxim: "reward is proportional to pain" ["le-fum za'ara 'agra"]. It is difficult and painful to search for the hidden will in Scripture; painful to be subjected to the influence of non-Pietist members of Jewish society; painful to experience great temptations of the body, mind and spirit. But if the Pietist succeeds in resisting these temptations and thereby selflessly fulfills the will of the Creator, the scales of God's justice will favor the Pietist with eternal reward.

The Qalonimides' perception of the ideal religious life as a trial sets off German-Jewish pietism from other Jewish views which conceive of the Pietist as a perfected human being. Rather than representing an achieved state of moral excellence, German Hasidism is portrayed as an ongoing process towards the achievement of perfection. Instead of being seen as the destination of a journey, German pietism is thought of as a path filled with roadblocks and detours. For the Qalonimides, the Pietist is not simply one who does no evil; rather, the Pietist is a Pietist only insofar as he obeys the larger will of the Creator while simultaneously resisting the divine trials posed by the evil impulse.

Focused on the non-Pietist Jewish community in Germany, Judah's critique judges other Jews and their communal and rabbinic leaders against his understanding of the pietistic Way and finds them wanting. His concern for the well-being of his Jewish community leads him to speak out and criticize social and economic abuses and to raise questions about the legitimacy of communal leaders who are non-Pietists and whom he accuses of ignoring injustice and of refusing to enforce measures of communal discipline such as the ban.

In addition to advocating a new social ideology as part of German pietism, Judah goes further and defines a new institutional context for the program. In *Sefer Hasidim* Judah's vehicle for the amelioration of German Jewry is a sectarian fellowship of Pietists, a counter-elite led, not by non-Pietist Jewish communal authorities, but by charismatic religious figures, the Sages, who serve the Pietist fellowship as surrogate communal and rabbinic leaders. The social world presupposed by *Sefer Hasidim* is divided into three groups: Christians, Pietist Jews and non-Pietist Jews. Jews may be rich or poor, scholarly or ignorant, powerful or common. All of these distinctions pale to insignificance compared to one distinction which cuts across the others: is a Jew a Priest or non-Pietist?

To be sure, the exclusivist character of Judah's Pietists was not absolute: a non-Pietist could become a Pietist by undergoing an initiation rite of ascetic atonement. To this end, Judah's *Sefer Hasidim* contains a penitential manual which is designed for the use of a Sage who functions as a confessor and dispenser of penances. This elaborate penitential ritual serves the sectarian functions either of disciplining Pietists who temporarily lapse from pietism or of enabling non-Pietists to "enter" or be initiated into it by means of a penitential rite of passage.

The Pietists depicted in *Sefer Hasidim* organized into a fellowship because they viewed non-Pietist Jewish society as illegitimate, and they adopted various political strategies, "the politics of pietism," to try to implement their programmatic vision of the complete divine will, or, at least, to contain the non-Pietists.

They tried either to take over the leadership of the Jewish community or to withdraw completely from it and form utopian communes of the godly. Both efforts failed. Throughout most of *Sefer Hasidim*, the predominant situation is of groups of Pietists who live in, but not of, the rest of the Jewish community; who try to work within that society while at the same time struggling to retain their fellowship and resist being absorbed or even influenced by the non-Pietist majority.

When the Pietists adhered to the dictates of pietism while living among the non-Pietist "wicked," the latter found the former to be insufferably self-righteous. To be a Pietist among non-Pietist Jews was often to be the butt of jokes, the target of ridicule, the victim of intemperate hostility. We find ample evidence in *Sefer Hasidim* of the social tensions engendered within the Jewish communities by the presence of those who were convinced that they, and they alone, knew how God wanted a Jew to live. In some respects, the German *hasidim* were the Puritans of early European Judaism.

When we compare Eleazar's pietistic writings to *Sefer Hasidim*, we see little, if any, criticism of social abuses or of non-Pietist communal leadership; nor is there evidence of religious factions within the Jewish community. Instead, Eleazar deals with relatively abstract discussions about how the individual Pietist or Jew (significantly, the distinction is breaking down) should proceed towards reaching the love of God in preparation for a mystical experience.

In marked contrast to the sectarian and political orientation of *Sefer Hasidim*, Eleazar's writings, like Samuel's, are addressed to the individual Pietist or Jew, and we never find a clear indication there of organized sub-groups of Pietists or of Sages. Instead, Eleazar reiterates the Qalonimide authors' shared understanding of pietism as a personalist eschatology. Eleazar's expression of pietism is personalist, not social; personalist, not sectarian; personalist, not political. But by articulating a personalist mode of pietism in the wake of Judah's attempt to effect a social as well as personal religious revival, Eleazar becomes a reactionary spokesman for a non-Judah, perhaps even a pre-Judah (i.e., Samuel) form of German-Jewish Hasidism.

The society which *Sefer Hasidim* presupposes consists of three groups: Pietists, non-Pietists and Christians. Throughout the book, Judah employs a variety of apparently interchangeable terms to refer to a group of Jews who are Pietists and another set of synonymous terms to describe the non-Pietists. If one looks at the way these sets of terms are used, it is apparent that Judah has created a cumbersome but technical vocabulary with which to describe not simply "good Jews" and "bad Jews," but rather two well-defined sub-groups within the Jewish communities of the Rhineland.

Judah calls Pietists *hasidim* [Pietists], *zaddqim* [Righteous], *hagunim* [Proper], *neqiim* [Clean], *yere'im* [God-fearers], *tovim* [Good]; and he calls non-Pietists *resha'im* [Wicked], *ra'im* [Evil], *pesulim* [Unfit], *perizim* [Violent]. etc. These terms are used to describe otherwise anonymously introduce people, or *exempla,* and sometimes several appear in the same paragraph or even the same sentence. Moreover, these terms are used as substantives, not adjectives. And while an expression like *tove ha-ʿir* [good men of the town] can be equivalent to the Latin *boni viri* and refer to the oligarchy of the local Jewish community, the terms enumerated above do not designate communal leaders, but members of a Pietist fraternity in distinction to all local non-Pietist Jews. A selection of passages will illustrate how these sets of terms operate in *Sefer Hasidim*. In each case we translate the term as a proper noun, with capitalization, but they are all to be understood as being functional equivalent to "Pietist" or "non-Pietist":

> A person should not live in a town where Violent (people) [perizim] eat and drink (SHP, par. 57).
>
> A person should not seat the Wicked [reshaʿim] next to the Righteous [zaddiqim]. Therefore, a person should not seat those who are drinking wine next to the Good [tovim] (par. 60).
>
> If you are walking along with the Good [ha-tovim] assume the best (about their pietism) even though you do not know what they are thinking (par. 108).
>
> Do not tell your dream to someone who does not love you but only to a God-fearer [yare' het] and a Sage [hakham] (par. 387).
>
> If there is in town a Righteous person [zaddig] and one who is not Righteous, a Proper person [hagun] and one who is not Proper who both know how to blow the ram's horn [shofar]....(par. 502).
>
> A certain Pietist [hasid] had many books and died. His heirs came and sold them all and the Righteous men [ha-zaddiqim] were upset....(par. 673).
>
> Jacob has (two) children: one does not lend his books to the Good [la-tovim] and the other willingly lends them to the Good [la-tovim]....(par. 675).
>
> The Righteous [zaddiqim] can impose fines and restrictions on Pietists [hasidim] and God-fearers [yere'im]....(par. 786).
>
> If that God-fearer ['oto yare' shamayim] says to him...(par. 790).
>
> If a man hides books and interpretations from thc Proper [hagunim] they will end up in the hands of the Evil [raʿim] and those who are not Proper [ve'enam hagunim]...(par. 1739), etc.

The Pietists are expected to behave in a variety of specified ways in relation to non-Pietists, and these expectations can be characterized as "sectarian." But if *hasidim, tovim,* etc., are to be thought of as interchangeable terms denoting the Pietists, how are we to understand the terms which denote non-Pietists? When *Sefer Hasidim* describes the Wicked, the Evil, the Violent, and so on, are we to understand that Jewish society was populated by criminals and other social deviants and that it is these scoundrels who are contrasted to the Pietists, the Righteous, and the Good?

In answering this question about the significance of the group which the Pietists describe as adversaries, we face the issue of interpreting the social meaning of the pietistic program. For it the criticism which the Pietists levelled against other Jews was in fact directed at social deviance, then the Pietists had a social as well as religious program of reform. If, on the other hand, we are to take the descriptions of the sinners as exaggerations or as references to Jews who simply did not follow the Pietist Way, then the social critique in the book becomes less obvious.

The question is, What is the character of the group portrayed in *Sefer Hasidim* as non-Pietists? Haym Soloveitchik has recently observed that *Sefer Hasidim* applies the term "wicked" to cases of learned rabbis who wrote liturgical poems [*piyyutim*] but who are simply non-Pietists, that this usage indicates that "wicked" denotes those who do not follow the Pietist Way, and that most references to sinners, corrupt communal leaders and criminals should be discounted or at least not taken at face value:

> No doubt [terms such as "wicked"] refer at times to violent and immoral individuals but the widespread presence of resha'im [wicked] according to the Hasidic account leads us to one of two conclusions: either the political and spiritual leadership in thirteenth-century Germany was frequently in the hands of evil men or the Pietists used this term after their own fashion.

Soloveitchik concludes that *Sefer Hasidim* does not contain a reformist program for the amelioration of society from social and economic wrongs. To him, the terms "wicked," and so on, refer mainly not to social but to religious deviance. Those to whom the author of *Sefer Hasidim* assigns such epithets are in the main simply non-Pietists, and the character of Jewish society in medieval Germany cannot be inferred from the way *Sefer Hasidim* describes non-Pietists.

There is merit in being cautious about how *Sefer Hasidim* should be used to write the social history of medieval German Jewry. The book, we too are arguing, is a program of a particular radical religious point of view, not a documentary record of everyday events written for its own sake. Caution is warranted, but evenhanded caution is in order. The difficulty with Soloveitchik's analysis is that while it insists on giving full weight to some data (those who wrote *piyyutim* are called "wicked") it advocates discounting other data (corrupt communal leaders are also called "wicked"). But there is no more reason for discounting the one than the other. The fact that scholars and synagogue poets are described as being "wicked" (which we agree clearly means "non-Pietists"), does not prove that all or even most cases of the wicked are to be levelled to mean simply "non-Pietists," regardless of the specific accusations made about their behavior. Allegations of murder, apostasy, obstruction of justice and other types of wrongdoing are no less (and no more) credible than references to talmudic scholars who wrote poems but who were not Pietists. Moreover, there is no way of classifying the majority of general references to the "wicked" which lack any detailed accusations, as being of the scholar-poet or criminal variety of non-Pietist.

Sefer Hasidim does describe Jewish society, but through the eyes of a radical perspective of Judaism which condemns all who deviate from that total way of life as outsiders, comparable in some respects to Christians. Although there is reason for being skeptical that what is described actually took place, there is no *a priori* reason for being more skeptical about some accusations than about others. Moralistic writings do not necessarily portray a society accurately and quantitative inferences about deviance are impossible to draw. Still, moralists do not all criticize the same behavior, and from the categories which trouble a particular writer and observer one can infer that there probably is a relationship between his perception and social reality. The author of *Sefer Hasidim*, for example, is not particularly concerned with some sins which have troubled other Jewish writers, such as gambling or ostentatious dress. For him, the problem areas are social and economic exploitation, sexual deviance, and law enforcement. It is difficult to imagine, for example, that Judah's creation of a cadre of Sages, functionally a counter-elite, has no bearing on his critique of the existing Jewish communal leadership.

Without suggesting that such social or economic conditions were exactly as Judah describes them or that they "caused" the emergence of Judah's social consciousness, it is not clear why his sectarian perspective necessarily precludes the value of *Sefer Hasidim* as a mirror of Judah's society. It could be argued that it was Judah's world view which enable him to become sensitive to and to "see" a particular set of problems around him. That his observations of the world were refracted through his ideological perspective docs not mean that he was hallucinating.

What was important for Judah—and for us—is that he described the Pietists, not as individuals but collectively as a group which he defines as the Righteous; all other Jews in his society are the Wicked. That distinction is sectarian.

The sectarian outlook of *Sefer Hasidim* is reflected not only in the polarization between the Pietists and non-Pietists but also in the former's claim to having a source of religious authority which transcends the authority of rabbinic Judaism. Judah argues that the authority of a learned scholar is insufficient for the Pietist; one must be learned in pietism as well as in rabbinic erudition. The latter without the former is worthless:

> If there are Righteous and Wicked in town and both are learned in Torah, even though the Wicked are intellectually more astute [yoter harifim], the Righteous should judge a case, not the Wicked....And if you should object and say that the Wicked is more erudite [yoter mufulpal] and will therefore render the correct judgment by virtue of his acumen, realize that the very opposite is the case. He will pervert (justice) and work hard to distort the truth and mislead the Just....

By advising the Pietist to value a Pietist judge more than a rabbinically learned one, more is being advocated than group solidarity. Underlying Judah's recommendation is a theory of Pietist authority, and it is his claim that Pietist scholars have a source of religious authority outside of rabbinic channels which constitutes a second expression of the sectarian outlook of *Sefer Hasidim.*

In actuality, the Pietist authors invoked two different, but complementary, sectarian modes of religious authority. On the one hand, they claimed to be the most recent recipients of a body of secret lore about how to interpret properly the liturgy and Scripture. This lore, they further held, was transmitted to them esoterically from Sinai. On the other hand, source of religious authority [transmitted or inspired] independent of the sources of authority of the larger community are both present in *Sefer Hasidim* and are transformed into something else in Eleazar's works. In *Sefer Hasidim*, the Pietists are the "good Jews"; the non-Pietists, "the wicked," comparable, in some respects, to Christians. In addition, Judah claims that the esoteric oral tradition about theosophical lore was given to "two or three initiates" and, second, it is the Pietists, like prophets, who are able to fathom the pietistic dimension of the will of the Creator. Neither group separateness nor the continuity of a private source of religious authority is characteristic of Eleazar's world.

Chapter 4
Religion and Economics in Medieval Judaism

Jacob Katz

The analysis of the economic role played by the Jews in Europe during the sixteenth to eighteenth centuries has not yet revealed any specifically Jewish trait, innate or acquired, which qualified them to fulfill the tasks that fell to their lot. Such objective data as their political position, their disposal of large financial resources, and their unity amidst geographical dispersion, would seem to provide sufficient motivation for the nature and scope of Jewish economic activity.

The question that remains to be answered is whether the Jewish religion, mentality, and outlook were also directly responsible for the character of Jewish economic activity. Religion might affect economic life through four other components: the practical performance of religious acts; the social doctrine of religion; its psycho-educational influence; and ethical and religious inspiration.

The Jewish community in this period was confronted with new opportunities for earning a livelihood. Some doubt arose as to whether several of these newly introduced activities did not violate Jewish religious prescription....The progressive integration of the Jews into the general economy led them to trade, directly or indirectly, in commodities which had not been sanctioned by religious law. Jewish merchants traded in non-kosher meat; Jewish estate managers provided their non-Jewish workers with forbidden foods. When engaged in the administration of villages and townships, they were often indirectly concerned with hog breeding. All these activities were forbidden according to the plain meaning of Jewish tradition. The complete and unqualified Sabbath rest specified in the religious codes often presented difficulties for those engaged in farming taxes, managing estates, particularly in retailing liquor, and certainly for transport agents. The same applied to those who leased flour mills, fish ponds, distilleries, potash producers, and the like. Many serious doubts arose concerning the permissibility of benefits accruing to Jews from leavened food stuff during the Passover week.

The conflicts between economic realities and religious prescription usually could be solved. This was due to two factors: the character of Jewish economic activity and the elasticity of halakhic casuistry. The first mitigating circumstance was the fact that a non-Jew could substitute for a Jew on holy days on which the latter was forbidden to work. However, the fact that the Jew did not actually engage in work on a religious day of rest did not satisfy the requirements of the Jewish code, since, from the halakhic point of view, a Jew was not allowed to benefit from work done by the non-Jew for him or in his interest or on commission or in an enterprise bearing his name. As this difficulty was mainly formal, it was removed by a formal solution, such as legal fictions in the contracts of partnerships with non-Jews. The main objective of the Jewish entrepreneur and the chief concern of the rabbinical authorities was to stay away from his place of business on a holy day.

The Jew intuitively shrank from actual engagement in normal weekday business on the Sabbath, even though he might have to act in some capacity. It thus became the practice in wide circles to attend to customers on the Sabbath, to sell them drinks, etc., but not to touch money. Rabbinical authority looked askance at such flimsy compliance with the letter of the law; yet in some cases, they would permit the Jew to be inconspicuously present on the Sabbath in order to keep an eye on the non-Jewish worker, provided that the business was not formally connected with him on this day. Thus he might be permitted to supervise collection of tolls from travellers, so that no advantage was taken of his absence. All these dispensations, whether of popular practice or of rabbinical authority, were based on the assumption that, by and large, the Jew would observe the Sabbath day to keep it holy, would refrain from any actual work, and would spend most of the day in a Sabbath atmosphere. A definite limit was set to the elasticity of the law where it was clear from the start that the basic character of the sabbath rest would have constantly to be violated. This applied to the employment of Jewish carriers in hauling merchandise over long distances and the like.

By distinguishing between direct, personal contact and impersonal, economic operations, rabbinic authority succeeded in working out a *modus operandi* permitting trading in food commodities that the Jew himself is ritually forbidden to eat. The objection to trading in non-kosher meat sprang from the feeling of revulsion aroused by the idea of dealing in "forbidden" food, or, in the more rationalistic formulation of the religious codes, to safeguard the dealer against eventually consuming it himself. Such a motivation was valid only when personal contact with forbidden food was involved. The feeling of revulsion abated in cases where Jews managed large estates on commission or administered large-scale enterprises and derived commercial benefit from these forbidden items without personal contact with them. We may see in this development an expression of the progressive rationalization of the economic process in which the traded goods lose their specific character and are considered merely as an object for profitable enterprise.

Inhibitions were most intense with respect to the enjoyment of the profits from pig-breeding, a traditionally accursed occupation shunned by Jews from time immemorial. Those authorities who remained adamant in forbidding any connection with pig-raising injected into their rulings a strong emotional appeal to the Jewish religious conscience. There are attested instances of Jews' endeavoring to remove the offending animals from the tenant farms during their period of management. However, in the farming districts of Volhynia and Galicia, Jewish leaseholders and contractors tolerated pig-breeding on the lands under their administration during the first part of the seventeenth century. Finally this practice found its halakhic advocate in Rabbi David ha-Levi of Ostrog, author of a gloss to the *Shulchan Arukh* (entitled *Torei Zahav*), who reasoned that pig-breeding was just one of the many branches of agricultural enterprises on the farm, "which did not bear the name of its Jewish administrator, nor does the Jew come into personal contact with this branch...."

The most obvious challenge to existing religious norms was posed by the problem of interest. The problem as such was not new. During the Middle Ages, the usual situation was that of a Jew lending at interest to a non-Jew. Some cases also involved the payment of interest between one Jew and another and required halakhic regulation. Various subterfuges were, indeed, evolved to circumvent the prohibition of usury which applied to both creditor and debtor alike, violation of which was viewed in a very serious light. Aside from the relative infrequency of such cases during the Middle Ages, certain extenuating circumstances facilitated the finding of a solution to the interest problem. Among these were the personal contact between creditor and debtor who made the loan effective by signing contracts or exchanging objects of security. The personal contact between the parties concerned made it feasible for the religious authorities to work out a legally acceptable procedure for the formulation of the contract. The loan contract was required to bear the character of a partnership in the enterprise financed by the loan that would promise the creditor-partner profits without any risks to his capital.

The novel aspect of this problem during the period in point is not the ways of circumventing the injunction against interest, but the emergence of conditions which militated against compliance with the formal regulations evolved by religious law in the past. It was no longer a question of merely advancing money in terms of a loan to be repaid with profit. It had become a practice to finance commercial projects, to make capital investments, to advance goods on credit, and to engage in all other forms of capitalist economy. It would appear that these economic activities favored the halakhic requirements by turning the legal fiction of the Middle Ages—i.e., the formulation of interest as partnership profits—into economic reality. The reality of what had been a legal fiction gave rise to new halakhic problems. The direct creditor-debtor relationship of the Middle Ages was replaced by credit activities through the medium of negotiable notes payable to an unknown bearer. The negotiability of these notes complicated the halakhic problems related to the interest derived from these transactions. Ultimately, only experts could handle such deals in compliance with the halakhic requirements; whereas the ordinary businessman, who was conversant with the elementary concepts of usury, only became confused and developed a cynical attitude towards the whole gamut of religious regulations governing this field.

This situation, which developed at the latest towards the close of the sixteenth century, caused religious authorities much concern. They tackled the problem in two ways: from the educational and administrative aspect and from that of legalistic reform. The former aspect is connected with the name of Rabbi Joshua Falk-Kohen, who held a prominent position in the meetings of the "Council of the Four Lands." He has recorded for us the resolutions, formulated by him, of the Council meeting, which convened in Lublin at the time of the Gramenitz Fair in 1607, with the rectors of the various yeshivot participating. In substance, these resolutions imposed controls upon the members of the Jewish communities that required them to execute transactions involving interest under the guidance of halakhic experts versed in the regulations and formulae governing the circumvention of the prohibition of usury. These expert counsellors were charged with the educational task of explaining "the reasons underlying the procedures adopted, in order to preclude ridicule of this and other matters." For the instruction of these counsellors, but also for the benefit of the ordinary businessman, Rabbi J. Falk composed a booklet setting forth the resolutions and regulations. This booklet contains two versions, one presenting the rules in the form of a manual and the other a learned treatise tracing the sources and outlining the train of thought that led to his rulings.

These enactments had no prospect of being realized in practice. Their authors doubted whether any businessman would be ready to divulge the nature of his transactions to the expert counsellors of his own community. They finally provided for an arrangement by which a counsellor could be appointed from each family, so that the businessman could at least consult his own kin. Obviously such an arrangement could not provide a permanent solution.

The second type of solution was directed, as we have described, at "legalistic reform," a term indicative of its inner character, though not of its self-declared purpose. In contradistinction to the educational, administrative type of solution propounded by the supreme forum of the Jewish communities in 1607, the legalistic formulae won immediate acceptance. Such formulae were already current even at the time when the Council issued the resolutions proposed by Rabbi Joshua Falk, and they were employed after the latter published his booklet, though they did not exactly conform with the procedures outlined therein. The dispensatory formulae propounded were based on varying halakhic grounds. Their common denominator was that they did not involve a detailed account of the proposed transaction and obviated the necessity of calling in expert religious advice in each and every case.

The Maharam formula, which transformed any gain by interest into partnership profit (*Hettar Isqa*), enjoyed the widest currency. Rabbi menachem Mendel

Avigdoris of Cracow issued a formulation which appeared in print even before the rectors of the yeshivot convened at the Council meeting in 1607. In the beginning, copies of these formulations were circulated and used in transactions. After they had become commonly accepted and known, the notes and agreements merely bore a standard clause stipulating that the transaction was to be valid in compliance with the instructions issued by Maharam, i.e. Rabbi Mendel of Cracow. These developments marked the lifting of the last halakhic reservations against the dynamic forces of the contemporary economic scene.

The evolution of the *Hettar Isqa* is but one of the most obvious examples of the process of adjustment called for by the rapidly growing business association among members of the Jewish community. The emergence of internal Jewish credit and its dynamism constituted the main changes that had to be contended with. The financial instrument of this credit was the so-called *memrami*, a promissory note payable to whomever presented it. The name *memrami*, and perhaps its legal content, were already known in the thirteenth century. It was, however, only from the sixteenth century onwards that the *memrami* evolved into the most characteristic instrument of the Jewish merchant in the internal, Jewish market. The employment of *memrami* definitely ran counter to talmudic precedent. According to this tradition, a promissory note was a personal obligation payable only to the party designated, and its negotiability was subject to a most complicated formal procedure. The dynamic economic conditions of the period called for a much more elastic approach to this problem. Again, the revocation of the talmudic tradition in this matter occurred almost unnoticed, and the completely new approach governing the negotiability of bills was adopted without a stir. Talmudic law proved itself remarkably adaptable to the changing needs of the times.

Since Jewish religious and legal tradition did not militate against the emergence of a capitalist economy, it may be asked whether it actually promoted and encouraged such development.

As far as social doctrines were concerned, contemporary Jewish thinking unhesitatingly approved the acquisition of wealth as a means to an end. Moralistic teachings did not ignore the dangers inherent in wealth; they considered both the temptation to employ improper means for its acquisition and the moral pitfalls that were its inevitable concomitants. The moralists reacted by redoubling their warnings against the temptations involved, admonishing their charges to be "honest in their business dealings." Their main concern was directed against unscrupulousness in business. They advised that profits be put to proper use and that the needy be given their due share. One should refrain from exploiting one's acts of generosity and consider the recipient's feelings.

The relationship between worldly success and virtue was undoubtedly the subject of differing evaluations. Some regarded success as a sign of Divine favor, a testimonial from "Him who dispenseth wealth." Ancient texts could easily be adduced in support of such an approach. Others refuted this connection between success and virtue, being prompted by their own personal antipathy to such preaching or by their own experience and social status. Religious tradition provided no clear clue either way. In any event, even those who doubted that wealth was a sign of virtue found no fault with the possession of worldly goods, nothing morally reprehensible in aspiring to worldly success and maintaining it. Poverty was considered a Divine tribulation which man had to suffer and bear. Even the most radical moralists never held up poverty as a virtue in itself for which man should strive. Ancient warrant for the ideal of poverty was not lacking. But supporting texts were either ignored or explained away by dialectic or homiletic argument.

The entire Jewish community depended for its everyday subsistence on profit-earning capital. This fact made it impossible for Jewish moralist doctrine to withhold its approval of such a situation. Far form having his acquisitive instinct checked, anyone growing up in the Jewish community of the sixteenth to eighteenth centuries was bound to absorb views which, after laying down due qualifications and controls, encouraged and promoted this tendency. We may, therefore, conclude that the social doctrine of Judaism during this period definitely favored the economic activities undertaken by the community.

It would be equally justified to regard Judaism—or rather its specific way of life—as affording a psychological and "rational" training for that type of economic activity. By "rational" is meant activity solely dictated by considerations of efficiency. Judaism inculcated purposeful living, demanded the planned utilization of one's time, and disapproved of uncontrolled emotional reactions. In other words, it trained the Jew to lead a carefully planned, rational life. The remarkable commercial talent of Jews may plausibly be traced to their religious upbringing, as has been maintained by some scholars. It should be borne in mind, however, that their religious background did no more than psychologically predispose them in this direction. Sociological research teaches us not to seek the key to an understanding of relationship between religion and economic activity in the sociological doctrines of any religion or in the formal psychological preparation it provides. We must also be careful not to overrate the psychological effect of rationalistic conduct in one sphere on that in another. The main impact of religion upon the social realm derives, as Max Weber has shown, from the very core of its beliefs and notion of personal salvation, matters which, at first sight, would seem to have little bearing upon anything outside the purely religious sphere.

This calls, therefore, for an investigation into the purely religious content of Judaism, the function it assigns to man in creation, and the way of life it directs him to follow on the road toward personal salvation. It would then be seen whether it predisposes men to engage in the kind of economic activity on which the Jewish community was based. In other words, did Judaism ascribe a positive role to economic activity in the struggle for salvation in the eyes of God, or, psychologically speaking, in man's own eyes as well? In our case, this central question—which Max Weber posed regarding Protestantism of that very same period—has to be answered, unlike Weber's reply in the case of Protestantism, in the absolute negative. Admittedly the acquisition of wealth was permitted, sometimes even commended, but worldly success was never served as the basic criterion of virtue in the sight of God and man. This could only be achieved by the practical performance of the precepts of Judaism and the cherishing of its ideals traditionally summed up in the threefold phrase: "Torah, worship, and good works." Money facilitated the achievement of religious ideals, but it was not an essential pre-condition. The study of Torah, the observance of the commandments, and, primarily, the performance of good works demanded some financial means. Torah study was furthered by removal of financial worry. The extent of good works and charity was determined by the financial means at one's disposal. This harnessing of wealth to religious purposes meant that it occupied only a subordinate role in the hierarchy of Jewish values. The accumulation and disposal of wealth could never become ends in themselves nor act as substitutes for virtue gained through authentic religious media. Economic success could, at best, be regarded as affording corroborative evidence of a person's merit. The crucial testimonial must derive from the purely religious sphere, based on strictly law-abiding and conscientious religious observance and the proper use of the worldly goods entrusted to man. Religion is bound to minimize the value of religious works if it wishes actively to promote chrematistic activities. Judaism never reached this stage. It developed an attitude of tolerance towards worldly occupations—but only as a last resort, according them *post facto* recognition, and then only in the form of special dispensations. Activities outside the purely religious sphere were never consecrated as ends in themselves.

It was theoretically possible for the faithful to discharge the sum total of religious observances demanded of them, in which religious practices reigned supreme, and still devote the remaining time to business as a sacred pursuit of secondary importance. But this was precluded by the existence of one precept, the duty to study the Torah, which monopolized by Divine prescription any time left after one's personal needs, livelihood, and other religious observances had been attended to. The study of Torah is obligatory at all times, whenever one is not engaged in an essential occupation. This obligation was, however, fully honored only by a small minority of scholars who dedicated their time without stint to the study of Torah. The majority studied Torah only in their leisure time. The average Jew found ample time to spare for business, and he energetically applied himself to it. Such application was, however, only condoned as a tolerated practice that required justification in the light of the principle that one should devote the maximum of one's time to Torah study. This obligation devolved on every Jew, layman, and scholar alike. The moralistic literature repeatedly stressed that even one who was incapable of profound study should gain from his text whatever his understanding allowed.

Anyone who devoted more time to the pursuit of worldly gain than was warranted to eke out his livelihood was guilty of idling his time away, a transgression tantamount to the neglect of Torah studies.

Profane occupations were justified in many ways. It was impossible to define clearly what came under the category of "essential occupations." Moreover, ways were found to vicariously engage in the prescribed religious studies by delegating them. He who contributed to the upkeep of Torah students, and, even more so, he who fully supported them, was regarded as a partner in their meritorious occupation. The heavenly reward was shared equally between them, as in all partnerships, since the precept could only be performed by the joint effort of student and patron.

Though the obligation of Torah study did not, in practice, militate against devotion to business and other occupations, it prevented their recognition as ends in themselves. Vocational occupations could not be gainsaid, but they remained workaday in character. Nothing short of a complete inversion of Jewish values could have won direct religious sanction for economic activities.

Chapter 5
A Marxist View of Hassidism

Raphael Mahler

NATIONAL OPPRESSION AND THE KEHILLAH RÉGIME

The abundant creative force accumulated by the teeming and seething masses of eastern European Jewry erupted for the first time in its full splendour with the Hassidic movement. For centuries, the literature of the Polish Jews had only differed from that of the neighbouring central European countries in the quantity of its creative output. Poland had been a major centre of orthodox Jewry from the sixteenth century and its influence had extended beyond the communities of Moravia, Bohemia and Germany into Alsace-Lorraine and Holland. However, its creative activity was confined to exegeses and commentaries on the Talmud and the Codifiers. The literature of ethics was also on the same pattern in Poland as in all other Ashkenazi Jewish settlements. The appearance of Hassidism revealed for the first time the uniqueness and originality of a culture deeply rooted in a colourful folk life, fashioned by a community of people which had been living in Poland and the countries around for many centuries. This body of Polish Jewry had moreover covered the cities, towns and villages of the country with a tight network of Kehillot. A mass religious movement such as this, which overwhelmed and inspired with enthusiasm vast numbers of Jews in Poland, Lithuania, White Russia and the Ukraine, was altogether inconceivable in central or western Europe: even in geographic terms, the tiny, scattered Jewish communities there, shut away in their ghettos and their separate streets, were not conducive to such a development. However, the differences in economic, social and political condition and cultural level between eastern and western European Jewry were more decisive with regard to Hassidism than the demographic and geographic factors. The spiritual exhaustion of religious orthodoxy and the decadence of the Kehillah and other organs of Jewish communal autonomy had become evident throughout the European Diaspora—East and West—by the second half of the eighteenth century. In western Europe, however, this period of enlightened absolutism saw the rise of capitalism so that western Jews found an outlet for their aspirations to transform public and cultural life in *Haskalah* and the movement for civil enfranchisement. By contrast, the social, economic and political backwardness of eastern Europe, with its intractable feudal system, caused the Jews there to express their hopes for social, national and cultural regeneration in a religious movement—Hassidism. Nonetheless, although Hassidism was confined to eastern Europe, it exerted the most pervasive influence of all Jewish religious movements during the centuries of exile. It was also the last such movement in the Jewish people's history. It represented the crowning achievement of religious Jewry and passed on to the modern, secular culture of the Jewish people what was best in the ancient culture which had for a long period (longer by far than in the case of other European nations) been exclusively dominated by religion.

Like all the religious movements amongst the Jewish people in the Diaspora, particularly the various mystical systems, Hassidism possessed all the characteristics of a redemption movement. Like them too, it developed and extended because of the yearning of a people living in captivity amongst gentiles for deliverance from exile and for restoration in Zion and Jerusalem. At every crisis in the diaspora history of the Jewish people—every increase in economic distress or national oppression, repressive legislation or persecution—the longing of the masses for deliverance became more acute. The expulsion of the Jews from Spain, Sicily, southern Italy, Provence and the cities of Germany at the end of the fifteenth century gave rise to the Kabbalah movement founded by Isaac Luria (HaARI) and his disciples at Safed. After the massacres of 1648 and 1649 in the Ukraine, Lithuania and White Russia, and the Czarniecki pogroms in Greater Poland, the Sabbetai Zvi messianic movement arose and caused such an upheaval in the Jewish world that its consequences were in evidence until the end of the eighteenth century. Hassidism was born during the "Saxon" period, when Polish Jewry was all but overwhelmed by persecution and oppression. At this time Poland was in the state of chaos that preceded its fall. The noblemen, who dominated the private cities, the towns and villages, indulged in atrocity towards the Jews, who were totally thrown at their mercy. During this period, the Catholic clergy too, had reached the height of its power in the state. Religious fanaticism against non-Catholics, and especially against the Protestants, was given free rein. Bloody assaults by students and apprentices under inflammatory Jesuit incitement were a daily occurrence for Jews inhabiting the Crown cities. The clergy re-introduced the system of public disputations—as if to revive the horrors of the Middle Ages. The most terrifying of the compulsory debates, those held with the Frankists at Kamenietz-Podolsk and Lwow, spread terror amongst all the Jews of Poland.

Innocent Jews were publicly executed on ritual murder charges in all the provinces of the state on an almost Inquisitional pattern. Finally, the Jews of the Ukraine were struck by the Haidamak peasant revolt. "The Terrible Tale of Uman," a massacre of Jews in the fortress of that city in 1768, seemed almost a repetition of episodes during the massacres of 1648. In 1768, too, the retrograde, fanatical and chauvinistic Polish nobility founded a union "For the Defence of the Faith and the Fatherland," the Bar Confederation. Its forces roamed through most of the districts of Poland for several years, regularly extorting war levies from the impoverished Jewish Kehillot.

During the closing decades of the eighteenth century when Hassidism experienced its greatest growth and expansion, the condition of Polish Jewry actually changed for the better in several respects. The government under the last king of Poland, Stanislaw August Poniatowski, reduced the power of the clergy, and ritual murder accusations and anti-Jewish riots occurred less frequently. But at the same time the legal position of the Jews in Poland deteriorated. The poll tax was raised several times after the liquidation of the Council of the Four Lands and the abolition of regional Jewish autonomy. Furthermore, the law of 1768 expelled the Jews from a number of cities; in the remaining Crown cities they had to wage a difficult struggle for the right to engage in trade and the crafts. As a result of the various repressions, the poverty of the Jewish population became even more desperate. Over a tenth of all Jewish family heads were totally without income and columns of beggars wandered from city to city, from Kehillah to Kehillah, begging for alms to keep themselves alive. The position of the village Jews, the lessees, innkeepers and liquor purveyors was undermined to an even greater extent than that of the urban Jews. Following changes in the management of manorial estates, tens of thousands of petty lessees were deprived of their leaseholds and left without employment. The same trend caused an arbitrary increase in rentals by the landed proprietors; lessees and their families who could not meet their contractual obligations were subject to incarceration and other forms of abuse by their masters. It is no coincidence that summary increases in lease rentals, the threat of expulsion from the villages, and the attendant "ransoming of captives" (the liberation of lessees held prisoner by estate owners) are recurrent themes in Hassidic legends about the miracle-working *Tzaddikim*.

The only improvement that took place at the beginning of the nineteenth century, under the absolutist régime of the three powers that had partitioned the Kingdom of Poland, was in the condition of the wholesale merchant class, the contractors and army suppliers. The burden of special taxes was even heavier than under independent Polish rule and weighed desperately heavily on the Jewish masses in the cities and villages. The double tax in Russia, the kosher meat tax in Galicia and the Grand Duchy of Warsaw, and the candle tax in Galicia sapped the vitality of the oppressed Jewish poor. The brunt of the repression fell on the rural Jews, as the partitioning powers paid special attention to implementing the enactments which Poland, on the verge of collapse, had not found the opportunity to enforce. Decrees expelling the Jews from the villages were issued in Russia, Austria and the Grand Duchy of Warsaw, and some were actually put into effect in Galicia and White Russia. The national oppression of the eastern European Jewish masses at the end of the Napoleonic period was as effective as in the days of Rabbi Israel Ba'al Shem Tov, during the reign of Poland's Saxon kings. Only the outward form was different.

It was not surprising, therefore, that Hassidic teaching interpreted "this bitter exile" as a total metaphysical, spiritual, ethical and even an economic antagonism between the Jewish people and the gentiles. Israel's position amongst the nations was compared with "a lamb amongst wolves." In their daily lives, the Jews encountered "the nations of the world" in the form of the arrogant, brutal and lustful *Paritz* or nobleman, the priests, with their hatred of the Jewish religion and their incitement of the mob against its adherents, the domineering, pompous officials whose goodwill could only be obtained by bribes, and the crude peasants who drank themselves into oblivion to escape from squalor and wretchedness. All the pent-up suffering and humiliation accumulated over the generations achieved a catharsis in the Hassidic doctrine of the Cosmic Axis, with its poles represented by Tyre and Jerusalem, Esau and Jacob, idolatry and the worship of God, defilement and purity, Satan's domain and the domain of Holiness. "Tyre was built up only through the Destruction of Jerusalem. . . . When the one falls, the other arises"—this was the key to the mystic interaction of supreme forces, which also affected livelihood and maintenance. Prayer, the study of the Law and the observance of the divine commandments functioned in such a way that ultimate affluence did not flow entirely towards the gentiles but was also allotted to the children of Israel. Their share of the bounty of the world increased to the extent that they proved themselves worthy. In this way too, the people of Israel were able to "assuage the sternness," to mitigate unfavourable decisions and decrees that the gentiles contrived against them and sometimes even to abolish those decrees completely.

The virtue of love for Israel was one of the cardinal tenets of Hassidism related to its consistent teaching of the identity between the people of Israel and the good positive and noble substance of the Universe. All the natural emotions of love for humanity and all the scriptural talmudic precepts, and those of ethical literature on the love of fellow-men were construed as references to the Jewish people—and not only as the chosen people but also as mankind personified. Love of Israel meant love of the people as a whole and of every living individual Jewish soul. It was as though the suffering of the Jewish people and its mission of reforming the world atoned for the sins of the entire community of Israel and of every Jew. When a people was troubled and in captivity and still served the one true God, its actions were not subject to minute scrutiny. Hassidic literature abounded in glorification of the people of Israel. One of the highest qualities that Hassidic lore attributed to all its *Tzaddikim* (the leaders of the movement beginning with Ba'al Shem Tov) was the vindication of Israel. Some of them were even crowned with the epithet *Ohev Yisrael*—a lover of Israel—(Moses Leib of Sasow, Davidl of Lelow, Levi Isaac of Berditchev, Abraham Joshua Heshel of Opator).

The "assuagement of sternness" and the bringing down of affluence represented only a modicum of salvation to a people exiled from its country—together with the *She'khinah* (the divine presence)—and delivered into the lands of the profane gentiles. Only complete deliverance would constitute total triumph in the contest between Israel and the nations of the world. In messianic times, the *She'khinah* would be redeemed from its exile to become a perfect entity with the Holy One Blessed Be He, the people of Israel would be restored to its own land, and the world would achieve its perfection (*Tikkun*) in the kingdom of the Almighty. The yearnings for deliverance, which had filled the hearts of the people throughout the generations of its long exile, became an overwhelmingly powerful and continuous longing amongst the masses who supported the Hassidic movement. Hassidism was, in fact, heir to all the religious folk movements in the history of the people, but it did not possess the attributes of a straightforward messianic movement in the accepted sense. On the contrary, from its inception its aim was a total negation of the Sabbetai Zvi movement and its offshoots, despite the fact that it adopted some of its mystic elements and even some of the customs from its mode of life.

Hassidism followed the pattern of the essentially evolutionary redemption movement and not that of the messianic movements, which had the character of national religious revolutions in the history of the exiled people. In that respect, Hassidism might rather be compared with the Karaite movement of some 1,000 years earlier. The emphasis that the Karaite movement placed on the striving for deliverance and the restoration of Zion was so great that it formed the basis for the principal divergence of opinion between it and rabbinical teaching on most of the religious laws and customs. Even so, Karaism did not fundamentally arise as a messianic movement but rather in opposition to the messianic movements that had preceded it, such as Abu Isa in Persia and Serene in Syria. The failure of these movements had strengthened Karaite belief that the end could not be hastened by acts of desperation, but that redemption lay in a wholehearted return to the God of Israel and literal observance of the Torah without the distortions of the talmudic sages and the rabbis. Analogically, Hassidism sought an answer and solution for the despondence and impotence which attacked large numbers of people after the defeat of the Sabbetai Zvi movement, sealed by Frankist treachery precisely when the new movement was beginning to grow. The founders of Hassidism counteracted the bitter disappointment that followed these attempts to hasten the end, by teaching that deliverance was a mystical-historical process in which each and every person in Israel was destined to play an active and decisive role. Every improvement in the soul of the individual through loving and worshipful adhesion (*De'vekut*) to God contributed to the attainment of perfection in the highest realms and thus accelerated the deliverance of the people and the *She'khinah* from exile. Prayer with intention (*Kavvanah*), the study of the Law for its own sake (*Torah Le'she'mah*), ardent observance of all precepts (*Mitzvot*) and the performance of acts of piety and charity would lead to individual wholeness and to communal redemption. As Hassidism revealed this truth concerning behaviour in the service of the Creator, its adherents were convinced that their movement was the messenger of deliverance—much in the same way as the publication of the *Zohar* had prompted the view amongst the Kabbalists that the age of deliverance had dawned with the revelation of Kabbalah. Proof that expectations of imminent deliverance existed and gained in strength as Hassidism grew was demonstrated by the Hassidic *aliyot* (ascents, i.e. migrations) to the Land of Israel led by the disciples of Ba'al Shem Tov and their pupils.

At the turn of the eighteenth and nineteenth centuries, the people gained new hope of the Messiah's advent from the cataclysmic events inaugurated by the French Revolution and the Napoleonic wars. But even amidst the spiritual tension of the time, Hassidism did not abandon its principles relating to the conditions for deliverance. It did not succumb to a spirit of adventurousness engendered by despair, but called for penitence as the only means of achieving the desired end.

Another common characteristic linking Hassidism to the other religious folk-movements in the history of the Jews was the fact that the forces motivating its aspiration for national redemption were inextricably connected with the dynamic factors of social development, and the aspiration on the part of the destitute and oppressed classes for social advancement, and with their struggle for liberation. As social pressures grew, the classes discriminated against by the Kehillah régime yearned for deliverance even in the widest sense: deliverance from bondage amongst the nations, from poverty, and from oppression by their own ruling classes. The yearning for national redemption, for an improvement in social conditions and for a reform of the régime were fused into one movement for total redemption, which called for a revival of the faith from its decadence and a purge of all its abuses. This social aspect of the redemption movement gave rise to violent hatred and ruthless persecution by the defenders of the existing régime and by the guardians of the traditional version of the Jewish religion.

In fact, the Kehillah régime in Poland had deteriorated to the lowest level of decadence during the period of the rise of Hassidism. The decay of the antiquated feudal order in the Kingdom had eroded the organs of Jewish autonomy, which were interlocked with its framework. The Kehillah had long ago ceased to discharge its functions of organizing the Jewish population to defend its rights and of ministering to its communal and cultural needs. It had become a tool of the monarchy and the noblemen who owned the towns. The rural Jews, including the wealthy lessees and suburban inhabitants, were denied electoral rights in the Kehillot and thus the right to hold Kehillah office, though they were required to pay all Kehillah rates and observe all its regulations. The authority of the Kehillot weighed heavily on towns in their immediate vicinity and their inhabitants were the victims of discrimination in the apportionment of government taxes. In the cities, not only the destitute but even Jews who were not actually prosperous were deprived of electoral rights.

Even wealth did not assure its owners of the official right to participate in Kehillah administration, as this had come under the control of cliques. The office of *Parnass* in the Kehillot had become a kind of concession (*arenda*), which, like other lesseeship transactions, depended on access to nobles and government officials. These leaders, with the support of the authorities, ruled the Kehillot like private estates. Their position sometimes provided a lucrative source of personal income for themselves, their relations and friends. The taxation system in the

Kehillot was almost entirely based on various indirect levies generically designated as the *korobka* and the full weight was borne by the working classes—artisans, storekeepers, the pedlars and the publicans. Charitable activities had been removed from the scope of Kehillah functions and long since entrusted to societies, the largest of which were in turn organized on the same hierarchical pattern as the Kehillah executive.

Generally, the rabbis not only failed to protect the people against oppression but actually lent their approval to the activities of the Kehillah leaders, established their own control over the people and prospered from their office. A rabbinical post could only be obtained in return for huge sums paid into the Kehillah treasury and its organs, and appointments were awarded to the candidate who paid most. Therefore, the office of rabbi was usually in the hands of the sons and sons-in-law of the wealthy who also controlled the position of *Parnass*. The rabbis lived on a similarly luxurious scale as their relations, and they recouped many times over in fees and obligatory gifts from their congregation the sums they had paid for their appointments. Nor were the Kehillah judges innocent of partiality during court proceedings or of accepting gifts from litigants, according to the critics of the time, the popular preachers (*darshanim*). The judges, like all Kehillah officials, received their appointment in return for a sum paid into the Kehillah treasury. The highest strata of the scholar class were tightly linked to the wealthy class which ruled the Kehillot. Even scholars who did not actually hold office were mostly related to the wealthy, either by social origin or by social position. The children of artisans and the poor usually had no opportunity to matriculate in the study of religious law and scholars were not common amongst the rural Jews, who were remote from rabbinical seminaries and religious schools. The rank of scholar not only conferred many rights in Kehillah institutions and societies—such as electoral rights or qualification to serve in public office—but also many honours within the synagogue (such as to be called to attend the reading of the Law) at ritual celebrations and similar occasions. As a result, the social position of the *am Ha'aretz** was of the lowest grade and they were even humiliated in their status as human beings. According to prevalent concepts an *am-Ha'aretz* could read the Scriptures but knew no *Gemara*. Even those who regularly studied Talmudic legends (the *Ein-Ya'akov Societies*) were classed amongst the lower orders. These caste distinctions isolated the lofty scholar from the broad masses.

The detachment and seclusion of the scholar class was also a symptom of the spiritual crisis that had developed amongst the Jews of Poland and orthodox Jewry as a whole. The fact that *pilpul* (casuistry) had become the predominant method in the study of the Talmud and the Codifiers proved that the Torah had ceased to be a rule for living and therefore correspondingly less of a guide to the masses of the Jewish people in Europe. It had become "a spade wherewith to dig" the means to a social career and distinction in the hierarchy of Jewish community life. This mode of *Halakhah* instruction had not given birth to any fruitful or enlightening concept

**am-Ha'aretz*, literally, the people of the land (*cf.* etymological connotation of the word *peasant*), hence a common or ignorant person, a boor.

and no innovations whatsoever had been made in the negative and positive laws, let alone in the religious way of life. All the precepts and prohibitions had been formulated and sanctified over the past two hundred years in the *Shulhan Arukh* and fortified for a hundred years by detailed commentaries. Any working man of Polish Jewry in the eighteenth century could justifiably have asked like Benjamin Assia, cited in the Talmud (*Sanhedrin, 99*) as a typical heretic "Of what use have our rabbis been to us? They have never permitted us to eat raven flesh nor forbidden us to eat dove . . ." Contemporary ethical literature had become permeated with the belief in demons, spirits and the transmigration of the soul under the influence of theurgic, or practical Kabbalah, and was equally incapable of supplying the spiritual mainstay of the people. Instead of encouraging them, raising their spirits, consoling them in their troubles and moral depression, and giving them renewed hope, the moralists urged them to forswear the vanities of this world, praised the virtue of asceticism and provided all the tortures of hell for the slightest transgression or suggestion of transgression.

During the final decades of the Polish Kingdom, when the spread of Hassidism had already made considerable headway, mass revolt broke out in the large Kehillot of Lithuania, White Russia and Volhynia (at Dubno), especially amongst the artisans, who organized themselves against the *Parnassim* and demanded a democratic Kehillah régime. The Hassidic movement was in sympathy with this mass uprising, though it never integrated with its organization and was not identified with its ideals. In some places, however, the Hassidim supported the rebellious masses in their demands for Kehillah reforms, and voiced complaints on their own behalf against abuses in Kehillah affairs (at Vilno and Minsk). Conversely, many of the oppressed who were in revolt against Kehillah despotism, were attracted by the democratic nature of the doctrines of Hassidism.

The theoretical basis of Hassidic doctrine rested on the Kabbalah, in all its phases of development, from the old *Sefer Ha'yetzirah* (*Book of Creation*) down to the concepts of the last Polish Kabbalists before the Ba'al Shem Tov. However, the Kabbalah system which influenced Hassidism most was that of Isaac Luria, as formulated by his disciple, Haim Vital. Until the rise of Hassidism, Kabbalah had only been a school of the occult in the mainstream of Judaism. Its sanctity was so widely recognized that none of the acknowledged sages dared challenge it, but its study was limited exclusively to individuals and circles concerned with the occult. Hassidism elevated Kabbalah to the rank of a superior doctrine, which endowed the revealed Law with meaning and purpose. Hassidism explained the mystic doctrine in such facile and simple terms that its secrets became a commonplace, an occult teaching which had, as it were, become a second version of revealed Law. The elements of Kabbalah assimilated by Hassidism became the property of the masses. The Hassidic movement ensured the publication of new editions of the principal Kabbalist books and also caused ancient manuscripts of the doctrine (*Sefer Ha'pe'lia—The Book of Miracles,* and *Sefer Ha'Kanah,* composed in the fourteenth century) to be printed for the first time. As a result, knowledge of Kabbalah and its original methods became widespread amongst the Jewish masses. The entire religious life of the Hassidim was permeated with Kabbalah doctrine after they had generally adopted the custom of conforming to Isaac Luria's method of preceding every prayer and every act of piety with a formula interpreting its mystic connotation. Furthermore, Hassidim were instructed by their masters never to depart from Kabbalah doctrine for a moment in their daily lives. In everything they did, they were conscious of the precept of adhesion to God and effecting perfection in the upper worlds. The influx of Kabbalist concepts into broad sections of the common people together with the spread of the Hassidic movement was reflected in the numerous Kabbalist terms which became an integral part of Yiddish vocabulary:*

> *Nitzotz Ke'dushah* (a spark of holiness of divine sanctity), *Sitra-Achra* (Aramaic: the "other side," i.e., the devil's domain); *Koah-Ha'tum'ah* (the force of defilement); *Ke'lipah* (the impure, or material shell); *Tikkun* (literally, a perfecting, or reforming; *cf. supra*); *metakken zein* (Yiddishized Hebrew, to effect *Tikkunim*); *madregah* (level, stage); *be'chinah* (category, criterion); *Olamot Elyonim* (the upper worlds); *Galut Ha'She'khinah* (exile of the abode of the divine presence).
>
> Likewise, the vernacular of eastern European Jewry absorbed expressions such as the following directly from Hassidic teachings: *Hitbodedut* (solitary communion; literally, being solitary); *de'vekut* (literally, adhesion, clinging; hence, devotion); *hitlahavut* (enthusiasm, fervour); *atzvut* (sadness, grief); *kavvanah* (literally, purpose; by implication in Hassidic contexts and by derivation in all acts involving application, concentration of purpose); *aliyat ha'ne'shamah* (ascent of the soul); *hitpa'alut* (ecstasy); *nitgaleh vern* (Yiddishized Hebrew phonetically: *nisgaleh vern*—to be revealed); *hitgalut* (becoming revealed, revelation).

The authority given to Kabbalah by Hassidism, as well as its spread and popularization by this movement, brought about a religious revolution—directly, through the propagation of a mystical outlook amongst the people and indirectly, by reducing the hegemony of Talmudic doctrine. However, Hassidism did not adopt Kabbalah unaltered. It discovered new facets of it and created a new system of mystics by its mode of presentation, its emphasis and its development of those ideas which were appropriate to the movement's aims. The central theme of Hassidic Kabbalah was not contained in the speculation on divinity and the nature of the upper worlds, or in the search for the "Story of the Divine Chariot" or "the Acts of Genesis." Its dominant interest was man, his conduct in reverence and his way of worshipping God.

SOCIAL CHARACTER OF THE MOVEMENT

An analysis of the social theme in Hassidic doctrine and legend reveals which social groups led the advance of the new religious movement. Social unrest as well as an intensified yearning for deliverance had gripped wide circles of the Jewish masses at the period when Hassidism was born. But the social stratum which

*All Hebrew, or Aramaic, words listed here as Yiddish vocabulary have been transliterated according to the accent commonly employed in modern Israel. In Yiddish they have actually undergone changes in phonetics and accent.

actually led the movement and determined its social complexion from the very outset was the underprivileged middle-class group in the Kehillot. It included the inhabitants of the suburbs and the small towns who were oppressed by the major Kehillot and also the villagers, the middle and petty lessees.

The continually deteriorating economic position of these lessees drove them to seek refuge and security in the idea of heavenly salvation and the righting of the balance of abundance forecast in the teachings of Hassidism. These middle classes in the villages, suburbs and towns were united in their opposition to the system of Kehillah exploitation which affected most of the population, including themselves. They also shared a mutual desire to be free of the humiliation of a status inferior to that of the scholars, who enjoyed pre-eminence in Kehillah society. This middle-class opposition found a broad social basis for its reform programme and religious policy amongst the lower middle class and the poor in the city and country. These masses, especially those who lived in the suburbs and towns, lent Hassidism its clearly democratic character and marked it with the popular quality of their religion, environment and customs. The Kehillah members in the cities and towns attracted to the new movement were the small shopkeepers, publicans, pedlars, hawkers, middlemen and all the unemployed who had no place whatsoever in economic life. The village Jews—the innkeepers, liquor-sellers and the middle and small lessees—for the most part also adopted Hassidism and firmly supported the movement at all stages of its development. In Lithuanian territories, where Hassidism only caught on in a few areas, it gained more adherents in White Russia, with its large rural Jewish population, than in Lithuania proper.

The rural and urban adherents of the Hassidic movement were not only brought close to each other by social conditions and by similar aspirations for greater equality in the Kehillah order and a more dignified status in the socio-religious sphere. The absence of deep economic roots affected both groups to the extent of rendering their livelihoods extremely precarious. The shopkeepers, publicans and particularly the hawkers, pedlars and middlemen earned a subsistence almost literally by "miracles" in the form of occasional customers. When their luck failed, they starved. Similarly, the village innkeepers and publicans depended for their income on the mercy of estate-owning noblemen; and "the nobleman's mercy," according to an apposite Polish proverb, "rides a striped horse." The sense of complete security that Hassidic doctrine provided, reflected the innate optimism of the people and encouraged them and gave them strength to face the future amidst their daily troubles.

Whereas lessees and publicans constituted the most frequent characters encountered in Hassidic legend, artisans were fairly rare. Even the earliest legends, compiled in *The Praises of Ba'al Shem Tov,* only mentioned a few. Despite the lowly status of the majority of artisans, their economic basis was far more stable than that of the Jewish small traders, middlemen and liquor-sellers. Their lack of privileges in the Kehillah régime was notorious, but they did not elect to remain passive or to put their faith in moral preachings. Instead, they organized active resistance against the Kehillah leaders wherever they were able, and especially in the large Kehillot of Lithuania and White Russia. In a number of Kehillot, the rebellious artisans at times found allies in the Hassidim, but for the most part they went their separate ways, as Hassidic teaching never at any time advocated actual class warfare as a means of changing the Kehillah régime. Furthermore, a distinct cultural and social demarcation divided the artisans from the lower middle class hawkers and liquor-sellers. The shopkeepers and the liquor purveyors customarily had their sons instructed in Gemara, while the sons of artisans usually completed their education at the age of confirmation—*barmitzvah*—and entered workshops as apprentices, even before they had acquired a knowledge of the Pentateuch. Unlike the shopkeepers and liquor sellers, whose wives could take their place in the store and the ale-house, the artisans could not observe the Hassidic customs of ritual personal hygiene which entailed frequent visits to the *mikveh* (ritual baths) and delayed prayer service. Often even the dress of a "master" (*ba'al-bayyit*, or *balle-buss*), though he might be nothing more than a hawker or a lowly liquor seller, differed from that of the artisan, who was considered an *am-ha'aretz*—an ignorant boor. In fact, the artisans were not amongst the devotees of Hassidism, despite its mass character, and although it would appear logical that they should have acknowledged its democratic aims in its quarrel with the Mitnagdim.

The men who moulded the ideas of the movement, the thinkers who expressed Hassidic ideology, came from the lower stratum of professional religious intellectuals. They were preachers and moralists, ritual slaughterers, cantors and teachers who were in closer touch with wide circles of the masses, both because of their profession and because of their own poverty. The active campaign that these underprivileged scholars led against the arrogant scholar class and the stern rejection of the Kehillah leaders who were robbing the common people expressed and reflected their own bitterness at their wretched status, as well as the popular opposition in the Kehillot as a whole. It was not surprising that the founder of Hassidism, Israel Ba'al Shem Tov had worked as an assistant to a village teacher, as a teacher and as a slaughterer, as well as in such undistinguished capacities as servant, watchman at a synagogue-school, clay-digger and bartender. It was even more typical that most of his disciples were preachers, moralists, teachers and slaughterers.* The group only included two or three ordained rabbis.

However, despite all its emphatic democratic tendencies, Hassidism never arrived at a lucid, outspoken programme of reforms in the Kehillah régime and social relationships. Hassidism, unlike non-Jewish socio-religious movements, lacked a solid social class (e.g. peasants, urban poor or proletariat) capable of undertaking the struggle from a clearly defined social and political platform. This was mainly because of the abnormal social and economic structure of the Jewish population, resulting from the absence of a territorial basis of its own, and the consequent absence of a national political life. Furthermore, national oppression

*Professor B. Z. Dinur (Dinaburg) has stressed the significance of the social composition of Ba'al Shem Tov's group of disciples, and emphasized the place held by the "intellectual proletariat" in the ascendant Hassidic movement, a phenomenon previously suggested by such historians as H. Graetz and S. Dubnov, *cf.* B. Z. Dinaburg, *The Beginnings of Hassidism, Its Social and Messianic Foundations* (in Hebrew), *Zion* Quarterly, Vols. 8–10, particularly Chapter 8, Vol. 9, pp. 89–108.

affected all classes of Jews, even though it weighed most heavily on the weak and impoverished groups. The affliction of exile, even within an oppositionist religious movement, was sufficient to relegate the social problem to a secondary position and to cause it to be absorbed into a general national aspiration for redemption—Messianic deliverance, envisaged only in the form of heavenly salvation.

The changes that Hassidism actually and successfully introduced were primarily in the sphere of rendering *social* life more democratic. Hassidism elevated the sense of human dignity and communal significance not only of the middle class, who ranked inferior to the scholars in learning, but also of the ordinary people, who had been denied both the distinction of wealth and the virtue of learning.

Hassidism was able to influence Kehillah affairs and public activities through its internal organization, a network which extended over numerous districts and, indeed, entire countries, far more than by direct action. In fact strong bonds of solidarity existed between supporters of the movement causing it, in some respects, to resemble a parallel organization to the Kehillah. This surprised its opponents and was mentioned in the reports of government officials. The principal task of the *Tzaddik* was to offer guidance in the worship of God and the way of righteousness. But he was also a congregational leader, on a par with the Kehillah Rabbi, and, furthermore, exercised absolute and unchallengeable authority over his flock. In this capacity, he attended to the affairs of the Jews in towns and villages, pronounced decisions in disputes between his followers, prevented infringement of rights of tenure by lessees and liquor sellers and usually defended the poor against extortion and exploitation. Their integral organization and exceptional unity made it possible for the Hassidim not only to influence decisions on the appointment of cantors, ritual slaughterers (by forbidding all slaughtering except with ground knives), preachers and even rabbis—even in Kehillot where they did not command a majority. At times they were even able to force their will on the Kehillah leaders in the regulation of Kehillah affairs.

The reforms instituted by Hassidism did *not* transcend the framework of the existing social order. The mass character of Hassidism was expressed in a powerful demand for justice and honesty on the basis of what it regarded as an unalterable system, in its attempts to soften the existing sharp social antagonism, and in charity and mutual aid to the poor. A principal feature of all Hassidic instruction on comportment in revering God demanded that business dealings be conducted honestly and faithfully, without "robbery" and deceit, and expressly included a prohibition on deceiving gentiles. The social pathos which animated the warnings against "robbery" and deprivation of the abjectly poor given by the preachers among Ba'al Shem Tov's disciples represented a continuation of the best in the ethical literature of the Middle Ages and modern times. The principle stressed in the new social morality of Hassidism was the unity of Israel, which could only be maintained through justice, as well as love of Israel, which required the practice of grace between men, before brotherhood and companionship amongst the people could be established.

Charity, as a means of redressing social wrongs, acquired a unique organization under the Hassidic system, in addition to the existing charitable societies. This was linked to the fact that congregational life centred on the *Tzaddik's* "court." It was the custom for the *Tzaddik's* friends, who constituted a sort of entourage, to share his meals. Even the term used to describe them, *yosh'vim* (sitters), proved the extent to which the Hassidic order was grounded in the feudal system of the state—precisely the same expression (in Latin, *residentes*) was customarily attached to impoverished nobles in Poland who resided in the palaces of their magnate relatives and patrons, literally living at their expense. The meals served to the Hassidic congregation in the *Tzaddik's* court on the Sabbath and on holidays, gave the local poor, who could not afford such feasts in their own homes, the opportunity to eat their fill. Charitable activities were concentrated in the hands of the *Tzaddik*, mainly because of the custom of paying a *pidyon* (redemption) to the *Tzaddik*, observed by Hassidim who came to pay homage and obtain help through his prayers. During the period of Hassidic ascendancy, these *pidyonot* served as a large welfare chest enabling the *Tzaddik* to distribute generous alms to the very poor. At that time, the *Tzaddikim* also organized special charitable activities in times of need. The legends in *The Praises of Ba'al Shem Tov* described his attempts on behalf of the *Redemption of Captives*—the release of lessees imprisoned by their masters for failure to pay their rentals punctually. During the second and third generation of Ba'al Shem Tov's disciples, *Tzaddikim* travelled about the country to raise funds for the impoverished ones. Hassidic legend also praised *Tzaddikim* who married off orphans of both sexes with their own funds (thereby fulfilling the commandment on the giving of the bride in marriage). The *Tzaddik* thus became the "bestower of abundance" not only in his mystical role as mediator between the people of Israel and the world of divine emanations, but also in a practical sense.

The *Tzaddik* undertook a similar double task in matters concerning bodily health and practical help in times of trouble. He not only aided the sick, the barren, and the afflicted, by the cogency of his prayer and adhesion to God, but he was also the practical consultant in times of distress and confusion and provided remedies and cures when required. Theosophic and theurgic Kabbalah had always been linked in mystical doctrine. They had already been united in the teaching and practice of the founder of Hassidism and his disciples and their pupils usually followed his example. The folk character of Hassidism also appeared in this field. The *Tzaddikim*, in their capacity as "the healers of the sick ones amongst His people of Israel" did not rely exclusively on the secrets of Kabbalah but occasionally also drew on popular experience in their diagnosis of illness and the application of simple remedies. Remedy lists, like that of Rabbi Pinehas of Koretz, were a combination of secret cures with actual medicines, tried and tested by popular quacks over generations. In fact, Hassidism marked a singular fusion between the profound study by generations of the dialectics of the law and theology and the naïve, superstitious beliefs current amongst the simple people. On the one hand, it expressed a consistent philosophical and mystical ideal, in an effort to comprehend the universe in a unified concept of idealistic monism, a subtlety of thought that rejected miracles in the crudest sense because they conflicted with the natural course of events. On the other hand, it clung to the simple and primitive beliefs of the people. This dual character impregnated the social composition of the movement, which united democratic scholars with the common people in the cities and towns.

As a popular movement, Hassidism adopted the characteristics peculiar to the people—their optimism, *joie de vivre,* fertile imagination, depth of feeling, gift of observation of the external scene and their wisdom born of experience. The theoretical works by Hassidic thinkers displayed amazing skill in their attempts to expound complex problems in occult science with the aid of the subtle dialectics of *pilpul.* But these thinkers were able to recount their parables with the narrative skill intrinsic to folk tales, and express them in the keenly humorous idiom of Jewish folklore. These qualities, together with the aim of national redemption, constituted the principal difference between Hassidism and gentile religious sects. Not one of the Christian folk sects ever became a popular religion, mainly because the dominant church, whether Catholic or Protestant, persecuted them relentlessly and forced them to exist illegally. Hassidism, on the other hand, never bore any trace of sectarianism. Its nature, aims and the scope of its activities marked it from the beginning as a movement fated to win over an entire people to its ideas.

The folk element in the movement's doctrine acquired singular importance in the lives of the Hassidic masses. They received the Hassidic system as a religion which was accessible to all men, which had brought the Torah down from heaven to earth and even brought God infinitely closer to the individual through His apostle and prophet, the *Tzaddik.* Hassidism gave the lower classes confidence in their difficult struggle to earn a living and strengthened their hope of attaining salvation together with the whole nation. But it also elevated them by mystic visions from the depression and inanities of daily life to the heights of the upper spheres, to a world that was all spirituality and divine radiance. Hopes of redemption and of the triumph of the oppressed people over the depraved nations grew with the increased pressure of the bondage in exile. As the life of the small trader and liquor seller became more wretched and melancholy, his yearning for flight and refuge in a higher source of beauty, splendour and majesty grew more powerful. Above all, however, Hassidism inspired the lives of the people with a spirit of joyfulness, of the warmth and good cheer of communal life, the buoyance of nature, and the pleasure a man could derive from his actions—all of which were licensed and approved in Israel's rejoicing in the Creator. The process was reciprocal: Hassidism was nourished by the spirit and emotions of the people, their innermost hopes, desires, and visions; in its turn, it wielded a tremendous influence on the people by bolstering their inclinations and ambitions, shackled for many generations by the dominant religion of the *Shulchan Arukh.* Hassidism roused the people from the religious frigidity of legalistic minutiae to the freshness of a religion exuberant with life and creativity. It released their creative ability, held in check for many centuries. The forces of their emotions and imagination were released and a wealth of art and wisdom burst forth. In the art of the people ecstasy to the point of "voiding one's existence" in Hassidic dances and an emotional outpouring that attained the "divestment of materiality" in music expressed Hassidic doctrine: a tumultuous joy in living tempered by gnawing economic problems and the sadness of bondage in exile, an overwhelming desire for redemption in Zion and for a beautiful, happy existence, an everlasting life amidst a liberated people.

Hassidism did not escape the unfavourable development that had in the long run overtaken all the religious movements of the world. Its development followed similar lines to the Gentile religious movements that had attained power. However, its initial lack of a crystallized social pattern made the process of transformation in Hassidism far easier and more rapid. As the movement began to acquire adherents among the well-to-do and wealthy, its doctrine was increasingly adapted to fit their specific social outlook. And the more drastically the doctrine was changed in order to subdue social opposition and the more prominence and emphasis were given to the principles of the system which were acceptable to the ruling Kehillah class, the more members of that class eagerly joined the spreading movement.

Some of the principles which the Hassidic movement proclaimed could, by altering their original significance, not only avoid antagonizing its opponents but actually serve them as arguments for strengthening the existing social order and its religion. Hassidism's aim of strengthening religious faith accorded with the aspirations of the ruling class more than all its other principles. The condemnatory attitude of the conservative *Mitnagdim* increasingly changed to approval as *Haskalah* "apostasy" began to gain adherents and spread through Poland. More than that, Hassidism not only provided a mainstay for religious faith, but also for community life on a religious basis. As the Kehillah was continually weakened by inner schisms and underminings from within as well as by the absolutist monarchy's restrictions on its institutional activities and authority, the conservative *Mitnagdim* perceived the efficiency of the new organizational pattern of the Hassidic congregation in the maintenance of religious institutions and the re-establishment of their authority within the Kehillah. As a result, Hassidism not only spread geographically at the end of the eighteenth and beginning of the nineteenth centuries, but also across class boundaries. It steadily pervaded the very wealthy circles and ruling Kehillah groups which had been determined to destroy it in its early days as a new religious movement.

In keeping with the change in its social composition, the doctrines of the Hassidic movement began to gloss over the ideals of democracy and social opposition which had reflected the aspirations of the lower middle class and the poor masses which constituted its social basis. Open criticism of the scholars as an aloof and haughty class became far less frequent in the Hassidic literature of the third generation, even though it was still repeatedly advised that Torah be studied for its own sake. With this decreased antagonism towards the scholar class, a change also took place in the attitude of Hassidism towards the study of the Law.

The change in the essential nature and characteristics of Hassidism was not only produced by relegating several of its cardinal principles to the background until they were forgotten or repudiated, but also by amplifying other ideas already present in the teachings of the fathers of Hassidism and presenting them in a new light. The role of the *Tzaddik* had already been fundamental to the doctrine in Ba'al Shem Tov's system. The *Tzaddik*, as Ba'al Shem Tov conceived him, was not only a counsellor to the people in the worship of God. He also possessed special mystical attributes: he transmitted the prayers of his congregation and sent up its sparks of holiness even when he only communed with it in his thoughts: and he was also the vehicle of supreme abundance. Ba'al Shem Tov, however, still believed that communion with the *She'khinah* and the "assuagement of sternness" was the duty of every individual Jew. He actually served frequent warnings to the effect that a Jew should not depend on the agent of the congregation but should pray in his own individual act of adhesion. Ba'al Shem Tov's disciple, Jacob Joseph, still did not differentiate between a *Tzaddik* and a scholar (*Talmid-Chakham*) who was attached to the mass of the people, and he employed both terms interchangeably. A generation later, the doctrine of *Tzaddikism* was definitely perfected in the system of Rabbi Elimelekh of Lezajsk. The *Tzaddik* was "omnipotent," and he lavished an abundance of wealth not only on the world as a whole but on every individual by praying for him, even merely by conversing with him. He also healed the afflicted through his prayer; the precondition for this function of the *Tzaddik* was that the person who came for help should have faith in him. The role of the *Tzaddik* had thus been transposed to that of an agent of divinity and a miracle-worker. He procured a livelihood, healed the sick and dispelled barrenness. What had begun as a prehumanist regeneration of religion in the form of a democratic folk religion, developed towards a mass religion permeated with magic, superstition, and idolatrous adulation of the all-powerful *Tzaddik*, the "Eye of God" on earth. *Tzaddikism* as a theoretical system reached its acme in the doctrine of Ba'al Shem Tov's great-grandson, Rabbi Nahman of Bratzlav, who regarded the *Tzaddik* as only slightly inferior to the Almighty. Hassidism had begun with aims directed towards a popular religious reformation. At the very height of its development it deteriorated to quasi-Catholic *Tzaddikism*. Opposition to the scholars on the grounds that they held themselves above the people, was succeeded by worship of the *Tzaddikim*, who exercised unlimited power over their congregations to an extent never attained by even the most brilliant learned men. The doctrine that the rabbi's office was a sacred rank to be bequeathed from father to son, caused the number of *Tzaddik* dynasties to multiply and branch out as fathers passed both their glory and their material assets on to their sons. A new aristocracy of "grandsons" thus gained ascendancy over the people, the sons of *Tzaddik* families, who for the most part even married only amongst themselves. The material wealth and way of life of this spiritual aristocracy in no way fell below the most opulent of the rabbis during their period of greatest prosperity.

The change in its social trend and tenor eventually caused Hassidism to follow a jealously conservative policy which obstructed the spiritual and cultural progress of the people. Its unalterably hostile attitude towards all secular science and enlightenment in its decline was far in excess of Talmudic orthodoxy.

It must be noted, however, that because of the very gradual geographic diffusion of Hassidism, there was no strict parallel between the stages of its development and decline in various localities. The process of decline first began in the Ukrainian districts where it had been conceived. In Lithuania and White Russia, where it had only caught on amongst a minority of communities, it never descended to the belief in miracles and the *Tzaddik* cult, such as it had reached in other eastern European countries. In central Poland, where the movement was late in spreading, it preserved much of the pristine freshness with which it had infused religious life as late as the beginning of the nineteenth century. Even in the middle of the nineteenth century some remains of its early dynamic intellectual power were still in evidence there. Similarly, wherever the movement still held sway during that period, there remained individual *Tzaddikim* who continued to propagate in their teaching and behaviour the finest elements of the popular Hassidism represented by Ba'al Shem Tov and Rabbi Moses Leib of Sassow. However, these variations in development and even the thin rivulets of original Hassidism in the mainstream of the movement were of no decisive historical significance. When the process finally came to an end, the entire movement had been imbued with unyielding conservatism and social and cultural reaction.

The *Haskalah* movement in eastern Europe furnished the progressive cultural trend destined to regenerate all spheres of the people's life. It was fostered by the modern Jewish middle class and gained ascendancy during the period of Hassidism's intellectual and social decline. Furthermore, the *Haskalah* movement in eastern Europe had no prospect of propagating its message except by a persistent struggle against the steadily deteriorating Hassidic movement. The superiority of the *Haskalah* movement in this struggle was the advantage enjoyed by capitalist progress over antiquated feudalism. It was only after the triumph of the *Haskalah* movement that historical reappraisal vindicated Hassidism. The Jewish people were only able to assess the movement's position in its cultural development and to evaluate the legacy of national and humanitarian values bequeathed by early Hassidism when it was no longer an active cause but a historical phenomenon. It was remembered as a religious movement that had wrestled with God for the deliverance of the people, and with man for equality and justice amongst the people, and had not prevailed.

PART II The Age of Diversity: Judaisms and Modernization, 1789–

Chapter 6
The Judaic Reformation as a Sociopolitical Process

Calvin Goldscheider and Alan Zuckerman

As the ordered society of estates eroded and new social and political institutions emerged, the religion of the Jews changed. New religious ideologies, changes in the forms of public worship, and declines in personal religious observance accompanied the initial phases of modernization. In Western Europe, Judaism became the legal, political, and ideological definition of the Jewish people. Did the new religious ideologies determine changes in the synagogues? Did they lead to declines in the religious practices of the Jewish masses? Did they, on the other hand, halt the slide of the Jews toward assimilation and apostasy? How is the modernization of Judaism related to the broader processes of transformation?*

Religious ideologies are the work of the intellectual elite. The philosophers and rabbis who organized the Reform movement, the Historical school, and Neoorthodoxy provided new understandings of the place of Jews and Judaism in a modernizing world. They responded to philosophical challenges met in the universities and brought them from there to the Jewish communities. The ideologies developed as their spokesmen competed to control communal institutions, not as the unfolding logic of ideas. New synagogues and changes in the form of public worship emerged in response to conflicts between lay leaders and rabbis. They also derived from changes in government policies toward general issues of modernization and the specific place of Jews and Judaism.

*References to the literature have been omitted in this selection.—Eds.

Neither the new ideologies nor the ritual changes was the direct consequence of the demands of the Jewish masses. In Western Europe most Jews opposed or were indifferent to religious reforms. During the period of greatest intellectual innovation, the first half of the nineteenth century, the new religious ideas reached the smallest number of Jews. The era of greatest visible impact on the Jewish masses occurred when the ideologies had lost their intellectual vitality.

The new ideologies and synagogues did not restructure the lives of the Jews. Religious decline resulted neither from the inability of old ideas to adapt to new conditions nor from the less demanding nature of some of the new religious ideologies, but from transformations in social conditions. Migrations to towns and cities with weak Jewish institutions, the growth of secular public education, and interaction with non-Jews in jobs and in new neighborhoods had much more to do with declining levels of personal religious observance. Similarly, continuing patterns of occupational and residential cohesion had more to do with the persistence of Jewish communities than the new religious ideologies. Our argument emphasizes the role of structural factors in determining ideological, institutional, and behavioral changes. The evidence we present rejects the assertion that ideological changes led the forces of religious modernization.

THE IDEOLOGY OF REFORM JUDAISM

Reform Judaism was the first of the new religious ideologies that emerged in Germany. It viewed Judaism as the Jews' unique quality. Jews were individuals with distinct religious beliefs but similar in all other ways to their Christian neighbors.

The movement's intellectual leaders persistently reiterated common themes: we have come not to diminish Judaism but to make it more meaningful to each Jew and to reach the increasingly indifferent masses, especially the youth. Sermons in German would uplift the spirit and the moral character, as would a service that is quiet, dignified, and orderly. These themes echoed the calls of reforming Protestant clergy. All these changes would combine to "edify" the Jew, and, thereby, bring him closer to the feelings of his Christian neighbors and the eternal tenets of Judaism.

They emphasized the religious feelings of individual Jews and their place in the changing Germany, while deemphasizing the importance of the Jews as a separate people and the distinctive Jewish ceremonies that would isolate Jews from modern society. Efforts to reform the prayer book rested on these principles: "That the people of Israel no longer lives, that Amalek has lost its significance for us, that Hebrew no longer lives, and that no hope is associated with Jerusalem." A response to the blood libel in Syria, in 1840, highlights the importance of Jewish entry into German society and rejects a broader conception of Jewish peoplehood: "That the Jews in Prussia may have the chance to become pharmacists or lawyers is much more important to me than the rescue of all the Jews of Asia and Africa, an undertaking with which I sympathize as a human being." The religious and lay leaders who joined the Reform efforts were particularly interested in smoothing the integration of Jews into German society.

The Reformers bemoaned the state of Jewry and Judaism. They claimed that the masses were religiously ignorant and performed the commandments by rote. They saw increasing rates of conversion to Christianity accompanying this religious indifference. The Reformers attacked the established rabbis for being unwilling and unable to respond to the exigencies of the times. Changes in religious norms, they argued, would reinvigorate religious practices. Many of their demands focused on the synagogue service and public worship. Decorum, sermons in the German language, clerical robes, choirs and music, they contended, would produce a properly dignified worship. All would result in the edification of the individual Jew, whose conscious acceptance of the commandments became the requisite for proper, religious behavior.

These ideas legitimated the most visible religious changes of the era, new synagogues and alterations in the worship service. In 1817, the group establishing the Reform temple in Hamburg proclaimed:

> Since public worship has for some time been neglected by so many, because of the ever decreasing knowledge of the language by which alone it has until now been conducted, and also because of many other shortcomings which have crept in at the same time—the undersigned, convinced of the necessity to restore public worship to its deserving dignity and importance, having joined . . . together to arrange . . . a dignified and well-ordered ritual . . . Specifically, there shall be introduced at such services a German sermon and choral singing to the accompaniment of an organ.

Other communal leaders reiterated the same claims.

Those seeking to change the worship service struggled to control the religious institutions. The legal proclamations issued in Cassel, Westphalia, in 1810, at the inauguration of the first of these new synagogues, introduced a set of directives that reappeared over and over again, emphasizing order, decorum, and dignity. The first paragraph permits services in only one synagogue in Cassel, a political statement of particular importance. The second paragraph establishes the role of the warden as the supervisor of the synagogue, and the next permits the employment of only one cantor-sexton, to be approved by the temple board. Other paragraphs proposed to enforce a dress code, prohibit children younger than four years of age from attending services, and establish the central role of the temple's cantor, and no others, in the worship service. Paragraph 16 sets out the new form of sermon: "Since rabbinical discussions do not belong in the synagogues, no rabbi is to deliver Talmudic or Kabbalistic or mystical discourses. He should speak about the teachings of religion or ethics only." Another paragraph limits the calling-up to the Torah to those who have taken family names, thereby fostering integration into the general society. This synagogue opened to a procession of dignity and pomp in which Jews and Gentiles entered together to the peal of church bells. The goal of the temples and new services was to establish a Judaism befitting the times and the equal place of Judaism in the emerging Germany.

THE RESPONSE OF THE ESTABLISHED RABBIS

The Reformers did not enter a Jewish community devoid of alternative ideologies and rabbis. The various Jewish communities were led by established rabbis, whose power rested on political as well as religious legitimacy. The established rabbis denied the Reformers' criticisms and plans. Most fundamentally, they denied the Reformers' right to an ideology. The members of various rabbinical courts responded to the intellectual and religious challenges as well as to the attacks on established authority. The Hamburg Rabbinical Court evoked these themes in 1815 as they responded to the new temple:

> These are the words of the covenant with Jacob, a law unto Israel, an eternal covenant; the word of God is one forever and forever. [These words are uttered] in accordance with the Torah and by judgment of the court of justice of the holy community of Hamburg—may the Lord bless it well—with the support of the leading men of learning in Germany, Poland, France, Italy, Bohemia, Moravia and Hungary. All of them join together . . . to abolish a *new law* [which was fabricated by several ignorant individuals unversed in the Torah] instituting practices which are not in keeping with the law of Moses and Israel.

Their political legitimacy derived, they maintained, from God and the Torah.

The court then prohibited the "three cardinal sins" of the Reformers: changes in the prayers, German sermons, and the use of musical instruments in the synagogues on Sabbaths and festivals. The rabbis based their injunction on their established authority as a court and not on the religious-legal sources of the halacha. The Reformers lacked the piety, holiness, and knowledge, so they argued, to effect religious changes. These were not only differences of ideological posture and attachment. These were mainly conflicts over authority. They concluded their pronouncement:

> Brethren, the children of Israel, it shall not be; Israel has not yet been abandoned. There are still judges in the land who are zealous for God's sake and who will rend the arm, crack the skull of him who pursues the sin of the Reformers. To these judges we shall hasten for aid. . . . Accordingly, we have girded our loins and written to the famous learned men of the holy communities of Germany, Poland, Bohemia, Moravia and Italy. We have sent them our legal judgment.

Calling on the police as well as the legal and religious authority of the established communities, these rabbis pronounced their negation of the Reformers' efforts.

Conflict between the established rabbis and the Reformers did not occur uniformly across Germany. Not all areas had movements for religious reform, and in those places the established rabbis did not take part in the conflict. They, therefore, did not develop any ideological response. Only in those areas where Reform emerged, as in Hamburg, was there an immediate reaction. Over time, these ideological disputes were translated into political maneuvering which involved large numbers of rabbis and their institutions.

When the established rabbis deigned to examine the Reformers' intellectual claims, they dismissed them out of hand. Since the commandments were established by God, their habitual performance was not necessarily a problem. Personal edification, in and of itself, was not the point of the prayer service. Legal authority prescribed that public prayer could be conducted in no language but Hebrew:

> Our sages of blessed memory said that the world was created in Hebrew. . . . If this is so, then this is the language of the Holy One, Blessed Be He, in which He gave us His Torah and it is inconceivable to speak before Him in our everyday language. Rather, we should speak the special language befitting His holy words. This is the opinion of the men of the Great Assembly who established the texts of the prayers and benedictions in the Holy Tongue.

Communal prayer is bound by the traditions and legal precedents of the community's courts.

The different styles of language that emerge in these documents reflect profound conceptual differences. In turn, these divergences tie to dissensus and conflict over communal authority. There were few halachic prohibitions on prayer in languages other than Hebrew, and legal precedent abounds in rabbinic literature to permit prayer in local languages. These precedents were not invoked. The issue was not only legal but political as well. The primary concern seems to have been less with theological correctness than with authority structure and political legitimacy.

As much as the established rabbis understood the political challenge of the Reformers, they misjudged their own strength. They could do little to shore up the erosion of their authority. Even a generation earlier, Berlin was not Vilna. As political conditions in the general and Jewish communities changed, so did the power of the established and Reform rabbis. Over time, others used new ideas and political techniques to defend the received religion. Conflict between the Neo-orthodox and the Reformers also occurred in the language of theology and religion. It derived, however, from efforts to control communal institutions.

IDEOLOGIES AND INSTITUTIONAL CHANGES

The established rabbis erred in another way. Although Reform rabbis called for changes in the rituals and worship services, their pronouncements were neither necessary nor sufficient conditions for these changes. In France, rabbis became preachers and pastors, not judges; they wore clerical robes, gave sermons in French, and introduced choirs into the worship service. More generally, the French rabbinate echoed the role and organizational structure of the Catholic Church. No conferences of Reform rabbis met in France, no journals of Reform theology were published, no new historical studies were completed, and yet the same changes that occurred in the religious service in Germany took place in France. Indeed, Reform Judaism, as an ideological movement, did not arrive in France until 1905, when church and state formally disassociated.

These same changes followed the extension of French rule and the establishment of consistories. Reforms in Cassel occurred when Westphalia was ruled by Jerome, Napoleon's brother, who permitted the new temple. When French rule ended in 1815, the consistory and temple collapsed. Similar changes occurred farther to the East. Napoleon's short-lived Grand Duchy of Warsaw also witnessed the inauguration of a Reform Temple, which dissolved when French rule ended. The comparison of areas under French and German governments makes clear that political change played a direct and central role in effecting change in religious institutions. Hence, an ideology of religious reform was not a necessary condition for the emergence of new synagogues.

What accounts for an ideology espousing religious reform in Germany and not in France? In part, the answer relates to dominant philosophical issues in the German universities as well as the employment patterns in these countries. The rise of a Reform ideology and movement reflected intellectual and employment problems particular to German university students, especially those in the arts and humanities. The giants of German philosophy, first Kant and then Hegel, attacked Judaism and challenged the faith of many Jewish students. At the same time, those who sought to pursue careers in philosophy and teaching were legally barred from employment in the gymnasia and universities. Many accepted positions in the newly created Jewish communal schools or as rabbis who could give sermons in the German language. The university world in France may have been as harsh on the faith of Jewish students, but it provided them with jobs in French schools. The rise of a new Jewish ideology required both new ideas and a mechanism for their diffusion into the Jewish community.

In the world of German universities at the end of the eighteenth century, no figure challenged Kant's intellectual supremacy. He provided the agenda for scholarly discussion and his answers dominated all others. His challenge to Judaism was direct and overpowering. Accepting Mendelssohn's definition of Judaism as a religion of laws and actions, not beliefs, Kant argued that Judaism was not a religion since it did not require conscious individual choice. The religion of Jewish students was not only the social, economic, and political burden that it had always been but it was now an intellectual embarrassment. "Kant's views on Judaism must have been especially agonizing for the Jewish intellectuals of the period. Not only did Judaism fail to compare favorably with Christianity, it was inferior even to polythesim." Jewish intellectuals could not repel his attack, and "agonizingly acquiesced."

Many of the fundamental ideas of the Reformers were responses to Kant. Not being able to refute his philosophical claims, they attacked the accuracy of his understanding of Judaism. Redefining the faith, they reduced the place of the commandments and increased the significance of personal meaning attached to religious action. Prayer and the worship service, they argued, must uplift the individual. It must, therefore, take place in a language that he understands. In Judaism, like all religions that fit Kant's definition, the individual must freely choose to do good. Obedience to external law, like the halacha, stands at the most distant edge of religion. Furthermore, Judaism is a set of principles and beliefs. It is not the religion of a particular nation or ethnic group. It does not require a halacha and a system of political controls to sustain its validity. Hence, it will persist as the religion of those who autonomously choose to live by its tenets, without their being a people and without political autonomy. Only this view, argued the Reformers, permits Judaism to stand as a philosophy of equal value to the other religions of Germany.

A generation later, Hegel provided an alternative to Kant's philosophy and another challenge to Jewish intellectuals. Hegel's ideas led to a new justification for Jews and Judaism, tying them to the historical link between ideas and people. According to the Hegelians, the idea-structure of Judaism was not necessarily religious and was not controlled by the rabbis. Rather, it emerged out of the life of the people and was best understood by the intellectuals. Reflecting their academic world, they formed the institutions of what would become known as the Historical School, The Society for the Preservation of the Jewish People, and the Society for the Culture and Science of the Jews (*Wissenschaft des Judentums*). They too were embarrassed by Judaism's intellectual weaknesses and adapted the dominant philosophy of their day to support their ideas. They attacked the intellectual bases of the established rabbis as well as their political power. The intellectuals who formed the Wissenschaft des Judentums offered a new understanding of the place of Jews and Judaism in the rapidly changing world of Germany.

The members of the Historical School remained a small group of scholars. Few were appointed rabbis or assistant rabbis; few controlled synagogues; at best their influence was felt in the community schools and the new rabbinical seminary in Breslau. They offered an intellectual challenge when only political success led to change in religious institutions. These intellectual issues affected very few Jewish students and, therefore, relatively few Jews. In any year during the first third of the nineteenth century, fewer than 1,000 Jews were among the 10,000–15,000 university students in Germany, and at the very most one-fifth of them studied in the faculties of humanities. We assume, therefore, that these intellectual challenges affected fewer than 200 Jewish students. Contemporary sources indicate even smaller numbers. A total of forty-two rabbis attended Reform rabbinical conferences in Germany in the 1840s. Hence, hardly any Jews took part in these intellectual debates.

The problems for these students extended beyond the realm of philosophy. The path to teaching in the gymnasia and universities was blocked to Jews who sought to pursue their philosophical interests. Several career options stood before them: they could forego their intellectual interests for a commercial career; they could leave Germany and pursue their scholarship in France; they could renounce their attachment to Judaism and convert to Christianity, thereby obtaining the "key to entrance into European civilization." If they maintained their attachment to philosophy, Judaism, and their families, they could pursue a career only within the educational and religious institutions of the Jewish community. Although most took careers in commerce, several chose Christianity and others migrated to France. Most remained in Germany as Jews.

The primary career possibilities in the Jewish community outside the world of commerce were teaching in the new schools, such as the Freischule in Dessau, and serving as rabbis in synagogues seeking clergy fluent in German. Hence, the intellectual and career sources of all Reform rabbis and members of the Historical School fit this pattern. The philosophical and occupational pressures on these intellectuals were necessary conditions for the formation and diffusion of these new ideologies.

The same pattern applies to those who became leaders of Neo-orthodoxy, the other religious ideology to form during the middle third of the century. Unlike the established rabbis, the leaders of Neo-orthodoxy attended universities and grappled with the same philosophical issues as the Reformers. Having resigned as Chief Rabbi of Bohemia and Moravia, Hirsch returned to Frankfurt to lead an independent synagogue. He installed an ideology and movement distinct from the Reformers and the traditional Orthodox. Hirsch insisted on a quiet, dignified service, and delivered sermons in German. Hirsch battled the Reformers with their own weapons. He wrote religious treatises in the idiom of German philosophy. Using their political tactics, he maneuvered within the Jewish and general communities, established newspapers, journals, separate schools, and synagogues.

The new ideologies—Reform, Neo-orthodox, and the Historical School—had little impact on the religious beliefs and practices of the Jewish masses in Germany. Most Jews fit into one of three types. (1) Those who would change no part of the worship service, retaining the prayers and observances handed to them by their fathers. Even at mid-century, this group probably amounted to a majority. (2) Those like the founders of the temples in Cassel, Hamburg, and Berlin, who sought a service sufficiently dignified and modern to enable them to stand proud in the general community. This group predominated among the commercial elite and the lay leaders of the communities. (3) A third group remained part of the Jewish community but did not follow any of the religious practices and knew little of the beliefs. None of these groups contained individuals with profound theological and philosophical concerns. The relative size of the groups varied by locale and over time, but the variations had little to do with the ideology espoused by the local rabbi. Similar patterns characterize French Jewry.

POLITICS AND CHANGE IN RELIGIOUS INSTITUTIONS

Political factors rather than ideologies or mass demands account for the diffusion of new temples and changes in religious services. In France, relatively high national unity, government centralization, and official ties between the state and the Jewish community through the consistories ensured that religious institutions changed in a generally uniform way across regions. Only resistance from some communities and rabbis in Alsace slowed this process. There is no evidence to support a claim that in Germany changes in a worship service occurred because the congregants sought a more meaningful form of prayer. Neither did the retention of the established service result from the preferences of the Jewish masses.

Was it economic or political factors which determined religious institutional change? Evidence indicates that there is no correlation between areas of economic expansion and the presence of Reform temples and rabbis. Nor does the size of the Jewish community vary systematically with type of synagogue present. Reform rabbis were as likely to serve rural small towns as large urban congregations. The areas of Western Germany, where most Jews were agricultural middlemen, were those with the largest number of Reform institutions.

Our emphasis on the centrality of political factors in determining the presence of new religious institutions helps clarify what appears puzzling and unexplained by previous research. Three political factors are critical: (1) a state government with a general policy of modernization and a specific policy fostering the use of the German language and the economic integration of Jews, (2) lay leaders who sought to further the integration of Jews by having a more impressive worship service with an emphasis on German sermons, (3) a rabbi who identified with the Reform movement. Where all three came together there were German sermons, clerical garb, choirs, decorum, and the other ritual changes of Reform. The regions of Nassau, Saxe-Weimar, Wurttemberg, and Baden were among the first to exhibit this pattern. Where all three opposed change—the government as part of a general reactionary policy, the lay leaders, and the rabbi too—these ritual reforms did not occur. After a start toward political modernization, Bavaria exemplifies this pattern for much of the century.

It is possible to rank these factors in their relative order of importance. The policy of the local government seems to be most important. It served as a necessary condition for religious reform and at times came close to being a sufficient condition as well. One key element was the law that lasted until mid-century that limited each Jewish community to one synagogue. Hence, control of the synagogue determined the nature of the worship service for all members of the community. The first and most obvious example of the effects of this law in Germany occurred in Cassel, Westphalia. Another government policy required rabbis to have university degrees and academic training. Modernizing governments in Baden, Hesse, and Wurttemberg, western areas with predominately rural Jewish populations engaged in cattle dealing, illustrate this pattern. In 1834, the Wurttemberg government dismissed forty-five rabbis who had not passed the state qualifying examination. Hence, once this political policy is taken into account, it is not at all surprising that the western areas of Germany had relatively large numbers of Reform rabbis. Modernizing civil servants bent on rationalizing governments and economies took as one of their policy goals the education and the reorganization of the local Jews.

Where government policy opposed all forms of change, it precluded the spread of religious reform among the Jews. The case of Berlin clearly illustrates this point. Given the history of the Prussian capital as an early center of the Jewish Enlightenment, and given the presence of a Reform temple there in 1815, it may seem surprising that Berlin did not emerge as a leading center of religious reform. Prussian political reaction, in general, and specific policies that followed Napoleon's defeat in 1815 explain the relative absence of the Reformers until after mid-century. The Prussian Emperor simply forbade religious reform among the Jews. In 1823, a Prussian court decreed that rabbis might not wear clerical robes or preach in German. These being Gentile customs, they must not be brought into the Jewish community. It took seventeen years of appeals for the Reformers to have the decision reversed. The Prussian government served as the court of last appeal in the struggles between the Reform and Orthodox and almost always favored the latter. It ruled, for example, that the Reformers might not enroll all the Jewish children in their schools. Thus, in regions of political reaction, government policy blocked all forms of change, including religious reform among the Jews.

Where the government had no policy, the desires of the lay leaders and the rabbi determined the nature of the worship service. Where they agreed, they prevailed. Resistance by local Jews could be overcome, and indifference certainly provided no barrier. Where the rabbi and local leaders split, then the rabbi's legal power allowed him to block their demands. The lay leaders required government intervention to overcome their rabbi's resistance. Where the rabbi opposed reform, lay leaders sought government permission to hire an assistant rabbi to preach in German. Where there was a Reform rabbi, the lay leaders turned to the legal authorities to dismiss him. Sometimes, only the establishment of a new synagogue resolved the conflict. This too required government approval. The Neo-orthodox success in Frankfurt used interest group politics to obtain from the Prussian government the right to secede from the legally sanctioned Jewish community. Hirsch succeeded in the face of massive opposition from the Jews of the city, whatever their religious ideology. Those who joined his synagogue either worked for him or, as Polish immigrants, had no ties to the local community. Hirsch did not ride the crest of a mass movement. Instead, having obtained legal independence, he used the institutional bases of a separate community, especially the schools and synagogue, to build the movement. Government policy and political maneuvering within the Jewish community helped to spread Neo-orthodoxy as well as Reform.

Over time, and particularly after mid-century, government policies played a smaller role in Jewish communal life. Increasing economic, educational, and linguistic integration of the Jews resulted in declining government intervention in the internal affairs of the Jewish community. Subsequent religious institutional change, therefore, derived less from government policies than from conflict and competition among Jews.

The religious ideologies were elite expressions. Where their spokesmen fought with each other, very few Jews entered the fray. The most well known of these battles occurred in Breslau in the middle of the nineteenth century and involved a vote among 1,500 householders (10 percent of the Jewish population). The Reformers lost. Where one group prevailed, there is little evidence that they actually affected the beliefs and practices of their congregants. The schools of the Reform and the Neo-orthodox initially reached relatively few Jewish students.

Nahman's windstorm, as we have seen, moved Jews into new homes and places of living, weakened old institutions, and created new ones. As the kehillot declined, adherence to the established religious norms rested on personal choices. The observance of religious commandments had previously rested on the absence of other alternatives and the sanctions of the established community. It is not surprising, therefore, that we find declines in the frequency and intensity of personal religious practices as new alternatives emerged and as traditional social, economic, and political sanctions weakened. As the Jewish population expanded, existing schools and synagogues were overwhelmed. As people moved to new cities, they encountered relatively few institutions of the Jewish community. In Paris, for example, there were four synagogues for the more than 50,000 Jews who lived there at mid-century. No more than 15 percent of the male adults could have attended synagogue services together in the French capital. The same pattern applies to other new centers of Jewish population. As long as the prohibition of more than one synagogue in the various German towns and cities held, most German Jews had little or no contact with that most important agency of a Jewish community. Hederim, private teachers, and new schools could not accommodate the growing number of Jewish children. New educational opportunities in general schools provided attractive alternatives. Informal Jewish education did not compensate for these new patterns of schooling. These transformations did not mainly reflect preferences for one type of education but the availability of alternative schools. The structure of opportunities and access, not values, determined educational choices.

Over time, those who studied in established, Neo-orthodox, and Reform schools were taught different curricula. More important, they developed allegiances to these branches of Judaism. Many had no formal Jewish education, and their Jewishness was likely to be associated with nonreligious communal institutions. Hence, synagogues and schools provided some bases for cohesion, while generating competition and conflict within the Jewish community. At the same time, the institutions maintained an image of a distinct body of Jews. They did not cause that distinction but helped to sustain it in the minds of Jews and non-Jews alike. The image neither determined nor impeded Jewish continuity. It legitimated and rationalized the broader changes that were unfolding.

The rise of new ideologies, declining personal religious observance, and the formation of new forms of public worship were all responses to political and social modernization. They paralleled similar developments in the broader society. Hence, while focusing on the Jews as a case study, our hypotheses derive from a general orientation to modernization and group cohesion. Our key explanatory factors are particular elements of political and educational modernization combined with population growth and urbanization. The new ideologies did not determine changes in religious behavior or institutions. The ideas of Reform, the Historical School, and Neo-orthodoxy are what must be explained. It is inadequate, therefore, to view the new religious ideologies and institutions as examples of assimilation. Similarly, those who obtained no Jewish education or rarely attended religious services had other bases for Jewish continuity. Communal organizations, socioeconomic, and residential patterns maintained Jewish cohesion in new forms. Modernization meant the differentiation of religious from other institutions as well as the creation of new supports for the Jewish community.

Chapter 7

The Rise and Reception of Zionism in the Nineteenth Century

Ben Halpern

The political ideas expressed by the concepts "national home" or "Jewish commonwealth" were neither uniformly nor unequivocally defined, even if we had no more to consider than Zionist theory itself. They were used as slogans in a political contest; and, in the struggle for advantage, each rival ideologist sought to appropriate the same popular conceptions by introducing his own shades of interpretation into them. But when opposing theorists engage in such dialectic, each is forced, at least, to take account of the other's usage; and he may have to modify his own so that it can be rationally defended against the other's, or effectively counteract its emotional appeal.

Moreover, the Zionist debate was not conducted in a closed circle. The public whose conversion was desired was the whole Jewish public. Consequently, although the "Jewish national home" and the "Jewish state" were terms invented and advocated by the Zionists alone, they were not free to formulate those ideas as they saw fit, without regard for the understanding of their concepts and the reactions to them among other Jews. The influence of Jewish non-Zionist and anti-Zionist ideas and attitudes must be understood in a historical-sociological analysis of Zionist political ideas.

Such influences to which Zionist theories responded were both traditional and contemporary. The Zionist conception of the Jewish homeland in Palestine always had overtones recalling traditional conceptions of Zion. As we shall see later, in these reminiscences of ancient symbols Zionism perceived itself as a rebellion against tradition quite as much as a continuation of it. Zionism also had to define and redefine its ideas and continually elaborate its mythic symbols in response to the rival opinions of its contemporaries. A constant dialectical development was required in order to oppose the anti-Zionists more effectively or find a suitable basis for compromise with the non-Zionists in the community.

These necessities were, perhaps, more pressing for Zionism than for other nationalist movements. As noted earlier, nationalism ordinarily develops in countries ruled by foreigners. The initiation of the movement by rebellious intellectuals, consequently, meets a ready response among the mass of the people; for they, too, are kept in constant, though latent, rebelliousness by a subjection never consecrated by including the rulers in a common social consensus. Just as any idea rapidly takes on overtones of meaning reflecting the experience of those to whom it is effectively communicated, so the ideologies of the nationalist elite, when communicated to a responsive mass, soon absorb the experiences and impulses, the frustrations and resentments, to which the mass is sensitive. In this way nationalism establishes itself as a new focus of social consensus for the subject people—an active consensus, which in many cases did not exist before, and which now fuses together the ideologies of the elite with the myth images of the mass in a single historic force and purpose.

Jewish nationalism, however, could not simply arouse a subject people against its oppressors. The Jewish situation was not that of a people oppressed in its own country by a foreign garrison and administration, or by landlords and nobles who had imposed their rule after conquest. The latent impulse of the mass of Jews in extremity was not to rebel—but to take flight, to emigrate. For the oppressors of the Jews were either the autochthonous majority of the land, or foreign rulers who enjoyed the support of the majority in their antiJewish policies. Consequently, while the emotional mood of Zionist rebellion might be echoed in some of the myth images of the Jewish mass, the positive Zionist proposals could not arouse such a concerted impulse as would establish an unquestioned consensus. In fact, Zionism aroused debate perhaps quite as much as it created a consensus.

Moreover, the Jews did not need to wait for Zionism to create an active consensus among them. The Jewish tradition, for one thing, was never reduced to a mass of mythic material, as happened to the traditions of many subjugated peoples; it always defined a clear historical (or transhistorical) purpose and exercised a decided historical force. Even if the tradition was a strictly conservative force among its most orthodox adherents, there was always an active rather than passive consensus among Jews, a purpose in history imposing a definite discipline upon Jewish attitudes and a definite direction upon Jewish impulses. In its relation to both Jewish tradition and the Jewish mass, then, Zionism was not called upon to activate a latent historic impulse. It had, instead, to overcome Jewish history and impose a new pattern upon the Jewish consensus.

Nationalist movements usually prefer to regard themselves not as historic innovations, but as movements for the *revival* of a national culture and the *restoration* of national sovereignty. Even when it is obvious that in actuality they have relatively insignificant ties to tradition, nationalists may seek to reconstruct bonds with the past, however great the effort of imagination and propaganda required to make them seem plausible. The attempted revival of Gaelic in Eire, the insistence on Gothic rather than Roman type faces during periods of nationalist enthusiasm in Germany, and the concerted drive for the adoption of Hebraic cognomens in newborn Israel are extreme and, perhaps, trivial examples. But the same tendency also manifests itself in territorial disputes based on the assertion of historic rights.

The attempt to reconstruct a tradition is facilitated in some ways by the decline of culture among suppressed and, particularly, degraded peoples. In such cases there may be no significant historical conceptions already established in the popular consensus which nationalism must seek to overcome in order to dominate. The nationalists frequently appeal simply for the revival of a culture that had fallen into oblivion or declined to the level of archaism or dialect; they strive to restore a sovereignty that had faded to a pale and ineffectual memory. The main opposition with which these ideologists have to contend is often the resistance of popular lethargy.

In this respect the problem Zionism faced from its very birth was quite different. Before Zionism arose there were already two distinct and well-established ideological positions, which we may call the ideologies of Western modernism and of Eastern traditionalism. For each of these ideologies, Jewish culture and Jewish sovereignty—which became the central concerns of Zionism—were significant problems, and each, in its historical development, had manifested a characteristic attitude toward those ideas. So, when Zionism undertook to revive a Jewish culture and restore Jewish sovereignty, it had not only popular lethargy to contend with. In its effort to implant its own attitudes in the popular consensus, it had to oppose other attitudes toward Jewish culture and Jewish sovereignty that had already more or less firmly taken root.

The position which Zionism eventually established in relation to its ideological opponents was not quite the same among Western and Eastern Jews. Certain rough distinctions are immediately obvious.

First, in the East the idea that the "problem of the Jews" must be treated as a national problem became dominant, and ideological issues between Zionists and anti-Zionists developed within a broad consensus on this point. In the West, whether or not the Jewish problem was a national problem remained an ideological issue between Zionists and non- and anti-Zionists.

The second distinction is a corollary of the first. In all countries, the characteristic Zionist attitude toward the "problem of Judaism" implied a return to the cultural situation characteristic of the East and a repudiation of the cultural trend of the West, which in the Zionist view had departed too far from the ethnic tradition.

Thirdly, in the West, Zionists and their opponents, who were divided over the national character of the problems "of the Jews" and "of Judaism," could unite in their practical concern for the settlement in Palestine. In the East, the latter was the bone of contention.

For a more accurate understanding of these differences and of the situations that produced them, we must consider, first, the circumstances under which Zionism emerged as an historic force.

I

The familiar division between Eastern and Western Jewries did not exist before the movement to emancipate the Jews in the late eighteenth century. Those whom we have learned to call Western Jews since that time are the Jewish communities that were effectively emancipated. Such communities, to the west of the Oder, adjusted their institutions to a status of civic equality. Their culture and customs responded to all the trends of general European culture since the Enlightenment. On the other hand, the title of "eastern European Jewry", while superficially denoting the Jews south of Vienna and east of Prague, Breslau, and Koenigsberg, refers essentially to communities that were never effectively emancipated in the nineteenth century.

Zionism arose as a historic force in response to the situation characteristic not of Western but of Eastern Jewry. In ideological terms, it was a reaction against the Emancipation, a denial of it as a rational solution of the Jewish problem.

Before this historic reaction, ideas subsequently crystallized by Zionism were not unknown. The doctrine of the emancipation of the Jews involved the view that their earlier status of subjection was no longer permissible; consequently, a "Jewish problem" existed. Given the existence of this problem, it was logically possible to seek a solution for it in two different ways: by granting the Jews a new status of equality either individually, as citizens of the countries where they lived, or collectively, as a modern nationality. The first to consider the latter possibility seriously, once the emancipation of the Jews began to be discussed in Western Europe, were not Jews but Gentiles.

That the Jews were a "nation" and not merely a "church" like other churches and that consequently their enfranchisement presented a particularly difficult problem was felt, among others, by ardent advocates of Emancipation like Abbé Henri Grégoire. However, this view was far more likely to be stressed by opponents of the Jews, who did not wish them admitted to civic equality, for in their case it served a polemical purpose. In the climate of opinion created by the French Revolution, it was common ground, accepted by every enlightened person, that a democratic nation, constituting itself anew, must respect the principle that all its members were equally endowed with the rights of man. Moreover, through the separation of church and state, religious differences were eliminated as obstacles to equal citizenship. On the other hand, it was also a valid position for all sides in the debate that an alien could be excluded from the rights of citizenship in a state where he happened to live, since he ought properly to exercise those rights in the nation to which he really belonged. Thus, if "church" was really equivalent to "nation" in the case of the Jews, there was a defensible case for denying them citizenship in France or in the Batavian Republic.

It was on this point that the Jews saw their advocates and opponents divide. The former urged that Jews be admitted to full citizenship in the countries where they lived; the latter argued, in effect, that through their long history as a distinct nation the Jews had already chosen to exclude themselves from the bodies politic of the lands in which they lived. As a practical conclusion from this, it was sometimes proposed to settle the Jews apart from the Gentiles as colonists in thinly populated, underdeveloped areas in France, Austria-Hungary, or Southern Russia. It was also suggested on occasion that it would be best for the Jews to be emancipated not as individual citizens in European countries, but as a people in Palestine. Such ideas of segregation and resettlement, put forward somewhat tentatively or even simply for polemical effect in the discussions arising directly in the wake of the French Revolution and its Napoleonic expansion, crystallized into seriously elaborated proposals among Russian and, to a degree, among Polish revolutionaries in succeeding decades.

The movement for emancipation and the ensuing debates caught the Jews of Europe unprepared. In their initial reaction, the Jews did not universally welcome the release from the old regime which was held out to them by the new. Within the familiar old restrictions they had built up institutions securing their traditions, and the uncertain benefits of the new regime left one thing quite certain: that much held dear by traditional Jews would have to go by the board in order that they might be emancipated. But as the debate among the Gentiles unfolded, the actual alternatives open to the Jews became clearer. Their old status, including the positive values they had built into its framework of restriction and deprival, was no longer a defensible position. The arguments *pro* and *contra* the Jews took place between the new alternatives—individual enfranchisement or collective segregation—formulated in the course of the emancipation debate; and it was in these terms that Jews were now called upon to defend their own interests as best they could. That they adopted the arguments of their defenders rather than of their detractors is not surprising; especially since the alternatives to emancipation which were proposed—regional colonization or restoration to Zion—bore very little semblance of practicability, and merely served in fact as a pretext for retaining the disabilities of the old regime.

Thus it was that, more at first out of compliance with the prevailing climate of opinion than out of such inner conviction as later matured in the religious Reform movement—even, indeed, out of sheer submission to a peremptory demand such as Napoleon placed before the assembly of Jewish notables in 1806—some Jews responded to the debates on their emancipation by formulating two new principles. The Jews, they said, were not a nation but a religious confession like any other—and if they were not yet completely like any other church, they would, under freedom, become so. As for the hopes of a Messianic Restoration of the Jews, some explained these away as symbolical or abstract, and others proposed that the whole theme be wiped out of the Jewish liturgy. So, even before Zionism arose, Western Jews, hoping to solve the Jewish problem by emancipation, formulated views implicitly opposed to Zionism.

However, throughout the nineteenth century, there were Jews as well as Gentiles who suggested solutions for the Jewish problem which were akin to Zionism. Even though Emancipation became the established basis of the Jewish community in the West, Western Jews were not wanting who, like their Gentile contemporaries, adopted a critical attitude to liberalism and the Enlightenment as a whole, and also to the Jewish Emancipation. From such a point of view, it was logical and natural to develop notions which anticipate the Zionist ideology in all but one respect: they were not intended to supplant but to complement the Emancipation. Because of this difference and, above all, because they gave rise to no movement of historical consequence, leading continuously to the establishment of Israel, we call them "proto-Zionist" rather than "Zionist."

Moses Hess conceived his view of a Jewish Zionist mission out of the conviction that the liberal, bourgeois, rationalist revolution had exhausted its historical function and brought mankind to a dead end. The whole world needed for its revival a fresh restatement of eternal verities, a religious rebirth, in fact, in which the Jews were called upon to play a crucial part: it was their historic mission to give the essentially social doctrine of Judaism a new and spontaneous development in free and sovereign self-expression in Palestine.

Such proto-Zionist doctrines remained nothing but stimulating eccentricities of opinion, favored by Jews more or less "marginal" in their relation to the community of Western Jewry. The more representative Western Jews were no less aware than the proto-Zionists of the setbacks to their dreams of redemption-through-liberalism. They, too, were sensitive to the anti-Semitic overtones in the Revolutionary and Napoleonic era itself, the reaction of 1815–1830, and the social upheavals of 1830 and 1848. But the Jewish emancipation seemed to them to be making steady strides, despite temporary retreats. As for the perfection of society as a whole, if this were the context of the discussion, then the Messianic role assigned to Judaism by the proto-Zionists was indeed a flattering idea, but the "representative" view of Western Jews was that it was a role to be performed in Europe. The idea of returning to Palestine in order to be able to live Judaism fully and spontaneously might be academically interesting, if it were not for the fact, that, in the minds of Western Jews, it was associated in a very practical way with the anti-Jewish propaganda of the opponents of emancipation. The Western Jews were still engaged, with confidence in their ultimate full success, in realizing their emancipation. The academic interest they might have in theories and projects of both Jewish and Christian proto-Zionists was consequently mixed with disapproval because of the apparent practical effects of such discussion.

A decisive historic difference made the Jews of Eastern Europe give to Zionism, when it developed among them, a wide and powerful response instead of the cool disinterest of the Western Jews. In Eastern Europe, Zionism arose in the context of an Enlightenment that had fallen short of its goal and an Emancipation that had been aborted—and of the Jewish problem that was defined by these circumstances. For those who had never stirred from the strict tradition, the problem was one of crude oppression which confined the Jews to a Pale of Settlement too poor and too congested to maintain them. It was the problem of a constant pressure for emigration, rendered acute by the coordinated pogroms that were condoned and abetted by the government. For the young and emancipated Jews who shared in the Hovevei-Zion movement, it was a more complicated problem.

The movement to emancipate the Jews, as part of the general Enlightenment, never went far enough or advanced steadily enough in nineteenth-century Russia to inspire anyone with confidence in its prospects. What it did succeed in doing was to raise up a thin layer of enlightened young Jews. But this generation, reaching maturity around 1860, pinned their faith on the ideal of Emancipation, both on the emancipation of their own people and of the Russian peasant, only to have their hopes cruelly and decisively disappointed in their own lifetimes. The traumatic event that brought this disappointment to a head was provided, of course, by the pogroms of the 1880's. What was the emotional reaction of enlightened Jews to this shock is illustrated by the diary notes of M. L. Lilienblum (1843–1910):

> May 7, 1881 . . . I am glad I have suffered. At least once in my life I have had the opportunity of feeling what my ancestors felt every day of their lives. Their lives were one long terror, so why should I experience nothing of that fright which they felt all their lives? I am their son, their sufferings are dear to me and I aspire to their glory.

A similar description of the mood of that time is given in Abraham Cahan's autobiography:

> As a result of the anti-Semitic riots there occurred such scenes as the following, for example: In Kiev a group of Jewish students came into a synagogue packed with mourning, weeping Jews. One of the group, a slender University student named Aleinikoff, got up at the reader's stand and addressed the people in Russian:
>
> "We are your brothers, we are Jews like you, we regret and repent that we considered ourselves Russians and not Jews until now. The events of the past weeks—the pogrom in Elisavetgrad, in Balta, here in Kiev, and in other cities—have shown us how tragically we were mistaken. Yes, we are Jews."
>
> It is needless to describe the impression that such words made on the community.

The ultimate adjustment to this traumatic moment was not the same for all intellectuals, of course. It was a "trauma," in fact, primarily for those who, since the turn to liberalism in Russia in the 60's, had hoped for a solution of the Jewish problem by Enlightenment. Others, younger men, in particular, who first awoke to dogmatic enthusiasm in the revolutionary movements of the late 70's, were sometimes too single-minded and too detached from the Jewish community for disillusionment. Some of these continued to fight for the revolutionary cause of the Russians, without regard for the cost to the Jews. Others, who had seen not only Czarist authorities supporting the pogromists but revolutionaries calculating whether it might not be wise to do the same, and sometimes doing so, were open, in revulsion, to new ideas. They found in Zionism the solution for what they now concluded was the inveterate and unalleviated Jewish problem. The personal situation which brought forth this new ideology, the crisis of disillusionment with the Enlightenment and Emancipation, was widespread enough so that Dr. Leo Pinsker's call for "auto-Emancipation" did not remain a mere eccentricity but evoked a wide response and consolidated a movement.

In Russia, moreover, as in all of Europe to the east of Germany, there had always been a far stronger resistance of traditional Jewry to the ideas of the Enlightenment and to the various aspects of partial Emancipation than in Western Europe. Thus, when Dr. Pinsker and other leaders of the new Hovevei-Zion movement declared Emancipation bankrupt and challenged the Jews to look to their own national resources for their national redemption, they initiated a *rapprochement* of the Zionist intelligentsia with the traditional leadership of Russian Jewry.

Moreover, the Zionists could present their movement as an expression of the powerful urge to emigrate from Russia to lands of freedom. The Zionist vision of social redemption, of the end of exile, was an echo of the dreams of masses who were on the move. As for the "official" leadership, dimly or clearly they sensed this: that in leaving Russia for the free West, the immigrants were going to lands of dangerous Enlightenment and "assimilation." The Zionist alternative, the prospect of migration to a home both free and Jewish, could not fail to attract them as a possible new safeguard against assimilation—though it was still prudent to wait until it became clear whether Zionism, too, were not merely a new subversion of tradition.

Actually, of course, it turned out that the Hovevei-Zion could not divert the stream of migration to any significant extent towards Palestine; and the bridge to tradition had to be built through a long process of polemics and strife from the beginning. Yet the Eastern Zionists were not listened to with merely academic interest as had been Moses Hess. Their underlying assumptions and the problem they grasped were, in one form or another, the assumptions of the bulk of the people of their time and the problem felt most painfully by all Eastern European Jewry: for the Jewish masses attested by their migration that they did not regard Russia as a home or haven for them; and the crisis of Jewish tradition as well as the failure of the Emancipation and the Enlightenment was everywhere felt. Consequently Zionism for the first time established itself as a recognized faction in the community, whose views and activities must, at any rate, be taken seriously.

For all that, no one could safely have prophesied at that time that Zionism would last and become historically memorable and effective. The Zionists, bred on Western ideas, felt isolated and odd so long as they remained a faction virtually restricted to Eastern European Jewry, with its basic hostility to every manifestation of Westernism. Furthermore, all their efforts to affect the fate of the mass of Jews, and the course of their migration, in a tangible way remained fruitless, for the stream went Westward, and not to Zion. Then Herzl arose and with his bold style and large conceptions made a way for Zionism in the West, too, giving the Eastern Zionists a share in a national movement of Jews throughout the entire Diaspora. Moreover, he raised the failing spirits of the Hovevei-Zion, by turning their efforts from practical colonization, whose limits had been painfully encountered in that period, to a new road of international political action. To be sure, in a short time this road too came to the end of its resources, but in the early days of Herzl, before its contemporary limits were plumbed, the new approach rekindled enthusiasm and released new energies among the old Zionists—till a new generation arose, inspired by its own new version of a road to Zion through labor, and reestablished Zionism's claim to become historic.

It remains true that, in his own Western Jewish community, Herzl, like Hess, was an essentially "marginal" figure; and if not for the prior existence of Eastern Zionism, he could not have achieved his decisive contribution towards making Zionism historic. For despite the long-drawn-out resistance of partisans of traditional institutions in Germany, to name only one example, what determined the situation and the character of Western Jewry was that the Enlightenment and the Emancipation had established a new cultural and institutional milieu in which the Jewish community now lived as of necessity. There was no failure of the Emancipation to be established, there was only sharp disappointment in the way it had been established: disappointment at the stubborn resistance to Jewish rights that was encountered from the start, at the "relapses" into anti-Semitism, and at the price which the Jews had to pay, in their own cultural confusion and communal disorganization, for so grudging a grant of freedom.

Such doubts and disturbance were transformed in the case of some individuals into a new proto-Zionist or Zionist ideology as a reaction to traumatic events. For Hess the Damascus and Mortara cases and the excitement of the Franco-Italian attack on the Holy Roman Empire, for Herzl the Dreyfus affair set off such a reaction. Each found a group of sympathetic readers with similar experiences among Western Jews. But the community as a whole could not take seriously any suggestion to seek a status other than civic emancipation in each country as its basis of existence—nor did any Western Zionist, until Herzl, forcefully present this position. But by the time Herzl arose to deny that the Emancipation was the solution of the Jewish problem, his Zionist proposals fell into a framework already established by the Hovevei-Zion societies that had spread among Jews from their origin in Russia. There the patent failure of the Emancipation had made Zionism something to be taken seriously by the community, a plausible alternative solution for a problem that urgently demanded to be solved.

Because Zionism was taken seriously in the East, Western Jews whom it attracted became not merely eccentrics, but adherents of a historic cause; and because of the accession of the Westerners, with their facilities for action, Zionism developed into something more than an episode—it became a historic movement. The Zionist movement now faced its first historic task: to convert its own basic views and attitudes into a national consensus shared by the entire people whom it hoped to revive. In this task, Zionism had to deal with substantially different problems in the Western and Eastern Jewish communities. It had to deal, first of all, with already well-formed and quite distinct attitudes of Western and Eastern Jewries to those ideas which were characteristically Zionist—the revival of Jewish culture as a solution for the "problem of Judaism" and the restoration of Jewish sovereignty in Zion as a solution for the "problem of the Jews."

While Jewish culture and Jewish sovereignty were matters of cardinal ideological significance for Zionism, they did not necessarily have equal importance for Western modernism or Eastern traditionalism. Before Zionism arose and sharpened these issues, "Zionist" ideas regarding Jewish sovereignty were sometimes voiced both among modernists and traditionalists. But Zionism could hardly have arisen at all if it had not sensed that, on those matters which it felt to be cardinal, the whole weight of the two already existing ideologies implied attitudes, nonrational as well as rational, which provoked the Zionists to rebellion. For Zionism, like any historic movement, was primarily a revulsion against what it found intolerable in the past. In the history of Zionist ideas, therefore, what is important is not the full range of the rather elastic views of its predecessors on questions Zionism regarded as crucial, but the more rigidly defined descriptions of those opposing views formulated by the Zionists themselves. And those formulations were molded under the polarizing force of the passion with which Zionists reacted to certain ideas, upon which, consequently, they demanded that everyone else take a definite, principled position.

When Zionism had confronted its ideological opponents with its own polemical descriptions of their views, these sometimes served as what a sociologist might call "self-validating definitions." Under the challenge of the fixed Zionist positions on Jewish culture and Jewish sovereignty, the modernist and traditionalist rivals of Zionism defined their own attitudes in more rigorous opposition—though the positions they took did not necessarily coincide point for point with the Zionist descriptions of them. Nor did Zionist ideology alone affect its rivals. The moods of the Zionist rebellion spread through mythic channels and exercised an influence not always parallel with the effect of Zionism as an intellectual challenge.

Our analysis begins, accordingly, with the traditionalist and modernist positions on Jewish culture and Jewish sovereignty as the Zionists perceived and reacted to them. The Hegelian dialectic provided the terms by which the late nineteenth-century European parties liked to describe themselves in relation to their opposing ideologies. Zionism, too, regarded traditionalism and modernism as the "thesis" and "antithesis" of a Hegelian dialectic, with Zionism itself appearing as the "synthesis" of its historic predecessors. That is to say Zionism recapitulated what it conceived to be the valid criticisms of tradition by modernism and of modernism by traditionalism. The element by which it hoped to transcend both was chiefly the new stress it laid on "auto-Emancipation" or, as we prefer to say, on sovereignty—a myth image whose conceptual content remained to be defined—as an indispensable requirement for the solution of the Jewish problem.

In the Zionist view, the valid historic contribution of the Western modernists had been the insistence that there was a Jewish problem that had to be solved rationally. The idea that the Jewish situation in the world is a problematic one is, of course, far from a modern discovery. According to the traditional view, the Jews are "in Exile," a conception which we today would unhesitatingly label as "ambivalent." Exile is a penance for which the Jews were singled out precisely because they are the "Chosen People." Hence, it is a sign of divine favor and a trial that must be piously and lovingly accepted. But Exile is also a penalty the Jews brought upon themselves and continue to suffer "because of our many sins." Hence, they must continually pray to be relieved of it and to be restored to Zion. To live in the light of such a conception is certainly to live problematically; but the problem involved is one which from the outset is conceived as beyond rational solution. It is at this point that what we have called modernism propounded a new idea: the modernists held that the condition of oppression and degradation involved in Exile could be and should be overcome by rational measures. This idea Zionism accepted and employed in its own criticism of traditionalism.

Out of their hostility to the pious, traditionalist acceptance of Exile, the Zionists adopted a familiar formula for the intellectual repudiation of a rival doctrine. They saw in the traditional conception of a millennial restoration by the Messiah, following the completion of the Jewish penance, only a cover for timid inaction—that is, they debunked it as mere "ideology."

Considered in terms of its logical sources, the Zionist hostility to traditionalism derives from the view that the Jewish problem can and must be rationally solved, and it expresses a consequent irritation with attitudes based on a nonrational view of the problem. But this is not the only kind of denunciation of traditionalism to which the same underlying opposition can logically lead. While Western modernism, as we have seen, also occasionally revolted against traditionalist passivity, it was far more characteristic of modernism to express its hostility in other terms. Obscurantism, not passivity, was the vice the modernists most frequently condemned in the representatives of traditional Jewry.

To condemn obscurantism as the vice that prevented a rational solution of the Jewish problem implied the view that the Gentiles had adopted, or would adopt, rational attitudes toward the Jews, and that the Jews must follow suit, or anticipate, by adopting corresponding rational attitudes. Consequently, in place of the vice of stubborn obscurantism the modernists preached the virtues of reasonableness and accommodation: the *acceptance* by the Jews of enlightened standards of culture and institutions of civil society, of an emancipation offered (if not yet everywhere in fact, then at least in conception) on the initiative of Gentile society. To condemn the traditionalists for passivity, as Zionism did, implies quite different assumptions and conclusions. It assumes that a rational solution of the Jewish problem demanded action *initiated* by the Jews, not by the Gentiles, perhaps even action by the Jews in the teeth of Gentile opposition. The virtues which Zionism, accordingly, preached were those of boldness and activity: the assertion of the individuality and the self-liberation—or, as it was called, the auto-Emancipation—of the Jews. To this it was hoped and expected that gentiles would concur, but the initiative necessarily had to be Jewish.

Quite as sharp an opposition between the conceptions of modernism and Zionism arose in relation to two other issues, Jewish culture and Jewish sovereignty, on which both departed from the traditional views.

What would be the effect of enlightenment and emancipation upon the individual tradition of Jewish culture and upon the traditional vision of Jewish sovereignty was not, perhaps, a cardinal problem but still a matter of concern to the modernists. One logical limit had to be observed by any *Jewish* modernism in seeking a rational accommodation with enlightened Gentile society: it could not accept a "solution" of the Jewish problem involving the total submergence of the Jews. In the generation following Moses Mendelssohn, a solution of this nature was proposed as a policy by some and adopted as an expedient by many who sought to escape the Jewish problem by conversion to Christianity. The Jewish modernists wished to erect a dam against such desertion by preserving those elements of Jewish culture and Jewish autonomy which were consistent with the standards of an enlightened Gentile world—and, of course, by discarding the others.

The Talmudic literature as well as the Yiddish language appeared at once to the Jewish Enlightenment as the kind of tradition that must be discarded. The Bible and the Hebrew language, on the other hand, deserved to be cherished on two accounts. These were, first of all, the classic foundations of the Mosaic cult, which the modernists defended as essentially rational. In addition, Biblical and Hebraic purism were valuable tools in the struggle against those strongholds of traditionalist obscurantism, the Yiddish "jargon" and rabbinic Talmudism. However, what actually happened in the wake of the Jewish Enlightenment in Germany was different from what was planned. Not only the obscurantist tradition and Yiddish language were discarded by the modernist reformers, but the projected neo-Biblical and neo-Hebraic Enlightenment culture swiftly vanished, remaining the hobby, at most, of a few scholarly specialists. Western Jews adopted the French and German cultural traditions as the most effective media of Enlightenment, while Jewish cultural individuality was restricted almost entirely to the synagogue.

The Zionists adopted toward the Enlightenment an attitude of condemnation like that of the traditionalists, who foresaw nothing but "shmad" (which translates roughly as "renegade apostasy") as the outcome of modernism. This traditionalist term of abuse was replaced in the nationalist vocabulary by another, "assimilationism," more neutral in its flavor but still heavily weighted with disapproval and bearing a connotation of "betrayal."

The common hostility of Zionism and traditionalism to the "renegade" tendencies of modernism was paralleled by a sense that the two were allied in defense of the Hebrew tradition. Significant differences divided them, of course, on this point. Tradition had cherished and succeeded in maintaining the Hebrew language as the medium of prayer and scholarship and also of general communication and solidarity between Jews and Jewish communities scattered in all quarters of the Exile. Zionism, however, wished to revive Hebrew as a spoken language so that the people—especially when it came together out of its Exile—would have a common mother tongue. In consequence of this, vernacular Hebrew would no longer be simply the vehicle of a "normative" religious culture such as had "created" Jews through successive generations. It would reverse that relationship for a more "normal" one. By expressing all the activities that spontaneously occur in a fully rounded society, it would become the medium through which the Jewish people would freely create its secular culture and thereby consolidate a national rather than religious consensus.

All these, however, were differences which crystallized in the course of time. When Zionism arose, the far more significant feeling was one of alliance with the traditionalists against the "assimilationism" of the modernists.

What concerned the nationalists even more was the position to which modernism was led on the questions of Jewish sovereignty and the restoration to Zion. We have noted how the Western Jews, in defence of their emancipation, were led to adopt the view that the Jews were not an ethnic group but a religious denomination no different from Christian denominations—or if not yet quite as divorced from any ethnic quality as the Christian denominations, certain to become so under a regime of civic equality. This involved a series of related propositions: that the traditional Messianic hope of Jewish restoration in Zion was at most a symbol or an abstract notion, perhaps best interpreted as no more than the reign of divine justice throughout the world; that the traditional idea of Exile had now been suspended by the grant of emancipation; and that the dispersion of the Jews was a providential act, signifying that the Jews had a mission to set the Gentiles an example of a pure, rational, prophetic, monotheistic faith.

The nationalist rejection of these views and their implied emotional correlates was passionate and decisive. Ahad Ha'am summed it up for his generation in an essay which, because of its emotional as well as intellectual conviction, crystallized the nationalist consensus with mythic force, so that its title, "Slavery in Freedom," cast the verdict against the West in a stereotype formula. The idea of a Jewish mission to be forever dispersed among the Gentiles in order to teach them prophetic monotheism, he dismisses with contempt. The Jews, he notes, are *not* a missionary people and they have long since renounced any idea of spreading their gospel by mass conversions to Judaism.

> We are no longer doing anything useful towards the fulfillment of our mission: the Scriptures, and consequently religious progress, are independent of us, and will do their work without us; we are nothing but a monument on the path of religious progress, which marches on to its consummation without our assistance.

How can enlightened men of our time, Ahad Ha'am goes on to ask, who have learned from Darwin that no purposes, divine or otherwise, but only determining causes control the course of history, believe in such nonsense? The obvious answer is that they don't really believe it; they only pretend to believe. Thus, just as Zionist critics attacked traditionalism as mere ideology, they made the same analysis of modernist beliefs. The critique was even fiercer in this instance, for the debunking of traditionalism was often tempered by respect for the profound faith which Zionists acknowledged among Orthodox believers, but no such consideration palliated the polemic against modernism.

> What, then, are those Jews to do who have nothing left but this theoretical religion, which is itself losing its hold on them? Are they to give up Judaism altogether, and become completely assimilated to their surroundings? . . . Where is the chain to which they can point as that which holds them fast to Judaism, and does not allow them to

> be free? Is it the instinctive national feeling which they have inherited, which is independent of religious beliefs, or practices? . . . But this answer, though it satisfies us, does not satisfy them. They have publicly renounced their Jewish nationality, and they cannot go back on their words; they cannot confess that they have sold that which was not theirs to sell.

So the modernists of the West had paid for their formal emancipation by selling themselves into intellectual and moral slavery. They dared not admit what they must have known to be true, that their professed religious belief was an ideological pretense, nor to confess what they must have felt to be true, that their Jewish loyalties were, in fact, a sentiment of nationality. In his conclusion, therefore, Ahad Ha'am places Eastern traditional Jewry on a higher plane than the Western modernists.

> Do I envy these fellow-Jews of mine their emancipation?—I answer, in all truth and sincerity: No! a thousand times No! The privileges are not worth the price! I may not be emancipated; but at least I have not sold my soul for emancipation. . . . I am my own, and my opinions and feelings are my own. I have no reason for concealing or denying them, for deceiving others or myself. And this spiritual freedom—scoff who will!—I would not exchange or barter for all the emancipation in the world.

Apart from the typical emotional revulsion against the modernists, these passages also convey a central nationalist doctrine: that emancipation is not a rational solution of the Jewish problem. The real danger to Jewish survival as a distinct group is not loss of religious belief, leading to assimilation. The Jews are an ethnic entity, and individual Jews consequently retain their loyalty and sense of solidarity even when no longer religious. However, modernism can injure the Jewish people severely. By forcing them to hide their natural ethnic feelings from others and even from themselves, it causes them to adopt false ideologies and to abandon their own historic myth. So, too, it leads them to rely on others to emancipate them, inculcating a false spirit of submission, instead of arousing the will to independence. This is the cardinal point in the Zionist critique; and in this regard, it condemns both traditionalism and modernism in almost the same terms. That pious acceptance of Exile which tradition exalted as a high penance, Zionism condemned as a supine surrender to oppression. So, too, the Zionists saw in the lofty Jewish mission proposed by the Western modernists only a high-sounding pretense, a "conventional lie" serving to hide "slavery in freedom."

The attitude of Zionism to modernism was, in other important respects, quite different from its attitude to traditionalism. The modernists were opposed because their views led to the abandonment of traditional Jewish culture and resulted in undermining the idea of Jewish independence and the will to achieve it. The Zionists had only this hope for the modernists: that they might be brought back again to the ranks of unestranged and uninhibited Jews.

The traditionalists, on the other hand, had never abandoned the heritage of Jewish culture or the historic myth of Jewish independence. They had been the mainstays of both, and preserved them alive through the centuries. At the same time, in the Zionist view, both Jewish culture and the idea of Jewish independence had been reduced by the traditionalists to a state of suspended animation in which they might be preserved, but were unable to be active and effectual. The Zionist hope, as to the traditionalists, was to persuade them to accept new views of Jewish culture and Jewish sovereignty based on the pursuit of independence as an immediate aim.

Reverting to the Hegelian formula, we may say that the Zionist "synthesis" stood directly opposed to the "antithesis," modernism, and sought a *rapprochement* with the original "thesis," traditionalism. For with modernism, Zionism shared the general principle that the Jewish problem required an immediate, rational solution; but it differed sharply—and emotionally—on the nature of the problem and the solution. With traditionalism, Zionism shared, as an emotional bond, the common vision of a solution by which the Exile would be transcended. Its task was to persuade the traditionalists to seek the desired solution immediately by inducing them to take a rational view of the existing situation.

Behind this difference in attitude lies the fact that Zionism arose as a historic movement in response to the situation of Eastern, not of Western Jewry. United with Western modernism in its resolve to achieve an immediate rational solution of the Jewish problem, Zionism found a different solution—because it addressed itself to a different situation. Opposed to traditionalism because it was impatient to solve the Jewish problem immediately and rationally, Zionism sought essentially the same solution, because it saw itself in the same situation: in exile. What seemed rational in terms of the Jewish situation as Western modernism saw it, and as the Western Jews defined it institutionally, seemed simply unrealistic in terms of the situation of Eastern Jews, as enlightened young men began to understand it after the 1880's.

II

These differences directly affected the different manners in which Zionism was received into the consensus of Western and Eastern Jewries. In the East, the crucial experience of the 1880's, and similar experiences that followed, made not only Zionists and traditionalists but the succeeding generations of Eastern modernists perceive their situation as one of national conflict. Even where Zionism led to the development of new ideologies opposed to its own tenets, some of the mythic components of the Zionist view—especially the stereotype of "assimilationism"—were accepted by the general consensus. In the West, however, the basic experience behind Zionism never dominated the consensus of the community. The Zionist myth was shared only by those won over to the Zionist ideology; and they often saw it as their primary task to bring their own community back into the consensus of Eastern Jewry.

For in the West, it was modernism that had had a dominant effect upon the communal consensus. With the rise of modernism, traditional Judaism did not, indeed, disappear; there was, in fact, an ideological revival of Jewish Orthodoxy in reaction against the doctrines of the modernists. Where modernist theologians like Abraham Geiger (1810–1874) demanded that traditional Jewish law and custom, as well as doctrine, bow to reason and contemporary history (which two they tended to identify), Orthodox theologians like Samson Raphael Hirsch (1808–1888) propounded the opposing view that the Torah, as a revealed law and doctrine, transcended history. But at the same time Western Orthodoxy shared the basic experience of the modernists and bowed to the force of their formulations. They, too, recognized that emancipation had established a new fundamental status for the Jews, that no return to the ghetto was possible, and that Jewish "secular" life must be conducted in a spirit of thorough accommodation to the standards of enlightenment which contemporary history had adopted. Only religion, and particularly the traditional ritual law, was defended against history, while a broad secular realm was recognized within which the Jews must live as fully and individually integrated nationals of the countries where they enjoyed civic equality. The characteristic attitude of Western Orthodoxy was summed up by S. R. Hirsch in the formula, "Torah together with *Derekh Eretz*." Interpreted, this meant the preservation of the traditional, particularly ritual, laws as above history, together with a full acceptance of prevailing non-Jewish contemporary standards in all secular affairs.

Before Zionism arose as an organized ideological movement and made a matter of principle of the idea of Jewish sovereignty, attitudes on this question could vary in spite of a basic acceptance of the Emancipation. Indeed, the 1860's saw a kind of proto-Zionism in Western Europe which took on almost the aspect of a historic movement: a theory of Jewish restoration was propounded, groups were organized and propaganda conducted on behalf of the return to Zion. It was among the Orthodox Jews of Germany and its bordering areas that this activity was most marked, in spite of the dictum of the leading Orthodox theorist, S. R. Hirsch, that the restoration to Zion was an event that could only occur beyond the bounds of history.

But two things must be noted about the proto-Zionism of those Western Orthodox Jews. The first is the striking fact that the movement enjoyed its greatest success and found its intellectual leaders among those in a "marginal" position in relation to Western Jewry, since in most cases they lived in the outskirts of the German cultural area (in Silesia or northern Prussia, or in Hungary) and shared as much in the life of the East as of the West. Yet the hopes of these proto-Zionists were pinned on Western Jewry—and the second striking characteristic of the movement reflects this orientation. The proto-Zionists of the 1860's did not begin with a programmatic assertion that the Jewish problem remained unsolved in spite of emancipation. They did not question the fundamental status of the Western Jews as an emancipated community, but sought an essentially religious supplement to emancipation through the restoration of the Jews in Zion.

Because it did not clearly challenge emancipation as the fundamental principle of Jewish status, the proto-Zionism of the 1860's fell short of becoming a historic movement based on ideological principles. It remained essentially a mythic variant within the attitude system of Western Orthodox Jews, a system that accepted emancipation as a principle that could solve the problems of Jewish secular status. No serious challenge of this view arose among Western Jews until Herzl. But, at the same time, the ideas of emancipation and enlightenment did not inspire intellectual enthusiasm for long. For while they had a decisive effect upon the Jewish consensus at a mythic as well as a rational level, their effect was a decisively negative, iconoclastic or, one may say, "antimythic" one.

Zionism did not succeed in "conquering the communities" in the West. The non-Zionist opposition, signalized by the Munich Jewish community's effective protest against convening the first Zionist congress in their city and based on ideological principles in statements issued by rabbis in Germany and even in far-off America, remained in control of the Western Jewries. Zionist intellectuals, like Herzl and Nordau, who sought a national consensus to respond to their appeal had to find it in those communities whose myth still perceived Jewry as an ethnic entity, the communities of Eastern European Jewry.

Some Western Zionist intellectuals, moreover, built into their ideology fashionable ideas repudiating rational Idealism. Zionism, through its rejection of Emancipation and Enlightenment as the adequate principles of Jewish life, enabled these men to seek what we now call existentialist doctrines in Jewish tradition and not outside it, and an organic community in the Jewish people, not outside it. The tradition of Orthodox Judaism, especially the mysticism of the Hassidic movement, was the new intellectual heritage, and the community of Eastern European Jewry was the new organic community they discovered.

Thus the over-all effect of the rise of Zionism in Western Europe was not the conquest of the communities there by the ideology of Zionist intellectuals. The effect was rather that Western Zionists, won over by the Zionist myth, found themselves in a new communion with Eastern Jewry. The assumption of the West had been hitherto that the Western situation of Emancipation and the Western principles of Enlightenment were the fundamental defining conditions of Jewish life in modern times; and that if Eastern Jewry did not yet live under those conditions, this was the result of backwardness that time would overcome. The new, Zionist assumption was that the Eastern situation of ethnic community, and the principle of auto-Emancipation that was demanded by such a situation, were the true defining conditions of the contemporary Jewish problem; and that the principles of Western Jewry represented a detour from the true course of Jewish history, and led to no rational solution of the Jewish problem.

The Zionists did not succeed completely in conquering the Eastern communities either. Even more than in the West, the rise of Zionism provoked a multiplication of opposing ideologies. But the underlying myth of Zionism did pervade the consensus of Eastern Jewry and was widely effective there. The general emotional reaction of Zionism to the historic events that give it birth in Eastern Europe was shared by many others, modernist and traditionalist alike; and the forms in which the Zionist rebellion was symbolized communicated a common sentiment and thus exerted an influence well beyond the Zionist group.

The most characteristic emotional mood of the Zionist myth was its militancy; and what militant Zionism found most odious in Eastern traditionalism and in Western modernism was their passive or accommodating submission to outer compulsions. But militant and rebellious moods in the face of oppression were, in fact, far from foreign to either traditionalists or modernists. Certainly, in Eastern Europe, the modernist youths who hoped to create by revolution a new Russia in which the Jewish problem would disappear (together with the Jewish community) did not lack militancy. In 1882 and in subsequent crises, they fought during pogroms in self-defense groups just as the young Zionists did; and their myth of revolutionary idealism provided the young Zionists with many figures of heroism. And in the West, the organization of Jewish self-defense in Eastern Europe found ready support among leaders of the community some of whom were anything but Zionist.

Resistance to pogroms found no less support in the traditionalist community. The self-defense groups could count not only on the cooperation of young workmen in the pious, poorer quarters but on the sympathy of traditionalists too old or too respectable to fight themselves. That it was Jewish militancy rather than Zionism which evoked this response is clear, because there was a similar warmth in the reaction of many traditionalist Jews in Russia—as well as of pillars of the Jewish community in the West—to the young Jewish social revolutionaries and terrorists. The views of these violent men were anathema and their actions damnable to such conservatives; if for no other reason, then simply because they imperilled the whole community. Yet it was balm for the helpless and humiliated anger of those who witnessed pogroms, from near at hand or from afar, to see the oppressor hurt. So, too, traditionalist Jews did not need to accept the Zionist view that the Jewish problem must be rationally solved in order to feel a life of pride (often mixed with distaste) when Jewish students suddenly undertook to display an un-Jewish prowess in duelling and athletic games. The adulation of Herzl in the crowded towns of Eastern Europe was certainly shared by many a Jew who had only a slight idea of his views, or who opposed them, but was moved by the legendary figure of this "King of the Jews."

From having touched a responsive chord among both modernists and traditionalists by its myth of militancy, Zionism still had a long course to cover in order to conquer the communal consensus for its more specific tenets. But among Eastern traditionalists and modernists alike, Zionism found understanding and acceptance of other aspects of its myth, of the way in which it perceived the critical experiences of its times, while it provoked sharp differences in the ideological conclusions that it drew.

Zionism strengthened its bonds with the traditionalists, in its mood of *rapprochement* with the past, by modeling its own symbols and symbolic actions in the style of tradition. Among the effects of the Zionist mood was a new appreciation of some of the traditional holidays, especially those that recalled heroic episodes in the national history of celebrated Palestinian harvest or sowing seasons. The first pamphlet issued for mass distribution in 1891 by the Zionist secret society B'nei Moshe was a Russian brochure on Hannuka, the festival of the

Maccabees; and the observance of the spring festival of Lag Ba'Omer as a Palestinian Arbor Day was accepted by the community throughout the Diaspora after the Zionists initiated this practice. Just as traditionalist Jews collected funds for Palestine in little tin boxes dedicated to "Rabbi Meir Baal ha-Ness," so the Zionists collected funds for Palestine in little blue-white boxes dedicated to the "Keren Kayemet le-Israel." Not only the name of the fund (and the colors of the box) struck a traditional note, but is statutes and purposes were in the authentic style. For the Keren Kayemet was a fund for the purchase of land in Palestine as the inalienable possession of the Jewish people as a whole; and the provisions under which it proposed to lease its holdings vaguely recalled ancient Biblical laws, commandments which tradition regarded as only fallen into disuse since the Jews left the Holy Land but still representing a sacred duty for all Jews to carry out. So, too, when new settlements of farmers were established in Palestine in the 1880's and 1890's, when Hebrew and Yiddish folksongs began to sing their praises, and one of these songs, "Hatikva," became a Zionist anthem; and when a new blue-white flag with a mystic six-cornered Star of David was adopted by the Zionists as the Jewish flag, all these adaptations of traditional materials and traditional styles penetrated far beyond the circle of avowed Zionists, and, indeed, were rejected only where clearly opposed ideologies arose.

Ideological issues which prevented the full *rapprochement* of traditionalism and Zionism soon did arise. The cultural program of those Zionists who were primarily concerned with solving "the problem of Judaism" could not be considered merely a matter of new Zionist symbols and ceremonial acts, of mythic variations in the traditional style, which traditionalists could accept as permissible innovations. It represented a full ideological attack on the very basis of traditionalism; for it proposed not merely to revive and reinvigorate, but to reform and reconstruct Jewish education, the Hebrew language and literature, and, indeed, the whole historic and ethical institutional structure of the tradition.

To such an enterprise the traditionalists could feel themselves drawn only in the early stages, and only in the hope that what began as a turn against the Enlightenment might end as a full return to tradition. When Ahad Ha'am set up his quasi-Masonic Zionist cultural order of B'nei Moshe, traditionalists joined it, and they proposed that the secret society bind itself at least to a *pro forma* acceptance of the most characteristic traditional customs; that much, as a beginning. In the agricultural settlements founded in Palestine in the 1880's, pious Jews were largely represented; and they hoped for the revival of ancient traditional rites in the colonies. So, too, the early pedagogical projects of the "cultural Zionists" in the Diaspora found many of the traditionalists ready to cooperate.

But it soon appeared that the Zionist *rapprochement* to tradition was not to be a one-sided movement. The revived tradition which the cultural Zionists envisaged was one that would meet the prodigal sons of Jewry halfway. It would have to be elastic enough to express without compromise of conscience the mood of nationalists who were, after all, stamped with the mark of the Enlightenment and who identified with Jewish tradition historically, not ecclesiastically. The demands of the traditionalists in regard to ritual and education were more than such men could meet, while, on the other hand, the ideological position of the secular Zionists provoked the Orthodox to set up their own ideological opposition.

Orthodox opposition to the secular Zionist cultural program in the course of time developed two forms, one Zionist and one anti-Zionist, each with its own ideology. Those who became Religious Zionists were united with other Zionists not only in their political aims but in sharing membership in the World Zionist Organization, while they differed with them in regard to the religious-cultural question. The Orthodox anti-Zionists, on the other hand, rejected membership in the World Zionist Organization on religious grounds, and at the same time developed a religious ideology politically opposed to Zionism.

Chapter 8
Judaism in America: The Social Crisis of Freedom

Jacob Neusner

America confronts Judaism with the challenge, and opportunity, of addressing Jews in a free society. The new politics defined by American freedom has reshaped the circumstance of Judaism and called forth revisions, reforms, and redefinitions of various kinds in response to the shifts in the political conditions in which successive generations of Jews in America formed their Judaisms. For the long centuries in which Jews lived as a separate and (usually) protected minority, from ancient times to the nineteenth century West, Judaism constructed a way of life and expressed a world view for a social group whose persistence seldom was called into question and could always be explained by appeal to the myth of exile and redemption, sanctification in the here and now, salvation at the end of time, for the holy people, the "Israel" of successive Judaisms. From their beginnings Christianity and Islam always recognized the legitimacy (if the inferiority, too) of Judaism, which Jews took to be self-evident. To be sure, Jews found their lives and property threatened. But Judaism could explain that fact and so find even reenforcement in it. More important, memories of times of stress flowed together with the experience of a world in which Jews found themselves living mainly among other Jews, by both mutual consent and political constraint.

In America by contrast the Jews' life together as a distinctive group has come to depend mainly upon inner assent, produced in decisions of individuals to make something of their origin. Less and less as time has passed, has "being Jewish" resulted from external compulsion. The reason is that in the condition of the open and free society constructed by Americans, Jews really did not find themselves much different from others. The distinguishing traits—whether imposed or voluntary—of a Jewish language, Jewish clothing, Jewish occupations and places and residence, which had marked the immediate predecessors of American Jews in Central and Eastern Europe, in America moreover were absent from the very beginning. Consequently, Jews, and therefore Judaism, found themselves in a circumstance hitherto not common in their history and the Judaisms that emerged in successive generations responded to the social experience that demanded explanation on the part of those cohorts.

FREEDOM'S CHALLENGE TO JUDAISM: THE SYSTEMIC QUESTION

The condition of freedom overtook the Jews only slowly, and then by generations. The numerous immigrants of the later nineteenth and early twentieth centuries (from 1880 to 1920, more than 3.5 million Jews came to the USA from Russia, Poland, Rumania, Hungary, and Austria) spoke Yiddish all their lives. They pursued a limited range of occupations. They lived mainly in crowded Jewish neighborhoods of a few great cities. So the facts of language, occupation, and residence reinforced their separateness. Judaism then explained it. In this period, moreover, other immigrant groups, together with their churches, likewise found themselves constituting tight enclaves of the old country in the new. How much freedom of choice a Yiddish-speaking Jewish immigrant from Poland actually exercised, or would have wanted to recognize, surely is limited. The children of the immigrants, that is, the second generation in America, by contrast, adopted the American language and American ways of life. But the second generation grew up and lived in a period of severe anti-Semitism at home and in Europe, especially in the 1930s and 1940s. While trying to forget the immigrant heritage, the second generation found the world a school for Jewish consciousness, and that of a distinctively negative sort. Coming to maturity in the depression and in World War II, the second generation did not have to decide whether or not to be "Jewish," nor were many decisions about what "being Jewish" demanded of them.

That set of decisions, amounting to the framing of a situation of genuine free choice, awaited the third generation, reaching its maturity after World War II. That generation found little psychological pressure, such as had faced its predecessors, in favor of "being Jewish." Surveys of anti-Semitic opinion turned up progressively diminishing levels of Jew-hatred. More important, while the second generation had strong memories of Yiddish-speaking parents and lives of a distinctively Jewish character, the third generation in the main did not. For in line with Hanson's law, the second generation made a vigorous effort to forget what it knew. The third generation had to make a decision to learn what it did not know, indeed, what it had no natural reason, in its upbringing and family heritage, to know. American Judaism as we know it today is the creation of that third generation, the result of its conscientious effort to remember what its parents equally deliberately forgot.

The decision was made in a free society and represented free and uncoerced choice. So the third generation forms the first generation of Judaism in a very long sequence of centuries to have the right to decide in an open society whether or not to be Jewish. More interesting, it is the first generation to define for itself what "being Jewish" would consist of, and how Judaism, as an inherited and received religious tradition, would be taken over as part of this definition.

THE GENERATIONS OF AMERICAN JUDAISM: THE SOCIAL SETTING OF AMERICAN JUDAISM

How so? To understand how the third generation of American Jews defined for itself a distinctive and fresh Judaic system, that is, a world view and way of life serving a distinct social group or class, we have to effect a striking contrast. It is between the state of Judaism at the point at which the second generation (1920–1950) had defined matters, with the equivalent condition of Judaism for the third generation (1950–1980) thirty years later, hence the Judaism of the 1940s and 1950s with the Judaism of the 1970s and 1980s. Beginning, for purposes of comparison and contrast, with the latter, we find a vast network of educational activities in Judaism, both formal and informal. There are, for example, camps devoted to the use of the Hebrew language in both prayer and every day activities, youth groups, programs of Judaic interest in Jewish community centers. A system of Judaic schooling based on afternoon and Sunday sessions now competes with the more intensive all-day schooling of Jewish parochial schools, many under Orthodox, some under Conservative auspices. The organized Jewish community in its philanthropic activities invests sizable sums in Judaic activities, youth programs, camps, and formal schooling. The religious observances of classical Judaism in Orthodox, Conservative, Reform, and Reconstructionist modes reach beyond the synagogue into the home, on the one side, and into formal community programs, on the other. Important historical events, such as the destruction of the Jews of Europe ("the Holocaust," in English, "Shoah," in Hebrew), receive massive community attention and commemoration. Even a program of quasi-religious pilgrimage, in the form of study-trips to the Holy Land, the State of Israel draws sizable proportions of participation of the community, old and young. Jewish organizations of an other-than-religious orientation (it is difficult to regard them as wholly secular) undertake these travel programs, generally imparting to them a strong religious-educational aspect. These same supposedly-secular organizations include in their programs study-sessions of a decidedly religious character, in which the Hebrew Scriptures and other Judaic texts or events of sacred history play an important role. Surveys of religious observance confirm a fairly broad level of popular participation in at least some Judaic rites, for example, the Passover Seder, though many other rites have become mere curiosities. Finally, alongside the neo-Judaic activism of the third generation comes the foundation, in the American Jewish community, of a quite distinct generation. Now a new first generation takes root, this one made up of survivors of the European catastrophe who came to the

USA in the late 1940s and early 1950s, with yet more recent immigrants from the State of Israel and oriental countries, on the one side, and the Soviet Union, on the other. The new first generation, beginning with its own history, has founded a broad range of vigorously Orthodox institutions and created a quite separate life for itself, in which Judaism as a classical religion defines the affairs of culture and society in every detail. The new first generation has had a deep impact on the orthodoxy of the third generation. It must be said that by the mid-1980s, therefore, a distinctively American expression of Judaism had come to full realization. What this meant is that a set of Judaic systems has come to definition in this country. That those who have defined them clearly have found effective ways of transmitting, to a fourth and fifth and a sixth generation, a rooted and on-going Judaism made in America.

Why that fact is noteworthy has now to be spelled out. The first generation (1890–1920), completing its migration and settling down in the 1920s, took for granted that its ways would not continue. How do we know? Because they did not try to preserve Yiddish. The Yiddish language within the first generation gave way to English, often in the home, and with it much else that had seemed definitely Jewish in the Central and East European setting. With the notion that Jews (like other immigrants) must become American, the immigrant generation tended to accept, not always benignly to be sure, what it perceived as the de-Judaization of its children. The parents kept the dietary taboos, the children did not. The parents practiced distinctively Jewish occupations, dominating only a few fields and absent in most others. The children spread out, so far as they could in the prevailing climate of anti-Semitism and exclusion. It follows, therefore, that the founding generation of Judaism in America did not define a system of Judaism, let alone a set of such systems, that it imagined it could transmit to the next generation. It contributed in rich and important ways to what the coming generation would inherit and utilize. But it defined nothing, except by negative example: the second generation (1920–1950) wanted to be American, therefore not Jewish. Judaism as an inherited religious tradition with rich theological perspectives and a demanding, enduring way of life bore little relevance to the American children of those Europeans who had walked on that path to God and lived by that mode of sanctification. And the immigrants took that fact for granted.

The second generation, for its part, accepted more from the founders than it planned. For while explicitly opting for "America" and against "Judaism," it implicitly defined life as a set of contrasts between the Jewish datum of life, on the one side, and everything else, on the other. Being Jewish was what defined existence for the second generation. That fact of life was so pervasive as not to demand articulation, let alone specific and concrete expression. The upshot was that the second generation would organize bowling leagues and athletic clubs, rather than prayer circles and study groups. But everyone in the bowling league would be Jewish, and they also would be neighbors and friends. The cultural distinctiveness that had characterized the first generation gave way to a Jewishness by association for the second. The associations, whether political or recreational or philanthropic, took for granted that the goal was non-sectarian. Little that proved definitively Jewish would mark the group's collective life. But how non-sectarian could an association become, when all its members live in pretty much the same neighborhood, pursued the same lines of work, and came from Yiddish-speaking parents? In fact the community life constructed on the basis of associationism characteristic of the second generation constituted a deeply Jewish mode. It took for granted exactly what the first generation had handed on, that is, the basic and definitive character of being Jewish, whatever, for the new generation, that might come to mean. The founding generation could not, and rarely tried to, articulate what being Jewish meant. But it imparted exactly the imprint of being Jewish that had become its hope to leave behind. The second generation was American and remained Jewish. More than that the first generation could not imagine.

The second generation did little to found camps, youth programs, and schools beyond a perfunctory sort. The institutions of the second generation recognized no need to make explicit, through either substantive or symbolic means, their Jewish character. There were few Jewish parochial schools. Jewish community centers regarded themselves as non-sectarian "community agencies." Jewish philanthropic agencies maintained a high wall of separation between "church" and "state." The result was that little public Jewish money went into Judaic activities of any kind. A great deal went into fighting anti-Semitism and maintaining non-sectarian hospitals. Proof of these contrasting modes of Judaic life comes readily to hand. Nearly all of the Judaizing programs and activities of the third generation, now received as the norm and permanent, date back only to the decades after World War II. Most of the earliest summer camps of Judaic character come from that period, especially camps under religious auspices (as distinct from Zionist and Hebraist ones). The several youth movements got under way in the late 1940s. The Jewish Federations and Welfare Funds in the 1960s fought the battle for a policy of sectarian investment in distinctively Jewish programs and activities. They undertook to treat as stylish anything markedly Judaic only from the 1970s. These and equivalent facts point to the passage from the second to the third generation as the age of decisive redefinition.

EXPLAINING THE GENERATIONS AND THEIR JUDAISMS

The factors that account for the shifts in generations begin in one simple, negative fact. The second generation did not need schools or youth groups in order to explain what being Jewish meant. Why not? It could rely on two more effective educational instruments: memory and experience. The second generation remembered things that the third generation could scarcely imagine: genuinely pious parents, for example. But, as we noted earlier, the second generation also came to maturity in an age in which America turned against the newest Americans. Universities open to Jews before World War I imposed rigid quotas against them afterward. More important, entire industries declared themselves off-limits to

Jewish employment. The fact that the climate of bigotry and exclusion affected others just as much as Jews, so that among the excluded minorities were a majority of Americans of the age, changed little for the mentality of excluded Jews. They may have moved to swim among an undifferentiated majority, had the waters been open to them; they were not welcome even on the beaches.

Far more profound than the experience of personal exclusion was the impact of the rise of political, organized anti-Semitism as an instrument of national policy in Germany, Poland, and other European countries, with its extension and counterpart in the Western democracies. What this meant was that the exclusion from a country club or an executive suite took on a still more ominous character, as the world at large took up the war against the Jews. Jewish immigration was barred when people fled for their lives. In such a setting Jews scarcely needed to find reasons to associate with one another; the world forced them together. They did not lack lessons on how and why to be Jewish, or what being Jewish meant. The world defined and taught those lessons with stern and tragic effect. All of the instrumentalities for explaining and propagating Jewishness, created for the third generation, and, in time, by the third generation, would earlier have proved superfluous.

The contrast, then, between the second and the third generation sets up the encounter with a hostile and threatening world, on the one side, against the experience of an essentially neutral and benign one, on the other. Yet that contrast proves somewhat misleading. For three other factors contributed to the renaissance of articulated and self-conscious Jewishness, along with a renewed search for Judaism, among third generation Americans of Jewish descent. The first was the rise of the State of Israel. The second was the discovery not of the murder of nearly six million Jews in Europe but of "the Holocaust." The third was the reethnicization of American life, that is to say, the resurgence of ethnic identification among the grandchildren of the immigrant generations, on the one side, and among blacks and other excluded groups that long ago had become American by force, on the other. Just as the Jewish third generation tried to remember what the second generation had wanted for forget, so the same pattern was exhibited elsewhere. Just as when black students demanded what they deemed ethnically characteristic food, so Jewish students discovered they wanted kosher food too.

All three factors, among the Jews, reinforced one another. We take as routine the importance of the State of Israel in American Jewish consciousness. But in the 1940s and 1950s, American Jewry had yet to translate its deep sympathy for the Jewish state into political activity, on the one side, and the shaping element for local cultural activity and sentiment, on the other. So too the memory of the destruction of European Jewry did not right away become "the Holocaust," as a formative event in contemporary Jewish consciousness. In fact the reethnicization of the Jews could not have taken the form that it did—a powerful identification with the State of Israel as the answer to the question of "the Holocaust"—without a single, catalytic event.

AN EXAMPLE OF A SELF-EVIDENTLY VALID ANSWER TO THE SYSTEMIC QUESTION OF AMERICAN JUDAISM: THE 1967 WAR IN AMERICAN JUDAISM

That event was the 1967 war between the State of Israel and its Arab neighbors. When, on June 5, after a long period of threat, the dreaded war of "all against one" began, American Jews feared the worst. Six days later they confronted an unimagined outcome, with the State of Israel standing on the Jordan River, the Nile, and the outskirts of Damascus. The trauma of the weeks preceding the war, when the Arabs promised to drive the Jews into the sea and no other power intervened or promised help, renewed for the third generation the nightmare of the second. Once more the streets and newspapers became the school for being Jewish. What do I mean? In the 1930s and 1940s, the age of Hitler's Germany and the murder of the European Jews in death factories, every day's newspaper brought lessons of Jewish history. Everybody knew that were he or she in Europe, death would be the sentence on account of the crime of Jewish birth. And the world was then indifferent. No avenues of escape were opened to Jews who wanted to flee, and many roads to life were deliberately blocked by anti-Semitic foreign service officials in the U.S., Canada, and other democracies' service. So too in 1967 the Arab states threatened to destroy the State of Israel and murder its citizens. The Israelis turned to the world. The world again ignored Jewish suffering, and a new "Holocaust" impended. But now the outcome was quite different. The entire history of the century at hand came under a new light. As we shall see below, a moment of powerful and salvific weight placed into a fresh perspective everything that had happened from the beginning to the present.

The third generation had found its memory and its hope. It now could confront the murder of the Jews of Europe, along with its parents' (and, for not a few, its own) experience of exclusion and bigotry. No longer was it necessary to avoid painful, intolerable memories. Now what had happened had to be remembered, because it bore within itself the entire message of the new day in Judaism. That is to say, putting together the murder of nearly six million Jews of Europe with the creation of the State of Israel transformed both events. One became "the Holocaust," the purest statement of evil in all of human history. The other became salvation in the form of "the first appearance of our redemption" (as the language of the Jewish prayer for the State of Israel has it). Accordingly, a moment of stark epiphany captured the entire experience of the age and imparted to it that meaning and order that a religious system has the power to express and make self-evident. The self-evident system of American Judaism, then, for the third generation encompassed a salvific myth deeply and personally relevant to the devotees. That myth made sense at a single instant equally of both the world and the self, of what the newspapers had to say, and of what the individual understood in personal life.

The distinctively American form of Judaism under description here clearly connects to classical Judaism. But it is not continuous with it. American Judaism draws upon some of the received religious tradition and claims to take up the whole of it. But in its stress upon the realization, in the here and now, of ultimate evil and salvation, and in its mythicization of contemporary history, American Judaism offers a distinctively American, therefore a new and unprecedented, reading of the received tradition. This is by definition. For when Jews have come to speak of fully realized salvation and an end of history, the result has commonly proved to be a new religion, connected to, but not continuous with, the received religion of Judaism. That is very much the case even now.

The ambiguity of American Judaism lies in sorting out what is old from what is new, in discovering, in the continuation of the familiar, what has changed, and in determining, in what appears to be new, what turns out to be entirely familiar and well-attested for centuries. In order to accomplish this work of analysis, we proceed to consider each of the primary categories of the received version of Judaism. When we allow the Judaism brought from Europe to tell us how to organize our data, we must speak of the categories out of which that system for a social group had constructed its world view and expressed that world view through a distinctive way of life. The simple categories, each beyond reduction to any more general or encompassing one, are these: (1) way of life (including every day mode of social organization, types of religious leadership), and (2) world view (where we are, what we believe). These then, in detail, allow us to speak of holy ways of life, holy man, holy people, and holy land. Our task is now to describe that distinctive system of Judaism produced in America, in particular by the third generation for the fourth and fifth generations, in terms of the categories just now defined.

HOLY WAY OF LIFE

In classical Judaism (including its contemporary expressions) the holy life—the things one did to conform to the will of God, or, in secular terms, the behavior patterns imposed by the Judaic tradition—was (and is) personal and participative. Every man, woman, and child had myriad deeds to do because he or she was a Jew. No one was exempt from following the holy way of living. Everyone expected to share in it equally. One did not speak of how others should keep the Sabbath. One kept the Sabbath, along with every one else in the community. People individually said their own prayers, advanced their own education in the tradition, did good deeds on their own part. Prayer, study and the practice of good deeds were personal and universal. To be a Jew meant to do a hundred mitzvot, holy actions, every day.

In modern America, to be a Jew primarily means to join an organization, but not personally to effect its purposes. The individual is lost in the collectivity. Joining means paying dues, providing sufficient funds so that other people may be hired to carry out the purposes of the organization. The "joining" is the opposite of what it means, for it is impersonal and does not bring people together, but verifies their separateness. The relationship of one person to the next is reduced to the payment of money. It is passive, for one does not actually do much, if anything at all. Universally condemned by the preachers, "checkbook Judaism" is everywhere the norm. What has happened is that the primary mode of being Jewish—living the "holy life"—has moved from the narrow circle of home, family, and small group to the great arena of public affairs and large institutions. The formation of large organizations, characteristic of modern life, tends to obliterate the effective role of the individual. In the Judaic situation, however, even the synagogue, with its substantial budget and massive membership, its professional leadership and surrogate religiosity, follows this pattern. If to be a Jew now means to take an active part in the "Jewish Community," then the holy life is lived chiefly by paying one's part of the budget of the organizations that call themselves the community. By contrast, Jews in other countries identify being Jewish with either synagogue membership (at home, in Johannesburg or Sydney or London) or becoming an Israeli (by emigrating to the State of Israel or by focusing one's Jewish life mainly upon Israeli matters), or both. In general, both modes of being Jewish involve personal participation, not simply money-giving.

People join organizations because they have been convinced that that is what "Judaism" expects of them. They think this primarily because of the patterns established, or already imposed, by others. The result is the concentration of power in the hands of the few who actually determine what organizations do. These few are not democratically elected, but generally come up out of an oligarchy of wealthy and influential men (only a few woman are included). But even these men do not actually effect the work of the community. They raise the funds and allocate them, but local funds are in fact spent by, and chiefly upon the salaries of the professional bureaucrats trained to do whatever it is that the organizations do. In general their work is to keep the organization alive and prosperous.

What has all this to do with "being Jewish"? Should we not have started with an account of what "the Jews believe" or what "Judaism teaches"? Indeed we should, if what Jews believed and what classical Judaism taught decisively shaped the contemporary realities that define what, in everyday life, it means to be a Jew. Since we ask what it means to be a Jew in America, the first thing we want to know is: What do people do because they are Jewish? And the answer is: They join organizations and give money. In this respect, what makes a person Jewish in American society primarily depends on which organization he or she joins and to what worthy cause he or she gives money.

That the "holy way" should have become the "culture of organizations" tells us that modernity has overtaken the Jews. What characterizes group life in modern times is the development of specialists for various tasks, the organizations of society for the accomplishment of tasks once performed individually and in an amateur way, the growth of professionalism, the reliance upon large institutions. What modern humanity gains in greater efficiency and higher levels of competence cannot be given up because of nostalgia for a way of life few now living in a traditional society would want to preserve. But as everyone recognizes, the cost of "progress" is impersonality and depersonalization. The real question is not whether to return to a more primitive way of living, but how to regain the humanity, personality, individual self-respect, and self-reliance necessarily lost of the new way.

HOLY MAN

The "professional Jews" who run the Jewish institutions and organizations that constitute for the ordinary folk the "holy way" are anonymous, faceless, wholly secular. People relate to them no differently from the way they do to other bureaucrats, in government offices, public schools, department stores. One Jewish functionary, however, the common people continue to regard as quintessentially "Jewish," important, and formative of values, and that is the least powerful and least effective figure, is the rabbi. For nearly twenty centuries the rabbi was the holy man of Judaic tradition. He became a rabbi through study of Torah, which comprehended not only the Hebrew Scriptures, but also the Oral Torah, believed to have been handed on in Mosaic revelation and eventually recorded in the pages of the Babylonian Talmud and related literature. The rabbi was a holy man consecrated not by prayer, though he prayed, nor by asceticism, though he assumed taxing disciplines, but by study and knowledge of Torah. That knowledge made him not merely learned or wise, but a saint, and endowed him with not only information, but also insight into the workings of the universe. Consequently, in former times rabbis were believed to have more than commonplace merits, therefore more than ordinary power over the world, and some of them, especially qualified by learning and piety, were seen able to pray more effectively than common people and to accomplish miracles.

Today the rabbi (now both women and men) will be an essentially peripheral figure in organized Jewish life, outside the framework of the synagogue. Dropping the rabbi out of the decision-making circles of the Jewish community merely took account of the rabbi's profoundly different role. Formerly judge, administrator, holy man, scholar, and saint, in American Judaism the rabbi at first served as a rather secular leader of a rather secular community, spokesman for Jews to Gentiles, representative of his synagogue to the larger Jewish group, agent of Zionist propaganda, and certifier of the values of the upperclass Jews who employed him. But as time passed these roles and tasks passed into the hands of others, better equipped for them because of community position, economic power, and public acceptance. By the 1950s a truly professional Jewish civil service was in control in the more enlightened communities. The rabbi was left to preside at circumcisions, weddings and funerals, to "conduct" religious worship, which, in traditional synagogues, meant to announce pages and tell people when to stand up and sit down, to counsel the troubled, and teach the children, in all a slightly anachronistic figure, a medicine man made obsolete by penicillin.

But that is not the whole story. With the decline of the effectiveness of education enterprises, the rabbi, who normally was nearly the only Jew in town who could read Hebrew and intelligently comprehend a Jewish book, stood apart for the same reason as in classical times. He was distinguished because of his learning. So far as access to Judaic tradition and capacity to comprehend Judaic thinking proved important, the rabbi continued to hold the key to the mind and intellect of Judaism. Second, and still more important, while the rabbi could be made into a pathetic remnant of ancient glories of his office, he remained the rabbi. The title and the role persisted in setting the rabbi apart from others, in making him a kind of holy man. In psychological terms, he continued to function as a surrogate father and God. Secularity did not, could not in the end, deprive him of his role as a religious figure, even leader. The holy man remained just that, even to the most secular people.

Today, the rabbi serves primarily his or her congregation. In a sense the rabbi has become a more religious figure than earlier. That means, to be sure, rabbis have less power in Jewish communal affairs. But it is likely that they now enjoy more influence than before, and influence in shaping the ideas and purposes of others represents significant power to achieve concrete ends. The rabbi does not stand at the head of organizations, of community bureaus. But the rabbi stands behind those who do, for Jewish leaders nearly universally belong to synagogues and rely upon religious rites at least at the time of crises—birth, puberty, marriage, death. They are accessible to the rabbi's words.

Above all, community leaders are under the spell of the rabbi as a holy person, in a way in which the passing generation was not. To be sure, lay people are as well educated as the rabbi in many ways. But in respect to the knowledge of Judaism, standards of literacy have so fallen that the rabbi now predominates in precisely the one area appropriate to his calling. So far as people remain Jews, they depend more than ever upon rabbis to explain to them why and what they should mean. It is the rabbi who retains the prestige and the learning to fill that empty commitment of Jews to being Jewish with purpose and meaning. The real foundations for the rabbinical position are the convictions people retain from archaic times about holy men, set aside for God and sanctified by sacred disciplines. In archaic times the rabbi was a holy man because of his mastery of Torah. Today the rabbi remains a holy man for that very reason. Thus far we have seen the sociological side of that holiness: The rabbi continues functionally to dominate because of his knowledge of Torah. With women now included, the rabbi has new opportunities for effective contemporary service.

The advent of women to the Reform and Conservative and Reconstructionist rabbinates has already given the Reform sector of the Jewish community access to talent formerly excluded from the pulpit. With the ordination of women in the Conservative rabbinate and the Reconstructionist one as well, the vast majority of American Jews—certainly 80% of the whole—now turn to women, as much as to men, as authority figures in Judaism. The renewed energy flowing from the formerly excluded half of the Jewish people already has made its mark. Women in synagogues find themselves more normal, more at home, than they could when only men occupied liturgical and other positions of symbolic importance and real power. Highly talented young women aspire to the rabbinate who formerly would have chosen other callings or professions. In these and other obvious ways, the advent of women to the rabbinate has redefined the profession and renewed its promise.

HOLY PEOPLE

The "holy people" in archaic times certainly knew who they were and confidently defined their relationship with Gentiles. Jews saw themselves as "Israel," the people to whom Torah had been revealed, now living in exile from their homeland.

"Israel" was a nation within other nations. But eventually Israel would return to the holy land, with the coming of the Messiah. Gentiles were outsiders, strangers to be respected but feared, honored but avoided except when necessary. Modern times were different. From the nineteenth century onward Western European Jews consciously entered the society of the nations among which they had lived for generations. They became German, French, and British citizens, ceased to form a separate community, and sought normal relationships both with Gentiles and with their culture. For the immigrants to America the nineteenth-century Western European experience repeated itself. At first the Jews formed separate, Yiddish-speaking enclaves in large cities, but as time passed, they and their children moved to less uniformly Jewish neighborhoods, entered less characteristically Jewish occupations, wholeheartedly adopted the language and culture of the America they had chosen. The assimilation of Jews into American culture continued apace in the second generation, and by the third it was virtually complete. Then the questions became, and now remain, What is a Jew? Who is Israel? What makes a person into a Jew? Are the Jews a religious group? Are they a "people"? A nation? The Jews thus have entered a lingering crisis of group identity, that is, they are not certain who they are or what is asked of them because of what they claim to be. And individual Jews face a severe dilemma of personal identity as well: Why should I be a Jew? What does it mean, if anything, that I am born of Jewish parents?

One important measure of modernity is the loss of the old certainties about who one is. The question of who is a Jew, always chronic, became critical in the 1940s and 1950s. The sense of a "crisis of identity" is a condition of being a modern person. Formerly, people suppose, men and women were confident of their place in the life of the community and certain of the definition of that community in the history of mankind. To be a Jew not only imposed social and economic roles, but it also conveyed a considerable supernatural story. Israel was the people of the Lord, bearer of revelation, engaged in a pilgrimage through history, en route to the promised land at the end of time. To be a Jew was to know not only who one was, but also what that meant in the economy of universal history. To identify oneself as a Jew was a privilege and a responsibility, but it was not a problem. The world posed problems to the Jew, particularly in the 1930s and 1940s; Judaism and "being Jewish," not separated from one another, solved those problems, explained felt-history, interpreted everyday reality in terms of a grand and encompassing vision of human history and destiny. "We are Israel, children of Abraham, Isaac, and Jacob, loyal sons of the Torah of Moses at Sinai, faithfully awaiting the anointed of God." What difference did it make that Gentiles treated Jews contemptuously, despised them, maligned their religion? In the end everyone would know the truth. Before the eyes of all the living would God redeem Israel and vindicate the patience and loyal faithfulness of its disagreeable experience in history, among men.

What strikingly characterizes the imagination of the classical Jew, practitioner of Judaism, is the centrality of Israel, the Jewish people, in human history, the certainty that being a Jew is the most important thing about oneself, and that Jewishness, meaning Judaism, was the dominant aspect of one's consciousness. The "holy people" today has disintegrated in its classical formulation. How so?

First, Jews are no longer certain just what makes them into a people. Second, they see themselves as anything but holy, they interpret in a negative way the things that make them Jewish and different from others, and above all, they introduce into their assessment of themselves the opinions of the Gentiles. So the advent of modernity seems to have changed everything. A group once sure of itself and convinced of its value under the aspect of eternity now is unsure of who it is and persuaded that the hostile judgments of outsiders must be true. The "children of Abraham, Isaac, and Jacob" have lost touch with the fathers. The people of the Lord seems to have forgotten why it has come into being. Everyday reality contains for ordinary Jews no hint of a great conception of human history. It has become a long succession of meaningless but uncongenial encounters. Sinai is a mountain. Tourists make the trip to climb it. The "Torah of Moses" is a scroll removed from its holy ark on the Sabbath, normally in the absence of the "loyal sons," who rarely see it, less often hear it, and cannot understand its language. The Messiah at the end of time is too far away to be discerned; anyhow, no one is looking in that direction.

It is easy enough to draw invidious contrasts between the virtues of the archaic world and the shortcomings of modernity. But since the old certainties and securities are mostly gone, one might observe that not only necessity, but choice moved Jews away from them. When Jews in Eastern Europe began to feel the birth pangs of modernity, all the more so when the emigrants came to America and plunged into the modern condition, they scarcely looked backward. Whatever virtues they knew in the old way of being did not restrain them. Something in the traditional life seemed to them to have failed, for in their thirst for whatever was new and contemporary they demonstrated that the old had not fulfilled their aspirations.

ORTHODOXY

It did not have to be so, and for some it was not. Let me qualify the description I have just given, which leads to the quite wrong impression that nearly all American Jews had given up on Judaism in its classical and on-going form, whether mediated through Orthodoxy or Conservatism or Reform synagogues and temples. There certainly was an Orthodox minority within American Jewry, and not all immigrants tried to raise their children only in English, to speak of both religious and cultural indicators. Orthodoxy characterized nearly all those immigrants who were religious, and Conservative Judaism, a modified form of Orthodoxy, certainly predominated for the second and the third generations. Both the emigrants of the 1890s and those who came after World War II included considerable numbers of Jews who remained loyal to the tradition in a wholly traditional way. The appeal of modernity was lost on them. Still others entered the modern situation and quickly turned their backs on it. They returned to classical Judaism. The return to religion in the decades after World War II saw considerable strengthening of orthodox commitment and conviction in American Judaism, and renascent orthodoxy did not take the modern form of surrogate religiosity, large synagogues, and impersonal professionalism, but the entirely traditional forms of personal commitment and maximum individual participation. Whether traditional Orthodox Judaism in America is traditional and orthodox in the same ways as in Eastern European Judaism hardly matters. The fact is that the classical Judaic perspective remains a completely acceptable choice for substantial numbers of American Jews. Those Jews who fully live the traditional life and adhere to the traditional way of faith seem to me to have made a negative judgment on modernity and its values. It becomes all the more striking that larger numbers—the vast majority of American Jewry—came to an affirmative opinion.

But in affirming the modern and accepting its dilemmas, American Jews of the third generation (1950–1980) continued in important modes to interpret themselves in the archaic ways. Most important, Jews continued to see themselves as Jews, to regard that fact as central to their very being, and to persist in that choice. That fact cannot be taken for granted. The Jews are not simply an ethnic group characterized by primarily external, wholly unarticulated and unself-conscious qualities. They are Jewish not merely because they happen to have inherited quaint customs, unimportant remains of an old heritage rapidly falling away. On the contrary, they hold very strong convictions about how they will continue to be Jews. Most of them hope their children will marry within the Jewish community. Most of them join synagogues and do so because they want their children to grow up as Jews. Above all, most of them regard the fact that they are Jewish as bearing great significance.

The American Jews of the third generation continue to see everyday life in terms different from their Gentile neighbors, beginning with the fact that to them, if not to their neighbors, their being Jewish seems an immensely important fact of life. The words they use to explain that fact, the symbols by which they express it, are quite different from those of archaic or classical Judaism. They speak of Jewishness, not Torah. They are obsessed with a crisis of identity, rather than with the tasks and responsibilities of "Israel." They are deeply concerned by the opinion of Gentiles.

JEWISH BUT NOT TOO JEWISH

In all, they are eager to be Jewish—but not too much so, not so much that they cannot also take their place within the undifferentiated humanity of which they fantasize. They confront a crisis not merely of identity but of commitment, for they do not choose to resolve the dilemma of separateness within an open society. In preferring separateness, they seem entirely within the archaic realm; in dreaming of an open society, they evidently aspire to a true accomplishment of the early promise of modernity. But if that truly open society should come to realization, one wonders whether the Jews would want wholly to enter it. For, standing at the threshold of more than two hundred years of assimilation into modern culture, of facing a lingering crisis of identity, who would have predicted what has happened?

The Jew continues to take with utmost seriousness the fact of his being Jewish, indeed to speak, precisely as did those in the classical tradition of Israel.

HOLY LAND

Archaic religions usually focus upon a holy place, where God and humanity come together, the focus for the sacred upon earth. In classical Judaism, Palestine ("the Land of Israel") was not merely the place where Jews lived, but the holy land. It could never legitimately be governed by pagans—thus, the continuing efforts of Jews to drive pagan rulers out of the land. There the Temple was built, the nexus of the God–man relationship in olden times. The mountains of the land were the highest in the earth. The land was the center of the world, of the universe. Jerusalem was most beautiful, most holy.

No element of the classical myth at the turn of the twentieth century could have seemed more remote from the likely preferences of American Judaism when it grew to maturity. When the emigrants left Russia, they could have gone southward, to Palestine, and a few of them did. But most went west, and of these, the largest number came to the United States. Since even then Zionism was an important option in Eastern European Judaism, one can hardly regard the emigrants as Zionists. A few who were stayed in America only a while, then left for Palestine. The vast majority of emigrants came and settled down.

Now, eighty or ninety years later, the vast majority of third- and fourth-generation American Jews support the State of Israel, and whether they are called Zionists hardly matters. The sole commitment shared by nearly all, uniquely capable of producing common action, is that the State of Israel must live. Zionism accounts for the predominance of the welfare funds. To American Jews, "never again"—referring to the slaughter of nearly six million European Jews—means that the State of Israel must not be permitted to perish. But there is a second, less often articulated fact about American Jewry. Alongside the nearly universal concern for the State of Israel is—by definition—the quite unanimous Jewish commitment to America, to remain Americans. Emigration to the State of Israel since 1948 has been negligible. Indeed, until the present time five times more Israelis have settled in America than American Jews in Israel.

Clearly, Zionism, with its focus upon the State of Israel, solves problems for American Jews. How does it do so, and why, then, do American Jews in the vast majority find Zionism so critical to their sense of themselves as a "holy people"? Zionism provides a reconstruction of Jewish identity, for it reaffirms the nationhood of Israel in the face of the disintegration of the religious bases of a Jewish peoplehood. If in times past the Jews saw themselves as a people because they were the children of the promise, the children of Abraham, Isaac, and Jacob, called together at Sinai, instructed by God through prophets, led by rabbis guided by the "whole Torah"—written and oral—of Sinai, then with the end of a singularly religious self-consciousness, the people lost its understanding of itself. The fact is that the people remained a community of fate, but, until the flourishing of Zionism, the facts of its continued existence were deprived of a heuristic foundation. Jews continued as a group, but could not persuasively say why or what this meant. Zionism provided the explanation: The Jews indeed remain a people, but the foundation of their peoplehood lies in the unity of their concern for Zion, devotion to rebuilding the land and establishing Jewish sovereignty in it. The realities of continuing emotional and social commitment to Jewish "grouphood" or separateness thus made sense. Mere secular difference, once seen to be destiny—"who has not made us like the nations"—once again stood forth as destiny.

THE AMBIGUITY OF ZIONISM IN AMERICAN JUDAISM

Herein lies the ambiguity of Zionism. It was supposedly a secular movement, yet in reinterpreting the classic mythic structures of Judaism, it compromised its secularity and exposed its fundamental unity with like attributes that do not necessarily represent "peoples" or "nations," and if the common attributes, in the Jewish case, are neither intrinsically Jewish (whatever that might mean) nor widely present to begin with, then the primary conviction of Zionism constitutes an extraordinary reaffirmation of the primary element in the classical mythic structure: salvation. What has happened in Zionism is that the old has been in one instant destroyed and resurrected. The "holy people" are no more, the nation-people take their place. How much has changed in the religious tradition, when the allegedly secular successor-continuator has preserved not only the essential perspective of the tradition, but done so pretty much in the tradition's own symbols and language?

Nor should it be supposed that the Zionist solution to the Jews' crisis of identity is a merely theological or ideological one. We cannot ignore the practical result of Zionist success in conquering the Jewish community. For the middle and older generations, as everyone knows, the Zionist enterprise provided the primary vehicle for Jewish identity. The Reform solution to the identity-problem—we are Americans by nationality, Jews by religion—was hardly congruent to the profound Jewish passion for the immigrant generations of their children. The former generations were not merely Jewish by religion. Religion was the least important aspect of their Jewishness. They deeply felt themselves Jewish in their bone and marrow and did not feel sufficiently marginal as Jews to need to affirm their Americanness/Judaism at all. Rather the first generation and the second (1890–1950) participated in a reality; they were in a situation so real and intimate as to make unnecessary such an uncomfortable, defensive affirmation. They did not doubt they were Americans. They did not need to explain what being Jewish had to do with it. Zionism for the second generation was congruent to these realities, and because of that fact, being Jewish and being Zionist were inextricably joined together.

But Zionism also constitutes a problem for Judaism. The mythic insufficiency of Zionism that renders its success a dilemma for contemporary American Jews, and for Israeli ones as well. Let us begin with the obvious. How can American Jews focus their spiritual lives solely on a land in which they do not live? It is one thing for that land to be in heaven, at the end of time. It is quite another to dream of a far-away place where everything is good—but where one may go if he wants. The realized eschaton is insufficient for a rich and interesting fantasy life, and, moreover, in this-worldly terms it is hypocritical. It means American Jews live off the capital of Israeli culture. The "enlandisement" of American Judaism—the focusing of its imaginative, inner life upon the land and State of Israel—therefore imposes an ersatz spiritual dimension: "We live here as if we lived there—but do not choose to migrate."

It furthermore diverts American Judaism from the concrete mythic issues it has yet to solve: Why should anyone be a Jew anymore, in the USA or in Israel? That question is not answered by the recommendation to participate in the spiritual adventures of people in a quite different situation. Since the primary mitzvot (commandments) of U.S. Judaism concern supplying funds, encouragement, and support for Israel, one wonders whether one must be a Jew at all in order to believe in and practice that form of Judaism. What is "being Jewish" now supposed to mean?

JEWISHNESS WITHOUT JUDAISM?

The underlying problem, which faces both Israeli and American Jews, is understanding what the ambiguous adjective Jewish is supposed to mean when the noun Judaism has been abandoned. To be sure, for some Israelis and American Jews to be a Jew is to be a citizen of the State of Israel—but that definition hardly serves when Israeli Moslems and Christians are taken into account. If one ignores the exceptions, the rule is still wanting. If to be a Jew is to be—or to dream of being—an Israeli, then the Israeli who chooses to settle in a foreign country ceases to be a Jew when he gives up Israeli citizenship for some other. If all Jews are on the road to Zion, then those who either do not get there or, once there, choose another way are to be abandoned. That makes Jewishness depend upon quite worldly issues: This one cannot make his living in Tel Aviv, that one does not like the climate of Affula, the other is frustrated by the bureaucracy of Jerusalem. Are they then supposed to give up their share in the "God of Israel"?

American Jews half a century ago would not have claimed "religious" as an appropriate adjective for their community. Today they insist upon it. The moralists' criticism of religion will always render ever more remote what is meant by "true religion," so we need not be detained by carping questions. But can there be religion with so minimal a quotient or supernatural experience, theological conviction, and evocative ritual, including prayer, as is revealed in American Judaism? If one draws the dividing line between belief in a supernatural God and atheism, then much of the American Jewry, also much of American Judaism, may stand on the far side of that line. If the dividing line is, in the words of Kristor Stendahl, "between the closed mind and spiritual sensibility and imagination," then American Jews and American Judaism may stand within the frontier of the religious, the sacred.

Let us begin with the substitution of organizations and group activity for a holy way of life lived by each individual. What the Jews have done in their revision of the holy way is to conform to, in their own way to embody, the American talent at actually accomplishing things. Americans organize. They do so not to keep themselves busy, but to accomplish efficiently and with an economy of effort a great many commendable goals. They hire "professionals" to do well what most individuals cannot do at all: heal the sick, care for the needy, tend the distressed at home and far away. In modern society people do not keep guns in their homes for self-protection. They have police. Nations do not rely upon the uncertain response of well-meaning volunteers. They form armies. The things American Jews seek to accomplish through their vast organizational life derive from their tradition: They want to educate the young and old, to contribute to the building of the ancient land, to see to it that prayers are said and holidays observed. Now hiring a religious virtuoso may seem less commendable than saying one's own prayers, but it is merely an extension of the specialization people take for granted elsewhere.

In archaic times people believed that salvation depended upon keeping to the holy way, so each person kept to it, made himself sufficiently expert to know how to carry out the law. In other religious communities today, that same viewpoint persists. Catholics and Protestants take for granted that they should go to church to pray. Jews regard communal prayer as less important, though Judaism has not changed its position on that matter. They tend to observe the religious way of life in diminishing measure, as the generations of American Jews pass on, from third to fourth to fifth. Today few believe that supernatural salvation inheres in prayers, dietary taboos, and Sabbath observance. It is therefore curious that the Jews nonetheless want to preserve the old salvific forms and symbols, as they certainly do. Few pray. Fewer still believe in prayer. It is astonishing that the synagogues persist in focusing their collective life upon liturgical functions. Perhaps the best analogy is to a museum, in which old art is preserved and displayed, though people do not paint that way any more, may not even comprehend what the painter did, the technical obstacles he overcame. The synagogue is a living museum and preserves the liturgical and ritual life of the old tradition. Why should Jews choose this way, when earlier in their American experience they seemed to move in a different direction? Is it nostalgia for a remembered, but unavailable experience of the sacred? Is the religious self-definition they have adopted merely an accommodation to American expectations? Or do they hope the archaic and the supernatural may continue to speak to them?

The figure of the rabbi calls forth the same wonderment. Why call oneself "rabbi" at all, if one (man or woman) is not a saint, a scholar, a judge? Given the ultimate mark of secularization—the complaint that rabbis no longer reach high places in the Jewish community—should we not ask, What is still sacred in the rabbi and his or her learning, calling, leadership? The answer would be, nothing whatsoever, were it not for peoples' relationships to the rabbi, their fantastic expectations of him or her. The rabbi, unsure of his or her role, at once self-isolated and complaining at his or her loneliness—whatever he is, he is he rabbi. He knows it. The people know it. They look to him as a kind of holy man. No nostalgia here:

The rabbi is a completely American adaptation of the ancient rabbinic role. But American society never imposed the peculiar, mainly secular definition of "Jewish clergyman" upon the modern rabbi. For two hundred years American Jewry had no rabbis at all. Leadership lay with uneducated men, businessmen mainly. And the rabbis they now have are not merely Judaic versions of Protestant ministers or Roman Catholic priests, but uniquely Judaic as well as exceptionally American. The remembrance of rabbis of past times—of the saints, scholars, and holy men of Europe—hardly persists into the fourth generation and beyond. The rabbi, profane and secular, is the holy man or woman they shall ever know. So onto him or her they fix their natural, human fantasies about men and women set apart by and for God.

The holy people, "Israel," of times past has become "the American Jewish community," uncertain what is Jewish about itself, still more unsure of what "Jewish" ought to mean at all. Surely the lingering crisis of self-definition, characteristic of modern men and women in many situations, marks the Jew as utterly modern and secular. Add to that the second component of the holy people's self-understanding: concern for what the Gentiles think of Jews, readiness to admit that negative opinion into the Jewishness assessment of the Jews. This submission to universal opinions and values hardly characterize a holy people, set apart from all others. Frail and uncomfortable, hating those "Jewish traits" in oneself that set Jews apart from everyone else, and wanting to be Jewish but not too much, not so much that they cannot also be undifferentiated Americans—this is the holy people that traversed 35 centuries of human history, proud, tenacious, alone? Can they claim their collectivity to be holy, separate and apart? Surely in the passage from the sacred to the secular, the holy people has disintegrated, become a random group of discrete, scarcely similar individuals. Yet while that may seem to be so, the one point Jews affirm is that they shall be Jews. This they have in common.

The very vigor of their activity together and the commonalities of a quite discrete folk suggest that the group, once a people, is still a people. The secular separateness of the Jews, their inner awareness of being a group, their outward view of themselves as in some ways apart from others—that separateness is probably all modern man can hope for socially to approximate "the holy." The archaic "holy people" has passed from the scene. In its place stands something different in all respects but the most important: its manifest and correct claim to continue as Jews, a different, separate group, and the claim that that difference is destiny. The relationship between secular Zionism and sacred messianism, modern nation building and the myth of the return to Zion at the end of time, is complex. It seems clear that the pattern recurs, perhaps most vividly, in the modern and secular modulation of the myth of the holy land.

Let us conclude with attention to doctrine, "Torah" in the mythic language of Judaism. The grandchildren of Jews who would not have understood what theologians do, not only write theology, but correctly claim it to be Judaic. The third generation produced religious intellectuals. This is the decisive evidence that something new has been created out of something old: Contemporary American Judaism, for all its distance from the classic forms of the past, its unbelief and secularity, constitutes a fundamentally new and autonomous development, not merely the last stages in the demise of something decadent. American Judaism calls forth, in the task of formulating a systematic account of its faith, the talents of philosophical sophistication and religious conviction, able to speak in the name, even in the words, of the classic tradition, but in a language alien to that tradition. To be sure, the Jews' response to Judaic theology thus far is routine and inconsequential. The best books reach a tiny audience, the worst only a slightly larger one. The finest theological journals are read chiefly by those who write for them, or aspire to. So the theological movement must stand by itself, as evidence of the modernity and secularity of the theologians, on the one side, but of their participation in the traditional sacred values and in the archaic texts, on the other.

American Judaism constitutes something more than the lingering end of olden ways and myths. It is the effort of modern men and women to make use of archaic ways and myths for the formation of a religious way of living appropriate to an unreligious time and community. Spiritual sensibility and, even more, the remnants of the archaic imagination are the sources for the unarticulate, but evident decision of American Jews to reconstruct out of the remnants of an evocative, but incongruous heritage the materials of a humanly viable, meaningful community of life. To have attempted the reconstitution of traditional villages in the metropolis and of archaic ways of seeing the world in the center of modernity would have been to deny the human value and pertinence of the tradition itself. But few wanted even to try. In the end the effort would have had no meaning. The Jews had the courage to insist that their life together must have more than ordinary meaning. In American Judaism they embarked upon the uncertain quest to find, if necessary to invent, to build that meaning. Despite their failures, the gross, grotesque form they have imposed upon the old tradition, that uncommon, courageous effort seems to be to testify to whatever is good and enduring in modernity. But whether good or not, abiding or ephemeral, all that modern men and women have, and all that they shall ever have, is the mature hope to persist in that quest.

PART III Toward the Twenty-First Century: Contemporary Judaisms in America and in the State of Israel

Chapter 9
Religion and Ethnicity in the American Jewish Community

Marshall Sklare

Perhaps the most remarkable aspect of our subject is the fact that American Jewry can be discussed as a living entity, and that the religious forms of American-Jewish life continue to exist. Such vitality was not foreseen by earlier generations of social scientists, for they believed that secularism would defeat religion, thus consuming Judaism in the process, and that the melting pot would triumph over pluralism, thus consuming Jewish ethnicity. Even academicians who criticized the melting-pot theory and were critical of the demands of "anglo-conformity"—as, for example, Milton Gordon in his book *Assimilation in American Life*—viewed those who would remain attached to Jewish religion and ethnicity (as well as others forms of subcommunal loyalty) as a kind of *lumpen* element, if not economically then at least culturally. The vanguard who would set the tone for the masses would be the intellectuals at the universities. Such intellectuals would not be interested in continuing loyalty to an ancestral religious group, whether Catholic, Protestant, or Jewish, or to an inherited ethnicity. While integration would start on the campus it would not be confined to the campus; rather, the campus would become the prototype for society at large.

This view is now under attack inasmuch as there is a new emphasis in contemporary sociological thinking on the continuing attachment to ancestral religious and ethnic loyalties. Perhaps the most noted proponent of this view is Andrew Greeley, a remarkable scholar who has retained his credentials as a member of the Catholic clergy in addition to pursuing a notable career as a sociologist. Both a highly productive researcher and a noted commentator on the American social trends, Greeley recently established the Center for the Study of American Pluralism at the University of Chicago. The center's establishment at the university carries with it a certain irony, for earlier generations of sociologists at the same institution had assumed that the "race-relations cycle" would result in the assimilation and amalgamation of American minorities. Greeley not only propounds the continued existence of subcommunities, but he regards such subcommunalism as healthy. Thus, unlike Gordon, Greeley feels that subcommunalism may make valuable contributions to American culture and is a vital part of American social structure; he does not regard it as necessarily retrogressive or reactionary.

If religion and ethnicity have been more hardy than earlier sociologists predicted, we may now turn to our special interest: the specific character of American-Jewish religious energy is more ethnic than religious. Frequently this has been said to be expressive of a general characteristic of American social structure: the tendency for ethnic differences to be expressed and sustained as religious differences.

Whatever the extent to which American-Jewish religion is sustained by Jewish ethnicity, the sociological study of religion generally conceives of religion as a uniting force which helps to strengthen the collective will, a force which helps to integrate individuals into a social system, as well as a force which gives legitimation to that system. Religion can be uniting because it is suprasocial—in a suprasocial system the bonds which hold the individual to the group are more than ephemeral, they are not easily cast asunder, they are not mere cultural styles. The bonds are ordained by God, and thus religion is enabled to function as a uniting force.

American-Jewish religion has in fact served such a uniting function. Of course this function has not been implemented in a simple and uncomplicated way. There have always been secularists in the American-Jewish community who have placed themselves beyond the reach of religion. But more to the point, American Jewry has not been monolithic. It is exceedingly diverse in its origins. There have been, and are, Sephardim and Ashkenazim; Western European Ashkenazim and Eastern European Ashkenazim; Lithuanian Ashkenazim, Galician Ashkenazim, and Hungarian Ashkenazim—the list of distinctions merely within the Ashkenazic group is multitudinous. Thus America, as well as Israel has had its ingathering of Jews, each with its own local or regional traditions. If these traditions are of declining significance today or have entirely eroded away, they were of significance in establishing the earlier forms of American Reform, Conservative, and Orthodox Judaism.

There have been other complications as well. Thus people from the same place arrived in America at different times. There were Polish Jews who arrived in the United States in the nineteenth century and Polish Jews who arrived during and after World War II. They each came from a different Poland and arrived in a different America. Furthermore, not only was the America of 1820 different from the America of 1880, or 1920, or 1940, or 1960, but there is considerable regional difference in America itself. The Polish Jew who left Poland in 1910, settled in the Bronx, and spent his life in the garment industry on Seventh Avenue is exposed to a different set of influences from those experienced by a similar Polish Jew who settled in Texas or California. All of these differences of origin, of time of arrival, of place of settlement, should be reflected in cultural or ideological differences. Such differences would have the result of creating religious distinctions and thus weakening the function of religion as a uniting force.

If religious uniformity cannot be expected of the American Jew, we must also realize that religion itself is capable of being a dividing as well as a uniting force. If we ponder the matter it becomes clear that the same elements in religion which make it a force for social cohesion are also capable of producing division. For example, because religion is suprasocial, differences which could ordinarily be readily contained can easily escalate. Furthermore, individuals who hold a different religious opinion from one's own are not only wrong but are sinful. It is difficult to acknowledge their right to exist, for such recognition may not only be tactically unwise, given the rivalry of religious groups, but it can also be regarded as sinful—acknowledgement involves conferring at least a minimal measure of legitimacy upon those who are different from oneself. To highlight what is involved we not only need to remember the well-known fact that Orthodoxy has its difficulties acknowledging Reform and Conservatism, but we must also recall that both Reform and Conservatism have responded by claiming that it is they who truly represent the rabbinic tradition. Both Reform and Conservatism have claimed that if Judaism had retained the openness to change which they see reflected in classical Jewish texts, their particular movement would represent the normative Judaism of today.

Given the existence of Reform, Conservative, and Orthodox Judaism in the United States, the possibility of religion functioning more as a dividing than as a uniting force has been ever-present. That religion has not split the American-Jewish community asunder is related, at least in part, to the very structure of the Jewish religion and of Jewish identity itself. The Jewish religion is extraordinarily ethnic in its thrust—it may in fact be the prototype of an ethnic religion. One aspect of such ethnicity is the feeling that whatever differences exist between Jew and Jew, they share more in common than does any given Jew with any given Gentile. They are members of a single clan—an extended kinship group. Furthermore, whatever differences divide Jew from Jew, only a fellow Jew can be relied upon as an ally; even the most friendly Gentile can turn into a fair-weather friend.

That religion has not split the Jewish community asunder is also related to the character of American culture and social structure. To be sure there have been American Jews who have conceived of America as Zion, and some who have considered the city of Cincinnati as Jerusalem. But even Reform Jews have covertly recognized that America is *galut*, and the more Classical Reform the Reform Jew, the greater his covert recognition of this fact. Thus neither the Reform Jew, the Conservative Jew, nor the Orthodox Jew has sought to mount a full-fledged campaign to change America into Zion. Each movement in its own way has recognized that America is Gentile and even Christian; they have divided on the question of what accommodations should be made to this fact of life. From one vantage point the Reform Jew has been less accommodating than the Orthodox Jew: while the Orthodox Jew tends to accept America's Christian character, the Reform Jew has tended to be ill-at-ease with this aspect of American culture.

There is the further fact that not only is America *galut*, but it is a nation which has a tradition of church-state separation. In theory the state interests itself in religious matters only minimally. In theory the state does not give religion in general, or religion in particular, official status. If the state does not recognize Protestant law, it certainly has no interest in refashioning its legal system so that it would conform to Jewish law. It follows, then, that in the United States adherence to *halacha* has remained a matter of private conviction rather than public obligation, though to be sure traditionalistic forces have sought to have American law take account of halachic precedent.[1]

In sum, since the United States is conceived by Jews to be *galut*, and because America has a long tradition of church-state separation, the problem of recognizing the legitimacy of Jewish religious movements other than one's own has not had to be confronted in a direct way. And since there has been minimal interest in having the state decide who is and who is not a Jew (or even in having the State collect statistics on Jewish population characteristics), some of the power of religion for divisiveness has thereby been reduced.

The reduction of the power of religion as a divisive force has been assisted by the fact that American social structure tends in the direction of a congregational rather than an episcopal form of religious organization. Thus, while episcopal forms exist, the emphasis is on the independence, equality, and freedom of each individual congregation. The anarchic and dysfunctional consequences of congregationalism has been a favorite theme of some American-Jewish religious thinkers, including Mordecai M. Kaplan, and this despite the fact that the Reconstructionist movement has been made possible by American congregationalism. In any case, it is the rare Jewish religious thinker who views congregationalism as a positive force inasmuch as it discourages confrontation, diffuses hostility, and, in the final analysis, makes possible unity on the basis of voluntary confederations of congregations as well as overall coordinating bodies.

The independence and equality of each individual congregation, which is free to determine its own ritual and to hire its own rabbi (and to fire him as well), may be productive of mischief or worse, but it has had the consequence that the divisions within Jewish religious life can be maintained without excessive *sturm und drang*. In this paper, Professor Katz made clear that this was not the case in Europe. He demonstrated how Samson Raphael Hirsch had to maneuver to get the right to establish his *gemeinde*. He also demonstrated that in Hungary Orthodox Jews were reduced to using the cry of freedom of individual conscience, of all things, in order to receive the right to establish their own institutional structure. Contrast this with the situation in the United States.

One very persuasive example of the character of American religious organization is that of the Breuer community in the section of Upper Manhattan known as Washington Heights. Despite the fact that this community arrived as late as the 1930s, it did not require the permission of existing Jewish institutions or of secular authorities to establish its *gemeinde*. Neither did it need to apply for permission to the head of the Union of Orthodox Jewish Congregations of America nor did it need to approach the borough president, the mayor, or the governor. Rather it proceeded to establish its own synagogue, its own educational institutions, its own *mikvaot*, and its own system of food supervision under the Breuer *hashgacha*. To be sure it is a bit difficult for the Breuer community to shut out the world of East European Orthodoxy, particularly inasmuch as the East Europeans preceded them in Washington Heights. Yeshiva University existed in Washington Heights before the first Jew from Frankfort arrived, and little can be done by the Breuer community in Washington Heights other than to say that East European Orthodoxy represents something which is different from "our" tradition. There is an irony here: both the ideology of Yeshiva University and that of the Breuer community share a common conviction that is not possible (and in some cases even desirable) to pursue secular knowledge as well as religious knowledge.

The final force which has served to blunt the divisive potentialities inherent in American-Jewish religious movements is their common affirmation of Israel as a Jewish state and their strong interest in its continued existence. In his presentation Professor Katz made the point that Rabbi Alkalay hoped that the Jews of his time who were of different religious persuasions could unite around a common love of Zion. This hope has been brought to fruition in the American-Jewish community. There is only a single organization with religious pretensions which is outside of the consensus about Israel—the American Council for Judaism—and it constitutes the exception which proves the rule. While in its youth the ACJ had some creditability in Classical Reform circles it is now inconsequential, being considered a mere eccentricity of Jews who are located at the margin of Jewish life.

To be sure, the affirmation of Israel by American Jews and their interest in its welfare is increasingly becoming a cause of division as well as a force for unity. Some of the religious differences which exist in Israel, including the question of the role of *halacha* in the life of the nation, have their repercussions in American-Jewish life. Furthermore, a two-way process takes place: religious groups in Israel look for support from American Jews, and at the same time American Jews have the wish to assist those in Israel to whom they feel closest. Reform and Conservative groups in America have experienced the pain of being outside the Israeli religious establishment. Nevertheless, both movements have established institutions in Israel and have located followers. Such followers include Americans who have made *aliyah*, Jews from other English-speaking countries, as well as Israelis coming from other nations—Israelis who find themselves seeking religion but are not attracted to the regnant forms of Israeli Orthodoxy.

Whatever the forces which unite, we must remember that inevitably religious movements seek to triumph over their opponents. They seek not merely to gain the advantage over opponents but to bury them as well. It is apparent that each religious movement in American-Jewish life—Reform, Conservative, Orthodox (and Reconstructionist as well) has dreamt the impossible dream: namely, that its competitors would die. Hopefully such death would be quick and merciful rather than slow and lingering. In any case, each movement has dreamt that it would be the surviving member of the clan.

You will notice that because of the complication introduced by ethnicity I hardly know how to refer to Reform, Conservatism, and Orthodoxy and have employed the term *movement*. Sociological language conventionally divides religious groups into either *denominations* or *sects*, but these terms hardly fit the Jewish case. Some students of American-Jewish life refer to Reform Conservatism, and Orthodoxy as "wings" of American Judaism—if Jews are thought to be *luftmenschen* the term *wings* may not be altogether inappropriate. But, however we designate Reform, Conservative, and Orthodox Judaism, and whatever their sense of alienation or closeness to each other, there is one understanding which they have always shared: a common opposition to conversion efforts by Christian churches. This issue has been the focus of some of our discussions here on Jewish life in European countries, particularly in France. We must therefore inquire into how American Jews have approached the problem of conversion.

It is fair to say that all three major Jewish religious groups in the United States have demonstrated horror and disdain of the *meshummed* in particular and of the Christian missionary in general. Interestingly enough, such horror and disdain have not been confined to Orthodoxy. Thus it is hard to find a stronger opponent of Christian missionary endeavors than Louis Marshall (1856–1929). In addition to all of his other offices, Marshall was a leader of Reform Judaism. His opposition to missionaries is particularly noteworthy since Marshall was a layman, and as such was under no compulsion to represent Judaism "officially" as would be the case if he had been a rabbi. Marshall, in fact, disliked all rabbis, whether Reform, Conservative, or Orthodox.[2] He thought most of them to be fools, but he even had little use for brilliant rabbis inasmuch as they too refused to live under what was called at the time "Marshall law." When the present edifice of Temple Emanu-El in New York City was being planned, Marshall, who was then president of what has become America's cathedral synagogue, fantasized that the architect could be induced to design a device whereby the president could press a button, a trap door would open, and the man standing behind the pulpit would disappear into the bowels of Fifth Avenue!

Marshall, however, hated missionaries more than he did rabbis. Although he was an ardent builder of interfaith amity, Marshall's dream for what later was to become the National Conference of Christians and Jews was that it would take on the task of convincing Christians that missionizing Jews was un-American, that such missionizing was, in effect, a violation of the civil rights of Jews. While Marshall was too good a constitutional lawyer to ever incorporate such notions in a legal brief, these ideas are manifest in the many documents which flowed from his fertile pen.[3]

To be sure, while Christian missionary activities were an irritant, and while several graduates of Hebrew Union College were actually converted to Christianity, conversion never developed into the threat that it became in Europe. How should the differences in this respect between Western Europe and the United States be interpreted? Should they be seen as a function of Jewish fortitude, or as a function of Jewish secularity, or should they be seen as a tribute to American tolerance as well as American pluralism? The last interpretation is perhaps the most strategic one.

If conversion has not constituted the same problem for Reform, Conservatism, and Orthodoxy as it did in Europe, in America there have been secular challenges to Jewish continuity of some magnitude and importance. For East European Jews such secular challenges have revolved around radical social movements. For German Jews they have taken other forms, especially an interesting movement established by the son of a rabbi. The rabbi's son I have reference to, of course, is Felix Adler, and the movement is Ethical Culture. If uptown could accuse downtown Orthodoxy of failing to enlist the loyalty of the immigrant and his children and thereby of being responsible for adherence to such un-American and un-Jewish movements as socialism, anarchism, and communism, downtown could accuse uptown Reform of aiding and abetting Ethical Culture.[4]

These minor confrontations should not deflect our attention from what was the major question: namely, what particular movement merited the support of American Jewry? What movement was best qualified to lead American Jewry away from the threat of assimilation, of intermarriage, and of conversion to Christianity, and thus able to insure the viability of American-Jewish life?

When this question emerged in the nineteenth century, Reform was best situated to advocate the position that it had the key to the American-Jewish future. The nineteenth century was the era of Reform triumphalism. All of the work of Isaac Mayer Wise was predicated upon the assumption that if Judaism were to survive in America it would have to be Reform Judaism. The establishment by Wise in 1873 of an organization which he named the Union of American Hebrew Congregations did not constitute an idle boast. His assumption and that of his co-workers was that if non-Reform congregations were to long endure they would inevitably have to transform themselves into Reform temples and ultimately would have to join the Union. American life would compel Jews to go through a kind of evolutionary cycle from lower to higher forms of religious life; a shift away from Orthodoxy and toward Reform was thus inevitable.

What happened, however, was that after its initial gains, the growth of the Union leveled off and very few new congregations joined its ranks. Eventually the size and number of Reform congregations was swelled by the influx of East Europeans, but this expansion involved a shift from Classical Reform to Neo-Reform, one aspect of which was a recognition of the role of ethnicity in Jewish life generally and in Jewish religion specifically. The new and expanded congregations of the East Europeans gave the Union greater viability, notwithstanding the fact that as a consequence some Classical Reform congregations seceded from the Union. However, most eventually returned and made their peace with Neo-Reform.

The recent celebration of the one-hundredth anniversary of the Union was not an overwhelming *simcha,* however. First there was the depressing fact that despite the prognostications of the founders, Conservatism and Orthodoxy still existed. Secondly, Reform's survival was due more to the fact that it had changed direction than to the attractiveness of its original vision. While Reform could claim that such change was a virtue rather than a vice, that change was the very thing for which Reform stood, it could not be denied that somehow the original vision of the founders had been clouded. And overall there was a feeling of *malaise,* a vague sense of ill-being and depression.

Perhaps the most obvious sign of Reform's feeling that something had gone wrong was the fact that instead of issuing anniversary volumes extolling Reform achievements, it felt compelled to call upon social scientists to diagnose its condition and to recommend a course of treatment. While the summoning of doctors who are social scientists can be interpreted as a sign of good sense, it can also be considered an act of desperation. From whence cometh our help? From social science. All of this is in contrast to Isaac Mayer Wise, who was a confident Reform Jew. He was firm in his conviction that the Almighty was a reality, that help from Him would be forthcoming, and that those of His children who were obedient to His wishes would find special favor in His eyes. In Wise's view it was, of course, Reform which qualified for Divine favor.

Two studies were commissioned to diagnose Reform's ills. One involved an analysis of the Reform rabbinate and the other a study of the laity and the congregations.[5] The *Reform Is a Verb* study proceeds on the assumption that secularization has made such deep inroads on Reform as to be irreversible, and that while a feeling of ethnic cohesion is still present in Reform synagogues, such a feeling will diminish unless the Reform congregation is restructured to serve a general human need. What is the need? Simply stated it is the need for community, the need to be protected against *anomie.* While the study agreed to the continuation of the present congregations, it recommended their restructuring into sub-units. These subunits would be essentially *havurot* serving adult middle-class families. As *havurot* they would provide mutual support, a surrogate extended family, and protection from the lonely crowd.

With the coming of the twentieth century, and more especially after World War I, the Conservative movement emerged. It too went through a period of triumphalism. Early advocates of Conservatism felt that the movement possessed a unique combination of features which would prove irresistibly attractive to the American Jew of East European decent. Conservatism would take the best of Jewish culture and combine it with the best of American culture. In its view it would be able to utilize the best of Jewish culture because, unlike Orthodoxy, it was not committed to perpetuate aspects of Jewish culture which were unacceptable to the modern temper. And unlike Reform it could be enthusiastically ethnic as well as "Jewish"—that is, in continuity with the main thrust of Jewish culture if not in conformity with all of its *mitzvoth.*

My understanding of Conservatism is that despite the movement's growth and predominance, Conservative triumphalism is a thing of the past. My belief is that the present mood of the movement may be characterized as at best sober and at the worst as somber. In another place I have sought to explain this sharp shift from the optimism and *élan* characteristic of an earlier Conservative generation.[6]

One of the reasons for the present mood of Conservatism is its assumption that Orthodoxy would be unable to survive on American soil. The first Conservative generation conceived itself as chosen to assume the crucial role of continuing the Jewish heritage in a new and threatening environment. This proclivity of Conservatism, then, leads us to consider the state of American Orthodoxy. Orthodoxy's death had long been predicted, and in the nineteenth century and in the early years of the twentieth century there were even Orthodox leaders who concurred in such a drastic prognosis. In the era since World War II, however, Orthodoxy has decided to live rather than to die; it has accordingly reasserted its claim to being the true conservator and guardian of Jewish tradition.

Orthodoxy has, in fact, gone further and asserted that while *it* would live, Reform and Conservatism would die, for only those who held to an authentic interpretation of Jewish tradition would have the qualities required for survival in the open society. In short, the post–World War II era has seen the emergence of a new triumphalism: Orthodox triumphalism. When the editors of the *American Jewish Year Book* published Charles Liebman's definitive article, "Orthodoxy in American Jewish Life," they introduced the article by characterizing the scholarly investigation of Orthodoxy as "a vital but hitherto neglected area of American Jewish life."[7] It was their way of saying that given Orthodoxy's new thrust and assertiveness, it was no longer possible to understand the dynamics of the contemporary religious scene by limiting oneself to knowledge about Reform and Conservative Judaism. It is apparent that if Orthodoxy's renewal surprised the editors of the *American Jewish Year Book,* its rise jolted the leaders of Reform and Conservative Judaism. Orthodox triumphalism has in fact served to bring Reform and Conservatism into a closer unity than ever before.

If each of American Jewry's religious movements has in turn succumbed to the dream that it would emerge as the truly legitimate and regnant form of American Judaism, American Jewry has nevertheless been able to abide religious pluralism. The reason for cohesion despite the division has been based on the uniting force of a common ethnicity. The most obvious marks of such ethnicity are that all Jews have considered themselves to be of the same ancestry, that those whose ancestry was not originally Jewish had been converted with due regard to halachic norms, and that all unmarried Jews were available to each other as potential mates.

Present-day developments raise the question of how long these assumptions can be maintained. There is not only the influence of Israeli Orthodoxy upon American Jewry, but there are also deep divisions within American Reform Judaism itself. As a consequence, the question of how long the ethnic mortar can continue to bind hangs in the balance. The practice of remarriage without a *get,* the performance of conversion without regard to halachic norms, and what has become the strongest irritant—the officiating by some rabbis at marriages between a Jew and a

Christian–are all facets of the same problem. In the past, whatever hostilities Orthodox, Conservative, or Reform Jews might have had toward one another (as well as whatever each might have thought of unaffiliated or nonidentifying Jews), for all practical purposes they were willing to concede each other's legitimacy in the sense that they assumed a common Jewishness. We may be at the beginning of an era when such legitimacy is no longer conceded—when all individuals who believe that they are Jewish are not in fact accepted by other Jews as Jewish.

If such a development takes place, the neat fit between Jewish religion and Jewish ethnicity will be no more. The mutual reinforcement of Jewish religion and ethnicity will be weakened, schism will develop, and religious warfare may break out. Since America is *galut*, and since in America there is a separation between synagogue and state, such warfare will not be bloody. However, anything which disturbs the delicate unity and mutual forbearance of those who identify with an American-Jewish subcommunity is capable of leading to serious consequences. By dividing brother from brother such disturbances could prove as deadly as the religious wars which occurred centuries ago within Christendom.

While many observers of the Jewish scene have repeatedly claimed that Jewish life follows the beat of the Christian drummer, there is the possibility that Jews may not be following the lead of Christianity toward greater ecumenism. One recent commentator on the Jewish religious scene has claimed that observers are unduly pessimistic about the state of Jewish religion in the United States because the "established churches are in crisis and Christian theology is in ferment. Jews are too easily tempted to view their situation in a Christian mirror."[8] Rabbi Kelman goes on to say that "Perhaps we should learn to measure Jewish reality in a more authentic Jewish context of qualified optimism and the mature posture of a people who have experienced 4,000 years of recorded history and civilization."[9]

While it may be correct to assume that the synagogue is more vigorous than the church at the present moment, it would be foolhardy to base communal policy on a recollection of Jewish longevity. Professor Katz has demonstrated for us that on the European continent the Jewish religion has served to divide as well as to unite Jews. Until now in the United States, the Jewish religion, in combination with the ethnicity which is an intimate part of Jewish religion, has been able to maintain a certain unity despite divided ranks. One of American Jewry's most difficult tasks in the present and immediate future will be to prevent the sundering of its fragile and uneasy solidarity.

NOTES

1. See Daniel J. Elazar and Stephen R. Goldstein, "The Legal Status of the American Jewish Community," *American Jewish Year Book, 1972*, Vol. 73, pp. 3–89.
2. See the many references in *Louis Marshall: Champion of Liberty; Selected Papers and Addresses*. ed. Charles Reznikoff, 2 vols. (Philadelphia: Jewish Publication Society of America, 1957).

3. See Marshall Sklare, "The Conversion of the Jews," *Commentary*, Vol. 56, No. 3 (September 1973), pp. 44–53.
4. See Michael A. Meyer, "Beyond Particularism: On Ethical Culture and Its Reconstructionists," *Commentary*, Vol. 51, No. 3 (March 1971), pp. 71–76.
5. See Theodore I. Lenn, *Rabbi and Synagogue in Reform Judaism* (New York: Central Conference of American Rabbis, 1972), and Leonard J. Fein *et al.*, *Reform Is a Verb: Notes on Reform and Reforming Jews* (New York: Union of American Hebrew Congregations, 1972).
6. See Marshall Sklare, *Conservative Judaism: An American Religious Movement* (New York: Schocken Books, 1972), pp. 253–82.
7. *American Jewish Year Book, 1965*, Vol. 66, p. v.
8. Wolfe Kelman, "The Synagogue in America," in *The Future of the Jewish Community in America*, ed. David Sidorsky (New York: Basic Books, 1973), p. 175.
9. *Ibid.*

Chapter 10
Civil Religion and the Modern Jewish Challenge

Jonathan Woocher

THE MODERN CHALLENGE TO JUDAISM

For two centuries Jews have struggled with a dual challenge: how and why to remain Jewish in the modern world? The questions "how" and "why" be Jewish are not in themselves new. But for the modern Jew they have carried an urgency and an uncertainty greater than that which most of his ancestors experienced. The post-Emancipation, post-Enlightenment history of Jewry and Judaism is one of continuous reformulation of the meaning of being Jewish. The process of reformulation has been complex and often contentious. Its products—the diverse forms of Jewishness manifest today—constitute tenuously successful responses to the dual challenge of Jewish self-definition in the modern world. But the challenge itself persists and repeatedly thrusts itself forward. It is the fundamental Jewish reality of our time, the text, as it were, to which modern Jews are writing and rewriting ever new commentary.

The story of this challenge and the Jewish responses to it has been recounted by numerous historians and social scientists.[1] Until the latter part of the eighteenth century, the vast majority of the world's Jews lived a life circumscribed by the authority of a corporate communal structure and a traditional religious culture. Jews were, in both a social and a psychological sense, in the world but not of it. The traditional community, the *kehillah*, mediated between the individual Jew and the surrounding society. This Jewish community was both a political and a religious entity. It served as the framework for Jewish self-governance (within boundaries permitted by gentile authority) and for the collective self-understanding which sustained and made meaningful the persistent Jewish struggle for continued existence as a distinctive national and religious group.

The *kehillah* was, in effect, a "state within a state." In pre-modern Europe, still largely comprised of social systems based on corporate subgroups, each with a distinct status, a semiautonomous Jewish collectivity was politically functional for both Jew and non-Jew. But the *kehillah* was not simply an externally dictated accommodation to the social structure of the period. For the Jew, it was a traditionally sanctioned instrumentality for maintaining a thoroughly Jewish way of life. Its source of authority was the *halakhah*, the Jewish legal system whose origins were traced back to the divine revelation of the Torah at Mt. Sinai. Thus, though Jews maintained economic and limited social relationships with non-Jews, they regarded themselves as a people apart. The religious and social institutions of the *kehillah* expressed, sustained, and symbolized that separateness.

The distinction between Jew and Gentile was accepted by both, and theologically legitimated by both. From the Jewish perspective, Jews were God's chosen people, living in exile from their homeland due to their own sins, but faithfully awaiting the expected messianic redemption which would vindicate their loyalty to Torah. For Christianity, the presence of Jews as a visible but subservient minority was living evidence of their rejection by God for having spurned his Son. Both theological perspectives demanded that Jews be marked off as a separate group. Thus, though Jews surely did not choose their living conditions, they could willingly accept them, as long as the traditional religious ideology which legitimated their distinctiveness held sway, and the surrounding society offered no alternative except repudiation of their Jewishness.

The revolution which transformed the Jewish world altered both of these conditions. The infiltration of new ideas, known generically as the Enlightenment, and the offer of a new civic status through political emancipation, beginning in the last years of the eighteenth century, set loose a wave of change which within a century would completely undermine the old order in Europe. Slowly, often in fits and spurts, but inexorably, Jews were drawn out of their traditional insulation. The autonomy and legal authority of the *kehillah* were increasingly circumscribed and eventually abolished. Intellectual modernization and secularization tore away at the fabric of the religious tradition itself. Most important of all, Jews became, at times reluctantly but often eagerly, participants in the dynamic cultural and social changes of the age. Their horizons were no longer those of a small group living, as it were, beyond time, but of actors on a vast stage filled with historical possibility.[2]

We cannot attempt here to describe this process of dramatic change in detail.[3] We can, however, identify four critical and closely linked areas in which the Emancipation/Enlightenment experience posed far-reaching challenges to European Jewry. The first was the question of identity: What does it mean to be a Jew in the new era? How does a Jew behave? What does he believe? How does he perceive the nature and significance of his Jewishness? The traditional religious answers to these questions were no longer persuasive for many Jews, but new answers were by no means obvious. As Jews entered the larger society they began to assume other identities as well—as Germans or Frenchmen, or later as liberals or socialists. Jewishness no longer was an all-encompassing identity, yet neither could its reality be entirely ignored. The post-Emancipation, post-Enlightenment Jew was forced to shape his Jewish identity in deliberate fashion, to "define its sphere and harmonize it with the other components of self," as historian Michael Meyer put it.[4]

At the same time as the individual Jew struggled with his or her identity, the collectivity of Jews struggled with its integrity and unity. In the pre-modern period, "Halakha provided the dispersed nation of Israel with a common religious framework that assured an enduring commonality and continuity to Jewish life despite the disparity of geography and of culture among the respective communities of the nation."[5] What the legal tradition did for Jewry as a whole, the political and social institutions of the *kehillah* did for the Jews in a given locality. But with the decline in the authority of the *halakhah* and the removal of authority from the *kehillah*, what could remain as a basis of Jewish unity? In the post-Emancipation environment, that unity rapidly gave way to diversity and even conflict, as partisans of various ideological programs sought to establish their authenticity as continuators of the Jewish tradition and to find new institutional bases for communal integrity.

The Emancipation confronted Jews with a further task of redefinition: redefining their relationship to non-Jews. Prior to Emancipation, that relationship was reasonably clear: the non-Jew was the "other," to be kept at arm's length. But such a relationship was impossible once Jews sought and received their rights as citizens. Napoleon asked the Assembly of French Jewish Notables which he convened in 1806 whether they regarded other Frenchmen "as brethren or as strangers." The notables answered unequivocally, "as brethren."[6] Yet, in the same set of responses, they expressed (delicately, to be sure) their continuing reluctance to countenance intermarriage with these "brethren." The dilemma of these notables was to be felt by nearly all Jews in many ways during the ensuing decades. The dominant thrust of Enlightenment ideas and Emancipation legislation was to minimize, if not to eliminate entirely, the distinction between Jews and non-Jews. Many Jews leaped eagerly at the chance to take their place alongside their new fellow citizens, to become part of the national body politic. They were not, however, prepared to give up completely a sense of Jewish distinctiveness, if only in religious terms. This posed a practical as well as theoretical question: How were they to maintain this distinctiveness and at the same time behave truly as "brethren" in their relationships to non-Jews? How could they be both a part of society and apart from it?[7]

The final question which the Emancipation and Enlightenment posed for the Jews was—and is—in many ways the most far-reaching in its implications. Why should Jews continue to seek to survive as Jews at all? In the face of a benighted and unwelcoming Christian world, and possessed of the certainty of his own special divinely-ordained place in the universe, the traditional European Jew need hardly have asked such a question. But for the modern Jew the question proved very real. What did the Jew gain by holding on to his or her Jewishness? As Joseph Blau points out, the secularization of society and the development of a "hyphenated," compartmentalized Jewish identity almost inevitably raise this question:

> If modern life is divided in this fashion, and if the compartment that contains a man's religion is just one box among many, and if this box is the only one in which a man differs significantly from other members of his society, it will not be long before he will question the need and the desirability of maintaining this distinctiveness.[8]

Any satisfactory Jewish ideological response to the Emancipation and Enlightenment had, therefore, to tell the Jew not only *how* to be Jewish under the radically new conditions of modernity, but *why* to be Jewish as well. The dual challenge was acute. For a Jewry increasingly cut off from traditional values and mores, without the support of authoritative and unifying communal institutions, the modern world was treacherously open. That openness was exhilarating for many who had felt stifled in the often narrow and decaying structures of the old order. But it demanded that Jews seek new landmarks and bulwarks if they were to survive at all in the new world of perpetual change.

RESPONSES TO THE CHALLENGE

The Jews of Europe responded to this challenge in diverse, even contradictory ways. Two responses need not concern us here: those of the Jews who believed that no essential change was called for, and of the Jews who were prepared to abandon Judaism altogether to ease their entry into the modern world. Between these two extremes, however, there remained a variety of programs which sought to blend accommodation to the modern world with fidelity to some interpretation of traditional Judaism. These programs were the progenitors of the contemporary Jewish religious denominations: Reform, Neo-Orthodoxy, and Conservatism. Each represents a particular strategy for meeting the interrelated challenges we have outlined above.

For the self-proclaimed Reformers who began to appear in Germany during the first half of the nineteenth century, the preservation of Jewish life demanded a radical reshaping of its substance and terms of reference. The program of religious reform which took hold in parts of Central Europe and spread to America as well had both practical and ideological components. The traditional liturgy and forms of worship were modified, with the introduction of regular sermons, prayer in the vernacular, mixed seating, choirs, and instrumental music, and the elimination of textual references to the return to Zion. Dietary laws and other practices which restricted participation in social intercourse were abandoned. Some radical Reformers even attempted to shift the Jewish Sabbath to Sunday.

Underlying these changes was a more far-reaching ideological innovation, one which redefined the nature and bases of Jewishness. Jews, the Reformers came to argue, must no longer regard themselves as a national group, but as a religious communion. They were now to see themselves as fully German, or Austrian, or American, differing from their fellow citizens only in their religious beliefs. These beliefs themselves, and the practices which accompanied them, were to be critically examined and modified where necessary in light of modern philosophical standards and spiritual sensibilities. The binding authority of the *halakhah* was denied. Instead, Reform leaders placed their emphasis on Judaism's "prophetic" ideals, the ethical values which were the essence of religion in their view and, therefore, perhaps not incidentally, the common possession of all enlightened religious individuals.

Perhaps the most significant change which Reform introduced came in response to the challenge of providing a rationale for the continued existence of Jews and Judaism itself. This challenge was especially acute for the Reformers precisely because they had rejected so much of the traditional differentiating structure of belief and practice. To validate the survival of Judaism without giving up their belief in the full integration of Jews into modern society, the leaders of Reform redefined a Jewish "mission" in the world which required precisely that involvement. They repudiated the traditional view of Diaspora existence as exilic punishment, and proclaimed it rather the divinely-ordained condition for the fulfillment of a Jewish mission to spread the ethical and spiritual ideals of Judaism among the nations. Freed from the necessity of maintaining an independent political existence, Jews could function as a pure religious group bringing the message of ethical monotheism to their fellows in every land. This concept of a universal mission represented a profound revaluation of the meaning of the traditional Jewish idea of "chosenness." Like the other innovations of the Reformers, it was offered not as a rejection of the Jewish past, but as a higher form of continuity with Judaism's religious ideals.

In looking back on the vigor with which such fundamental changes were pursued, it is easy to draw the mistaken conclusion that the Reformers were merely assimilationists in disguise. This, however, would be a significant misunderstanding of Reform's intent. The Reformers, by and large, acted out of a sincere belief that only substantial changes could preserve Judaism in the new era, and out of a genuine sense that, in the words of an early Reform group in Berlin, "our religion failed gradually to give us that satisfaction which was the comfort and the happiness of our ancestors."[9] The choice, many Reform leaders believed, was between change and complete disintegration.

In their own way, these leaders were often sensitive to the threat their efforts represented to Jewish unity. They sought, through frequent Rabbinic synods, to preserve a measure of unity at least among those with some sympathy for their platform. But ultimately, the entire thrust and tenor of their position, placing the authority to redefine Jewish practice and belief in the hands of those who could claim to be most in tune with the times, rendered this hope unrealizable.

That this would be so became clear from the vigorous opposition which the Reformers received, not only from those who rejected change in any aspect of Jewish life, but also from forces which accepted the idea of accommodation with modernity, but not the Reform program for achieving this accommodation. The reality of the challenges which Jews confronted required that this latter group restate the premises of the traditionalism which they wished to maintain, as well as the terms under which they would participate in post-Emancipation, post-Enlightenment society. The most notable such restatement came from Samson Raphael Hirsch, the nineteenth century German rabbi generally regarded as the founder of modern Neo-Orthodoxy. Hirsch took as his motto the Talmudic phrase "*Torah im derekh eretz*," which he translated as meaning "traditional Judaism together with the civilization of the times." Traditional Judaism meant unswerving fidelity to the *halakhah*. The civilization of the times meant acceptance of citizenship, social intercourse with non-Jews, and philosophical exploration of the meaning of Jewishness in and for the modern world.

Like the Reformers, Hirsch believed that Jews had a mission among the nations which required their dispersal and an effort to bring together the values of modern society and of Judaism. Unlike the Reformers, he believed that Jews must maintain a spiritual segregation from the world in order to fulfill their mission, and that Torah must remain the standard by which modernity is judged rather than vice versa. Thus, the Neo-Orthodox insisted that *halakhah* continue to serve as the basis for Jewish unity and the vehicle through which Jews pursued their mission of demonstrating how man must and can devote his life to divine service.

Despite this assertion of continuity with the past, Hirsch himself confronted the necessity of defining Neo-Orthodoxy as a party within a divided Jewry, no longer the unself-conscious religious expression of a unified community. When the official Jewish communal institutions in several German cities were "captured" by Reformers, Hirsch did not hesitate to advocate secession from these communities. The Neo-Orthodox fought for government recognition as a separate religious grouping, and in so doing they helped to reemphasize the distance which Jews had traveled in the post-Emancipation period. If religious ideology and practice were the fundamental defining characteristics of a Jew, then, indeed, one could question whether Reform and Neo-Orthodox still constituted a single religious group. To be sure, the sense of commonality among Jews even of different denominational loyalties never dissipated entirely, but such an absolute split was conceivable within the terms of reference which both the Reformers and their Neo-Orthodox opponents employed.

Not all those, however, who were uncomfortable with Reform's open dismissal of the authority of *halakhah* were prepared to assert the Law's unchanging character. Nor were all rabbinic leaders sympathetic to the need for change ready to discard the notion that Jews constituted a people with a national homeland. Standing between the Reformers and the Neo-Orthodox there developed a third program of response to the challenges of modernity. In Germany it was called the Historical School; in America it became the Conservative movement. The core of its position rested on a new understanding of the character of traditional Judaism. Utilizing the tools of the new "scientific" approach to history, the Historical School found in Judaism a continuous process of evolution guided by the internal dynamics of a developing *halakhah*. Change was, in effect, built into the tradition, and therefore could be effected without denying the tradition's authority.

But what was to be the mechanism for determining which changes were in fact acceptable and which violated the tradition's spirit? Since, according to the proponents of this viewpoint, Judaism represented the record of the Jewish people's divinely inspired responses to their changing life experiences, it would be the people—what American Conservative leader Solomon Schechter called "catholic Israel"—which would serve as the ultimate arbiter. This position was not quite as democratic as it seemed, because the ideologists of the movement generally added an important qualifier: the people in a position to decide were only those who accepted and identified with the tradition and could therefore presume to accurately represent its spirit.

Despite this qualification, the Conservative movement, as it developed, came to place far more emphasis than either the Reform or Neo-Orthodox on the maintenance of Jewish community as a vital response in its own right to the challenges of modernity. In effect, it placed its faith not in ideology—whether liberal or traditionalist—but in the primordial affinity of Jews for one another and in their common history as the vehicles for sustaining Jewish identity and unity in the modern era.[10] The ambiguity of its own ideology enabled Jews with diverse beliefs and practices to gather under its banner, but that banner could not embrace those on either side who sought a clear break with the past or its unequivocal reaffirmation.

FROM RELIGION TO NATIONHOOD

Reform, Neo-Orthodoxy, and Conservatism were philosophical and denominational antagonists, but in several respects they were in fact ideological allies. All affirmed the possibility and necessity of maintaining Jewish identity and communality in the modern world. At the same time, all affirmed that the social and intellectual canons of modernity could be embraced by the Jew without undermining his Jewishness. They differed on how to maintain Jewish identity and communality and on the terms under which modernity could be appropriated, but they shared a fundamental strategy for Jewish survival in the post-Emancipation world: the reconstitution of Jewry as a religious group.

In the context of nineteenth century Germany, most of the rest of Western and Central Europe, and the United States, this strategy appeared to make sense. As a religious community Jews could justly assert an undivided nationality, that of their homeland. They could locate their distinctiveness in an arena—that of faith—which accorded it social legitimacy without demanding social isolation. And by linking that distinctiveness to spiritual and ethical values, they gave it a prima facie rationale as purposive, not merely accidental and therefore dispensable. Bitter though the dispute among the denominational proponents may have been, it was, to borrow the traditional Jewish phrase, "for the sake of heaven," for a conception of Jewish life in the modern world which placed religion at its center.

Such a strategy could not, however, appeal to all Jews. Even in the West, the inroads of secularization rendered a Jewish religious identity irrelevant to those who had rejected religion itself. Further, the fundamental proposition underlying religious reconstitution—the assertion that as a religious group Jews would find full acceptance in the emerging post-Emancipation national societies—proved problematic. Not only did religiously based disabilities disappear more slowly than anticipated, but the entire intellectual atmosphere of Europe was transformed by the emergence of a more romantic form of nationalism which emphasized "folkist" and even racial conceptions of national identity from which Jews were excluded.

In Eastern Europe, where millions of Jews lived, the entire drama of challenge and response which we have sketched out above was played out in very different terms. Jews living under the Czar (as most did after the Polish partitions of the late eighteenth century) did not experience even the promise of freedom which the Emancipation offered their Western counterparts. Instead, they were subject to a policy which sought to undermine their traditional communal institutions, transform their economic role, and often forcibly assimilate them to Russian culture, while keeping them restricted geographically and socially. Religious reform, as such, held little attraction or utility. Neither, for most, did assimilation to a Russian culture which was not notably superior to their own and was characterized by a deep strain of anti-Semitism. In the multiethnic, multicultural milieu of the Czarist empire Jews retained a stronger consciousness of their distinctiveness in these domains, even as their communities began to disintegrate and their religious traditionalism to weaken in the face of spreading secularism.[11]

Thus, the responses of Eastern European Jews to their crisis of modernization were by and large different from those in the West. There were efforts to reinvigorate religious life, primarily within the framework of traditionalism (for example, the Musar movement which sought to revitalize Jewish ethical piety through educational reform). There were also Jews who sought a radical transformation of the Jewish condition through social and political revolution. For some of these radicals the continuity of Jewish identity was irrelevant. They embraced instead the ideals of proletarian internationalism and, in practice, Russian culture. For others, the vocabulary of Jewish culture was a language through which to reach the Jewish masses, of instrumental if not ultimate value. Other socialists, however, regarded revolution as a precondition for the free development and expression of a secular Jewish culture, which retained significance in its own right.

Undoubtedly the most important response to modernity within Eastern European Jewry, however, was the emergence of Jewish nationalism. Jewish nationalists took what was in their eyes a self-evident fact, that Jews possessed a distinct ethnicity and culture in addition to their religious faith (or lack thereof), and made it the cornerstone of a program for revitalizing the people and securing a place for it in the modern world. Jews, they believed, should seek acceptance and self-respect as a ethno-cultural-national group alongside other such groups. The national culture would replace traditional religion as the glue holding Jewry together. Its values would provide the spiritual substance necessary to sustain Jewish morale. This program was as far-reaching in its context as religious reform had been in the West in terms of redefining the basis and nature of Jewish identity and communality. The redefinitions proposed were in apparent diametrical opposition, but the goal of each strategy was the same: to enable Jews to live in the modern world on its terms, but as Jews.

Several forms of Jewish nationalism existed, often—as among Jewish socialists—in bitter rivalry with one another. One group envisioned Jews as a culturally autonomous minority enjoying full individual civic and political rights within the countries in which they lived. Others went further and championed some form of minority political, in addition to cultural, autonomy. The most radical form of Jewish nationalism to emerge in Eastern Europe was Zionism. Russian Jews were not the only ones to embrace the conclusion that Jews required a national homeland of their own. Theodor Herzl, Zionism's first great political leader, was, after all, an assimilated Western Jew. But Eastern Europe provided the soil within which the Zionist seed could take root and flourish. More than a decade before Herzl fashioned his proposal for a Jewish state, the *Hovevei Zion* (Lovers of Zion) movement had already taken shape in Russia, and Pinsker had already published his pamphlet "Auto-Emancipation," which anticipated many of Herzl's ideas.

Historians have often debated how to characterize Zionism as an ideological movement. Does it represent, as many have suggested, a revival in a secular vein of traditional Judaism's messianic aspiration for a return to the national homeland in Eretz Yisrael? Or is it primarily an echo of nineteenth century European nationalism, a Jewish *risorgimento?* Does Zionism provide a basis for continuity with the Jewish past, or is it a revolutionary repudiation of what has gone before?[12] Regardless of exactly how one assesses the relationship of Zionism to traditional Judaism and modern nationalism, it is clear that, as Joseph Blau has asserted, it must "be understood as another of the constructive attempts of Judaism in confrontation with the modern world."[13] Zionism, like the other such attempts we have outlined, sought to permit Jews to live in the modern world with the same rights and civil status as others enjoyed, while preserving a measure of Jewish distinctiveness and communality. The Zionists argued that these conditions could never be met as long as Jews were a dispersed minority, that neither political emancipation, religious reform, social revolution, nor cultural autonomy could overcome the dual specter of assimilation and anti-Semitism. Only in a Jewish national home could Jews be secure, be "like all the (modern) nations," and at the same time express their unique national spirit.

These claims made Zionism highly controversial in its early years. More than most modern Jewish ideologies, it was itself internally differentiated, with multiple visions and versions of the core ideology competing for hegemony within the movement. Zionism was wedded to socialism, to liberalism, to religious Orthodoxy, to vitalism, producing a bewildering array of variants. Even more, it was the target of attacks from virtually every other camp in the increasingly divided Jewish world. Like nearly all of the responses to modernity's challenges which preceded and accompanied it, Zionism held forth a vision of a united Jewry, but took its place as one among many competing programs which insured that Jews would, with respect to fundamental issues of self-definition and direction, remain disunited.

Yet, in another sense, the development of Zionism reinforced an underlying thrust in the several major Jewish responses to modernity which casts their admittedly substantial differences in a somewhat different light. The original Reform program for reconstituting Jews as a denationalized religious community and the Zionist program for building a modern, secularized Jewish nation-state stood in diametrical opposition to one another. Yet, as Jacob Neusner has noted, in one respect at least, they shared a common focus. Both concentrate

> upon the meaning of great events. Reform Judaism and Zionism take with utmost seriousness the history of the modern world, each interpreting that history, those events, in its own way, but in common agreeing that the world was changing and moving towards a climax.[14]

Reform Judaism and Zionism were in this sense messianic ideologies. They took the fundamental fact of modern Jewish existence—the Jewish return into history—and made it the focal point for their programs of internal revitalization and external adjustment. They averred that Jews could, through a self-conscious effort to restructure their relationship to the world, meet the challenges of modernity, and indeed play a central role in the world's progress.

Not all of the programs of response which we have outlined above were quite so bold in this assertion as classical Reform Judaism and Zionism. But nearly all shared the conviction that the return to history offered Jews an opportunity to enjoy the fruits of a new-found freedom, while rediscovering a purposive focus for their continued Jewishness. When it came to the point of defining the terms under which this vision might be consummated, the various ideological programs took their disparate paths. But in their belief that the modern world could accommodate an ongoing Jewish presence, and in their conviction that Jews could make that presence a satisfying and meaningful one, they were more united than their respective partisans might ever have acknowledged.

IDEOLOGICAL DIVERSITY AND JEWISH CIVIL RELIGION

In this Jewish world of active, but not necessarily eternal, disharmony, American Jewry began to come of age. The Jews who came to America throughout the nineteenth and early twentieth centuries brought with them every program and ideology which European Jews had devised. In America the partisans of these programs encountered one another in an atmosphere of unprecedented openness to Jews and to Jewish self-expression. With no old order to assault, no official community structures to seize or contest, no government arbitration of Jewish disputes, America provided a virtual blank slate on which Jews could write whatever story they wished about who they were and why they were.

And so they did write. As the waves of immigration—from the West and then the East—ebbed and flowed, ideological or ethnic groupings made their grasp for hegemony and unity, and fell back in face of the stubborn diversity of America's

Jews. Reform leaders proclaimed the inevitable triumph of their theological standpoint, while proponents of Jewish national identity invoked, with equal confidence, their vision of American Jewry's destiny. In 1908, David Philipson could assure his Reform rabbinic colleagues that the Russian Jewish immigrants would soon be Americanized; that ghettoism, neo-nationalsim, and Neo-Orthodoxy would soon fade, "and that which shall remain will be the great fundamental ideal of the mission of Jews...as a people of religion and of Judaism as a religious force through all the world."[15] Seven years later, the writer and activist Chaim Zhitlovsky could predict with firm conviction that "the basis of our life in America will not be the Jewish religion, but rather our Jewish nationality."[16]

Again, however, it is not only the utter divergence of these predictions that should be noted, but a hidden commonality as well: in this case, the belief that American Jews must find a basis for unity which would at once locate them securely in their American environment, and legitimate their continued existence as a group. Both the fact of Jewish diversity and the American emphasis on freedom of belief made unity behind any of the ideological programs of the day impossible. In the American context neither religion nor ethnicity alone could serve as the foundation for encompassing Jewish community. Yet neither were American Jews prepared to abandon the sense that they were, ultimately, members of a single group. They were, therefore, unwilling to give up the quest for at least a partial expression of that unity.

Joseph Blau describes how the leaders of the Historical School in America sought to grapple with this problem. They came to recognize that for American Jews "unity would have to be one that transcended differences in the interpretation of Judaism, and that recognized the right to differ in belief, and even in practice, as a fundamental right of the Jew."[17] What had to be emphasized were those things which American Jews did have in common:

> All Jews, regardless of their "party" affiliations, shared in the millennial Jewish tradition, had a common concern for the fate of Jewry in the present age, and bore a responsibility for the transmission and preservation of Judaism in the future. Historical continuity itself is the factor transcending contemporary divergences and, therefore, the constitutive principle of the Jewish community.[18]

The leaders who recognized in this approach a path to unity were, in fact, accurate in their assessment. But even the Conservative movement was too particularistic in its own ideological program to serve as the vehicle for its realization. A basis for American Jewish unity indeed existed, but none of the specific religious or national ideologies arrayed alongside or against one another could effect or adequately express that unity.

The dilemma which American Jews faced, and continue to face, is not unique. One of the fundamental realities of the modern era is religious pluralism—members of the same society espouse different, even conflicting, ultimate meaning systems. Yet, they recognize themselves as participants in a common social order as well. Out of this sense of unity may arise a new religious quest: an effort to endow the commonality which is felt and the actions which are undertaken as a society with transcendent significance in their own right. Where this quest takes hold, "civil religion"—a religious meaning system which symbolically expresses and sustains the unity of the society (or nation, or group), even in the face of religious diversity—emerges.[19]

For the Jews of America, the quest for a shared religious self-understanding could not be met by any of the Jewish ideological movements which competed in offering systems of meaning. Yet the possibility existed for the emergence of something else—an American Jewish civil religion, a civil religion which would draw out the meaning implicit in those domains of experience and activity where Jewish commonality *was* manifest, and define an overarching identity for American Jews which would transcend the divisions of belief and practice that characterized American Jewry.

THE NATURE OF CIVIL RELIGION

The concept of civil religion has emerged as a major theme in the contemporary sociology of religion and in the study of American Religious history. The publication of Robert Bellah's seminal essay, "Civil Religion in America," in 1967 initiated a wave of discussion about the nature of civil religion, the historical and intellectual roots of the concept, and its applicability to a variety of phenomena ranging from contemporary American political rhetoric to medieval Japanese society. While there is even today no consensus on many of the historical and interpretive issues which have arisen, there is sufficient agreement on the reality of civil religion that we can feel comfortable in attempting to utilize the concept to illuminate the American Jewish experience in this century.[20]

The fundamental nature of civil religion can perhaps best be understood in terms of Durkheim's conception of religion in general as the symbolic expression of a group's sense of unity: "Men who feel themselves united, partially by bonds of blood, but still more by a community of interest and tradition, assemble and become conscious of their moral unity."[21] Religion—belief and ceremony—serves both to represent this unity and to reinforce it by linking the group to a transcendent order of reality. The group comes to envision itself not merely as a conglomeration of individuals, but as a moral community, a purposive entity with shared values and conceptions, with a life and destiny of its own beyond that of the individuals who comprise it.[22] That sense of transcendentally rooted and purposefully directed group unity becomes available to the group as it seeks to legitimate its collective endeavors and mobilize individuals' support for them. Religion is thus, in effect, the cement which bonds a group together. Where unity exists, religion arises; and where religion takes hold, unity is reaffirmed.

Modern society, however, is characterized, as we noted above, by a disjuncture between the unified political order of the nation-state and the plurality of religious meaning systems generally espoused by its citizens. Religious pluralism involves more than simply the existence of multiple religious groups in society. It means the presence within the social order of different, sometimes (though certainly not always) conflicting, frames of reference concerning the "moral architecture" of social life. Because religion defines the fundamental understandings that individuals and groups hold of their place in the world and supports their moral commitments, religious pluralism constitutes a potential threat to social discourse and to the unity of the political-social order itself. As long as that order is not entirely undermined, however, the desire of even a religiously diverse people to invest their common undertakings with meaning keeps open another unifying option. The political-social order itself may become the focus of religious sentiments. Alongside and apart from whatever religious convictions individual citizens and sub-communities (e.g., churches) may profess, the nation-state and/or its political institutions can themselves serve as the bases for the elaboration of a religious meaning system.[23] Such a system of shared beliefs and public rituals, defining and symbolizing the nation or polity as a moral community, is a civil religion.[24] United by such a civil religious faith, a society is assured of securing the degree of shared moral commitment required to tolerate a plurality of private meaning systems.

The great force of Bellah's original article on American civil religion lay in its demonstration through the citation of key historic texts that American political leaders spoke of the nation—of its origins, its trials, its purposes, and its destiny—in unquestionably religious, but not denominational, terms. The American civil religion is, as Michael Novak has defined it,

> a public perception of our national experience, in the light of universal and transcendent claims upon human beings, but especially upon Americans; a set of values, symbols, and rituals institutionalized as the cohesive force and center of meaning uniting our many peoples.[25]

The civil religion speaks to Americans not as members of particular faith communities or ethnic groups, but as participants in a common national historical venture. It sacralizes and interprets the elements of that common experience so as to link them to transcendent purposes and moral values. In so doing, the civil religion neither challenges the legitimacy of the churches as they continue to address questions beyond the purview of the civil religion's concerns, nor does it merely adopt the common denominator of the churches' beliefs. Rather, the civil religion operates in a sphere of its own, that of the nation's identity and destiny, and seeks to invest that sphere with religious meaning. Often, it borrows its language—its symbols and metaphors—from the vocabulary of the religious traditions of the churches (especially the Bible). Often, the churches themselves share in the attribution of religious meaning to the national experience. But the American civil religion, Bellah and others suggest, is a meaning system in its own right, with a unique vision and a unique role to play in shaping American life.

Although America has provided the setting for most discussion of the phenomenon of civil religion, the concept has, as we noted above, been applied in a variety of other contexts as well. Charles Liebman and Eliezer Don-Yehiya, for example, have utilized the notion to illuminate the changing ideological underpinnings of the Israeli polity. They define civil religion in functional terms, "as a symbol system that provides sacred legitimation of the social order."[26] More specifically, civil religion helps to perform three major functions in and for the social-political order:

> (1) integration (uniting the society by involving its members in a set of common ceremonies and myths, which are themselves integrative and in turn express a sense of a common past, a common condition, and a common destiny on the part of the participants); (2) legitimation (transmitting the sense of an inherent justness or rightness in the nature of the social order and in the goals pursued by the society); and (3) mobilization (galvanizing the efforts and energies of society's members on behalf of socially approved tasks and responsibilities).[27]

Civil religion, like traditional religion, serves to link the ethos of a group to a worldview which renders that ethos supportable, and which is at the same time itself made plausible by the behaviors and sentiments it inspires.[28] The beliefs which a civil religion propounds and the mode of conduct it prescribes sustain one another and together offer a coherent way of understanding and responding to the conditions of group life. These beliefs are often embodied in myths, sacred stories which recount paradigmatic events in the life of the group. They are reinforced in rituals which call attention to the special character of particular values and moments in the group's experience and invest these with symbolic meaning. Civil religion integrates, legitimates, and mobilizes by producing in its adherents the sentiment that the society or group is tied to a sacred order, that its history and activity point beyond themselves to a higher realm of purpose and significance. Thus, the members of the society are induced to support its endeavors, to protect its unity, and to find meaning for their own lives through identification with the collective's ventures.

Not every group or social-political order either requires or is capable of generating a civil religion. Societies which are religiously homogeneous may draw sufficient legitimation from traditional religious institutions and ideologies. For centuries, traditional Judaism served also, in effect, as the "civil religion" of the Jewish people. Conversely, groups or societies which lack (or lose) the sense of themselves as moral communities will be unlikely to generate a civil religion (or to sustain one inherited from the past).[29] Other means of integration may be available for such societies, e.g., integration through the domination of a ruling class or caste, or through the functional relationships of the economic system. The vision of society as a moral community is itself not the only possible ideological standpoint. In the political realm, the position which regards the polity as a moral entity contests with at least two others: the liberal constitutional view, which sees the primary function of the state as the preservation of public order and maintenance of the conditions in which a free marketplace in goods and ideas can flourish; and the welfare state philosophy, which defines the role of the state in terms of the satisfaction of citizen demands and mediation among interest groups. It is unclear whether either the liberal or the welfare state approach is, by itself, conducive to the development of civil religion within a society.[30]

Where civil religion does develop, it assumes a functional and structural configuration much like that of traditional religion, but with two critical distinctions. First, civil religion's focus and locus is in the civic and political institutions of the community, not in the conventionally religious realm. Though it may invoke the concept of divinity, civil religion is not primarily concerned with God (or the Transcendent). It is concerned with the ultimate meaning of social and historical experience, especially as that experience is focused in the political domain. The prime bearers of civil religion are thus not, as we have noted, clergy or religious institutions, but the institutions of the polity itself and political leaders. Civil religion exists because the social-political order has a particular self-understanding as a moral entity which it seeks to sanctify and to legitimate. Civil religion provides a "meta-ideology" for the political community in a sacred key.

By introducing this transcendent component, however, civil religion also differentiates itself, at least partially, from the political regime at any given moment, and even from the political order and nation itself. Civil religion is a statement about the meaning of society's political institutions in an ultimate frame. Thus, it transcends any specific institution's or leader's political program or vision.[31] To be sure, this differentiation in theory is not always achieved in practice. Nor is the character of the transcendent component which civil religion introduces into the polity's self-understanding fixed. Writing of the American situation, Martin Marty has suggested that there are "two kinds of two kinds of civil religion." One axis of differentiation, Marty proposes, divides the civil religion which "sees the nation 'under God,' " from that which stresses "national self-transcendence." In the former there is an objective transcendent reference point which stands beyond the nation; in the latter, the vocabulary of transcendence and faith is retained, but it is the nation itself and/or its political values which are seen as embodying transcendent significance. The second line of distinction separates "priestly" civil religion—"celebrative, affirmative, culture-building"—from a "prophetic" mode which is dialectical and often judgmental.[32]

These categories are, of course, analytical constructs. Specific articulations of civil religion do not always fit easily into one box or another. Nevertheless, Marty's typology is a valuable reminder that a civil religion may embrace several variants with different theological shadings and social implications. Civil religion, like traditional religion, is less a single unchanging set of ideas than a family of beliefs and sentiments capable of multiple interpretations.[33] In nearly every instance, however, civil religion establishes a context of meaning for group life which transcends the political situation of the moment, even as it helps to illuminate that situation. Civil religion constitutes the nation's or polity's window on the larger reality beyond it. If it lacks traditional religion's capacity to depict the human situation from a trans-human perspective, it can at least enable a society to see itself in a light projected from beyond its own present boundaries.

The second major way in which civil religion differs from traditional religion is linked to the first, but is even more far-reaching. Because civil religion is concerned primarily with the integrity and meaningfulness of the social-political order, its scope is narrowed and its impact truncated in comparison with traditional religion. The social-political domain is, after all, only one of life's spheres. Often it is of relatively little immediate consequence to many individuals. Traditional religion reaches to embrace the totality of human existence and of life's concerns. Civil religion generally does not. That is its strength as a social "meta-ideology." Because it seeks to embrace only that part of life which is public, it can integrate individuals and groups with diverse personal beliefs and tolerate the existence of alternative meaning-systems. But this is also civil religion's weakness. It cannot hope to displace these alternative systems, nor can it anchor its own claims convincingly in an all-embracing world-view which promises personal as well as social integration and fulfillment. Lacking such a worldview, civil religion rarely develops an elaborate or systematic theology. At most, one can expect to find a few theological tropes; often, civil religion is theoretically mute.

For these reasons, it is common for civil religion to establish a modus vivendi with traditional religious institutions. What the civil religion requires from these institutions is essentially reinforcement of its themes in the areas of its concern. This is usually not difficult to obtain. Civil religion, where it succeeds in taking hold, cannot be simply an artificial construct. It expresses the genuine integration and self-understanding which a group or society has achieved. As such, it generally enjoys a base of popular support. Indeed, civil religion often draws upon popular religious sentiments—the "folk religion"—for some of its central content. In this respect, its theological inarticulateness may indeed be an asset, since it can reflect and utilize folk myths and ceremonies without having to subject these to rigorous intellectual critique. Traditional churches and denominations have, at least in the American case, found it acceptable and at times advantageous to identify with the civil religion and offer it support.

At the same time, however, traditional religious institutions and leaders can play other roles with respect to the civil religion. Martin Marty has drawn the distinction between civil religion and "public theology."[34] The latter represents an attempt to elaborate on the theological import and meaning of civil religious themes and symbols. It is a public, but "unofficial" effort to add depth and substance to the vocabulary and content of civil religion, which its own articulators from within the political system often leave vague. This public theologizing may emanate from particularly thoughtful leaders in the political domain, but often it comes from church leaders who accept the fundamental direction of the civil religion, but wish to see its insights sharpened and critiqued. When the civil religion itself becomes too "priestly," or the sense of being "under God" threatens to become lost, it may be from the domain of "public theology" that a prophetic voice is heard. Such need not be the case; in American history some of the most celebratory, uncritical, and expansive visions of national self-transcendence have emanated from church leaders. But the relationship between civil religion and traditional religion can be dialectical without becoming oppositionary.

That dialetical relationship—and the inherent limitations of civil religion—are evidenced in other ways as well. We noted above that civil religion often relies upon and borrows from traditional religion for its primary symbols and metaphors. The prominence of biblical images in American civil religion—indeed America's core religious self-understanding as a "new Israel"—are evidence of this. So too is the use of traditional Jewish symbolism by contemporary Israeli civil religion.[35] The way in which such symbols are employed varies. Sometimes they are explicitly revalued, i.e., given radically new meanings and stripped of their old ones, as, for example, the socialist pioneers in Israel did with the festivals of the Jewish year. More often, they are assimilated to the new situation they are intended to significate without their original meanings being denied. This process is important in achoring civil religion to a familiar religious vocabulary and in intensifying the emotional resonances it produces. Civil religion "borrows" legitimacy from traditional religion in this fashion, but also gives these symbols new potency and immediacy. Traditional religious institutions must then decide if they too will accept the new symbolic referents, or risk having their symbols captured altogether by the civil religion.

As civil religion moves to incorporate elements of traditional religious symbolism, however, it also highlights its own weakness as a generator and interpreter of religious meaning. Because the force of transcendent reality is often attenuated in its own beliefs, myths, and rituals, these rarely have the same impact on the lives of adherents as do traditional forms on those who accept them. Coupled with civil religion's failure to address the full range of personal human concerns, the limited impact of its self-generated symbols places civil religion in a tenuous position. Its fortunes as a meaning system are very much linked to the events and social environment of the day. At a time when the political atmosphere is highly charged and the history of the hour dramatic and compelling, civil religion can dominate the consciousness and commitment of an entire society or nation. When events become routinized and concerns more private, then civil religion may fade into the background.

CIVIL JUDAISM: THE CIVIL RELIGION OF AMERICAN JEWS

American Jews did not set out to develop a basis for unity in the midst of their ideological diversity by deliberately fashioning a civil religion. Yet, with the benefit of hindsight, we can see that over the course of the last century just such a Jewish civil religion has emerged. American Jews shared in all of the problematics of Jewish existence in the modern world. They confronted the problem of identity—of how to define their Jewishness. They faced the challenge of establishing their relationship to non-Jewish Americans and to American society as a whole. They asked the question "why?"—why seek to maintain a distinctive Jewish identity, why not accept the implicit invitation to immerse themselves in the most inviting melting pot the world could offer. The programmatic answers which nineteenth century Europe bequeathed to American Jewry were helpful, but insufficient. Above all, those answers could not enlist the common assent necessary to sustain their plausibility in the American environment. Each had something to offer, to at least one important segment of American Jewry if not to all. None had the power to express both the commonality which American Jews, despite their differences, felt, and the mix of certainties and uncertainties which characterized their attempts at a unique *American* Jewish self-definition.

Without fully recognizing that they were doing so, American Jews embarked on a strikingly successful venture in the early decades of the twentieth century. They began to create an American Jewish polity, a matrix of voluntary organizations and associations which carry out functions of communitywide concern.[36] The initial steps in this direction were relatively small and seemingly without significant ideological consequence. But the development of a Jewish civil sphere, institutionally distinct from (though not in opposition to) the domain of religious activities conducted by the synagogues and rabbinic leadership, constituted a critical point of departure for the development of something else: an American Jewish civil religion.

As the American Jewish polity evolved and took shape, it began to express, as well, a characteristic understanding of who its "citizens" were, of what purposes it pursued and what kind of world it pursued them in. It discovered a raison d'être and a mission, and these in turn became central to large numbers of American Jews who otherwise remained divided in their denominational loyalties and affiliations. The evolving ideology of the American Jewish polity became a type of American Jewish common faith, a "civil Judaism." This faith expressed and sustained the unity American Jews felt among themselves, legitimated the endeavors of the community to maintain Jewish group life while promoting maximal involvement in American society, and inspired Jews to contribute to the support of other Jews and the pursuit of social justice. In this civil Judaism many American Jews have found persuasive answers to the fundamental questions which have vexed modern Jews since the Emancipation. The American Jewish civil religion prescribes a model of Jewishness which synthesizes ethnicity and religiosity and places both firmly within the embrace of American pluralism. It links American Jews to the totality of the Jewish people at a level beyond ideological diversity. Perhaps most important, it gives American Jews transcendent purposiveness by holding out to them a vision of Jewish destiny and mission in which they have a central role to fulfill.

American Jews do not constitute a nation or a society in their own right. To speak, therefore, of an American Jewish civil religion may seem to be stretching the use of the concept beyond reasonable boundaries. Yet, we would suggest that no other concept makes as much sense of the constellation of beliefs and practices, myths and rituals, which animates the organized American Jewish community today. That community is indeed a sophisticated political system, with hundreds of local and national organizations operating through a complex network of linkages to raise and expend hundreds of millions of dollars to carry out the "public" business of American Jewry: support for the state of Israel, assistance to Jews abroad, maintenance of social welfare, recreational, educational and cultural programs for American Jews, insurance of Jewish security and involvement in American society. This voluntary political system is the expression of American Jewry's identity as a moral community. The American Jewish polity embodies American Jewry's sense of purpose and priorities, its conviction about the type of world Jews live in and the response to it they are called upon to make. It is, therefore, not really surprising that polity institutions and leaders have come to give voice to these convictions in civil religious terms. In the statements of these leaders and institutions, in the symbols they evoke, we can locate American Jewry's shared understanding of its place in the world and its part in Jewish destiny. This understanding in turn gives transcendent meaning to the work of that polity and to the lives of the individuals who share in it. It is American Jewry's civil religion.

NOTES

1. See, among others: Jacob Katz, *Tradition and Crisis: Jewish Society at the End of the Middle Ages* (New York: Free Press of Glencoe, 1961) and *Out of the Ghetto: The Social Background of Jewish Emancipation* (Cambridge: Harvard University Press, 1973); Michael Meyer, *The Origins of the Modern Jew: Jewish Identity and European Culture in Germany, 1749–1824* (Detroit: Wayne State University Press, 1979); Joseph L. Blau, *Modern Varieties of Judaism* (New York: Columbia University Press, 1964); Steven M. Cohen, *American Modernity and Jewish Identity* (New York: Tavistock Publications, 1983); Calvin Goldscheider and Alan S. Zuckerman, *The Transformation of the Jews* (Chicago: The University of Chicago Press, 1984).
2. Cf. Jacob Neusner, *Between Time and Eternity: The Essentials of Judaism* (Encino, California: Dickenson Publishing Company, 1975), p. 116.
3. For a detailed account of the modernization process and its effects on Jewish demography, ideologies, economic, and political life, see Goldscheider and Zuckerman, pp. 29–153.
4. Meyer, p. 8.
5. Paul R. Mendes-Flohr and Jehuda Reinharz, eds., *The Jew in the Modern World: A Documentary History* (New York and Oxford: Oxford University Press, 1980), p. 241.
6. Mendes-Flohr and Reinharz, pp. 114, 118.
7. Cf. Arnold M. Eisen, *The Chosen People in America: A Study in Jewish Religious Ideology* (Bloomington: Indiana University Press, 1983), chap. 1.
8. Blau, p. 25.
9. Eliezer L. Ehrmann, ed., *Readings in Modern Jewish History: From the American Revolution to the Present* (New York: Ktav Publishing House, 1977), p. 33.
10. Cf. Blau, p. 98.
11. Mendes-Flohr and Reinharz, p. 300ff.
12. Cf. the discussion on this question in Arthur Hertzberg's Introduction to his anthology *The Zionist Idea: A Historical Analysis and Reader* (New York: Atheneum, 1971), pp. 15–100.
13. Blau, p. 128.
14. Neusner, pp. 129–30.
15. Mendes-Flohr and Reinharz, p. 388.
16. Ibid.
17. Blau, p. 97.
18. Ibid. p. 98.
19. For a full discussion see Phillip E. Hammond, "The Rudimentary Forms of Civil Religion," and "Pluralism and Law in the Formation of American Civil Religion," in Robert N. Bellah and Phillip E. Hammond, *Varieties of Civil Religion* (San Francisco: Harper & Row, 1980), pp. 121–37, 138–63.

20. The literature on civil religion, and especially American civil religion is voluminous, and often contentious. The analysis which follows largely adopts the definitional and empirical approach of Bellah, Hammond, and others who regard civil religion as an important and enduring religious phenomenon. Critiques of Bellah's work have generally been of two types: (1) Normative critics have questioned Bellah's characterization and positive appraisal of the theological content and functional role of American civil religion. This has been especially characteristic of some denominational religious leaders who do not accept Bellah's claim that the civil religion represents a viable transcendent faith. (2) Sociological critics, most notably Richard Fenn, have argued that Bellah's picture of a unifying American faith, while possibly valid at one point in the nation's history, is no longer supportable. These critics fail to find any overarching moral order or transcendent meaning system uniting all of modern, secularized society, and hence regard civil religion as at best a phase in the long-term process of social differentiation and secularization. We will not attempt in this work to enter into these debates in any depth, since they focus largely on the specific phenomenon of American civil religion—if it is and what it is. For statements and analyses of the various positions, see the following: Robert N. Bellah, "Civil Religion in America," *Daedalus* (Winter 1967): 1–21; the reprint of this essay with comments by D. W. Brogan, Leo Pfeffer, John R. Whitney, Phillip E. Hammond, and a reply by Bellah in *The Religious Situation: 1968*, ed. Donald R. Cutler (Boston: Beacon Press, 1968), pp. 331–93; John Coleman, "Civil Religion," *Sociological Analysis* (Summer 1970): 67–77; Robert N. Bellah, *The Broken Covenant: American Civil Religion in Time of Trial* (New York: Seabury, 1975); Russell B. Richey and Donald G. Jones, eds., *American Civil Religion* (New York: Harper & Row, 1974); Richard K. Fenn, *Toward a Theory of Secularization* (Storrs, Conn.: Society for the Scientific Study of Religion, 1978); Bellah and Hammond, *Varieties of Civil Religion;* Gail Gehrig, *American Civil Religion: An Assessment* (Storrs, Conn.: Society for the Scientific Study of Religion, 1979); Michael W. Hughey, *Civil Religion and Moral Order: Theoretical and Historical Dimensions* (Westport, Conn.: Greenwood Press, 1983); as well as symposia in *Sociological Analysis* (Summer 1976): 111–82; *Religious Education* (September–October 1975) and (May–June 1976).
21. Hammond, "Pluralism and Law," p. 139.
22. Cf. Charles S. Liebman and Eliezer Don-Yehiya, *Civil Religion in Israel: Traditional Judaism and Political Culture in the Jewish State* (Berkeley: University of California Press, 1983), p. 214.
23. Hammond, "The Rudimentary Forms," pp. 121–37; "Pluralism and Law," pp. 141–44. Hammond suggests that religious sentiments are likely to be attached to precisely those institutions which are most effective in resolving social conflicts, i.e., which provide concrete foci of unity in the society. The legal system, he argues, often plays this role within American society and hence is a prime locus of American civil religion. A similar role, we contend, has been played by philanthropy in American Jewish life. Thus, as we will describe in detail in the next chapter, its emergence as the institutional and ideological core of American Jewish civil religion is in line with Hammond's argument.
24. The first use of the term "civil religion" is usually credited to the French political philosopher Jean-Jacques Rousseau, who included a chapter "Of Civil Religion" in *The Social Contract*. Rousseau viewed the existence of a set of universally affirmed, though theologically minimalist, dogmas of faith as a requisite for sustaining the cohesion of the social order and for inculcating citizens with appropriate civic virtues. He urged political leaders to promulgate such a faith. This notion of civil religion as a deliberately engineered political faith differs somewhat from the Durkheimean approach which focuses on the natural emergence of religion as the symbolic expression of social unity. Both approaches are relevant to the depiction of civil religion's place in contemporary society, and, as we shall see, among American Jewry. In our understanding, a healthy, functioning civil religion can be neither simply an expression of popular sentiment nor

an artificially contrived ideology imposed for the purpose of maintaining social cohesion. While rooted in a sense of unity which must be to some degree natural and organic, a civil religion represents as well a conscious program for sustaining and directing that solidarity toward socially worthy ends. The tension implicit in the alternative perspectives of Durkheim and Rousseau is, nevertheless, worth keeping in mind. In various times and places, civil religion may hew more toward one or another of the two models, and should the gap between popular self-understanding and political program grow too great, civil religion itself may be impossible to sustain. On this point, see N. J. Demerath III and Rhys H. Williams, "Civil Religion in an Uncivil Society," *The Annals of the American Academy of Political and Social Science*, vol. 480, Religion in America Today, ed. Wade Clark Roof (Beverly Hills: Sage Publications, July 1985), pp. 154–66.

25. Michael Novak, *Choosing Our King: Powerful Symbols in Presidential Politics* (New York: Macmillan Publishing Company, 1974), p. 127. Gail Gehrig, basing her definition on that of John Coleman, defines American civil religion as "the religious symbol system which relates the citizen's role and American society's place in space, time, and history to the conditions of ultimate existence and meaning" (p. 18). Bellah defines civil religion in general as "that religious dimension...through which [a people] interprets its historical experience in the light of transcendent reality" (*The Broken Covenant*, p. 3). All of these definitions treat civil religion as a transcendent faith with universal dimensions. This is not, however, the only sense in which the term has been used. In the introduction to their collection of readings on American civil religion, Richey and Jones cite five different meanings given to the concept: (1) civil religion as "folk religion," (2) civil religion as religious nationalism, (3) civil religion as the democratic faith, (4) civil religion as Protestant civic piety, and (5) civil religion as the transcendent universal religion of the nation (pp. 14–18). We agree with Gehrig and others that the last of these is the most encompassing and conceptually significant of the understandings of civil religion. The others may be regarded as variants which can indeed be attested in the American historical experience, but which fall short of the full meaning of the concept. (Cf. Gehrig, pp. 2–4, 17–19.)
26. Liebman and Don Yehiya, p. 5.
27. Ibid. Gehrig too lists integration and legitimation as central functions of civil religion (indeed, of any religion). In keeping with her definition of civil religion in transcendent, universal terms, she posits a third function which she labels the "prophetic" role of religion (judging and criticizing a society which strays too far from the professed values of its religious faith). Whether American civil religion in fact performs a prophetic function is a major source of debate among various scholars.
28. This formulation is based on the definition of religion given by the anthropologist Clifford Geertz. See "Religion as a Cultural System," in *The Interpretation of Cultures* (New York: Basic Books, 1973), pp. 87–125.
29. This assertion is, as we noted above, the basis for a major critique of Bellah's work. Is America still a society which is integrated by a shared moral order? If not, the critics contend, then the civil religion of which Bellah writes is an historical anachronism or an elite ideology, not a functioning meaning system for the nation as a whole. Two issues embedded within the debate between Bellah and his critics have relevance to our consideration of Jewish civil religion. The first is the question of whether a civil religion must be recognized and affirmed as such by a broad segment of the populace in order actually to function as integrator and legitimator of the polity. There is disagreement, but not a great deal of empirical evidence, as to whether Americans at large do in fact endorse the tenets of the belief system which Bellah identifies as America's historic civil religion. The second issue focuses on the question of whether civil religion should be defined in functional or substantive terms. If one defines civil religion in terms of its presumed functions (i.e., as a meaning system which integrates

and legitimates the social order), then the empirical judgment that no such integrating moral order can be found in contemporary society indeed defines civil religion out of existence. Bellah, on the other hand, defines civil religion in substantive terms, as a particular set of beliefs about the nation and its relationship to transcendent reality. Therefore, he regards the capacity of the civil religion to serve as a unifying force in American society as historically contingent. At times, especially times of crisis, Americans may indeed rally around the beliefs of the civil religion. But at other times, the prophetic message of the civil religion may fail to win uniform assent, even be divisive. The tenets of the civil religion are likely to be interpreted in different ways by different subgroups (denominational, ethnic, and class) in American society. (Indeed, as Demerath and Williams suggest, the symbols and rhetoric of the civil religion, like those of any religion, are available for mobilization as weapons in social and political conflict.) Thus, rather than always unifying society, civil religion may at times be crippled and ineffectual. (Bellah views the present as one such period in American life and speaks of the civil religion as a "broken covenant." See *The Broken Covenant* and "Response to the Panel on Civil Religion," *Sociological Analysis* [Summer 1976]: 153–59.) We would agree that the extent to which any civil religious system actually fulfills an integrative (or legitimating, or mobilizing) function is historically variable. That it is not or is only partially successful in performing these functions at any given moment does not, however, imply that the civil religion no longer exists as an identifiable meaning and symbol system, nor that it will never again emerge as a powerful social force.

30. Cf. Bellah, "Religion and the Legitimation of the American Republic," *Varieties of Civil Religion*, pp. 3–23; and Liebman and Don Yehiya, p. 215.

31. Thus, one can speak of a civil religious meaning system in the same way one speaks of "Judaism" or "Christianity" (as in "Judaism teaches…"). There is, to be sure, a measure of reification in such usage which does violence to the fact that all expressions of religious belief ultimately constitute particular, situated statements. There is in reality no such thing as "the American Jewish civil religion," just as there is no such thing as "Judaism." Yet, there is enough validity in the construct to justify our adopting the language convention of treating "the civil religion" as an entity with a life of its own.

32. Martin Marty, "Two Kinds of Two Kinds of Civil Religion," in *American Civil Religion*, ed. Richey and Jones, pp. 139–57.

33. This caution applies as well to the analysis of American Jewish civil religion which follows. The focus of that analysis will be on the civil religion as it has been embodied and interpreted primarily within the domain of Jewish Federations and the United Jewish Appeal. Although most other institutions and segments of the American Jewish community would, we believe, affirm the same fundamental tenets, they undoubtedly do so with some variation in emphasis and interpretation. Thus, we will be discussing one version of American Jewish civil religion, albeit the one which is the most widely articulated and influential today.

34. Cited in Bellah, "Religion and the Legitimation of the American Republic," p. 14.

35. See Liebman and Don Yehiya, especially pp. 123–61.

36. The description and analysis of the American Jewish community as a voluntary polity has been pioneered by Daniel J. Elazar. See especially *Community and Polity: The Organizational Dynamics of American Jewry* (Philadelphia: The Jewish Publication Society of America, 1976). Elazar uses the term "polity" to designate the entire American Jewish institutional structure—including its explicitly religious institutions—in its political dimension. This is entirely appropriate, since the religious-congregational sphere does play a role in the political processes of the Jewish community, just as the churches do in American life as a whole. In the discussion which follows, however, our emphasis in using the term "polity" is on the network of Jewish organizations and

agencies which are conventionally thought of as non-religious, especially the Jewish federations and the local and national institutions closely linked to them. It is these organizations which serve as the functional equivalent of a Jewish "state" in America, and which are generally recognized as standing somewhat apart from the Jewish "churches."

Chapter 11
Synagogue Life in America

Samuel Heilman

"Jewish worship embraces the study of Torah."[1] "Torah" stands as the dominant symbol of the corpus of law, lore, and rabbinic commentary which tradition considers divinely inspired and revealed. It includes, first, the Pentateuch (the five books of Moses, which constitute the entire Torah scroll), the writings of the prophets (including the books of Joshua, Judges, Samuel, Kings, Isaiah, Jeremiah, Ezekiel, and the twelve minor prophets), and the scriptures (including the Psalms, Proverbs, Job, the Song of Solomon, Ruth, Lamentations, Ecclesiastes, Esther, Daniel, Ezra, Nehemiah, and Chronicles). The three together are referred to acrostically as Tanach, after their Hebrew names: *torah, navi-im,* and *kesuvin.* Second, and in terms of actual study perhaps more important, the Torah includes the Mishna and the Talmud, codified oral law, together with its rabbinic analysis and commentary. Third, contemporary rabbinic scholia and responsa may under certain circumstances qualify as Torah. Finally, mystical as well as exegetical texts have over time slowly been incorporated into the general definition of Torah. The study of any of these four areas may fulfill the ritual and religious obligation to study Torah.

Informally, Torah has come to symbolize and stand for the very fiber of Jewishness. To "follow the Torah" is to abide by the principles and emphases of the Jewish people and its doctrines. For the religious Jew, that alone describes the purpose and substance of life.

From almost the moment of his awakening, the observant Jew testifies to the central role which Torah plays in his life. In the liturgy which begins his morning prayers, the first blessing recited after those pertaining to the fulfillment of bodily needs is one which affirms the gift of the Torah. Moreover, as pointed out earlier, the liturgy itself is interspersed with numerous and lengthy excerpts from the Torah, which become repeated in much the same way as prayers. Moreover, the halacha states that one engaged in the study of Torah is exempt from the simultaneous obligation to fulfill other commandments. Legend even has it that one may not die while engaged in Torah study. Finally, reading from the Torah scroll and from the prophets and scriptures makes up a part of the service at regular intervals.

The preeminence of Torah study in the life of the dutiful Jew is emphasized in other ways as well. For example, as stated early in this study, no Orthodox Jewish community is complete without access to some day school where children may be educated in the ways of Torah. By the age of five the male youngster is expected to have a rudimentary knowledge of the Hebrew alphabet and to have learned (i.e., to recite and understand) a few prayers. By the age of seven he should have begun the study of the Pentateuch; and before bar mitzva, at age thirteen, the child is expected to be well along in the study of Talmud and Mishna. Throughout life these early study habits are supposed to be reinforced. What holds true for the child should remain so for his father.

For the modern Orthodox Jews of Kehillat Kodesh, many of whom are products of substantial formal Jewish education, the study of Torah remains an important principle of religious doctrine. In practice, however, relatively few attend the regular weekly formal study groups which the shul and other Orthodox institutions sponsor. Instead, members exercise their concern for Torah study in other ways—through private individual study, in conversation, through frequent halachic inquiries, and in other ways that will presently be discussed. More precisely, while shul members spend more time in Torah study than their less observant brethren, such time is not necessarily spent in formal study groups.

This neglect is not taken lightly by the members themselves, since it seems to stand as blatant evidence of an unconscionable disparity between principles of belief and realities of practice: by sponsoring and organizing formal study groups, the congregation displays its adherence to doctrine; by low attendance levels, members exhibit their deviance from that doctrine. Accordingly, the group continually calls for new classes, which disintegrate when relatively few persons attend; this leads in turn to a call for more new classes, ad infinitum. Yet always some classes exist.

For the most part it is Orthodox men who engage in Torah study. Just as women are exempt from the ritual responsibilities of prayer, so too they are exempt from Torah study. According to Jewish tradition, the woman is exempt from this obligation because her other duties leave her little time for scholarly pursuits. The *modern* Orthodox woman, like her contemporary sisters, finds that she in fact does have both time and the inclination for other than housewifely duties. Accordingly, Kehillat Kodesh women have organized several study groups of their own (groups which in longevity and size far exceed those organized by the men). These groups, however, unlike the men's, do not meet in the shul but rather, on a rotational basis, in various members' homes.

Only during lecture classes devoted to some special topic, which both sexes may attend, do women engage in Torah study in shul. Interestingly, at such times the women sit separately in the back, just as they do during prayer. They are participants—but only by invitation, not by right. In study as well as in prayer, the shul is clearly a man's world, in which the women can share only so long as the men let them.

Formal Torah study for Kehillat Kodesh members may take any of four forms: (1) small weekly study groups, (2) regular lectures on a set text, which take place between mincha and ma'ariv on Sabbath afternoons, (3) lectures on special topics, and (4) individual study. Let us look more closely at each of these types in order to decipher the primary activity of the shul as house of study.

WEEKLY STUDY GROUPS

The small study groups, all of which meet in the shul, have a fairly consistent format. Each has a teacher-leader who controls the proceedings. He is the one who makes the final decision on what will be studied, how long the class will last, and what issues will be emphasized. All questions are addressed to him; and although various participants may offer their own responses, the teacher's answer has the ring of final authority. Like a chazan, the teacher gives cues as to when to move on in the text, when to end digressions, and when to reiterate or amplify any point.

The props for such classes are of two types: those formally required by the dominant activity of Torah study and those informally attached to it through the other involvements associated with the class. The text is the primary formal requirement. Others besides the teacher will usually have copies of it. Indeed, regular members of such classes are often persons who have large scholarly libraries at home, and each therefore has a copy of the work under study. In fact, the class, in addition to being an opportunity for using these books, often acts as a setting where one's bibliothecal wealth may be displayed—with all the attendant advantages of any display of wealth. Members may frequently spend the warming-up period before the beginning of the class in perusing and comparing one another's books. One man finds that another has a rare and impressive volume with a great many esoteric commentaries. Another has a new edition, set in a new style of type. Still another has a cheap edition, while the last has one which was his grandfather's and which survived the Nazi holocaust. For each book there is a story; and, as the books are compared, the stories are exchanged.

Some members may not have copies of a particular text, and to them the shul offers its library. As with individual libraries, the ownership of books is an indication of the importance of study in the life of the library's owner. The ownership of books takes on added significance for the shul library. Just as the minyan indicates the strength of the religious community, so the size and variety of a library *may* express the communal commitment to study. Accordingly, members may commemorate significant occasions in their personal lives by donating books to the shul's library. The condition of the library is also important. Books that appear unused, or too old or too damaged for use, fail to express an active commitment to Torah study. The Kehillat Kodesh library is small. Complaints on this score sometimes arise, and their frequency seems to be in direct proportion to the strength of the minyan. It is as if the first worry is to project an image of a strong house of prayer. Once that image has been satisfactorily expressed, concern about the house of study can and does emerge.

Another prop, in addition to the text, is the shulchan or table. Most of the small study groups are held upstairs, in the kiddush room. The six or seven men who attend sit around a long table, their books spread out before them. By its contact with the sacred texts the table acquires a degree of sanctity (the texts themselves must be approached with circumspection, kissed if dropped, and generally be kept from profane contact).

While certain profane objects, like pipes or ashtrays—the informal props of the activity—may be placed on the table, others, like coats and hats, which are irrelevant to the action, are removed. One has only to place the wrong objects on the table to see them quickly and quietly disappear. The sanctity of the table, however, remains understated, not, for example, as formally institutionalized and surrounded with religious ritual, as is the holy ark.

Other props, particular to the Kehillat Kodesh setting, change from time to time. At one class they may consist of extra chairs for coats and hats; at another, a supply of cigarettes, matches, and ashtrays; and, at yet another, refreshments from the nearby kitchen. These props, the arranging of which often occupies much of the warming-up period, have less to do with the formal activity of Torah study and more to do with the informal interactional needs of the particular participants at this focused gathering.[2]

Consider, for example, the distribution of cigarettes. For a long time this chore accounted for at least the first ten minutes of each class. In a ritualized manner, one or two members would pull out one or even two packs of cigarettes and place them on the table. While these men offered smokes to everyone present, beginning with Rabbi Reblem, the teacher from the Sprawl City Yeshiva, who had volunteered to lead this Talmud study group, others began a search for ashtrays and matches. When all the materials had been gathered, the smokers would light up, remark on the advantages and disadvantages of smoking, joke, share community news, and finally talk about Torah.

Almost imperceptibly, while such materials are being gathered, conversations which often last well into the first cigarette move from being concerned with pure sociability to discussions about Torah. As if warming up for the subject at hand, one member might mention a rabbinic commentary he had studied during the week, while another might bring up a question that had long been puzzling him. Still another might use this time for making a halachic inquiry about ritual practice, receiving an answer which could stimulate a long and complicated discussion among the members. When, for example, one man once asked the rabbi what should be done with beer before the Passover holy day, the question and its answer raised issues which were debated for almost the entire classtime. Topics raised during the warming-up period often resurface later in the class in the form of digressions. As such they continue to be part of the substance of the class.

Perhaps a useful way of considering such classes is in terms of Pike's conceptions of *spectacle, game,* and *miscellaneous overlapping personal hierarchies of activity.*[3] Using the example of a football game and its surrounding simultaneous and intermittent activity, Pike delineates various foci of concern. The "spectacle" includes all activities and involvements which, while related to and dependent upon the existence of the official game, are not, strictly speaking, a part of it. These include (but are by no means limited to) the pre- and postgame activities, as well as events at halftime. The spectacle is more inclusive than the "game" and occurs around it. The game remains what Pike calls "the predominant focus unit"[4] (in the present study called the "basic involvement"); still, it is by no means the only thing going on in the setting. In addition to both the spectacle and the game are other miscellaneous personal hierarchies of activity which, although ego-oriented, may temporarily merge or overlap with the spectacle. Pike mentions the cheering students in the stands, for whom participation in the spectacle is but one activity in a long series of individual involvements which he calls their "personal hierarchies of activity."

One might similarly describe the study group (to say nothing of the prayer service). The formal involvement in textual study may be seen as analogous to the "game." This is the predominant-focus unit, or basic involvement, which serves as both the stimulus for the gathering and the common activity upon which those present most regularly refocus their individual attention. The conversations, passing of cigarettes, asking of questions unrelated to the text, digressions, and exchange of gossip and jokes may, from the point of view of an observer, all be considered as part of the "spectacle." As with football, such peripheral activities may and often do take up more time and attention than the actual game and occur simultaneously or intermittently with it. Indeed, for some, if not all, persons the spectacle is more absorbing than the game.

Each man has come to the class for reasons of his own. For some, study of this kind belongs to their conception of Jewish religious observance. For others, the class offers a chance to get away from wife and family. One man admitted that by coming to the class he had found another way to get in the smoking that his wife would not let him do at home. For still others, such gatherings offer an opportunity to exchange gossip or to engage in sociability. These exemplify the "miscellaneous overlapping personal activities" in which the class is but one item in one's repertoire of active involvements. Moreover, because in the class—unlike the football game—observers are also full-fledged participants, the personal activities of one participant (e.g., his joking) become, from the point of view of the others present, *part* of the spectacle.

The group begins its formal work at the teacher's signal, commonly accomplished by his opening the text, silently perusing it, and then recapitulating the material covered during the last class. His leadership is maintained throughout the class. Whenever the group digresses from the subject at hand, it is he who brings them back to the text, most simply and frequently by reading aloud from it during a lull in the digression. Like a chazan, the teacher acts to cue the basic involvement.

As in prayer, those present try to indicate that they are knowledgeable, involved, and attuned to the activity. Such displays serve not only to advertise one's intellectual abilities but also to signal the teacher that he has made his point and can move on to the next issue. Just as quasi-chazanic activity serves many of these display and cuing functions in prayer, so reiteration and restatement do in class. For example, consider the following description:

> Reblem is explaining a fairly difficult section of the text. In silence we all follow along as he unravels the argument and explains the phrases of the Talmud. Some members are nodding, as if to indicate that they have assimilated and understood each point. Occasionally one or two will smile, signifying a fascination with the logic and a total comprehension of it. In the silences between various parts of the *sugia* [textual episode], the students remain silent, allowing Reblem to structure his remarks. Now, as the sugia nears its end, various participants begin to restate and reiterate Reblem's arguments.
>
> "So then, the *gemara* [Talmud] is saying that a man has to be responsible for his *sheliach* [representative]?" Riff asks. "That's right," Reblem replies. One by one the various members repeat in their own words the points that Reblem has elucidated.
>
> Not everyone reiterates, especially one or two of the members who seldom seem able to follow the line of the text. Reiterations over, Reblem begins again to read from the text.

Members may indicate their comprehension in other ways as well. Beyond restatement and reiteration, they may respond to the material by outlining its implications. Here the student can display his ability not only to follow the line of the text but to penetrate its logic and underlying theory. Such comments win for the student a greater prestige than simple reiteration. The student who can go beyond the text shows that he is on the way to mastery of the material. Such statements must be made with care and are subject to ratification by the teacher. Without his agreement and confirmation, the effect of a remark may be quite the opposite of what its author intended. The student who draws a faulty conclusion and spins out wrong implications indicates not only that he has misunderstood the point of the text but also that he is perhaps less capable and comprehending than those who have remained silent. Accordingly, only students who have scored some successes in their reiterative remarks will follow these up with statements of conjecture.

The description cited from my notes makes reference to other means of demonstrating comprehension. Many of these are nonverbal and gestural. Nods, smiles, and facial expressions may all serve notice to the other students, as well as to the teacher, that one has followed and understood the text. Of course, such gestures, which attempt to manage an impression of comprehension, must at some point be ratified and confirmed by reiteration; otherwise, doubt will arise as to the genuineness of one's comprehension.

Yet study is more than reiteration. "Learning," as talmudic study is called, consists also of the asking and answering of questions. In part this format springs from the approach of the text itself. Made up of rabbinic questions, answers, debates, and comments, the Talmud sets up an atmosphere of questioning. Not only does the text ask and answer questions; the teachers and students do, too. As if using the text as a dramatic script, class participants anticipate questions and answers, debate them, and thus bring the page before them to life. While one speaker argues one position, another offers its opposite. When the text moves off on tangents, so do the students. The artful teacher elicits such reactions from his students, or, failing to receive responses from them, plays out the drama himself by asking questions in a rhetorical manner: "But how can a person be responsible for a sheliach if he does not know what the sheliach is planning to do?" asks one member. "That's just what the gemara is really asking," the teacher replies, indicating that the student has kept up precisely with the Talmud. And so it goes, each point in the text being clarified in a gradual unfolding of questions and answers, each sugia increasingly embroiling the class members in the drama of its development.

In such a framework of questions and answers, a student's question can serve him in much the same way as a reiteration. The uncomprehending student asks digressive or misplaced questions. A proper question either anticipates the text, thus acting not only as a sign of intellectual apprehension but as a cue for the teacher to continue in the textual development, or it goes beyond the text, stimulating scholarly discussion. Questions of the latter type are the province of the more advanced students. Such questions stimulate answers and comments not only from the teacher but from the other students, who may use the discussion as an opportunity to exhibit their Jewish scholarship. Here, however, as elsewhere, the teacher retains the right to the last word; without his ratification, even a comment which may sound very learned will remain at the level of conjecture.

Questions which go beyond the text allow one to display not only one's Jewish scholarship but also one's secular knowledge. For example, during one discussion of the dietary laws of kashrut, the question of the organic composition of green olives was raised. Are such olives, because they contain lactic acid, *milchic* (dairy) or *pareve* (neutral, and thus permissible)? One member exploited the issue by indicating his special expertise in chemistry; offering a long dissertation on the composition of olives and the nature of lactic acid, he concluded, "The lactic acid in them is so broken down that it's not like milk any more." Even such comments, however, are subject to some ratifying remark by the teacher. In this case, the teacher concluded, "If that's the case, then *takeh* [indeed], we could learn up that olives are *mutor* [permissible] here."

The odd English in this last remark raises another issue inherent in the practice of learning at Kehillat Kodesh, namely, that the class context transforms language. Not only does English become intermingled with Hebrew, Yiddish, and the language of the Talmud, Aramaic; its syntax is also altered. For want of a better word, such English may be called "Yiddishized English" or, for denotative purposes, "Yinglish." The domination of Yinglish is awesome in scope. Indeed, one class member, a professor of English at a nearby university, whose command of English syntax is undoubtedly adequate, will, when engaged in Torah study, come out with a phrase like, "How *medakdek* [careful] do you have to be in learning out this *posuk* [verse]?"

This transformation of language is in part explained by the fact that the study of Torah and its transmission have for many years been in the hands of teachers whose English (Polish, German, etc.) has been less than fluent—men whose spoken language is in fact a mixture of Yiddish, Hebrew, and Aramaic, with Yiddish predominating. Thus, most students' early experiences in learning have always been in this mixed language, the use of which may in time have become habitual.

Such an explanation, however, seems to beg the sociological question. It may explain the origins of the usage but not its continuation, which seems instead to have deeper social-psychological roots. Any thoughts on the nature of such roots must, however, remain at the level of conjecture. One might speculate that because study and scholarship were and have remained essentially esoteric activities, engaged in by a limited and specialized group of virtuosi (in *spite* of being universally encouraged by religious precept), their transmission and practice have evolved a language of their own, known only by the initiated. Such a special language, like a secret code, would act to distinguish insiders from interlopers. Indeed, Yinglish has this quality. The newcomer to learning very quickly identifies himself through his accent, syntax, and inability to jumble language in the way that insiders do. Only the person who has studied the Talmud in a yeshiva or with people who have studied it there knows how to use the lingo properly. For example, the occasional Conservative Jew who makes his way into a Kehillat Kodesh class immediately exhibits his Jewish identity through his meticulous pronunciation of Hebrew and his use of unjumbled English.

To adequately decode the use of language and syntax in shul classes (and, one might add, in classes at other Orthodox institutions), one would have to begin with a precise analysis of the speech patterns of such classes. Such work requires a full and exact treatment and collection of all Yinglish terms utilized. Analysis of this sort is beyond the scope of this study and outside the ken of this writer and remains as an area for further study by social linguists. Some tentative remarks are, however, in order.

The Talmud in its text makes use of shorthand terms for various of its conceptualizations. Such terms act as representations of complex Judaic legal arguments. When translated literally, they make little or no sense, since they are usually composed of key words of the argument. Although these words could be translated into English abstractions, to do so would destroy their codical and referent qualities. Moreover, such efforts are intellectually gratuitous, since they often obliterate important nuances of meaning in the interests of coining some pithy neologism. Accordingly, such terms remain untranslated. For example, in the sentence "*Hasholayach es ha kayn* is the principle working here," the first words refer to a legal principle which mandates one to chase away a mother bird from a nest before taking away her eggs. The words themselves make little sense if literally translated. However, they act as simple referents to the complex argument of which they are the opening words. In much the same way as a pope's encyclical may be referred to by its opening words, so certain legal and talmudic principles become epigrammatized. Familiarity with many of these terms is another indication of scholarship and the mark of one who is an insider to the class, if not to the study of Talmud in general. This particular use of non-English is thus explained both by the conventions of talmudic terminology and by the strategic displays of status which occur in the social context of Talmud study.

Other non-English terms defy such relatively simple explanation. In many cases the non-English term is one that might be considered to be emotionally or socially charged: *moichel* is used instead of "forgiven"; *chiyuv ahava* appears instead of "the obligation to love"; *pilegesh* in the place of "concubine." Why such terms are spoken in non-English is not immediately clear. One is tempted to make vaguely psychoanalytic statements pertaining to the associated guilt, fear, and shame upon which ritual behavior, including study, is presumed to be predicated, but such comments are not warranted by the ethnographic data; that is, no corroborative evidence of such feelings was displayed.

Moreover, not all non-English terms are so blatantly affective. The use of *hachonos* rather than "preparations" or *zochur* instead of "male" defies psychological explanation. Many of these are idiomatic and stylized expressions which have become a part of Torah study. To "be *makdim*" instead of "to preface," to "give a *payrush*" instead of "offering an explanation," is to speak in Yiddishisms transplanted from a Judeo-European world in which they were marks of cultural eloquence. In their accentuation and in the context of Yinglish these expressions have, however, lost their original veneer of eloquence. Like a noble lost on a linguistic skid row, such phrases are memories of a language that once was. To the speaker these are often formulaic phrases of whose historic linguistic roots he is unaware.

The question of Yinglish syntax is perhaps the most intriguing of all and the hardest to answer. The speculation above, regarding the segregationary and distinguishing qualities of such language, does not unravel the puzzle of its specific rules of usage, nor does it account for the fact that those who use Yinglish vocabulary and syntax are commonly unaware of what they are doing to language. Switching from one language to another within the same sentence, the speakers seem oblivious of their shifts.[5] In their minds, they are speaking only one language, consistently throughout the class. Only when he is stopped in mid-sentence and asked to account for his phrasing and language will the speaker realize the composite character of his speech. Laughing sheepishly, one member responded to an inquiry of this kind by saying, "Well, you know, gemara is a special language."

In part, some language-shifting is mandated by the exegetical quality of Torah study, for much of the classwork consists in translating text and commentaries into the contemporary, and hence more comprehensible, language of the student. While one might properly expect this approach to promote the use of contemporary syntax and a predominance of English, one finds instead that the translations blend Yinglish with English. One possible explanation might view this mix as symbolic of the mix between the parochial and the secular so characteristic of modern Orthodox Jewishness. While the more frum continue to study in

Hebrew, Aramaic, and Yiddish and the less frum study primarily if not completely in English, these shul Jews, living at once in the modern English-speaking world and the traditional Jewish world, study in Yinglish, that linguistic blend which reflects their character and situation.

One final point should be made in regard to this multilinguistic behavior, namely, that those who engage in it in class are often quite capable of speaking perfect English; some are even native-born Americans. Outside the frame of the class such individuals are seldom heard speaking extensively in Yinglish. In fact, its only other regular use occurs during informal conversations held in shul, possibly for many of the same reasons it occurs in class. The modern Orthodox shul, one might suggest, is in its social dimension generally a crossroads between the contemporary world and the traditional Jewish one. Often the teacher, as group leader, sets the argot for the event. His phrases, set out early in the proceedings, are repeated in students' questions and reiterations, making him seem like a director of a drama, who, by setting out the phrases and words to be used in class provides the fundamentals of the script.

The series of involvements defining the situation of these small, formal study groups is affected by the small number of participants in them. With at most seven people in any given class, the group can ill afford the luxury of allowing *individual* participants to shift their involvement from the primary activity (i.e., basic involvement) so as to create a definitional anarchy. Consequently, the small study groups are characterized by what Goffman calls "tightness." That is, they are situations in which "each person present may be obliged to show constant orientation to the gathering as a whole and constant devotion to the spirit of the occasion" in order to maintain the relatively fragile *group* definition of the situation.[6] The few participants present retain expectations of mutual involvement in the subject at hand, because deviations from such involvement threaten disruption of the paramount reality. Consequently, when persons shift involvement away from the primary task of learning the text, they do so with great circumspection and detachment, so that they will be able to return quickly and easily to the primary involvement. They do so both out of fidelity to the situation and in order to avoid the negative repercussions of defiant deviance. Thus, for example, personal conversations are whispered and brief.

Yet, in spite of the pressures of tightness, involvements other than those of study occur here, just as in other shul situations. In this frame of action, however, contextual shifts, when they do occur, involve the entire collectivity. That is, shifts suggested by engagement in involvements other than the primary one either include everyone present or else dissipate themselves shortly after being initiated. The entire class stops its primary involvement in textual study and does something else. Such collective shifts may be called *digressions*. Although digressions in class are primarily verbal in nature (i.e., digressive discussions), they may at times be digressions of action—gathering props, servicing the setting, smoking, and so on.

The first point to be made in connection with digressive discussions is that such talks do not irreparably disrupt the primary involvement in study. Indeed, the teacher, like the chazan, is often the one who calls the participants back to the primary involvement. For the informed, "learning," the activity of Torah study, ineluctably includes such digressions. Moreover, classes that are replete with digressions turn out to be the ones that participants describe as "one of the best classes we've had in a long time."

The topics raised during digressive discussions often act as hints to the character of the assembled collectivity. When the members of the group perceive the gathering as essentially a social occasion, they indicate this by broad-ranging digressions which at times have no clear connection to the text. When those present sense the learning dimension of the class, digressions tend to be scholarly in nature. Moreover, groups composed of young professionals, the most modern, tend to digress into their areas of secular interest, while the more traditional older members digress to less contemporary (though not necessarily less esoteric) topics. Just as warming-up periods reflect participants, situational definitions, and plans of action, so digressions indicate the kind of involvement desired. Together, digression, warming up, and, of course, the primary activity help the observer to decipher the direction and character of the action.

As suggested, not all classes digress in the same way. Digressions in the small Talmud groups meeting at Happiton are quite different from those in the Kehillat Kodesh class led by Rabbi Reblem. Each reflects its respective membership. The former contains more novices to Torah study, while the latter consists of former yeshiva students. Not surprisingly, digressions in the former group are not patently related to Torah, while, in the latter, group deviations from text study often include the asking of halachic questions, the sharing of Torah scholarship, and discussion of various ritual observances, as well as occasional jokes and news. Where the Happiton class is study sandwiched between jokes and anecdotes, the Reblem class is study interspersed with other scholarly involvements.

Having already described the Talmud-class proceedings as a drama which mirrors the text and brings it to life in the actions and involvements of the students, one should note that the digressions are also a part of that drama. The Talmud, in itself digressive, weaving its text with the most tenuous of connecting threads, creates an atmosphere of digression. While the wanderings of the students do not necessarily parallel those of the text in content, they do so in large measure in structure. Both text and students go off on tangents.

No treatment of digressive discussion would be complete without a presentation of some clarifying examples. Accordingly, I offer, below, eleven episodes that occurred during one ninety-minute class. Although these examples are not completely representative of the full scope and variety of digressions, they display their general character. Some seem to be stimulated by subjects raised in the text, while others simply spring spontaneously out of the silence that occurs between readings in the text and the elaborations made on them. Some of the spontaneous digressions turn out to be continuations of broken-off conversations begun during the warming-up period.

1. The rabbi, having just made reference to Jewish practice during "rabbinic times," is bombarded with several questions about such practices. Although he could easily

delay answering by saying that such a discussion would be digressive, he does not do so. The conversation quickly moves far afield as the entire group begins to talk about Jewish practice then and now.

2. At a particular mention of an anecdote about a rabbi in the text, the teacher leaves the text and tells a joke about the rabbinic role. Self-deprecatory in nature, this digression is brief, the other class members offering one-word or one-line rejoinders before allowing the teacher to return to the text.
3. Prior to this class one of the members has raised a question about preparations for the upcoming Passover holy day. Now, during a lull in the class, another member bounces back with further inquiry about Passover procedures. Instead of answering this question directly, the rabbi and the others launch into a recitation of the list of places in Sprawl City where special Passover-preparation seminars will be held in the coming weeks.
4. Directly stimulated by the text, which outlines an important halachic principle, one member suggests that this principle is similar to one outlined in a recent state supreme-court decision. As he sets forth the details of the case, but before its legal principles can be deciphered, the other members begin to ask all sorts of questions about the particulars—almost as if they were gathering gossip information. In the end, the case seems to have very little if anything in common with the principle stated in the Talmud text under study.
5. A talmudic tale is recounted by the rabbi in response to a point made in the text. This digressive talk does not, strictly speaking, completely abandon involvement in the text; it might qualify as an effort to elaborate it. The tale may, however, be considered digressive because many of its details and much of its substance seem completely off the original subject.
6. A mention of the law of yartzeit prompts a long series of questions and tales of personal experience related to this observance.
7. The mention of the law of atonement brings about a rather lengthy discussion of Christian versus Jewish modes of atonement. The underlying theme of these comparisons delineates the emotional superiority of Jewish atonement.
8. The text has just mentioned the Exodus from Egypt. Now members try to construct a detailed map of the forty-year journey through the wilderness. The map is first described in terms of the countries inhabiting the land in Mosaic times, then in terms of the contemporary map. The subject stimulates much debate and disagreement, which the rabbi's opinion seems to end.
9. Soon after the digressive discussion described above, a member stops the discussion of the text with, "I know this is off the subject, but I was just thinking...." He proceeds to detail what to him appears an inconsistency in the description of the Exodus: the fact that one source describes all the Jews as having maintained the rites of circumcision throughout their forty-year journey, while another source asserts that Joshua saw the entire nation circumcised just prior to its entry into Canaan. "How can both sources be correct?" the member asks. This question, discussed with a sense of urgency, stimulates a great deal of discussion, with various members guessing and hypothesizing replies. The rabbi, puzzled as well, stops the class to fetch another book, which might provide an answer. All watch him and wait, occasionally reiterating their own hypotheses. Finally, the rabbi provides an answer which seems to reconcile the two sources, and the group, satisfied, returns with him to the text.
10. The subject of Passover is raised again during a silent moment. Now all sorts of questions break out about procedures. Some of these are answered and discussed. Finally, a decision is reached to devote the next few classes to Passover study.
11. After this last digression, with the class nearly over, the rabbi returns to the text only to be struck, almost at once, with another digressive discussion. This one is another

> continuation of material discussed during the warming-up period. The subject now concerns the various types of tefillin, or phylacteries, worn by various persuasions of Jews. After this digression, the teacher closes his book, a signal that the class is over.

During the class, it is often the case that digressions become more numerous and protracted as time passes; thus, by the end of the class, digressions have often taken up more time than the references to the text. The observer gets the impression that classes have two endings: the first occurring when the group signals, by its constant digressions, that it can no longer be held by the text for any extended period of time, the second occurring afterward, when the teacher, reciting one more point from the text, either closes his book or formally indicates closure. Always, it is the teacher who either explicitly, or, as here, indirectly, signals and ratifies the conclusion of the formal period of study.

Two more important points, each related to the other, must be made with reference to the small formal study group. The first concerns the fact that it is the teacher who chooses the material to be studied. Implied in this is the fact that, no matter what text is chosen and what subject of study, people will attend. Some members may be deterred from talmudic study because of a lack of expertise and ability, but this is not necessarily the case. Indeed, Talmud classes are often attended by members who could never study such material on their own. They do so because the regular study of Torah is a ritual activity. What one studies is less important than that one continue to study *something*. Only with great admissions of guilt do members admit that they have missed a particular chance to study. Like prayer, Torah study, in some form, is expected of all men. As with prayer, different people involve themselves in the activity in different ways. Yet somehow, either in small study groups or in other formats, people "learn."

The second and related point concerns the fact that men study Torah in shuls. Just as their prayer is often in shul, so their study is there. The women need not come to shul to pray, so, analogously, their study, which also is not legally mandated, takes place in private homes, away from the public shul. The house of study, like the house of prayer, remains a male territory, where others may sojourn but never nest.

SABBATH-AFTERNOON LECTURES

The small attendance at the small formal study groups suggests that, if shul members engage in Torah study, they must do so for the most part in other formats. One of these is the brief lecture on the Torah (again usually the Talmud) given during the break between mincha and ma'ariv on Sabbath afternoons. Before anything can be said about this class, the special nature of this time must be made clear.

Although the Sabbath begins at sunset on Friday afternoon, it does not end until nightfall on Saturday night. Practically, this means that ma'ariv, the first prayer of the week after Sabbath, cannot begin one moment too early, while mincha, the last prayer of Sabbath, cannot begin too late, lest it end after Sabbath. Institutionally, this halachic issue has been handled by scheduling mincha in the late afternoon; this makes for a break of forty-five minutes, lasting through the twilight hours of dusk, between the end of mincha and the beginning of the ma'ariv service. This gap (which does not occur during the week for more than a few minutes, unless members are deep in conversation) is filled with Torah study.[7]

The substance and nature of this study is somewhat different from the formal type. First, it always takes place in the sanctuary, with the teacher, Rabbi Housmann, standing at the bimah, facing what to an outsider seems very much like an audience. Unlike the participants in the small study groups, these people have not manifestly come to shul to study. Rather, they have come for tefilah sheh be tzibbur, with all of its associated activities—only one of which may be study. Many are thus a captive audience, and many often refuse to define the situation as being a class. Some, rebelling against their captivity, repair to the foyers or the yard for conversation. Others may simply go to the back of the sanctuary or upstairs, to engage in private study, poring over some volume of the Talmud, and completely ignore the class.

Those who do attend do not remain constantly involved in the text and thus define the situation as "loose"—a situation "in which the regulation barely constrain[s] the participants to display their respect for the gathering."[8] A condition of looseness allows participants to engage in a series of individual involvements, including some which do not absolutely conform to the basic activity. Hence, members may talk among themselves, read, stand (to catch up on prayers they have missed), or otherwise openly deviate from involvement in the class. In short, during Housmann's class one observes many of the same sorts of involvements that occur during the loose periods in tefilah sheh be tzibbur. There one returns to the basic involvement by returning to prayer; here, however, one returns to listening to Housmann. The same man who seems engrossed in conversation with his neighbor will in a moment turn his attention to Housmann and may even raise a question or reiterate a point made. Collective digressions occur, more frequently when the number of people attending this class is small. When the group reaches fifteen or more, the situation becomes loose enough to allow for individual involvement shifts. When these occur, the situation seems at one moment defined as a sociable assembly, at another as an extension of mincha prayers, and at a third as indisputably a class in the Talmud.

Another distinction obtains between the small formal study groups and these short lecture periods. Here only a minority of the participants hold copies of the text that is being studied. This further facilitates situational looseness. Forced into the role of passive auditors who cannot on their own delve into the meaning of the text, students are implicitly encouraged in their involvement-shifting.

Although the class is regular and is always taught by Housmann, those attending it vary from week to week. A man who, for example, one week finds people with whom to go out for conversation will, the next week, find himself alone, with little else to do but remain inside for the class. Accordingly, the class lacks a sense of continuity, and this also tends to foster looseness.

In spite of the loose nature of the class situation, Housmann retains many of the prerogatives of the teacher role. It is he who calls the beginning and end of the class, accomplishing the former by standing up and opening the text and the latter by closing it. Often the participants insistently signal him to end. A rising tide of involvements other than attentive study shows him that he cannot long maintain the class as a legitimate baseline definition of the situation. Terminal squirms, an increasing volume of talk, and joking amens also serve to express the students' impatience. Finally, an influx of members returning from the foyers may force Housmann to close his text. Nevertheless, without his signal, the class is still on, regardless of others' lack of participation. Like the chazan, the teacher declares when the event has reached its formal conclusion. Like the chazan, however, he must be sensitive to cues from the group if he is to continue as its leader.

For many members, this Sabbath class is a chance to fulfill the ritual obligation to study. However, widespread dissatisfaction with its character ("This is really just a chance for Housmann to make speeches," one member admitted) has given the class a reputation that makes it difficult for a member to point to his attendance at it as an adequate fulfillment of his obligation.

LECTURES ON SPECIAL TOPICS

There is a third type of class, which, although infrequent, enables members to express, exhibit, and feel as if they have met the obligation of Torah study: the lecture on a special topic. Essentially such occasions are programmatic events dealing with a specific and circumscribed subject. Commonly held for only one session, they may occasionally be part of a regular but relatively infrequent lecture series. Although such seminars may occur at any time during the year, they are most common during the period immediately preceding holy days. Indeed, on two occasions of the year such special classes have become a part of Ashkenazic Jewish tradition.[9] Before Yom Kippur, on Shabbos Shuva, the Sabbath of Repentful Return, and prior to Passover, on Shabbos Hagadol, the Great Sabbath, Torah discourses have become an institutionalized ritual of shul life. Such class lectures are attended by all segments of the community—even by the women and children.

The substance of the seminars preceding holy days tends to be fairly similar from year to year. These classes must be distinguished from the sermons which also occur during these periods, but usually during a prayer service, for the classes are special occasions set aside distinctly for study and not for homily. Seminars before Passover inevitably deal with dietary-law observance. Before Yom Kippur, lessons focus on Atonement. Before Succos, the Holy Day of Booths, classes pertain to the laws of building and using the booth.

A point about the symbolic character of these annual classes can be made, particularly with reference to the Succos class. According to Jewish tradition, Succos commemorates the journey of the Jewish people following their Exodus from Egypt. During that time the people dwelt in booths (*succos*), small huts with three or more walls and a roof made of branches or reeds, through which the sky was visible. In order to relive this experience, Jews are to "dwell" (i.e., eat, study and—in some cases—sleep) in succos during the seven days of the holy-day period.

For the urban Jew, Succos presents logistical, but not insurmountable, difficulties, since he finds few spots outdoors where he can build a booth. Accordingly, the synagogue often provides a community succah (booth) for all its members to use. While Kehillat Kodesh offers such a facility—which members help construct and decorate each year, just before the start of the holy day—many members, living in private homes which have back yards, build their own succos and invite those lacking one to join them for meals in the succah. Consequently, the shul succah remains relatively unused—a good sign from the point of view of the members, since it indicates a self-sufficient community which sees to it that the obligations of the holy day are fulfilled. To "prove" that the shul succah is empty, not out of neglect of tradition but because of the members' scrupulous care in fulfilling by themselves the demands of the holy day, the community sponsors and attends the special-topic classes on the laws of Succos, a matter of interest only for the actively observant—i.e., Orthodox Jews. Attendance at such classes has thus the latent function of indicating a general communal frumkeit in the face of an empty shul succah. Hence, *building* a shul succah indicates to the outside, non-Orthodox world—for example, passersby on the street who may see the structure—the communal concern for observing the laws of the holy day. Leaving it *empty*, along with the ritualized attendance at the anticipatory classes, symbolizes, to the insider, the same sort of concern.

Let us examine in greater detail one of these special-topic classes, one dealing with the laws and observances of Passover, in order to get a clearer understanding of their nature, structure, and function. The seminars preceding Passover are the most common and perhaps the best-attended events of their kind. More than any other holy day, Passover, during which all *chometz* (leavened foodstuffs) must be systematically removed from one's possession, requires anticipatory adjustment and preparation. For the Orthodox Jewish woman, whose dominion over the workings of the home is in some spheres nearly absolute, this period is therefore filled with comprehensive cleaning and preparation. While this is not the place to summarize the many and complex laws of Passover, we may generally say that for those who strictly observe halacha the tasks are gargantuan.

As might well be expected, those preparing for the holy day must have a practical and fairly thorough familiarity with the laws of Passover. In many cases such knowledge is accumulated through years of experience. One often hears explanations of procedures phrased in terms of, "My father or my mother did things this way." The laws are, however, so complex, and the coefficients of modern life so unsettled, that new questions, requiring authoritative legal responsa, may sometimes arise.

For such questions, as well as for review of traditional preparatory practices, Passover seminars have become institutionalized. Upon closer analysis, however, one finds that in spite of the manifest educational justification for seminar attendance—"to learn the laws of Pesach [Passover]"—few of the annual questions are new, and most of the time is spent in the reiteration of laws already known and complied with. The purpose of the class must thus go beyond instruction. Indeed, the class becomes, as will be apparent, no less a symbolic and ritual event than the class held before Succos.

The announcement of a special Passover seminar to be taught by Rabbi Shofetman, a teacher from the very large yeshiva in Bayberg, 250 miles south of Sprawl City, came two weeks before Passover. If people had been waiting for such a class before making their Passover preparations, they would have been caught with too little time. The cleanings and anticipatory arrangements had to begin at least four weeks earlier in order to be satisfactorily completed by the beginning of the holy day, which, by the time the class met, would be less than a week away. If anything, the seminar would, from the practical point of view, serve at best as a checklist event and at worst as a notification that, when it was too late to change, everything had been done wrong—a possibility which few if any people expected.

The occasion of Shofetman's seminar was announced by Velvel on the two preceding Sabbaths, while notification for the rest of Sprawl City Orthodoxy went out by newsletters and word of mouth. In addition, Sprawl City Yeshiva students were urged to attend, since Shofetman was renowned for his expertise in the matters of practical halacha. Although women were invited as well, they were told that there would be separate seating for them (in deference to the more frum—including the speaker). They could, therefore, expect to take a back seat in the proceedings—symbolically as well as in fact. Thus, although the affair was to be held in the shul sanctuary, it would not, strictly speaking, be a completely Kehillat Kodesh event.

The talk was scheduled for 8:00 P.M., with a ma'ariv service posted for 7:45 P.M. Latecomers who had missed the prayers organized a second minyan at the conclusion of the class. The alignment of these two events is neither unusual nor serendipitous. Traditionally and halachically the relationship between prayer and study is a close one, so that a house of study may also be considered a proper place for communal prayer. Moreover, halacha requires that all public study sessions where at least ten males have gathered be followed by some recitation of prayer. Finally, as mentioned earlier, much prayer consists of repeating the same texts that in other contexts one studies.

Before the beginning of the lecture, people, as always, warmed up, talking about Torah more than is usually the case before tefilah sheh be tzibbur. More than the usual number of members perused volumes of the Talmud and other scholarly books. Women whose conversations I could overhear also seemed to talk a great deal about the halachic questions that they had about Passover preparations (many of which had been resolved long before Shofetman's arrival). The few local yeshiva students set themselves up with paper and pencil, ready to take notes. Two students had even brought a tape recorder, which they installed in front.

As always, gossip was exchanged. With so many outsiders present, most of the information passed was of the news variety. Who was sick, who was out of town and not to be expected—this made up the substance of such conversation. News is of course by definition open to anyone present, but only shul members, among those present, seemed at all interested in the details about Kehillat Kodesh, particularly in the matter of who would and would not be coming tonight.

Any insider could easily catalogue and identify the various participants. In front sat the men, divided into the following groups. Yeshiva students sat together near the front, on the left side of the sanctuary, while shul members sat at the back, on the right, close to the mechitza. The large middle section was occupied by a miscellany of outsiders, most of whom were members of the Aguda, an Orthodox association which had partially sponsored the lecture. The women, fewer in number, sat behind the mechitza in groups much like the men's. Most of them were members' wives (single women are seldom responsible for preparing a home for Passover and hence have no manifest reason to attend a lecture of this kind).

The various participants further identified themselves and their association by their clothing. Yeshiva students, in traditional dark suit and backward-tilted hat, where the easiest to spot. Other nonmembers, most of whom, as Aguda members, were more traditionally Orthodox than shul members, also wore hats, but without the yeshiva tilt. Shul members wore yarmulkes, the skullcaps which the more frum usually reserve for wear in the home. Women wore headcoverings; since they were barred from view and careful observation, I noticed no other features of their dress.

Of all the distinctions among the participants in the setting, the most interesting, sociologically, seemed to be in the nature and content of the questions each group asked. The format of the class consisted of a short lecture by Shofetman followed by a longer period of questioning.

Shofetman spoke mainly about two common legal problems of the season. The first concerned the halachic procedures involved in holding onto chometz whose value is sufficiently high that to remove it from one's premises and ownership constitutes a substantial financial loss and hardship. Traditionally, halachic virtuosi have found loopholes in the law to mitigate and in some cases avoid such hardships. One such loophole, the selling of chometz to a Gentile for the entire eight days of Passover, only to repurchase it after the holy day, has become an institutionalized procedure. To use it invariably requires the help of a rabbi, who acts as an agent for the sale and repurchase. Although every Orthodox and observant Jew knows the general aspects of this procedure, it is complex enough so that explanation of it can always make for part of a seminar. As could be expected, Shofetman described this procedure in detail. He colored his words with humor, as if realizing that the facts themselves were not as important as their repetition. Almost as in telling a folktale, one could repeat the laws either directly and without embellishment or with new nuances and flair. By choosing the latter, Shofetman set the tone for a successful and popular presentation. He described the hypothetical befuddlement of the Gentile who had to be "pulled out of a bar by a rabbi and confused with all this business about buying and then selling chometz." The participants enthusiastically chuckled, obviously enjoying the humor, which made the recitation of what was well known appear new and fresh.

In addition to the laws of selling and buying chometz, Shofetman described procedures for using dishes on Passover—dishes which might be cleansed of their "chometzdik" qualities and thus become acceptable. In all his comments, Shofetman made clear that he was maikail, a fact which would be reemphasized as the evening progressed. He did not, for example, require women to move heavy refrigerators in order to check for chometz which might have fallen behind. Such chometz was "buried," he said, and did not require any further attention. The members with whom I sat nodded and whispered approvingly at many of these lenient decisions.

With the end of the formal remarks, questions began to be called out by the participants. Shofetman fielded all these without hesitation, the only exception occurring on the occasion of the first question called out by one of the invisible ladies. Exhibiting what appeared to be some reticence at answering the lady in public (women are, after all, not to be included actively in yeshiva study—but this was no yeshiva), Shofetman at first seemed to ignore the question. When a Kehillat Kodesh member called out to the women, "A little louder, he couldn't hear you," Shofetman answered, obviously realizing that he was expected to respond to the women as well as the men. From then on questions and answers continued unhesitatingly and unabated for almost two hours.

As stated earlier, the various participants in the class defined and identified themselves through the content of their questions. Women's questions were all practical ones, relating to tasks of housework and the cleaning of kitchens in preparation for the Passover. Women made inquiries such as "Will you discuss the use of ovens on Passover?"; "May baking pans be lined with waxed paper and be baked in?"; "Is yeast chometz?"; and "Do cabinets have to be lined with paper before Passover?" To each of these questions Shofetman had a succinct and ready reply. From the practical standpoint most of these questions must be seen as superfluous, since the women had for the most part already acted on these matters. After all, these were not women who were observing and preparing Passover for the first time in their lives. Instead the women seemed to be asking the questions almost ritually, as part of what Eliade might call "the ceaseless repetition of gestures"—in this case, verbal ones.[10]

The men, especially the modern Orthodox ones of Kehillat Kodesh, also asked practical questions, but of a larger scope. Just as the women were physically preparing the home for Passover, the men seemed to be preparing themselves to act as specialized virtuosi in halacha, consultants who could provide solutions for the questions most likely to arise. These men asked such questions as "What is the case with chometz brought into a man's place of business?," "What is the reason for not eating *gebrochts* [dunking unleavened foodstuff into liquid] on Passover?," "How long after Passover before you can buy chometz from a Jewish shopkeeper?," "Can more than one kind of wine be used for the four required cups at the Passover seder?," and "Why is the law so strict on the use of ovens?" These questions and others like them seemed aimed at amassing a store of knowledge which could be dispensed when necessary throughout the holy-day period. Here again, as was true for the women, many if not all of the inquirers had observed Passover before and knew or had once heard answers to these questions, so again the asking may be seen as more important than the receiving of answers; for it is the asking—and the preliminary thought which it implies—which exhibits one's preparations for Passover, as well as one's ongoing involvement in Torah study. Such involvement in learning, perhaps more than the actual substance of what is learned, is what counts. Indeed, according to tradition, if one has finished studying the entire Torah, one begins again. What is studied is never quite as important as the act of studying.

The Sprawl City Yeshiva students and some of the adults, as immersed in study as any student in a yeshiva, asked questions of a different order. Theirs were intricate and esoteric legal inquiries aimed at acquiring and displaying the special knowledge of a halachic virtuoso. Such questions are to be expected of yeshiva students. Trained as they are for ultimate ordination, Torah study is more than just a ritual act; it is part of their active daily life. Accordingly, the seminar and its questions are a part of their course of study. Put simply, for yeshiva students (and to some extent for their adult counterparts), Torah questions are shoptalk. Examples of their questions include: "Is there a *chiyuv* [obligation] to eat two *kezaisim* [a unit of measure] even if there are too many people present for all of them to have enough?," "How long before someone has to swallow the matzah in his mouth?," "Should you rush to end the *seder* [Passover meal] before *chatzos* [midnight]?," and "How do you appoint someone else to appoint a rabbi to sell your chometz?" To each such inquiry Shofetman would reply with a smile, adding once, "I'm used to these *yeshivadik* [yeshiva-like] questions." While many people laughed at some of these questions, no one challenged their legitimacy; nor did the rabbi try to ignore or inadequately answer them. For the students, as for the others, the act of asking and the content of one's question were at least as important as the substance of the information received. Through the act of questioning, that archetypical vehicle of Jewish scholarship, they became actively involved in the learning; through the content of the question, they acted to identify themselves.

If one searches for one remark which hints at the instrumental and symbolic qualities of the session as being even more important to the participants than the actual substance of it, none could be more suggestive than one made by Shofetman at the conclusion of the evening as he walked out among the women in their foyer. Many people were following him with specific questions that they had not had an opportunity to ask. In an almost offhand manner, Shofetman at one point said, "Look, no one really listens to *rabonim* [rabbis] anyhow. You all come to classes, but you'll do what you want anyway." He smiled, as did those who heard him. Learning Torah around holy-day time has an importance all of its own, independent of any questions of its substance.

Perhaps one final point should be emphasized. Although many of the questions asked during the seminar seemed to be technical or even obscurely legalistic, such questions are the very tissue of Jewish religious study and learning. While some classes allow for homily and theological sermonizing, especially around the time of various holy days, for the Orthodox Jew, true Torah learning consists of intellectual navigations in halacha. No high-flown theology or homiletic expostulation exists without the halachic nexus. What to do when one man's bull gores someone in a third man's meadow, how to become another's agent, how to prepare dishes for Passover use—these inquiries are the stuff of Torah learning, from which prodigious and monumental theological implications may emerge. But the latter can never stand without a firm basis in halacha.

INDIVIDUAL STUDY

There is a fourth type of study at Kehillat Kodesh: individual Torah study. Although persons may engage in such study in shul, it is not confined to shul, and no special time is institutionally set aside for it. Rather, each man must find his own way of integrating such study into his everyday life. For the modern Orthodox Jews of Kehillat Kodesh, daily Torah study is difficult and sometimes impossible. Many, however, try to set aside some time during the week which they devote to Torah study. Sabbath afternoons and Friday evenings are the most common times reserved. Reviewing the biblical reading for the week, exploring a difficult talmudic argument, and reviewing the laws of Sabbath or holy days are examples of the subject matter common to individual study.

In the shul, the primary locus of my observations, persons engage in individual Torah study most commonly within the context of, or immediately before and after, tefilah sheh be tzibbur. Instead of picking up a prayer book upon entering the shul, some members grab a scholarly book to peruse as they recite the words of the prayers, which they have already committed to memory. Many of them chant words from the scholarly text with the same Sprechgesang used for prayer.[11] Moreover, such persons often spend much if not all of their warming-up period immersed in study, indicating by this that the time for praying is not to be completely separated from the time for studying.

Such involvement is not always devoted purely to study. Other ends may be served as well. For example, immersion in Torah study during the warming-up period serves latently to avoid sociability. The person involved in Torah study is shielded by it from other kinds of involvement. This quality is particularly useful for the stranger who knows no one else in the setting. By immersing himself in Torah study, he avoids the uncomfortable and vulnerable position of appearing open to invasion and conversational intrusion. Furthermore, he also displays his status as a knowledgeable Jew. Finally, he exhibits his familiarity with the shul setting, with what is legitimate or "occasioned activity" in it.[12] He knows that study is appropriate in shul, especially during the warming-up period before prayers. Just as the stranger who engages in quasi-chazanic activity exhibits his familiarity with the "activities that are intrinsically part of the occasion,"[13] so too does the stranger who involves himself in individual study (or at least appears to be so involved).

While no one in the shul setting negatively sanctions individual Torah study, efforts to disrupt such auto-involvement are pronounced and frequent.[14] The person who uses individual Torah study to remove himself from involvement in a setting which is essentially group-oriented and dominated is deplored. Thus, a man engaged in such study may often be approached by others with inquiries about the subject of his study. This draws him back into the group, and what was individual study turns into group study. Indeed, he may himself realize the group's claims upon him and volunteer scholarly insights even before being asked for them. To fail to do so is to risk the disfavor of the group and isolation in one form or another.

Turning the individual study into a group effort is not the only way of disrupting such auto-involvement. Sometimes the student may be approached by others who seek to completely reorient his involvement and interest. The joker, the gossiper, the friend may all act to force the student to close his book and chat. Many are the members who begin warming up with study but end up in conversation, their book lying closed on a nearby seat.

CONTEMPORIZATION

One more point should be made in connection with Torah study in its specific setting among the modern Orthodox Jews of Kehillat Kodesh, and that is that the material studied is constantly undergoing a process that might be termed "contemporization." By contemporization I mean the explanation, exemplification, and elaboration of Torah material in present-day terms. Even the most archaic-seeming and obscure references are supplied with contemporary parallels. Sensitive to accusations of intellectual obsolescence, the modern Orthodox Jewish Torah student enthusiastically delineates such analogues and examples. The Torah seems for him enhanced with added significance and power when its seemingly parochial concerns can be discovered to be not completely removed from present reality and to speak to contemporary concerns. Such contemporization is, therefore, frequently observable in Kehillat Kodesh classes. On one occasion, for example, during a class studying the Haggadah, the rabbinic text used as a guide for the traditional Passover seder, one of the participants pointed out with great enthusiasm:

> "The Haggadah is really a great textbook in education. Look how it goes: first, background; then reinforcement and motivation, stimulation, stories and legends—midrash—and finally praise of God."

The others present were quite impressed with this insight, reiterating its major points and at times elaborating them. With this statement, something they already believed was once again confirmed—that Torah belongs in the contemporary world. For persons who invest a great deal of emotional and physical energy in maintaining simultaneously allegiance to both a modern and a traditionally Jewish set of guiding principles, finding such parallels is of no small importance.

Recall the comment quoted earlier in this chapter in which one class participant compared a point made in the Talmud with a recent state supreme-court decision. That reference aroused a great deal of interest and discussion, even causing digression from the original text. Making the parallel stick is often a crucial part of modern Orthodox Jewish study. In short, while the study of Torah has intrinsic religious and ritual value, the advantages in finding that it applies to the contemporary world and can be presented and understood in those terms are not to be overlooked.

There is the other side, or complement, of contemporization as well. Not only can one in the course of Torah study find parallels and applications to the modern world, but one is also never so fully engrossed in contemporary life that one is not on occasion reminded of the wisdom of the Torah. The Orthodox Jew, accordingly, often appears as the narrator of maxims, the citer of texts. His mind is forever in search of and finding text analogues for the vagaries of contemporary life. An oversight at work reminds one of a talmudic quotation on how to avoid forgetfulness; a mistake in procedure can be described as one would describe the procedures of making food kosher, and so on. These references to the Torah are frequent reminders of one's adherence to Jewishness in the midst of a modern-world involvement.

Even during what appear to be the most mundane of conversations, speakers may suddenly shift to "talking Torah." The man who is at one moment gossiping, joking, or otherwise engaged may in the next find himself deeply immersed in a discussion of Torah. Thus, when one member was chatting with another about problems he was having in securing the support of his coworkers, the other responded, "Yeah, it's just like with Moshe Rabeinu [Moses, Our Teacher]; no matter how hard he worked, he couldn't count on help from the others." That comment stimulated an extended conversation about Moses, his relations with the Israelites, and other related issues of Torah. For shul members, such serendipitous conversations are often the most vigorous forms of Torah study.

Finally, questions about halachic performance inevitably arise in the course of daily religious and ritual observance. These questions, along with their response, may also serve as stimuli and occasions for Torah study. In order to properly formulate a question, a member may have to delve into the Torah. To comprehend an answer, he may have to do the same. Indeed, one rabbi, in constant search of ways to enlist his congregation in study, refuses to answer any halachic questions without obtaining a promise that the questioner will join him in the scholarly search for an answer. In this way he ensures that the desire to maintain halacha in the contemporary world is coupled with active Torah learning.

That Torah learning is not to be separated from other religious and ritual obligations is recognized by shul members. While relatively few of these moderns are immersed and involved in regular formal Torah study groups, almost all agree on the need to continue shul sponsorship of such opportunities for learning. As one member plainly put it, "An Orthodox shul ought to have regular *shiurim* [Torah classes]." Learning is a ritual responsibility which a synagogue ought to make practicable.

Like all ritual acts, Torah study can transform those who perform it. At no time more than the eve of the Passover holy day is this fact more clearly exemplified. At this time all first-born Jewish males are required to fast. However, if these males attend a Torah class where some volume of study is completed, they are freed from the obligation to fast. Torah study has changed their state of being.

Indeed, all young Orthodox Jews learn very early in life that the way to become a good Jew is to study Torah. The study of Torah is a way to atone for sin, to achieve sainthood, to change one's position in the cosmos. Yet, just as modernity makes the minyan suffer from poor attendance, so does it affect study groups. Just as everyone—including those who seldom attend—wants the minyan to continue to stand, as a monument to both the religiosity and the existence of the group, so do they want the formal study groups to flourish. Torah study affirms the existence of a shul; regular Torah study affirms the Orthodoxy of that shul and its members.

As should by now be clear, the congregation in its informal life exudes an involvement in Torah. The conversations, the inquiries, the one-session classes make up the lifeblood and tissue of everyday shul life. Every Torah-dominated conversation can thus be seen as an act which defines a situation as one of Torah study and transforms the location into a house of study. When shul men assemble and talk Torah, their place of gathering becomes not only a house of assembly but also a house of study. In this way, perhaps more than any other, the congregation in its house seeks to fulfill the talmudic dictum: "Make the study of Torah a regular habit."

NOTES

1. A. E. Milgram, *Jewish Worship* (Philadelphia: Jewish Publication Society, 1971), p. 15.
2. For the term "focused gathering," see Erving Goffman, *Behavior in Public Places: Notes on the Social Organization of Gatherings* (New York: Free Press, 1963), p. 24.
3. K. Pike, *Language in Relation to a Unified Theory of the Structure of Human Behavior* (Glendale, Cal.: Summer Institute of Linguistics, 1955), pp. 44–48.
4. Ibid., p. 48.
5. Indeed, because I too had assimilated and acquired skill in such language-switching, it was one of the last observations that I was to make in my study of the setting and the behavior in it. The discovery was quite serendipitous and came only as I began to look at various quotations I had gathered in my notes of the classes.
6. Goffman, *Behavior in Public Places*, p. 199.
7. In many congregations this period is filled with *seudah shelishis*, the third ritual meal of the Sabbath, during which eating is complemented with Torah study and sociability. The financial burden of providing such refreshments is too great for the small Kehillat Kodesh congregation to bear. Accordingly, perhaps to compensate for this ritual nonobservance, the group has substituted the ritual activity of study.
8. Goffman, *Behavior in Public Places*, p. 198.
9. The ritual nature of these classes is captured in the following joke told by one of my informants, a rabbi:

   A rabbi who had been giving the same biannual lecture for seventeen years finally decided that he had had enough. Accordingly, one Shabbos Shuva he asked his congregants:

   "I've been making the same points year after year for seventeen years; do you all understand it now?"

   Not wanting to appear dumb, all responded: "Yes."

   "If so, then I need not make them any more," the rabbi replied with a smile.

Recognizing that the rabbi was trying to get out of his job and deprive them of an opportunity for study, the members decided that if he should ask the same question on Shabbos Hagadol, they would answer "No," so that he would have to continue the classes. Accordingly, when the rabbi asked the same question six months later, everyone answered "No."

"If in seventeen years you didn't understand these points, then there is no sense in my continuing to teach you," the rabbi replied, again with a sly smile.

The congregation planned their strategy anew, deciding that, the next time, half the members would answer "Yes," while the others would answer "No," in order to foil the rabbi and maintain the ritual of Torah study. Accordingly, after six months, when again on Shabbos Shuva the rabbi asked his expected question, the members gave him their mixed reply.

"Good. Those who understood, please explain the matters to those who did not," the rabbi remarked, laughing heartily.

Beyond the one-upmanship here, the story displays the efforts to keep the class going. In spite of the fact that they were learning nothing new, the members of the congregation were committed to the ritualized continuation of the class. This is the case at Kehillat Kodesh also.

10. Mircea Eliade, *Cosmos and History* (New York: Harcourt, Brace, 1965), p. 5.
11. Traditional Torah study, especially as it is practiced in yeshivas, requires a kind of Sprechgesang throughout. Indeed, the untrained ear often cannot be sure, on hearing men at study, whether they are praying or studying. The trained one recognizes subtle tonal differences, to say nothing of specific words. This similarity between the two involvements is but one more hint at the religious and ritual qualities of study—it even sounds like praying.
12. See Goffman, *Behavior in Public Places*, p. 36.
13. Ibid., p. 35.
14. For a fuller discussion of the concept of auto-involvement, see ibid., pp. 64–65.

Chapter 12
Ethnicity, American Judaism, and Jewish Cohesion

Calvin Goldscheider

Socioeconomic transformations, and changes in family structure, residential concentration, and mobility patterns, have resulted in new forms of Jewish community networks and associational ties. As an ethnic group, the community has changed its character. As a group sharing a religious tradition and culture, we ask: What changes have occurred in the religion of modern American Jews? How has secularization affected Jewish continuity? Have new forms of Jewish expression emerged to serve as anchors for cohesion among America's Jews? We focus on two themes: (1) the patterns of secularization in Jewish religious behavior and identification and (2) the emergence of alternative forms of Jewish expression. The overriding concern is with the ways in which Jewish cohesion and continuity are manifest in the community.

Previous research has documented extensively the decline of religious behavior, ritual observances, and traditional Orthodox identification among American Jews. The transformation of the more religiously oriented immigrant generation to the secularized second and third generation has been one of the master themes in the sociology of Jews in the United States. In turn, these changes have been associated with broader processes of assimilation and acculturation. Some of the fundamental patterns are well known. There is, however, less consensus in the interpretation of the evidence and the inferred connections to assimilation.

The most widespread interpretation of these patterns of generational change in the various dimensions of religiosity derives from the secularization-modernization framework. The argument is that changes in religious behavior and attitudes are part of the assimilation process. As Jews become more American and more modernized in America, they shed their religious particularism. They become less religious in their behavior, view religion as less central in their lives, and mold their religious observances to fit in with the dominant American culture. What remains, therefore, of traditional Judaism are forms of religious expression which do not conflict with the Americanization of the Jews. Family rituals predominate; dietary regulations are observed less frequently; Chanukah and Seder celebrations fit well with children and family-centeredness and parallel Christmas and Easter; Sabbath observances and regular synagogue attendance are more difficult to sustain, since they compete with leisure and occupational activities. In sum, one argument is that Judaism declines with modernization. The residual observances reflect acculturation and imitation of dominant American forms. Alternative activities, such as participation in Jewish communal organizations, are viewed as poor substitutes for traditional religious institutions and behavior. Indeed, these are often included under the rubric "civil religion." In this context, therefore, changes in religious identification and behavior are interpreted as the weakening of the religious sources of Jewish continuity. Religious leaders and institutions are the most likely to equate the decline of Judaism with the demise of the Jewish community.

There is another view which understands the processes of secularization as part of the broader transformation of Jews in modern society. In this perspective, the decline in the centrality of religion must be seen in the context of the emergence of new forms of Jewish expression. Before one can equate the decline of traditional forms with the loss of community, it is important to examine whether alternative ways to express Jewishness emerge. In the past, religion and Jewishness were inseparable. Changes in Judaism were indeed threatening to Jewish continuity and cohesion. However, in the process of expansion of community size and institutions, and the integration of Jews in the social, economic, political, and cultural patterns of the broader society, opportunities for new forms of expressing Jewishness have developed as alternative ways to reinforce Jewish cohesion, even as links between religion and Jewishness have weakened.

These new forms provide a wide range of options for expressing Jewishness among those at different points in their life cycle. For some, religion remains central; for most, Jewishness is a combination of family, communal, religious, and ethnic forms of Jewish expression. At times, Jewishness revolves around educational experiences; for families with children, the expression of Jewishness is usually in synagogue-related and children-oriented celebrations. For almost all, it is the combination of family, friends, community activities, organizations, and reading about and visiting Israel. Many ways have developed to express Jewishness, and some have become more important than others at different points in the life cycle, in different places, and with different exposures to Jewishness.

In this perspective, the examination of changes in one set of Jewish expressions must be balanced by an investigation of other Jewish expressions. Hence, a decline in ritual observance, synagogue attendance, or Jewish organizational participation must be viewed in the context of the total array of Jewish-related activities and associations. It is the balance of the range of expressions which allows for the evaluation of Jewish continuity. Thus, connections between secularization (in the sense of changing forms of religious expression and declines in ritual observances) and broader Jewish continuity (including a wide range of Jewish-related attitudes, values, and activities which are not necessarily religiously oriented) need to be studied directly rather than by inference.

Two methodological considerations emerge from this view. First, since the ways in which Jews express their Jewishness vary over the life cycle, we cannot use life cycle variation as the major indicator of generational decline. Variation in Jewishness over the life cycle may imply the different ways young singles, married couples, and older people relate to Judaism and Jewishness. Inferences from cross-sectional age variation about the "decline" in a particular dimension of Jewishness need to be made with caution. Disentangling life-cycle from generational effects is very complex using cross-sectional data. Longitudinal studies are needed to fully investigate these patterns as they unfold. In their absence, retrospective longitudinal designs (i.e., asking about past behavior and earlier generations) are appropriate.

A second methodological issue relates to the emergence of new forms of Jewish expression. While we can identify the decline of traditional forms of Judaism, we have no clear way of examining the development of new expressions of communal activities. For example, we have identified in the Boston study, as in previous research, declining Orthodox identification and observances of dietary regulations of Kashrut. But the changing concerns about Israel, Jewish communal activities, and other forms of Jewish expression which are new on the American scene cannot be measured against the past, where they did not exist. As a result, the tendency is to focus on those items which are traditionally associated with Jewishness. We shall attempt to move beyond that focus to include some different dimensions. Nevertheless, much more research needs to be carried out on these alternative forms of Jewish expression which are not continuous with the past but may have a major impact on Jewish continuity in the future.

SECULARIZATION AND THE DECLINE OF RITUAL OBSERVANCES

One implication of the secularization-modernization thesis is that there have been shifts in the denominational identification of American Jews. The linear model of assimilation predicts the change from Orthodox identification among first-generation Jewish immigrants to Conservative and Reform Judaism among their children and grandchildren. If followed to its logical conclusion, the fourth generation, growing up in the 1960s and 1970s, should be heavily concentrated among the nondenominational. Nonaffiliation with one of the three major denominations within Judaism is interpreted as the final step toward total assimilation.

There are three ways to document and analyze these changes in religious denomination: (1) comparisons of the two cross-sections 1965 and 1975; (2) changes inferred from age variation in religious denominational identification; and (3) changing denominational affiliation by generation from retrospective longitudinal data. Each has methodological limitations; together they present a consistent pattern.

In 1965, the Boston community was characterized by a larger proportion of Orthodox and Conservative Jews and a smaller proportion of Reform and nonaffiliated Jews than in 1975. During this decade, the proportion Orthodox declined from 14 percent to 5 percent, while the proportion nonaffiliated increased from 14 percent to 25 percent. The age data in 1965 showed a drop in Orthodoxy and an increase in the nondenominational. Some of the changes relate to the changing composition of the community, its demographic structure, migration patterns, and marriage formation patterns, as well as the continual secularization and change of the population. By 1975, most of those age 20–29 in 1965 will be married; some will have moved out of the community, others will have moved in, and those remaining will have been exposed to a wide range of personal, community, and Jewish changes. These cannot be easily disentangled. Comparing, for example, those age 21–29 in 1965 with those age 30–39 in 1975 shows that the proportion with no denominational affiliation was about the same (22 percent), while the proportion Orthodox declined from 6 percent to 3 percent and the proportion Conservative declined from 43 to 35 percent. The proportion Reform increased from 26 percent to 39 percent. Although the net expected pattern appears, it is difficult to understand what actually happened, and thus predict with any confidence future trends from cross-sectional comparisons over time at the aggregate level. Such an analysis cannot adequately deal with whether these changes reflect life cycle effects, the differential impact of selective migration streams into and out of the community, the changing attractiveness of Reform Judaism, or hundreds of events and alterations in individuals or communities during this decade. We therefore focus our attention on the most recent study for a detailed analysis.

The data from the 1975 survey show that one-fourth of the adult Jewish population did not identify with any of the three major denominations within Judaism, only 5 percent identified as Orthodox, and the rest were about equally distributed between Conservative and Reform. It is difficult to argue assimilation and disintegration when three-fourths of the adult Jews identify denominationally. Similarly, while synagogue attendance is not high for most Jews, only 23 percent never attend. Turned around, over three-fourths attend synagogue services sometime during the year, mainly high holidays and some festivals or family-social occasions. Furthermore, fully 80 percent observe at least some personal religious rituals—keeping kosher, reciting prayers, lighting Sabbath candles, fasting on Yom Kippur, affixing a *Mezzuzah* on the door, or observing dietary rules on Passover.*

*A factor analysis disclosed that a single scale emerges from the combination of the six items: (1) keeping Kosher at home; (2) reciting a daily prayer or worshipping at home or at a synagogue; (3) lighting Sabbath candles; (4) putting a Mezzuzah on the door; (5) fasting on Yom Kippur; and (6) observing dietary rules on Passover. These were each given equal weight in one overall index of religious ritual observances.

Indeed, in cross-section, the Boston Jewish community exhibits a high level of religious commitment. The only serious indication of low levels of religiosity is the extent of membership in synagogues and temples: only 37 percent of the adult Jewish population are synagogue or temple members. Twice as many Jews identify denominationally as join synagogues. Nevertheless, formal membership is a reflection much more of life cycle and communal attachments than of religiosity per se. There is no basis for arguing that nonmembership indicates the lack of commitment to Jewish continuity.

The issue of changing religious vitality is of course a question of change relative to the actual past, not necessarily to an ideal. In this regard, the data by age show clear patterns of decline in Orthodox identification, some decline in Conservative identification, general stability in the proportion identifying as Reform among those 18–60 years of age, and a monotonic increase in the proportion nondenominational. The data for the youngest cohort are difficult to interpret, since there is a life cycle effect on religious-denominational identification. The level of identification increases with marriage and childbearing. Hence, it is reasonable to expect an increase in denominational identification as those age 18–29 marry. A general estimate of the level of nondenominational identification among the young would be around 25 percent, i.e., the level of those age 30–39. That is the same proportion characteristic of those age 21–29 in the 1965 study. We are thus tempted to see this level as a reasonable estimate for this cohort, suggesting that even among the young, between two-thirds and three-fourths are identified with a specific religious denomination within Judaism. The same set of assumptions would characterize synagogue attendance and membership and the observance of religious rituals.

If we take the cohort age 30–39 as the level of religiosity of young Jewish families, we can infer that only about 20–25 percent are religiously secular, i.e., do not identify denominationally, never attend the synagogue, and observe no personal religious rituals. An even larger number (perhaps the majority) are not members of religious institutions.

Overall, therefore, these data show some systematic variation, largely over time and partly over the life cycle, in Jewish religiosity. They also show patterns of continuity and vitality in Jewish religious identification and behavior.

Another aspect of the secularization theme focuses on the education-religiosity connection. Again the simple argument is that higher levels of educational attainment result in lower levels of religiosity. This connection is based on the assumed process of liberalization associated with education, exposure to ideas which challenge traditional beliefs, and the role of college and university education in changing family attachments and particularistic attitudes and behavior. The data in Table 1 only partially support these connections. There is a systematic inverse relationship between educational attainment and the nonobservance of religious rituals and synagogue membership. However, there are no significant differences in the proportions nondenominational among those with high-school, some college, and completed college educations. Differences between those with the highest level of education and others reflect age factors, since when it is

TABLE 1. Proportion—Low Jewishness on Selected Measures by Education

	HIGH SCHOOL	SOME COLLEGE	COLLEGE GRADUATE	POST-GRADUATE
Percent				
Nondenominational	20.2	19.0	22.7	33.0
Never attending synagogue	22.8	20.0	23.0	24.3
Nonmember of synagogue	57.6	57.8	60.5	73.6
Nonobservance of rituals	11.7	18.2	21.8	21.9
Low Jewish values	12.2	16.5	27.9	26.4
Nonobservance of family rituals	8.9	12.0	6.7	12.6
No community-ethnic association	44.7	47.0	41.0	36.5
Mostly non-Jewish friends	19.0	15.4	12.4	11.6

controlled, no systematic differences emerge. The same is true for the relationship between educational attainment and synagogue attendance. In short, life cycle and generational factors affect these measures of religiosity more than educational attainment. Moreover, it is clear from these data that higher levels of educational attainment are not an important threat to Jewish religious continuity.

GENERATIONAL DENOMINATIONAL ROOTS AND CHANGES

These cross-sectional data focus on aggregate changes inferred from age variation. Most previous research has used that or a generational model to highlight changes over time in religiosity. Another way to examine these changes is to compare the denominational identification of respondents directly with that of their parents. In the Boston study, a question was included on the religious denomination of the respondent's parents. This question measures a subjective dimension imputed by the respondent. It should not be taken as an unbiased distributional measure of the denominational affiliation of the parental generation. A series of methodological limitations makes this assessment of parental denominational affiliation problematic.* There are differences between the denominational affiliation attributed by children to parents and the self-identification of parents. Children may ascribe more-traditional affiliation to parents, particularly in periods of rapid change. Moreover, denominational affiliation is not an ascribed characteristic, constant throughout the life cycle. Hence, it is reasonable to assume that changes in denominational affiliation characterized parents over their life cycle, and perhaps the religious denomination attributed by children to parents varies over the children's life cycle. Taken together, we assume that there is some error in treating attributed identification as equivalent to self-identification. Nevertheless, the uniqueness of these data for an assessment of generational change and the denom-

*Differential fertility, mortality, and migration have effects on survivorship. These limitations apply as well to our discussion of generational changes in socioeconomic and demographic processes.

TABLE 2. Comparison between Religious Denominational Self-Identification and Imputed Identification, Selected Ages

	ORTHODOX	CONSERVATIVE	REFORM	TOTAL PERCENTAGE
Religious denominational identification[a] of those currently age 40–59	4.0	46.8	49.1	100.0
Parental denominational identification imputed by children age 18–29	3.5	49.5	47.0	100.0
Religious denominational identification[a] of those currently age 60+	19.5	53.5	27.0	100.0
Parental denominational identification imputed by children age 30–39	26.1	46.8	27.2	100.0

[a]Eliminating the proportion who currently are nondenominational.

inational roots of current religious identification at the individual level, argue strongly for the analysis of these data.

Furthermore, comparing the denominational distribution attributed to parents by children age 18–29 and 30–39 to the distribution of the self-identification of those currently age 40–59 and 60 and over reveals striking parallels (Table 2). Eliminating the nondenominational, the data show almost identical distributions of those currently age 40–59 with the parents of those 18–29 and of those currently age 60 and over with the parents of those age 30–39. Including the nondenominational makes the comparison less similar but still a reasonable approximation.

What are the denominational roots of those who currently identify themselves as Orthodox, Conservative, Reform, or other? For the total sample in 1975, 25 percent identified their parents as Reform, and the remainder were equally divided between Orthodox and Conservative. There were so few who identified their parents as nondenominational (or "other") that we did not have enough cases for analysis. Perhaps the children of parents who were nondenominational disproportionately migrate out of Boston or no longer identify as Jews; or, perhaps, those who identified as "others" were childless. We do not have sufficient evidence to confirm any of these explanations. On the basis of the nondenominational of the current generation, neither their Jewishness nor their fertility or migration patterns provide much support for those arguments. The low proportion nondenominational imputed by children to their parents probably reflects nothing more than the tendency to place parents (and others) into convenient categories. If these parents had been asked directly, a larger proportion would probably have responded "other." Indeed, 12 percent of those age 60 and over in the sample did not identify with one of the three major religious divisions within Judaism.

Generational changes away from Orthodox affiliation are striking when examined by current denominational identification. Of those who are currently

Orthodox, almost all described their parents as Orthodox. In contrast, less than half of those who are Conservative describe their parents as Conservative; the same characterizes the Reform Jews. What are the denominational origins of Conservative and Reform Jews? Most of the Conservative Jews are from Orthodox families; Reform Jews are equally divided between parents who are Orthodox and Conservative. There is a clear general tendency intergenerationally to move from Orthodox to Conservative or Reform, and from Conservative to Reform.

The denominational sources of the nondenominationally identified are complex. They do not overwhelmingly come from Reform parents. Indeed, more identify their parents as Conservative than Reform, and a substantial number define their parents as Orthodox (21 percent). The nondenominational are, therefore, not mainly the children of Reform parents, although they disproportionately identify their parents as Conservative and Reform compared to the total population.

Viewed from the perspective of generational outflows, these data suggest that most Orthodox parents have children who are either Conservative or Reform. The low levels of generational inheritance of Orthodox identification (only 14 percent of the parents who are Orthodox have children who are Orthodox) imply major declines over time in this traditional category. In contrast, there is a much higher level of generational inheritance among Reform and Conservative Jews. Fully 70 percent of the parents who are Reform have children who are Reform, and 46 percent of the Conservative parents have children who identify as Conservative Jews. The outflow generationally is therefore clearly away from Orthodoxy; most of the Orthodox (and most of the Conservative) Jews have shifted to Conservative identification. There is the same outflow to nondenominational identification from Conservative and Reform parents: about one-fourth of Conservative and Reform parents have children who do not identify with one of the three religious denominations within Judaism.

Thus, the Orthodox have shifted generationally much more to Conservative than to Reform, and few have become nondenominational. The children of Conservative Jews who are not also Conservative tend to be equally divided between Reform and nondenominational. In contrast, Reform parents are more likely to have children who are nondenominational than children who are Conservative or Orthodox and are most likely to have children who identify themselves as Reform Jews.

In general, these patterns characterize males and females. Denominational continuity is weaker among males than females: the proportion of women who are two-generational Orthodox, Conservative, or Reform is higher in each case than that of men. Similarly, the number who shift generationally from one of the three denominations to nondenominational is higher among males than females. For example, about 20 percent of Conservative and Reform parents had daughters who do not identify denominationally; about 30 percent had sons who did not identify denominationally.

More important, there is a much higher level of generational continuity in denominational identification among the youngest cohort. Most young Conservative Jews identify their parents as Conservative Jews (86 percent); most young Reform Jews have parents whom they identify as Reform Jews (71 percent). Those who do not identify denominationally are about equally from Conservative and Reform families. One implication of this generational continuity parallels our argument about education, occupation, fertility, and family processes: there is a growing homogeneity among younger Jews, which forges bonds of continuity and interaction between generations and among age peers. The data for younger cohorts suggest little generational conflict in religious identification. Even the backgrounds of those who are nondenominational (i.e., equally from Conservative and Reform families) do not split them away from their age peers who have similar religious backgrounds.*

These patterns of generational continuity are characteristic of the youngest cohorts and are relatively new. In the past, generational differences in denominational identification were much greater. For example, only 20 percent of Conservative Jews 60 years of age and older identified their parents as Conservative Jews; this proportion increases to 32 percent among those age 40–59, 56 percent among those age 30–39, and 86 percent among the youngest cohort. There is a similar pattern among Reform Jews: from 21 percent among those 40–59 years of age to 71 percent among the youngest cohort.

An examination of the changing denominational roots of nondenominational Jews reveals an increasing equal distribution between Conservative and Reform parents. In the older generation, almost all of those who are nondenominational identified their parents as Orthodox. For the next age group (40–59), there was a greater balance toward Orthodox and Conservative parental roots. Comparing the two youngest cohorts reveals clearly the shift toward a more equal division between Conservative and Reform parents away from mostly Conservative parents.

Most of those who are Orthodox identify their parents as Orthodox. Data on the Orthodoxy of the younger generation are not complete because of the small number included. Generational continuity among those who are currently Orthodox is significant precisely because of the major shifts generationally away from Orthodoxy. While there have been major outflows from Orthodox to non-Orthodox denominations, those who are currently Orthodox are almost exclusively from Orthodox families. There is no evidence from these data of inflows to Orthodoxy from the non-Orthodox.

The critical variable in the continuity of denominational identification between generations is age. That is expected, given the age variation we noted earlier in the cross-section and the patterns of denominational changes in the aggregate from Orthodox to Conservative and Reform. The patterns are striking: of those who are currently 60 years of age and over, three-fourths describe their parents as Orthodox, 15 percent as Conservative, and 9 percent as Reform. These attributed denominations decline among the younger cohorts: 56 percent of those age 40–59 identified their parents as Orthodox, compared to 26 percent among those 30–39 years of age and less than 4 percent among those age 18–29. Concomitantly, the proportion Conservative

*It should be noted that the level of Jewish education is high in the Jewish community of Boston and has remained high in both the 1965 and 1975 studies. Indeed, most Jews receive some Jewish education, and there has been a slight increase among young adults (cf. Fowler 1977). This pattern should also be viewed in the context of generational continuities.

and Reform increases monotonically with age: from 15 percent to 50 percent Conservative parents among those age 60 and over to the youngest cohort; from 9 percent to 47 percent Reform parents for the same age comparisons.

Denominational changes between generations do not vary systematically by education. The general transformation of religious identification is not specific to an educational level. Nor are the recruitment or inheritance patterns more pronounced among the more- or less-educated. As socio-economic patterns have been transformed, so has denominational identification between generations.

In an attempt to capture in summary form the details of these patterns, we calculated the proportions who had the same religious denomination as the one they attributed to their parents, i.e., two-generational Orthodox, Conservative, and Reform. We subdivided the remainder into those who generationally moved "up" (from nondenominational, Reform or Conservative to Orthodox, from nondenominational or Reform to Conservative, and from nondenominational to Reform) and those who moved "down" (from Orthodox, Conservative, or Reform to none, from Orthodox or Conservative to Reform, from Conservative to Reform). We do not want to convey any judgment in this classification except a direction away from, or toward, traditional Jewish religious identification. (We use *traditional* in its social-normative, not Halachic, sense.)

There is a built-in bias, however, in that so few are reported by their children as nondenominational in the parental generation, and therefore, those who are currently nondenominational must be placed in the "down" category. In this way, each generation feels it moves "down" by comparing its reality with remembered ideals. Nevertheless, this situation is at least in part a reflection of reality and cannot be totally dismissed.

Overall, the data show that 40 percent of the adult Jews have the same denominational identification as their parents (Table 3). Almost none moved "up" religiously, and 59 percent moved away generationally from more traditional religious identification. (When the nondenominational are eliminated, there is a 50 percent continuity level between generations.) The age patterns are most revealing. Over time, there has been a substantial *increase* in the extent of generational continuity in denominational affiliation. Three-fourths of those age 40–59 had a different denominational identification from that of their parents, and almost all moved away from tradition. Among the youngest cohort, the number who identify with the same denomination as their parents exceeds 50 percent; excluding those who are not yet identified, the proportion generationally similar of the three denominations among the young is 77 percent. Hence, at the same time that there are clear indications of secularization away from religious tradition, there are powerful signs of increasing generational continuity. There are also some indications, although slight, of an increase in the proportion who have moved "up," from less than 1 percent among the oldest cohort to over 2 percent among the young. The change from a pattern of 75 percent downward mobility away from religious traditional identification among the older generation to 77 percent of the younger generation who have the same religious denomination as their parents (if they identify denominationally) is nothing less than a radical transformation. We

TABLE 3. Generational Denominational Identification: Summary Patterns

	PERCENT SAME	PERCENT "UP"	PERCENT "DOWN"	TOTAL PERCENT	N
TOTAL	40.0	1.5	58.5	100	1,818
Sex					
Male	36.2	0.7	63.1	100	840
Female	43.4	2.0	54.6	100	978
Age					
18–29	52.7	2.2	45.1	100	624
30–39	44.6	1.4	54.0	100	291
40–59	25.3	1.0	73.7	100	509
60+	35.1	0.8	64.9	100	366
Income					
$10,000	47.8	3.2	49.0	100	474
10–20,000	45.7	0.3	54.0	100	368
20–35,000	45.0	1.3	53.7	100	315
35,000+	26.9	0.4	72.7	100	270
Education					
High school	32.3	0.4	67.3	100	477
Some college	37.8	1.8	60.4	100	338
College graduate	43.1	2.9	54.0	100	511
Postgraduate	46.3	0.6	53.1	100	483

postulate that this increasing level of generational continuity in religious denominational identification has become an additional source of Jewish cohesion. It is reinforced by other forms of generational continuity, including socioeconomic status and family patterns. Taken together, these social processes are powerful sources of American Jewish continuity in the 1980s.

We note in addition that stability generationally is somewhat higher for women than for men, as is the proportion who move "up." Of greater importance is the higher proportions generationally similar among the more educated. The positive relationship between generational denominational continuity and educational attainment partly reflects age patterns but operates even within age groups. This pattern supports the general findings that generational continuity is high among the younger cohorts and the most educated. These are the future of the American Jewish community.

ALTERNATIVE SOURCES OF JEWISH COHESION

Religiosity is only one of the ways in which Jews express their Jewishness. In the past, Judaism and Jewishness were intertwined, so that any change in religious expression represented a threat to Jewish continuity. That is no longer the case

TABLE 4. Selected Measures of Jewishness by Age (Percent)

	TOTAL	18–29	30–39	40–59	60+
Jewish Values					
Low	21.6	30.5	26.0	17.3	7.3
High	58.6	45.9	48.9	63.9	74.7
Family Observances	71.2	68.2	64.2	75.6	75.8
Ethnic-Community Associations					
None	42.0	53.0	38.9	39.6	27.7
Many	30.2	21.3	27.1	31.6	46.3
Proportion Jewish Friends					
Most	49.7	32.4	46.7	62.8	68.9
Few or none	14.8	24.5	13.6	3.7	12.1

among contemporary Jewish communities. Our focus here is on tapping the Boston study for clues about some of these alternative sources of Jewish cohesion which are not religious forms in the narrow sense. We shall focus on Jewish values, family observances, ethnic-community associations, and Jewish friends. These measures of cohesion indicate contexts of interaction, sources of particularistic values, and anchors of ethnic identity. As such, they complement the religious dimension of Jewish cohesion.

A series of questions was included about Jewish values and the meaning of being Jewish. A statistical analysis selected four elements that combined to yield one overall factor. These included the following values: (1) It is important for every Jewish child to be given a serious continuing Jewish education; (2) It is important to observe traditional Jewish religious practices; (3) I feel proud of being a Jew when I hear or read about accomplishments of Jews; (4) The existence of Israel is essential for the continuation of American Jewish life.

A high proportion of Jews expressed most of these values (Table 4). About 60 percent agreed with at least three out of four of these items. The critical issue is, of course, some indication of change. The age data show some increase in the proportion scoring low and a decrease in the proportion scoring high. Still, 70 percent of those age 18–29 had medium to high scores on this scale.

An equally impressive level of Jewishness emerges from an examination of the celebration of Jewish holidays with family.* Over 70 percent of the adult Jewish community participate in religious holiday celebrations with family. There is some indication of decline, from 76 percent among the two oldest cohorts to about 65 percent among the youngest cohort. Nevertheless, the overwhelming impression is that most adult Jews, young and old, connect up with other family members for

*This index combines two questions which were isolated in a factor analysis as a single dimension of family observances: (1) taking part in a Passover Seder; (2) getting together with relatives to celebrate any Jewish holidays in the past year.

Jewish-family-related celebrations. In turn, these celebrations have become major sources of group cohesion and anchors of Jewish continuity.

A third set of items which also emerged out of a factor analysis relates to ethnic-community issues. These included: (1) attending lectures or classes of Jewish interest: (2) visiting Israel; and (3) reading newspapers or magazines of Jewish content. Again the pattern is similar: some indications of decline in identifying Jewishly through Israel and direct involvement with the community, but nevertheless an impressive level of some type of community identification.

A final item is the extent to which Jews interact with Jews and non-Jews. The question was: "About how many of your friends are Jewish—all, most, about half, or are most of your friends not Jewish?" Fully 85 percent of the respondents said that at least half of their friends were Jewish, and 50 percent said that most or all of their friends were Jewish. There is a decline in the proportions who say most of their friends are Jewish, and an increase in the proportion with few or no Jewish friends, with decreasing age. Nevertheless, three-fourths of those age 18–29 and 85 percent of those age 30–39 indicated that at least half of their friends were Jewish. (See Figure 1, where these patterns are compared to the changing observance of Jewish ritual.) For the older age cohorts, there is a more exclusive pattern of ethnic friendship, where about two thirds had mostly Jewish friends. The pattern among the younger cohorts seems to be a greater balance between Jewish and non-Jewish friends. It is inconsistent to argue on the basis of this evidence that younger Jews do not have important networks of friendship which tie them to other Jews. These networks may be less linked to the organized Jewish community, to formal Jewish organization, or to religious institutions. However, they are tied to new forms of Jewish continuity, and have important relationships to economic, residential, lifestyle, and related values.

How are these ethnic-community aspects of Jewishness related to education? The expression of traditional Jewish values is clearly linked inversely to education—the higher the education, the lower the proportion expressing Jewish values (Table 1). These patterns characterize the youngest cohort but reverse among those age 30–39. In that cohort, only 22 percent of the most educated express low Jewish values, compared to 36 percent among the college-educated. For family ritual observance and ethnic-community associations, the patterns by education either are unclear or show that the most educated have the greater links to Jewishness. For example, the more educated rank higher on the community-ethnic dimension than the less educated, and these findings are accentuated within age controls. Detailed data not shown reveal that over three-fourths of the most educated ranked medium to high on this dimension, compared to 40 percent of the college-educated.

A similar pattern may be observed with the proportion with mostly non-Jewish friends. Those with postgraduate educations have the *lowest* proportion who said most of their friends are not Jewish. These patterns are even clearer by age. While one-fourth to one-fifth of the college-educated age 18–29 had mostly non-Jewish friends, only 13 percent of the postgraduates had mostly non-Jewish friends. Similarly, for the 30–39 cohort, 38 percent of those with some college

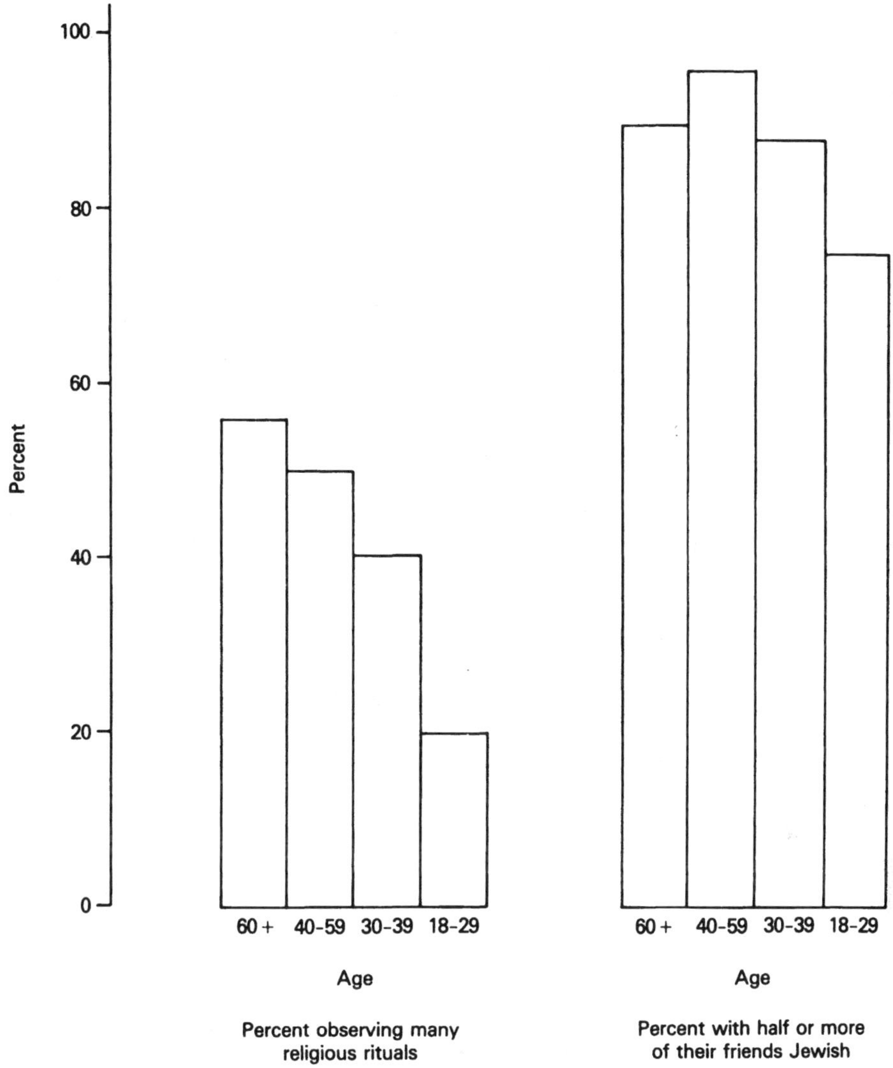

FIGURE 1. A comparison between religious rituals and Jewish friends by age.

education had mostly non-Jewish friends, compared to 11 percent of the college graduates and less than five percent of the postgraduates.

These ethnic-associational patterns by education are consistent with the earlier data on religiosity. Educational attainment is not the source of Jewish secularization, nor does it lead to alienation and disaffection from the community. The data support the argument that new Jewish networks have emerged which are based less on traditional modes of behavior and institutional associations. They are based on lifestyle and jobs, education, residence, and family; they are reinforced by religious observances which have become family-community-based. While religion has lost its centrality and dominance in the modern, secular American community, it continues to play a supportive role in linking educational, family, economic, and lifestyle issues to broader communal, ethnic (Israel), and Jewish continuity issues.

JEWISH CONTINUITY OF THE NONDENOMINATIONAL

The nondenominational represent about 25 percent of the adult Jewish population and are more concentrated among the younger age cohorts. Are they "lost" to the Jewish community? Does religious nondenominationalism imply the absence of alternative ways of expressing Jewishness?

The evidence suggests that significant segments of the religiously nonaffiliated are linked to Jewishness in a variety of ways. The overwhelming majority of the nondenominational are not synagogue members, and those that are belong to Reform temples. The proportions who are members and who attend religious services are significantly lower among those who do not identify themselves with a religious denomination than among those who are denominationally identified. Nevertheless, almost half of those who are nondenominational attend religious services sometime during the year. Those who do not identify denominationally also are less likely to express traditional Jewish values and will observe fewer religious rituals. Nevertheless, again, fully three-fourths of the nondenominational participate in religious family celebrations, and half are involved with some ethnic-community activities. Only 25 percent of the nondenominational have mostly non-Jewish friends—a slightly higher proportion than among Reform Jews. This tendency is more characteristic of younger Jews age 18–29, where one-third have mostly non-Jewish friends. Nevertheless, for the cohort age 30–39, the percentage of nondenominational drops off very rapidly, and the proportion of those who have mostly non-Jewish friends is lower than among Reform Jews of that age cohort.

In short, the patterns are relatively clear and consistent: most Jews have a wide range of ties to Jewishness. The overwhelming majority have some connections to Judaism and religious institutions. Those whose religious links are weakest have alternative ties to Jewish friends, family, and communal-ethnic activities. While the young tend to have weaker links to religious and social dimensions of Jewishness, they exhibit strong family ties, friendship patterns, and ethnic-Jewish attachments. It is of significance that these ties are not only generationally but life-cycle related. That suggests that the Jewishness of the young is not an ascribed characteristic, nor is it constant over time. They will change as marriages occur and families are formed, as new households are established and new communities are settled, and will continue to change as new educational, occupational, and residential networks emerge.

RELIGION AND ETHNIC FACTORS

Religion and ethnic factors are particularistic features of the Jewish community. They are the defining quality of American Jewish life and the source of communal consensus. The secularization of Judaism and Jews has long been observed in America. The critical issue, however, is whether alternative sources of group cohesion have emerged as religious centrality has declined. Religious and ethnic forms of Jewishness have changed in America. Interpreting these changes and understanding their link to the future of the American Jewish community are a key analytic concern.

The data document the changing manifestation of religious forms of cohesion. They also clearly indicate how forms of religious and ethnic cohesion provide a wide range of options for Jews at different points in the life cycle. For some, religion in its Americanized form is of central importance in their Jewishness; for most Jews, social, communal, ethnic, and religious dimensions of Jewishness are combined. It is most problematic to specify and measure the "quality" of Jewish life, since there is no theoretical or empirical consensus about it. Nevertheless, it is clear that the decline in religiosity per se must be viewed in the context of the emergence of these alternative forms of Jewishness. Secularization in the religious sense is not necessarily equal to the decline of the Jewish community, to its assimilation or demise. By treating Jews as members of a community in the broad sense, we recognize religion as one dimension of the total array of factors, but not as equivalent to the whole.

Despite the evidence of secularization, there remains a strong sense of religious identification among Jews. Fully three-fourths of Boston Jewry define themselves denominationally, attend synagogue sometimes during the year, and observe some personal religious rituals. This high level of religious identification is not matched by formal membership in religious institutions. Hence, membership per se is not an adequate indicator of religious identification. Life-cycle- and family-related factors determine membership patterns. Nonmembership does not seem to imply the lack of commitment to Jewish continuity.

These patterns characterize the younger as well as the older generations, men and women, and appear to be a pervasive feature throughout the Jewish community. In particular, there are no clear relationships between educational level and religiosity or between other social class indicators and Jewishness. Hence, neither the attainment of high levels of education nor upward mobility can be viewed as a "threat" to Jewish continuity.

For recent generations, there are high levels of religious denominational continuity, albeit in less traditional and usually less intense forms. Similarities in affiliation across generations forge bonds of interaction and reduce conflict over religious issues. Even those not affiliated denominationally are similar in background to the denominational, thereby not splitting them from their age peers. The increasing generational homogeneity in religious denominational affiliation, in which three-fourths of the younger generation have the same denominational affiliation as their parents, while three-fourths of the older generation were "downwardly" religiously mobile, is an additional source of cohesion in the community.

This generational continuity in religious denominational affiliation parallels the continuity in social class and family life. Over and above the effects of religious affiliation on Jewish continuity, generational continuity per se has become an additional basis of Jewish cohesion. This socioeconomic, family, and religious continuity implies high levels of consensus between generations in lifestyle, interests, kin networks, economic linkages, values, and norms. It also implies fewer sources of generational conflict. Again, we argue that the more the bases of cohesion, the stronger the community and the firmer the anchors for continuity. This continuity takes on particular significance, since it characterizes the young and most-educated, the future of the American Jewish community.

These indicators of religious continuity and the importance of religion as one distinguishing feature of Jewish communal life are reinforced by ethnic-communal forms of Jewish cohesion. Jewish networks have emerged which are based not on traditional modes of behavior but on lifestyle, jobs, residence, education, and family ties—cemented by religious observance and identification. The new forms of Jewishness are family- and community-based. While religion has lost its centrality and dominance in the Jewish world, it continues to play a supportive role in linking educational, family, economic, and lifestyle issues to broader communal issues.

Among those who are religiously anchored and who share family, social-class, and residential ties with other Jews, the issues of continuity are not problematic. In this context, the question of the future of the nondenominational, those not affiliated or identified religiously, has been raised. Most of the conclusions in previous research about the nondenominational have been inferential: if Jews do not identify religiously, they are lost to the community. Nondenominationalism is an indicator of (or a first step toward) total assimilation.

The evidence does not confirm this inference. The causal connections between nondenominationalism and other social processes are difficult to establish. In particular, nondenominationalism is linked to life cycle changes. Hence, higher rates among the young do not necessarily imply generational decline, but life cycle effects which will change as the young marry and have children. Most important, there is no systematic relationship between nondenominationalism and the variety of communal and ethnic ties characteristic of the Jewish community.

The incomplete and limited data which we have analyzed together with the body of previous cumulative research lead to the overall conclusion that there is much greater cohesiveness in the Jewish community than is often portrayed. It is consistent with the data (although beyond its power to confirm fully) that the Jewish community is characterized by multiple bases of cohesion. On both quantitative and qualitative grounds, the American Jewish community of the late twentieth century has a variety of sources of continuity. The changes and transformations over the last several decades have resulted in greater ties and networks among Jews. These connect Jews to each other in kinship relationships, jobs, neighborhoods, lifestyles, and values. Change—whether referred to as assimilation or acculturation—has reinforced ethnic-communal identification. The modernization of American Jews has been so far a challenge, not a threat, to continuity.

The longer-range question is whether these social networks and the emerging constellation of family, ethnic, and religious ties will persist as bases of cohesion for the Jewish community in the twenty-first century. How much secularization and erosion of traditional religious practices can occur without having a major impact on the Jewishness of the younger generation? Are the new forms of Jewish ethnicity able to balance secularization? Will the "return" to Judaism or the development of creative expressions of Jewish religious fellowship become the new core of generational continuity? These questions emerge from our study, although they cannot be addressed with any data available.

Nevertheless, the response to modernization as threatening, as the road to total assimilation and the end of the Jewish people, is not consistent with the evidence. The Jewish community in America has changed; indeed has been transformed. But in that process, it has emerged as a dynamic source of networks and resources binding together family, friends, and neighbors, ethnically and religiously. As a community, Jews are surviving in America, even as some individuals enter and leave the community. Indeed, in every way the American Jewish community represents for Jews and other ethnic minorities a paradigm of continuity and change in modern pluralistic society.

Chapter 13

The Social Foundation of Israeli Judaism

Shlomo Deshen

INTRODUCTION[1]

A great deal has been written on Israeli religious institutions, activities, and problems, but the treatment of the subject leaves much to be desired.[2] Many studies focus primarily on a specific topic within the subject—the relationship between the polity and religion as reflected in institutional arrangements.[3] But this problem is not coterminous with the subject as a whole. While the problem of relations between synagogue and state can be discussed as a formal constitutional problem, it cannot be understood sociologically, because it merely represents the tip of an iceberg, so to speak. The iceberg itself, still to be uncovered, consists of religious phenomena—the variegated activities of various groups whereby they relate to religious symbols. People engage in these activities in many ways, causing the emergence of various features of society, and the relationship between synagogue

[1]This essay was originally dedicated to the memory of Max Gluckman.—Eds.

[2]See Shelah, Harlap and Weiss (1971: 49–55) for an interesting, though not exhaustive bibliography; Singer (1967), Petuchowski (1971), and Zenner (1965*a*) for brief introductory accounts; for recent essays see Yaron (1975) and Liebman (1977).

[3]The following are just a few of the numerous studies on this problem: Birnbaum (1970), Rubinstein (1967), Goldman (1964), Eisenstadt (1967: 309–320), Don-Yihye and Liebman (1972), and Gutman (1972). For descriptions of the interrelations between politics and religion at the grass-roots level see Willner (1965), Aronoff (1973), and Deshen (1970).

and state is only one of them. Another limitation of present writing on religion in Israel lies in the bias whereby the Israeli situation is often evaluated according to a model of separation of church and state of the American or French type. Many writers demonstrate impatience and lack of sympathy when discussing the religious establishment and the current role of religion in the Israeli state.

There are also methodological reservations concerning the conventional use of the variable 'religion' in those Israeli studies that attempt a quantitative approach to the subject (see, e.g., Dittes 1973: 328–349; Robertson 1972). The survey analysts manipulate the variable by comparing crude categories, such as 'observant', 'nonobservant', and 'partly observant' (often incongruously termed 'traditional').[4] The categories are usually founded on the respondents' reports of their religious observances (for example, the number of periodic visits to the synagogue), and sometimes even on the respondents' self-assessment. Different respondents may invest a single concept, such as 'observant', with completely disparate meanings, and the researcher by lumping these together may create a category of dubious sociological significance. Antonovsky (1963) concludes that 30 per cent of the population is religious, 24 per cent irreligious, the bulk falling between the two extremes. Katz and Gurevitch (1973), in their more recent study, place only 20 per cent in the religious category, and their other extreme category also comprises a smaller number—16 per cent. Arian (1973) provides another set of figures differing in detail. Such data while informative are not very enlightening. Beyond the superficial quantitative information, we gain no insight into the nature and meaning of the respondents' religiosity or irreligiosity. Furthermore, even when the categorization is based on objective behavioral factors, such as figures on synagogue attendance, we may still be constructing deficient categories through failure to isolate the varied meanings people may attribute to a certain pattern of behavior. There is, of course, little point in looking for correlations that are based, at least in part, on spurious categories.

In this account, attempting to avoid some of the pitfalls of the existing approaches to the subject, I seek to contribute to a general sociological understanding of Judaism as it is currently evolving in Israel. I try to isolate the major patterns of religiosity which make up Israeli Judaism. In these patterns I include both the formally religious and those who define themselves as irreligious, heterodox, or agnostic. The rationale for this inclusiveness will become clear as I develop my argument.

In brief, I maintain that all the present patterns of Judaism in Israel are comparatively recent developments and in that sense they are nontraditional. This is as true for the orthodox as it is for the heterodox. On the other hand, these patterns all emerged from a common source of traditional Judaism. The various patterns differ in many subtle ways and, therefore, differences in quantitative observance, while present, do not adequately reflect this variety. To uncover the nature of people's religiosity necessitates drawing upon the insight that humanis-

[4]See Antonovsky (1963, 1972: 99–108), Arian (1973: 64–67), Herman (1970), E. Katz and Gurevitch (1973), Matras (1965: 66–73); also Weller and Tabory (1972) and Rim and Kurzweil (1965). See Weller (1974: 210–228) for a review of some of the work of this nature.

tic disciplines, such as history and social anthropology, can provide. Proceeding from the relevant background, I isolate the sectors of the Israeli population that evolved diverse religious patterns, and then continue by delineating the nature of these patterns.

THE DIASPORA BACKGROUND

Israel is mainly a society of immigrants. Discussing the religion of various social groups necessarily leads us to the recent past in their countries of origin where the present religious and cultural patterns emerged. A relevant categorization of Israeli Jews for the purposes of this discussion is that of immigrants from Christian countries and immigrants from Muslim countries. Numerically, the categories are more or less equal.[5] In terms of social status, however, immigrants from Christian countries predominate. The reason for this is that during the late nineteenth and early twentieth centuries immigration from Muslim countries lagged. A steady stream of immigrants from Europe kept coming to the country, whereas comparatively large numbers from the Orient immigrated only after 1948. Of the 70,000 immigrants who arrived during the first two decades of the twentieth century—crucially formative years for Israeli society—almost all were from Russian territories. This means that immigrants from Muslim countries, the Orientals as we shall now term them, came to a society whose institutions were already formed and were manned by immigrants of the earlier wave. Therefore, they had to adapt perforce, whether to a greater or to a lesser extent, to the institutions and norms they found in the new country. The crucial historical background of the society is thus that of the Europeans.

For many centuries, Jews had lived as corporate autonomous communities within Christian and Muslim societies.[6] The host societies were, of course, not mass societies of a democratic type, but societies in the line of contemporary premodern models. Living as Jews in these societies entailed many specific sociocultural features—such as making one's living along certain lines, having the choice of area of residence and friends delimited, the use of a particular language, having recourse to particular legal institutions, and many others. Thus, in addition to their own religious practices, Jews were engaged in many particular social and cultural practices, as were members of other strata of premodern society. Through the centuries, Jewish religion became intertwined with these practices, many of them gaining the legitimation and actual sanction of religion. Analytically, it is often very difficult to decide where in Judaism a religious practice ends and mere custom and social exigency begin.

[5]This estimate is based on the findings of Peres (1976) who, on the basis of data from 1969, extrapolated the proportions of the population originating in Europe and in Muslim countries. According to his study, the respective figures are 51.7 per cent and 48.3 per cent. They include Israeli-born descendants of the immigrants.

[6]In the historical resume that follows, I am indebted to the works of Jacob Katz (1968, 1973) and his pupil Moshe Samet (1969, 1970).

This social situation has changed since the late eighteenth century. Premodern states evolved into mass societies whose tolerance for the legal and cultural autonomy of groups and strata was comparatively minimal.[7] In the course of these radical social changes, the status of members of Jewish communities has tended to be transformed from that of 'Jews' to that of 'citizens of the Jewish faith'. The transition implied the granting of universal rights while at the same time annulling ancient rights (such as autonomy in the dispensing of justice) pertaining to membership in the particular stratum of Jews. These ancient rights were, however, intertwined with the Jewish religion and Jewish social practices. To the Jews, the societies undergoing change posed acute and profound dilemmas. As ghetto walls began to crumble, Jews faced the predicament of reorganizing their lives in society at large. This process of political and social modernization of the Jews, or of 'the Emancipation' as it was called in the nineteenth century, started first in Western Europe in the late eighteenth century, gradually moved to Central Europe, and much later to some of the Muslim countries. The process did not develop consistently and radically, however, as later events, culminating in the German massacre of European Jewry, tragically attest. Powerful social forces from both sides of the old ghetto walls—the Jewish and the Gentile—operated to obstruct the total dismantling of partitions. But the social, cultural, and religious problems inherent in the terms of the Emancipation faced all Jews.

The various responses to these problems constitute the core of the internal Jewish conflicts of modern times. To understand the current Israeli religiocultural situation, we must follow the main trends of the clashing Diaspora responses that have been carried over into latter-day Israel. They all grapple with the root problem of outlining Jewish positions on the question of assimilation to Gentile society on the one hand, and the question of adherence to traditional Jewish life on the other. While the two are mutually exclusive, and some circles opted for a stand on one side or the other, many chose to make for themselves an ideological and existential niche at some place along the continuum between the extremes. The varied responses, far from being abstract philosophical exercises, entailed grappling with acute personal problems concerning life-styles and practices. They were programs for mapping out one's existence on many levels, practical and ideological: in worship, in one's choice of occupation, in the company of strangers, and in one's kitchen. Some of these programs were carried over more or less intact by immigrants to the new society. Three major trends of Diaspora responses are notable: (1) nationalism, (2) neo-orthodoxy, and (3) orthodoxy.

The Jewish national movement, which in time came to be instrumental in the formation of the State of Israel, strove for the reconstitution of formal elements of national existence: primarily the return to the ancient homeland, the revival of the Hebrew language, and the creation of a stratum of farmers deemed essential for national existence. These aims became absolute values. The nationalists rejected the fundamental, traditional, G-d-centered, ideological rationale for Jewish exis-

[7] The vicissitudes of the modern Mennonites, even in the traditionally tolerant New World, are quite typical in this context.

tence. Their ideology was founded on the belief in a Jewish national genius that expressed itself through the ages in the craving for existence as a people. The precise nature of this genius and of Jewish identity generally were accepted as self-evident and consequently remained vague and confused.

On the plane of religious practice, nationalism, particularly that branch of the movement that came to dominate the Israeli scene after the early 1900s, combines radical antinomian tendencies with profound traditionalism. While the early nationalist pioneers who settled in Palestine were, in many ways, radically heterodox, they nevertheless transplanted many practices from their traditional Diaspora homes which they deemed compatible with their new roles and tasks as pioneers. Thus, the Jewish calendar with its cycle of festivals and Sabbath days continued, fundamentally, to regulate time. Traditional Jewish literary materials remained, albeit most selectively, the core of culture and schooling. Many religious practices, such as circumcision and food ritual (refraining from raising hogs and many similar matters) stayed in force. Through the use of the Hebrew language, numerous traditional symbols, sentiments, and association survived, though the symbols often underwent change and profanation. Even the essential utopian elements of traditional Messianism remained, and only the more unrealistic and supernatural beliefs were abandoned.[8]

Neo-orthodoxy, the second major Diaspora response to the nineteenth-century predicament, sought to divorce religious practices from other cultural elements of traditional Judaism. Religion was to be retained while many of the other elements, such as the restricted range of occupations, or the use of the Yiddish language, were to be discarded. Because of the age-old minimal differentiation of religion from other elements of culture, the task neo-orthodoxy set itself was highly problematic. The protagonists of neo-orthodoxy moved on the continuum, out of the ghetto toward modernity, as far as religion in the strictest sense of the word (barren of cultural appendages) permitted. They remained punctilious in their adherence to the practices of traditional religion as strictly defined. At the same time, the neo-orthodox accepted the dissolution of the ancient institutions, such as the autonomous judicial, political, and educational organs of the corporate communities. Immigrating during the 1920s and 1930s, the neo-orthodox strove for and welcomed the nationalist state. As religious nationalists, they participated actively in the roles and tasks of society, all the while remaining loyal to traditional Jewish religion as strictly defined.

One innovation of neo-orthodoxy is particularly notable in the context of the argument that I develop in this paper. In traditional Judaism the study of Torah ('the divine teaching'), in the form of talmudic literature, was a major act of religious merit. At the same time, it was also a standard cultural and leisure activity, and this had important ramifications in the areas of occupation, education, and the social life of traditional Jewry. In neo-orthodoxy, the worth that came to be attached to advanced technical training and to non-Jewish culture generally led to a deemphasis of the study of Torah as an act of value in itself. People engaged less

[8]For an insightful treatment of late nineteenth-century Jewish nationalism see Katz (1968).

in Torah study and devoted time to other cultural activities. This shift has never attained clear religious legitimation in neo-orthodox thought and has therefore remained a source of religious malaise that we shall come across again in our discussion. Neo-orthodoxy as a way of life also entails many problems in religious practice. I cite one broad range of problems. Traditionally, Jews did not normally engage in certain occupations, notably army and police service, farming, heavy industry, and the maintenance of essential public services (e.g., the provision of water and power). Inherent in all these activities are clashes with the norms of the traditional way of life and of religion specifically, as, for example, in matters of Sabbath observance. But religious nationalists, because of their commitment to the general society, do not want to shun these activities. Ways therefore are sought to adapt the practice of these occupations to religious norms, and rabbinical figures associated with the movement grapple with the problems. But many remain intractable (see Fishman 1957; Singer 1967).

In orthodoxy, the third major Diaspora response to nineteenth-century problems, the traditional way of life, gains value as a total system for its own sake. As distinct from neo-orthodoxy, orthodoxy does not seek to isolate the specifically religious elements in tradition. It is a conservative movement in the full sense of the word, and at the same time a novel phenomenon in Judaism. In the traditional past, Judaism had been characterized by a precarious balance between this-worldliness and other-worldliness. At the side of the basic orientation to spiritual life there was high value, albeit qualified and delimited, placed on achievement in material matters and on secular scholarship. By the late nineteenth century, as a result of two major Jewish religious movements in Eastern Europe, Hassidut and Musar, the balance tilted in favor of spirituality and other-worldliness.

One of the concrete expressions of the shift in the world view of orthodoxy was in the area of traditional learning. In the traditional past, East European learning in Torah had had a standing roughly analogous to that of classical humanistic learning—a requisite for a self-respecting Jew—and, because of its religious importance, it was universally practiced at various levels. There existed a two-stage degree system operated by senior scholars (in a fashion again analogous to contemporary university honors). Specific religious roles, such as community rabbis, were esteemed and called for ranking scholars.

In latter-day orthodoxy, however, learning in Torah attained a more elevated, quasi-mystical standing. The theme of learning for its own sake, without thought of degree or professional reward, not to mention actual ulterior material and social motives, was emphasized with unprecedented force. In the context of Eastern European Jewish society, where traditional bonds were wearing thin, learning in Torah among the orthodox came to be conceived of as insurance that secured Judaism against erosion. Adults proceeded with their studies, practically unsupported, while raising their growing families, and self-privation among the orthodox became a familiar feature. A new variant of the Jewish religious ideal character, in the form of the unworldly and ascetic Torah scholar, relatively oblivious to professional and realistic elements in his study, thus became more and more common during the nineteenth century. At the same time, among the neo-orthodox, because of their increasing involvement in the modern economy and in modern culture generally, the study of Torah actually declined.

The vicissitudes of the old ideal of learning in Torah among various sectors of nineteenth-century Jewry lead us to a point of major importance. Both nationalists and neo-orthodox were ambivalent, although in different ways and to different extents, about traditional Judaism. To a certain extent, they dissociated themselves from tradition, whereas orthodoxy, notwithstanding its own considerable innovations, professed to perpetuate tradition and formulated a conservative ideology. The orthodox claim that it constitutes the main-road continuation of traditional Judaism has never been consistently challenged by protagonists of other Jewish trends. The neo-orthodox, in view of their relative situation in matters of Torah learning and the attainment of the new religious ideal, have always been apologetic and on the defensive vis-à-vis orthodoxy. Even the nationalists, repudiating much of tradition themselves, by and large accepted the orthodox claim to historical continuity. This means, in effect, that whatever one's views on tradition, only those of orthodoxy have the weight of subjective legitimacy.

While recognizing that about half the Israeli population stems from Muslim or Oriental countries, I have thus far focused on the background of that half of the population which originated in Europe. There is justification in this up to a point, because the Orientals, mostly latecomers to the country, have not had a formative impact on most of the institutions of Israeli society. By and large, these immigrants came from traditional communities, such as in Iraq, Morocco, Iran, and Tunisia, which were only beginning to disintegrate socially and culturally at the time of emigration. Although the traditional Jewish background of communities from both Europe and the Muslim Orient is similar in many ways (see Katz 1960), there are salient differences between the immigrants of European and of Oriental origin. The reason for this lies primarily in the time lag between the occurrence of events, which in themselves were not entirely disparate, in Europe and in the Orient—the disintegration of traditional Jewry in the West started in the eighteenth century, while the same process in Muslim countries, specifically in Algeria and in Turkey, began over a century later. In many Muslim countries, traditional Jewry remained viable well into the present century and in some regions, such as the Yemen and parts of the Maghreb, it remained so right up to the time of emigration.

The European religiocultural movements that have concerned us—nationalism, neo-orthodoxy, and orthodoxy—are the organized and studied responses of people who experienced the crumbling of their societies gradually and while mostly still located in their old homes. Oriental immigrants, however, while abroad, hardly sensed the problems and constraints that aroused these particular movements.[9] Innovative Jewish religious movements were almost nonexistent in Muslim countries, where the Zionist movement emerged late and then only embryonically in a few communities that were beginning to disintegrate culturally, most characteristically in Iraq (see Cohen n.d.). Therefore most Oriental Jews, upon

[9]See Sharot (1974) for further considerations in support of the conception that Oriental immigrants constitute a disparate sociocultural category.

immigrating to Israel in the 1950s, were catapulted into a cultural situation much more secular, heterogeneous, and problematic than they had previously experienced. The religious reaction of Oriental immigrants to this situation is discussed in the final section of this paper.

THE ISRAELI BACKGROUND

On the current Israeli scene, nationalism, neo-orthodoxy, and orthodoxy are the three major contributions of European Jewry to Israeli Judaism. Oriental Jewry has contributed a fourth distinctive pattern. Each of the four patterns is adhered to by a whole range of groups distinguished by other detailed and subtle religious distinctions. These must, of course, be considered in a full treatment of Israeli religion. But from a broad cultural and historical perspective, the four patterns that I have isolated are crucially distinct, and for the present I deliberately eschew details that might blur the main outlines of the picture.

In Israel the names and labels of the various religious patterns change constantly, while the essential phenomena remain stable. A sociological understanding of current Israeli Judaism demands the elucidation of the characteristics of these religious patterns and of their mutual relationships. The three European movements emerged finally on the Israeli scene during the 1920s in the form of social movements cum political parties. The orthodox position was represented by the Agudat Yisrael party, the nationalist by the nationalist, so-called secular Zionist, parties, and the neo-orthodox by the Mafdal party. The neo-orthodox position, as organized in the Mafdal party, was also nationalist-Zionist. But it was a complex, hyphenated position—it was both nationalist and neo-orthodox. I choose to discuss the Mafdal position under the neo-orthodox label because that is where its distinctiveness lies, whereas the other nationalists are much more radically removed from tradition, and often consider themselves socialist Zionists. The Orientals have not consistently organized themselves for political action. During the prestate period, attempts of this nature were somewhat sustained. In recent decades, the attempts have become ephemeral, and the Orientals participate in the various political parties that have emerged from the European social and religious movements.

Numerically, the adherents of the various religious patterns are very disparate. One can obtain a very rough idea of their relative numbers from general election returns, keeping in mind the limitations of such a survey analysis. The Agudat Yisrael party usually wins about 5 per cent of the general Jewish vote, a figure that more or less represents the actual percentage of the orthodox in the population; Mafdal usually gains about 10 per cent, probably the optimal figure for Israeli neo-orthodoxy.[10] I estimate that the rest, the 85 per cent returned by the

[10]Mafdal draws a great deal of its support from the Oriental electorate, which represents a different religious pattern from that of the neo-orthodox. On the other hand, some neo-orthodox people support nonreligious parties. The latter are, however, much fewer than the Orientals who vote for Mafdal. Therefore the 10 per cent figure I have given tends, if anything, to be exaggerated.

nonreligious parties, is drawn more or less equally from the Oriental and the nationalist sectors. This places the Oriental and the nationalist figures each at around 40 per cent of the population. The smallness of the orthodox and neo-orthodox figures should not lead us to underestimate the intrinsic importance of the religious patterns they represent. Orthodoxy is recognized as carrying the weight of legitimate Jewish tradition, and as will become clearer below, this gives the views of orthodox circles an importance disproportionate to their numbers.

In contrast with the immigrant background of the 'secular' and Mafdal parties, the core of Agudat Yisrael lies in the ancient traditional Jerusalem community that preceded the nationalist immigration. Both Agudat Yisrael and Mafdal were rather weak parties during the prestate period: Agudat Yisrael because of its lack of involvement and its self-insulation from the nationalist immigrant movements that exerted themselves in laying the foundations of the embryonic State; Mafdal because of its comparatively late appearance on the scene. The social life and culture of the country, owing to the revolutionary element in Zionism, had an antiorthodox and antitraditional atmosphere. Intolerance and impatience toward the observant, and particularly toward the Agudat Yisrael circles, were in the air. For their part, the Agudat Yisrael circles dissociated themselves from the nationalists and their political aims and institutions. They did not, for example, participate in the Jewish paramilitary defense force.

On the other hand, beginning in the late 1920s, a political partnership developed between Mafdal and most of the other major parties (the latter merging later to form the Labor party), all of which had a good deal in common as nationalist parties. The partnership was founded, *inter alia,* on a theological legitimization developed by Rabbi Kook, a spiritual figure of great stature who associated himself with Mafdal. The major parties were not averse to religion in the neo-orthodox form, and this had one particularly important ramification: the institutionalization of the Chief Rabbinate. During the state period, the Chief Rabbinate was to become an important institution. Yet in the 1920s and 1930s, although the newly created office was manned by as impressive a personality as Rabbi Kook, it was weak and ineffectual. One can hardly speak of the Chief Rabbinate of that period as an authority; it was accepted only by the small Mafdal circle then beginning to strike roots in the country, ignored by the secular circles, and vociferously opposed by the orthodox.[11]

The effective opposition of the orthodox to Rabbi Kook and the Mafdal circles is particularly notable on the following issue. Rabbi Kook and the Mafdal circles repeatedly tried to establish a seminary for the training of rabbis of modern outlook, as the neo-orthodox had done in the Diaspora. Their efforts were thwarted by Agudat Yisrael rabbis, who fought for the supremacy of their conception of the rabbinical role, but the issue has remained alive. When later, in the 1950s, the religious Bar-Ilan University was founded by Mafdal circles, the orthodox again ensured that the university, paradoxically, would not establish a school of rabbin-

[11]For accounts of the Chief Rabbinate see Friedman (1972) and Morgenstern (1973).

ics. In contrast with Mafdal, Agudat Yisrael rabbis have crucial institutionalized powers as members of the party's Council of Torah Sages, which has the decisive voice in the party's general policy and concrete decisions. Not infrequently does the council figure as a rival to the Chief Rabbinate. The views and decisions of its rabbis also often echo in Mafdal circles, and, though not always accepted, they cause uneasiness and soul-searching.

Agudat Yisrael's greater influence is not rooted in any substantial socio-economic or political power. To a small extent, it derives from the capability of the orthodox circles to rouse emotional demonstrations of various kinds (sometimes peppered with a little violence). More fundamentally, however, it lies in Mafdal's basic lack of self-confidence, or 'weakness of nerve', derived from the problem of religious legitimacy. The Mafdal failure on the issue of rabbinical training has perpetuated the problem, and, until very recently, religious nationalist circles have by and large not trained their own leaders. More often than not, Mafdal-associated rabbis receive their training and religiosocial outlook from orthodox scholars in *talmudei torah*, *yeshivot*, and *kolelim*, rabbinical seminaries of varying levels oriented toward Agudat Yisrael circles. Some of the most senior of their scholars are members of the Council of Torah Sages. Naturally the graduates of the yeshivot often look back over their shoulders to their alma mater when deciding on controversial matters.

The social life of Mafdal people during the 1930s and the 1940s had a good deal in common with that of other nationalists. They intermingled as neighbors in many localities throughout the country, particularly in the growing towns and in the larger villages that were beginning to lose their rural character. Religious observance in these localities, insofar as it did not concern practice upon which everyone agreed, tended largely to be a matter for the individual. Mafdal circles as such were not very forceful in pressing—certainly not in pressing successfully—religious policies. In localities with large, concentrated orthodox communities, particularly in Jerusalem, it was different. Here the Agudat Yisrael circles struggled with the secular parties over the religious and cultural character of public life. Demonstrations, at times agitated and at times more restrained, over such issues as the desecration of the Sabbath in public, the opening of modern schools, and the enfranchisement of women, were endemic.

In the sphere of educational activities, there also were notable differences among the various social circles. The nationalist circles developed a modern schooling system in which biblical literature played an important, but far from major role. The schools sought to provide a broad, diversified curriculum, but in matters of religious practice, they inculcated indifference (and sometimes an actively antireligious attitude). While basically all nationalist schools were structured similarly, Mafdal circles created a network of schools that differed on two counts: traditional studies were quantitatively more prominent (but again not predominant), and religious practice was actively taught and encouraged. Agudat Yisrael circles, by and large, carried on and developed the traditional schools (the *talmud torah*, *yeshiva*, and *kolel*) with their paramount emphasis on talmudic studies. The rift between the educational patterns of the orthodox and the neo-orthodox is in many ways deeper than that between the educational patterns of the neo-orthodox and nationalists. This rift has profound religious ramifications.

Examining the Agudat Yisrael educational pattern in greater detail will lead us to an understanding of some of the crucial characteristics of orthodox and neo-orthodox religiosity.

THE ORTHODOX PATTERN

As Israeli secularism grew through nationalist immigration during the first decades of the century, the traditional schooling system became ideologically buttressed by a new conservative ideology, causing it to react to innovations. At a time when schools everywhere were becoming sensitive to the need for technical training, Agudat Yisrael educators were reluctant to introduce changes in the traditional curriculum. It is probably because of the social insulation of Agudat Yisrael circles that their youth accepted the limitations of the curriculum. Consequently, the Agudat Yisrael circles were quite successful in perpetuating themselves through their schooling system. Mafdal circles, on the other hand, apparently withstood secularism less successfully; during the 1930s and 1940s, many of their youth abandoned religious practices and joined the other nationalist circles. Since the mid-1940s, in the wake of two very dramatic events—the German massacre of European Jewry and the attainment of Israeli independence—much of that has changed. While the more profound effects of the European massacre on Jewish religion and spirituality still remain to be explored, the following crucial development is clear.

At the end of World War II, the major remnants of European Jewish orthodoxy were in eastern Hungary and in Romania. In the past, most of this region had constituted one Jewish culture area, a bastion of orthodoxy that had a history of acute conflict with other trends of modern Judaism (Katz 1974). Hungarian Jews, vociferously anti-Zionist, were now driven to migrate. Many came to Israel where they joined both the old Jerusalem community and new religious communities (such as the Tel Aviv suburb of Benei-Brak). Israeli orthodoxy thus came to include a new and aggressively conservative element, people whose conservatism was compounded by the experience of having seen their communities shattered and who now strove to reconstruct them in emulation of the past.

The events in Europe also prompted many of the surviving orthodox rabbis and talmudic scholars to move to Israel and to establish numerous yeshivot and kolelim, institutions of advanced talmudic learning, in various localities throughout the country, including the new towns founded by the nationalists. The combination of an immigrant rabbinical leadership of ranking stature and the Hungarian immigration elicited much religious vitality. The new yeshivot flourished quantitatively and qualitatively, attracting increasing numbers of students, so many that yeshivot now perforce sometimes reject applicants, contrary to all traditional practice.[12] The new Israeli yeshivot have become the world center of traditional Jewish learning, taking over from the Lithuanian and Polish yeshivot which had filled this role before World War II. They are looked up to by observant Jews throughout the world and even attract students from communities—such as in New York—which are themselves major centers of traditional learning. The yeshivot are the core of orthodoxy, and their flourishing is one of the most crucial features of Israeli Judaism. Characteristically, the yeshivot, while maintaining high academic standards, practice talmudic scholarship in a completely traditional way, consciously shunning modern scholarship in the field.

The scholars of the yeshivot are concerned with religious problems in a manner that is a continuation of their nineteenth-century Lithuanian and Polish forebears. There are considerable productivity and publication in the discussion of problems of ritual, custom, and law, both in the abstract and in the context of present-day technological and social contingencies. The work of ranking yeshiva scholars has relevance for Israeli society generally because the rabbinical courts, which exercise religious law (*halakha*), have exclusive jurisdiction over marital affairs. The ultimate interpretation of religious law, while theoretically resting with the Mafdal-oriented Chief Rabbinate, in fact resides to a very considerable extent in the hands of eminent scholars of yeshiva circles. Members of the High Rabbinical Court pay attention to the informally expressed opinions of these scholars, despite their lack of formal authority. Though there are ancient historical precedents to this kind of mutual regard among rabbinical authorities, in Israel it is also nurtured by the disparity in legitimacy and self-assurance between orthodox and neo-orthodox interpreters of tradition.

The most recent development, within the last few years, is a tendency for yeshiva-oriented rabbis to gain dominant positions within the Chief Rabbinate itself. In this context it is notable that the yeshiva scholars have a tendency to interpret halakhic requirements, in many different areas, in increasingly strict and unequivocal terms.[13] Consistent with this tendency is the new, occasional practice of Israeli halakhic authorities to substantiate their rulings by declaring them to be authoritative *da'at Torah* (Torah Wisdom), along a pattern reminiscent of Catholic pontifical ex cathedra pronouncements. Traditionally, halakhic rulings, even when handed down by most eminent authorities, would always have been annotated with the rational explication of pertinent legal considerations and would consequently have been open for discussion.

Traditionally, abstract religious thought has not been consistently emphasized in Judaism; it is therefore not unusual that the productivity of yeshiva scholars in this area is comparatively poor. Given this background, the fair amount of productivity in the area of ethnics is notable; a small number of new moralistic works appears constantly. The social scope of the works emanating from yeshiva

[12]In 1973 some 15,600 male adults and boys were reported studying in orthodox yeshivot; of these 5,400, who presumably have their own dependent families, were in kolelim. See Ministry of Religious Affairs (1974) as a source for these, and other, data cited below.

[13]See Rabinowitz (1971) and M. Elon (1973: 22–28) for descriptions of this tendency through analyses of the mutations of legal opinion of particular scholars over particular issues.

circles is, however, largely restricted to orthodox circles. The halakhic tracts, insofar as they are not juridical or concretely textual, mainly discuss matters that are only of concern to strictly observant people. The ethical works are even more restricted. They mostly focus on the problems of the yeshiva student, not on the mundane problems of the observant after termination of his full-time studies.

Yeshiva circles constitute in many ways an enclosed, self-sufficient subculture. Terms such as 'religious order' and 'monasticism', while only grossly approximate, do denote some of the features of most Israeli yeshiva circles. Characteristic is a feeling of corporateness and difference from other people and a powerful sensation of superior religious status that sometimes expresses itself in actual haughtiness. This feeling evolved from the shift, previously noted, in nineteenth-century Eastern European Judaism toward other-worldly spirituality. Yeshiva culture often nurtures the Yiddish language of traditional Europe. Although foreign to many students, they pick up the language in the course of their studies, at least to the extent that they can follow lectures. But even the common Hebrew speech of yeshiva students has many particular characteristics, both in vocabulary and in pronunciation, making yeshiva Hebrew rather distinctive. These peculiarities derive from the Yiddish language, frequently used in scholarly and daily discourse, and the Aramaic language of the talmudic texts. Yeshiva students dress almost uniformly—dark suit and hat, and white shirt usually with a dark tie. This kind of attire, immaculate and formal, considering Israeli culture and the country's subtropical climate, renders yeshiva students a highly visible and self-conscious group.

The distinctiveness of yeshiva life also reaches into the sphere of marital and household activities. Owing to the consistent traditional segregation of the sexes at all stages of socialization, marital bonds are formed through the traditional mode of matchmaking. Ties are thus established not only between orthodox couples in Israel, but between people living in Israel and in orthodox communities overseas as well. The strong hold of yeshiva life on the students also molds the structure of the family. The wives very often are as keen as their husbands that the latter continue their studies indefinitely. Consequently, a pattern has developed whereby the wife is the main breadwinner through such work as elementary school teaching. At the same time, little family planning is practised, so that families grow very fast. Because of the wife's occupation, the husband is much involved in child care, probably comparatively more than in the traditional Jewish family. The students receive only very small stipends, so that the general standard and style of life in yeshiva circles is modest, sometimes virtually ascetic. Gradually, most of them are driven by financial need and domestic pressures to terminate full-time, and eventually part-time, studies and to move into teaching, commerce, or lower-grade clerical work. Socially and culturally, however, they maintain many of their characteristics, and their lives continue to revolve around the yeshivot and their spiritual leaders.

Agudat Yisrael circles also include a handful of people who, despite the drawback of not having received a higher secular education, have attained relatively advanced positions in the economy. They have also attracted a trickle of American and Western immigrants of neo-orthodox background (some of them in advanced professional positions), who, with immigration, shifted their religious orientation. Their numbers, however, are not very significant, and, more crucially, these people submit to the religious authority of the yeshivot.

The relative insulation of yeshiva circles from broad social concerns and cultural trends is fostered by two major factors: exemption from army service and the structure of yeshiva finances. Yeshiva students serve in the army only to a very limited extent, or not at all. The yeshiva heads, supported by the religious parties, have insisted on exemption for their students, their feeling being that military service would expose the students to cultural and social influences which might eventually lead them to move away from yeshiva life.[14] It can be assumed that the present flowering of yeshivot in Israel is linked to the military service exemption that yeshiva students can enjoy.[15]

The insulation of yeshiva circles is further reinforced by the structure of yeshiva financing. The main source of funds generally rests with the philanthropy of American and Western orthodoxy. Distance and the relative anonymity of the benefactors render the yeshivot rather independent in the management of their affairs; a fact that, most significantly, sponsors a sense of separation and self-sufficiency vis-à-vis the immediate Israeli environment. Although the Israeli government is in fact an important financial source of support, it does not have actual controlling power or even much influence over the yeshivot, as the case of exemption from military service shows. The government grants support only because of the political power of the religious parties that back the yeshivot, and its concessions probably do not stem from a conviction of the moral right of yeshiva circles to preferential treatment. As a result of this situation, yeshiva circles do not feel obligated to the government—at the most, perhaps, to the Mafdal party that sustains the concessions. Plagued by its fundamental lack of self-assurance, Mafdal, far from controlling the yeshivot, is, in fact, much under their influence. The peculiarities of yeshiva financing and the minimal civic participation of latter-day yeshiva circles cultivate in them a tendency to aloofness and lack of rapport with society. These characteristics are again rooted in the particular spiritualistic and other-worldly turn that Eastern European Jewish religiosity took in the nineteenth century.[16]

I have emphasized the importance of the new yeshiva circles in Israeli orthodoxy. They are distinctive in having been formed by recent immigrants who are involved in the mainstream of the nationalist economy. Characteristically, the new yeshiva circles are centered in the Tel Aviv area, the dynamic economic and

[14]See Horowitz and Kimmerling (1974) for a discussion on the important function that Israeli military reserves service plays in social integration.

[15]This assumption is based on my impression that orthodox circles in Western countries, which otherwise have much in common with their Israeli counterparts, maintain comparatively few yeshivot and kolelim and provide for a much shorter yeshiva education. Their youth move quite soon either into commerce or to studying a profession.

[16]My very informal, comparative impressions of yeshiva circles in Israel and in Britain lead me to the conclusion that in Britain, where the yeshivot are in close rapport with their sources of munificence, relations with the community are generally much closer, and yeshiva circles are not as clearly delimited, culturally and socially, from other sectors of the community.

social center of the population, and they are more consistently militant as conservatives than their older Jerusalem counterparts. Many features of the Israeli rabbinate that have been pointed out by both neo-orthodox and secular critics, particularly the limited concern with social and moral issues in contrast with the preoccupation with ritual and legal matters (see Singer 1967 and many others), can be traced to the rabbis' personal roots in yeshiva circles. The phenomena are only deceptively exotic; they lie on the main road of present-day Israeli Judaism.

THE NEO-ORTHODOX PATTERN

The reassertion of orthodoxy is contemporaneous with comparable developments in the neo-orthodox circles. In the past, Mafdal adherents had intermingled with nonobservant Jews as neighbours and had educated their children in schools only marginally different from those of their neighbors. Since the late 1940s, a tendency has developed in Mafdal and Agudat Yisrael circles to draw together and establish their own residential housing projects. Thus, at a time when the general population multiplied greatly, the observant population of many localities remained constant or decreased, while in a few localities it increased to such an extent that these gained the characteristics of religious quarters.

Specific religious problems rooted in Judaism underwrite the preference of the observant for a neighborhood of people of their own kind. An observant person would prefer to live among neighbors who, for instance, do not drive, play the radio loudly, or smoke in public on the Sabbath, and who do not dress in a way he considers immodest. It is striking that the observant have become more sensitive in these matters. People who lived in religiously mixed neighborhoods in the 1930s and 1940s moved during the period under discussion to comparatively homogeneous localities, or at least to localities where there were large communities of the observant.

Another recent development, in the sphere of schooling, is a new network of Mafdal-oriented educational institutions which competes with the old Mafdal network. The new network comprises 'high school yeshivot' (boarding schools for the high school grades) which, as the name implies, have much in common with the Agudat Yisrael yeshivot in matters of curriculum and religious atmosphere. The high school yeshivot also offer a program of secular studies leading to matriculation. Secular studies, however, are considered necessary only to the extent that matriculation examinations require them. The inculcation of culture and values, insofar as it is effected by the school, is carried out exclusively through the religious program. Secular culture and studies are deemphasized and largely denuded of cultural and educational value. Since the early 1950s, the high school yeshivot have attracted increasing numbers.[17] At first, the new schools were for

[17]The following figures convey an impression of quantitative growth: in 1954 only 700 boys studied in high school yeshivot; in 1963 the number was 3,453; and in 1973 it was 7,455 (Ocks 1973). It should be noted that these figures isolate, to a certain extent, the factor of general population growth, because the bulk of immigration came before the period covered by these figures. Also, Oriental immigrants, who constitute the majority of immigrants in recent decades, are underrepresented in the new schools. These figures, therefore, indicate a true shift in neo-orthodox educational patterns.

boys only, but in the 1960s demand for parallel schooling for girls led to the establishment of institutions of the high school yeshiva type for girls.[18] The most recent trend in Mafdal education is the extension of the yeshivot network to cover the younger ages—boys aged twelve to fourteen. At the senior pole of the new Mafdal network, new advanced yeshivot have been founded, and they attract some of the graduates of the high school yeshivot.

The new advanced yeshivot also have much in common with the traditional yeshivot of Agudat Yisrael circles. The major difference between the two is that the Mafdal yeshivot have an arrangement with the military authorities whereby their students serve in the army, and can periodically, during their term of conscription, resume yeshiva studies. This arrangement has significant implications relevant to personal life-styles. Presently, 1,200 students are reported studying in the Mafdal-oriented advanced yeshivot.

With the rise of this new, comparatively traditional educational network, the older Mafdal educational system has stagnated, particularly at the high-school level. The old system laid more stress on the secular curriculum and the general educational emphasis was also more secular. A natural process of selection has now developed whereby, to put it very generally, academically superior students study in the new network, and inferior students in the old network.[19] This trend in education among the neo-orthodox is of major import. It implies a consistent move in Israeli neo-orthodoxy toward the religious and cultural patterns of orthodoxy. It is linked with the failure of the old Mafdal schooling system of the 1930s and 1940s—relative to the Agudat Yisrael yeshivot—in its aim to produce religiously observant graduates similar to the parent generation. The shifts in educational and neighborhood preferences are also linked with the basic trauma of recent Jewish history, the destruction of European Jewry. The zest for spiritual, cultural, and social experimentation has consequently abated, and instead people increasingly seek existential moorings in practices they consider to have been vindicated by time. The current developments express a reassessment of values, and more profoundly, to use Gilbert Murray's phrase, a neo-orthodox 'failure of nerve'.

The graduates of the new Mafdal system and those whom it has influenced evince distinctive religious and cultural characteristics. They are self-assured, confident, perhaps even self-satisfied, and their morale is high.[20] In this respect they have much in common with the orthodox yeshiva circles, and are distinct from their elders and other contemporaries. While from the point of view of religious practice the young Mafdal adherents are similar to, or slightly more observant than, their parents, their theoretical conception of the role of religion in society is radically different. The young Mafdal people coalesce politically as a vigorous faction (named the 'Young Mafdal') within the Mafdal party. They believe

[18]In the old Mafdal schooling system the sexes were usually not segregated.

[19]The new institutions, because of the comparatively large number of candidates, are able to select their students through entrance examinations. Secondary schools of the older type are usually reduced to accepting most applicants. There is also a marked tendency for students of European background to study in the new network and for students of Oriental background to study in the old network.

[20]For a profile of a student in a high school yeshiva see Herman (1970: 152–165).

that religious (halakhic) considerations should be consistently explicated and be made to penetrate all areas of public life, most of which are presently governed by purely pragmatic or secular considerations. They seek to explicate and to formulate the requirements of religious law in areas such as foreign policy, labor relations, and social welfare. The ideal is to have a specifically religious foreign policy, religious labor relations, and a religious social welfare policy, and they strive to realize these policies in practice. Yet despite their extreme religious orientation in public affairs, people of the Young Mafdal circles maintain a personal Jewish life of neo-orthodox cast: religion plays a delimited, circumscribed role, and it does not dictate as many aspects of daily life as among Agudat Yisrael-oriented yeshiva circles. Personally, the Young Mafdal are well attuned to nonobservant persons and secular living in the modern style,[21] but at the same time they have moved far in the direction of orthodoxy as a public position. They maintain closer ties with rabbinical figures than do their elders, and they take more serious note of rabbinical views in their politics, in a manner reminiscent of the Agudat Yisrael attitude to the Council of Torah Sages. The Young Mafdal are intransigent and 'hawkish' in terms both of relations between the state and religion and of external affairs, constituting the extreme right wing in the current political spectrum. On territorial issues, their position is far more uncomprising than that of most leading orthodox rabbis or their elders. While extremist positions in external and internal affairs can be rooted in secular considerations of *realpolitik*, the Young Mafdal's views are, in fact, religiously motivated. These views, passionately propagated through reference to a wealth of religious symbols—the divine promise, the holiness of the land, and so on—and through concrete biblical associations with particular localities, are an essential element of the particular new pattern of Israeli Judaism evolved by the Young Mafdal. Remarkable indeed is the contrast with the views of most rabbinical authorities who, while cognizant of the symbols that fire the Young Mafdal, interpret them in more ambiguous terms.

The Young Mafdal circles, as a religious phenomenon, represent a development within Israeli Judaism that awaits full elucidation. Tentatively, I suggest following interpretation: The Young Mafdal positions, consisting in the explication of religious requirements for new areas of life (and within this context their intransigent stand in external and internal affairs), are responses to the old neo-orthodox malaise—the sensation of religious shortcoming and questionable legitimacy. While the Young Mafdal positions are distinctly orthodox and conservative in character, these particular positions were never formulated by the orthodox themselves. These positions should be viewed in conjunction with the adoption of various cultural and educational traits from orthodox circles, as are seen in the new Mafdal educational system and the new residential pattern. Yet the Young Mafdal people are far from accepting the orthodox personal life-styles of yeshiva circles, and in many ways they oppose them. The phenomenon should be seen in terms

[21]See reports in the Hebrew press by the journalist Sylvy Keshet for some pugnacious and biased accounts of this aspect of Young Mafdal circles (Keshet 1969: 119–124). Despite these reservations, the material has some insight.

of a response to the old fundamental problem of Jewish neo-orthodoxy. It presents for the first time in many decades an offensive position vis-à-vis orthodoxy in that it is a combination of modern life-style in daily living and a radically orthodox ideology in public affairs. This combination can stake a claim for the legitimacy that has heretofore eluded the ideologists of neo-orthodoxy.[22]

THE NATIONALIST PATTERN

In contrast with the relatively small orthodox and neo-orthodox circles, the 'secular' nationalist circles, the third major pattern of Israeli Judaism, form a much larger and more complex sector of the population. The particular religious pattern of this sector was formatively influenced by Ahad Ha'am, a turn-of-the-century Zionist ideologist, whose views were paramount in nationalist circles for many decades.

The ideology of Ahad Ha'am contains profoundly traditional elements such as the concept of national election, the ideal of a stern morality, and many other points of traditional belief and practice. But the traditional elements have been loosened from their old theological moorings: national election is no longer divine election, and morality lacks the religious rationale. Ahad Ha'am set forth new, atheistic anchors for the traditional elements, such as the concept of 'the national spirit', which stems from late nineteenth-century positivist thought. It is the Jewish 'national spirit' that generates the people's view of its unique, elected destiny, creates its lofty moral teachings, and nurtures the attachment to the historical homeland. Ahad Ha'am catalyzed the fusion of tradition and heterodoxy that has come to be characteristic of Zionism. The way was thus cleared for the development of secularism which, paradoxically, is couched in traditional symbols and language. The Bible is prominent in the culture and education of Zionist circles, but its standing is of a national historical–literary heritage, not of a divine testament. Messianism, to take another example, is present in Zionist ideology, but its restraining transcendental anchor has been removed. Hopes and ideals, such as the idea that the Jewish State should eventually become a social model for universal emulation, are vital; but the national destiny is not seen in traditional religious terms.

The combination of a traditional symbolic idiom with a secular nationalist ideology led to religiosymbolic innovations. The nationalists reinterpreted many traditional symbols by infusing them with an atheistic–nationalist content. I cite just one example. At an Independence Day parade in the early 1950s, the following slogan was unfurled across the parade route: 'Israel, Trust in the Army! It is the Help and Shield!' This is a parody of a biblical verse (Psalms 115:9) that figures in the liturgy, where the object of trust is, of course, G-d and not the army.[23] Nation-

[22]For another approach to the Young Mafdal phenomenon see Liebman (1977).

[23]For further examples of profanation in the context of Ahad Ha'am's thought see Yaron (1975: 15–21).

alist circles engaged in symbolic innovations most consistently and creatively in the socialist *kibbutzim*. Here the traditional festivals were radically transformed. They were largely expurgated of their traditional religious content and became infused with new nationalist meaning, which is indeed present in tradition, but often in an understated idiom and always within a broader religious context. The relative importance of the festivals also changed in line with their potential for the expression of nationalist values. For instance, Hanuka, traditionally a festival of a markedly earthy nationalist character, attained increased and novel importance, whereas the Day of Atonement, traditionally the holiest of all days and the most transcendentally oriented, fell practically into desuetude.

The power to realize national aims now rests not in divine intervention, but exclusively in human action. The concrete needs of Nation and State have become the ultimate values. This equation is at the root of the symbolic innovations of nationalism where the nation now takes the place formerly held by Divinity. The equation of nationalism with ultimate values implies political and social ideas and policies that, if consistently developed, lead to étatist conclusions typical of modern nationalist movements in general.[24]

Since the attainment of independence, secular nationalism as an ideological and symbolic system has been on the decline. The new festivals of the nationalist circles flowered for only a comparatively short period, during the 1930s and the 1940s. Since then, people have been losing interest and some of the customs, including most of the agricultural rites, have been abandoned. Lilker (1973) describes in detail some of the ceremonies of what he calls 'kibbutz Judaism', their decline and transformation. In addition, Israeli literature of the last two decades expresses a malaise and gropes for values. The innocent assurance that characterized the prestate generation of nationalists seems gone. A whole range of attitudes populates the cultural spectrum—from destructive, and sometimes vulgar, nihilism, to an introspective and sensitive ethic—all having in common a sense of disillusion with classical nationalism of the Ahad Ha'am type.[25]

On the other hand, we find among secular nationalists a new attraction to activities such as archaeological research in Israel, which are by all accounts expressive of the quest for new existential and ideological bearings (see A. Elon 1971: 279–289).[26] We also often have traditional content being reintroduced into various areas of life, both on the public and private planes. In kibbutz Judaism, traditional content now frequently fills the vacuum left by the agricultural rites that lost their resonance. For one kibbutz we have a graphic description of this development (Kressel 1974: 44): until 1964 the members of the kibbutz celebrated

[24]See A. Elon (1971) for a pertinent general characterization of the Israeli nationalist 'founding fathers' and of their views on relations between Arabs and Jews.

[25]See the work of the literary critic Kurzweil (1966), and, on a more popular plane, that of Leslie (1971: 72–89) and of A. Elon (1971: 256–279). See Reich (1972) for a detailed account of the vicissitudes of Passover celebrations in kibbutzim.

[26]Max Gluckman pointed out that the current popularity of archaeology seems to be a wider phenomenon, which is common to many countries besides Israel, such as Britain. The explanation of the particular Israeli case may have a wider applicability.

the feast of Shavuot with a wagon procession displaying agricultural produce. The celebration culminated in the ceremonial donation of the produce to a public national fund. In 1966 the kibbutz held only an agricultural exhibition, and people gathered for a picnic. In 1969 and 1970 just a picnic was held; and in 1971, for the first time, a traditional religious theme was introduced—a lecture on Shavuot as the traditional anniversary of the giving of the Torah on Mount Sinai.[27]

Tendencies of this kind are also noticeable in other sections of the secular nationalist circles, for example, in middle class suburbs. Here one gains the impression that people increasingly celebrate rites of passage in synagogues in the traditional manner, which fewer would have done in the past. Many people tend to mill around synagogues, if not actually to attend services, on the Day of Atonement. Although completely disregarding religious norms in most contexts, they will revert to tradition in matters such as death and mourning. They will, more or less uncomplainingly, accept religious practice in various areas of life to the extent that it is required by Israeli law. Protest against the fusion of civil and halakhic law is limited to comparatively small groups, and is expressed inconsistently and in subdued form. At the same time, it is notable that modernistic religious movements, of such types as the American Jewish Conservative movement and Reform Judaism, have so far made little headway in Israel.[28] They have no more than a handful of congregations in the country (though more than existed before the State period). Quantitatively, there is no substantial trend toward acceptance of full orthodox or neo-orthodox patterns, although again, there have been individual cases in recent years.[29] Latter-day Israeli secular nationalism, as a form of Judaism, cannot be characterized unambiguously.

Also on the general societal level, ever since the formation of the State, we find nationalist ideologists and politicians turning to traditional religious sources, and traditional symbols now figure in various nationalist roles and activities. Thus, all State presidents since the presidential elections of 1952 have been conceived of as figures who, to an extent, exemplify Jewish tradition. The president's participation in synagogue worship and similar activities is well publicized,[30] and it would now be inconceivable for a president publicly to express atheistic views of the

[27]But see Rosner and Ovnat (n.d.) who argue that the religious trend exemplified by such symbolic changes is characteristic of the moderate, rather than of the extreme Marxist, wing of the kibbutz movement. The kibbutz described by Kressel is of the former type.

[28]These movements are basically structured to answer the needs of essentially traditional minority communities struggling against assimilation in the midst of hospitable majorities in Western countries (see Sklare 1955, for a sociological analysis of their emergence). It is not surprising that these movements have not struck roots among Israelis whose backgrounds are radically different (see also Zenner 1965*a*), as comparatively few of them originate in Western countries. There is, of course, also the factor of the inimical attitude of the Israeli rabbinical establishment whose administrative power has consistently stymied the modernistic movements. In its sociological context, this factor should, however, be seen as only secondary.

[29]See again Rosner and Ovnat (n.d.) for a balanced view of the background of such kibbutz cases.

[30]This is true even for incumbent President Katzir, who, by temperament and background, is personally much further removed from religious observance than his predecessors.

classical nationalist type. This would not, however, have been the case for Israeli leaders before independence, nor for Chaim Weizmann, the first president.[31]

These complex developments are still too fresh to afford us a complete assessment, but there are some overt explanatory factors. The successful attainment of the major Zionist aim with State independence fundamentally undermined the classical secular nationalist ideology, and the crisis was compounded with the disillusion and frustration inherent in any realized social vision. Another factor was the destruction of European Jewry during World War II. This catastrophe muted earlier Zionist criticism of the immediate past that was now irrevocably gone. Particularly the older generation, which remembers the fullness of prewar European Jewish life, has developed a new sentimental attachment to various bits and pieces of tradition.

The traditional ideas and folkways, moored in nineteenth-century positivism, which characterize nationalism of the classical Ahad Ha'am type, were now bolstered by unabashed sentimentalism. On the other hand, the practical exigencies of a vision that has essentially materialized have caused a mellowing and cutting to size of the messianic element in the ideology (see Decalo 1974). The nationalists' conception of statehood has been transformed into an instrumental goal whose ultimate aim is to provide a haven for all Jews. The decline of messianism in Israeli nationalism and the concomitant increasing realism have moral ramifications.[32] The destruction of European Jewry also sharpened the nationalists' awareness of their ties with Diaspora Jewry and of their need for moral and not only material support. The intensified consciousness of the Diaspora inevitably implies a heightened appreciation for traditional religion since it plays a central role in the existence of Diaspora Jewry.[33]

The eclipse of classical secular nationalism is contemporaneous with the reassertion of orthodoxy and with the Mafdal 'failure of nerve' that expressed itself in the Mafdal educational shift and in the phenomenon of the Young Mafdal. All these transformations occurred in the same environment and are fed by basically similar forces—primarily, the emotional upheaval stemming from the destruction of European Jewry; secondarily, the attainment of independence.

THE ORIENTAL PATTERN

On the scene characterized by the three broad religious and cultural movements that I have described appeared the masses of Oriental immigrants who came in the 1950s, after the establishment of the state. In sharp contrast to the European immigrants, the

[31]Liebman (1975), in a discussion of data of this kind from the aspect of general political integration, has suggested that there may be developing in Israel 'a civil religion' on the lines of Bellah's American counterpart. My analysis does not support that view.

[32]See Ben-Ezer (1974) for a collection of interviews, some of them very fascinating, on these themes and on secular nationalism in general; in particular see the interviews with Scholem and Alter. See also Har-Even (1970) and Rotenstreich (1965: 325–329); for a somewhat idealized profile of secular nationalist youth see Herman (1970: 165–177).

[33]See again A. Elon (1971: 198–215) for a description of present-day awareness of European World War II events.

Oriental newcomers, most of whom had escaped the trauma of German atrocities, did not experience in a searing personal way the situation that the Holocaust had brought about (despite, of course, their knowledge of the events). This is one of the crucial cultural factors that differentiates Oriental from European Israelis and is operative in the quite different courses subsequent religiocultural developments have taken among these two major sectors of the population.

Oriental immigrants have undergone a different but also very disturbing experience of their own, however, an experience rooted in their particular sociocultural situation: the abrupt, overnight transition from traditional life in backward Muslim societies to life in a confused, hectic, heterogeneous, and worldly new country. The immigrants had no ready solutions for the problems inherent in this situation. Worse, they were confronted with a range of solutions (outlined earlier) that European Jews had evolved long ago to cope with their own versions of those problems. The solutions, now in the form of specific socio-religio-political movements and patterns of living, were not tailored to the particular needs of the Oriental immigrants. The mere existence of these delimited solutions stultified the religious creativity of the Orientals which, given time, might otherwise have expressed itself in the formulation of their own original responses to the situation.

Oriental immigrants compose a large, complex population. For the purpose of this discussion, however, I view them within the frame of a single religious pattern, because the distinguishing sociohistorical factors considered above are crucial. These factors are paramount in molding the religious response of Oriental immigrants to their new environment. While there are differences within the Oriental pattern, they are not sufficiently clear-cut to warrant discussion on the same plane as those of the major patterns. As we shall see, a religious distinction may possibly be emerging between the first and the second generations of Oriental immigrants, but we do not yet have enough empirical research to argue this definitively.

In Israel, many of the Oriental immigrants became fascinated by the socioeconomic superiority associated with Western culture and by its external, more spectacular and vulgar expressions, such as the trappings of material affluence. Their exposure to the influence of mass media eroded their own variants of traditional culture. Moreover, the confrontation of the Oriental immigrants with the existing religious movements had overt political expression. The various political parties that represent these movements vied among themselves to attract the new Oriental and other immigrants. Because their background was so different from that of the Europeans, Oriental immigrants often failed to understand the genuine religious and cultural forces at the root of the political bickering that went on about them. The fundamentally cultural and religious issues were frequently interpreted, or misinterpreted, as pure struggles for power, and the overt religious policies as slogans manipulated cynically for political ends.[34] Traditional religion, consequently, lost much of its appeal.

[34]See my accounts of electioneering among the Oriental electorate (Deshen 1970, 1972), and particularly Deshen and Shokeid (1974: ch. 5) and Deshen (1976), where I document religious responses to this situation.

The gulf between the younger and the older generations of Oriental immigrants is now very deep. Generally speaking, the older generation retains very little prestige, and is often pathetically lacking even in self-respect. Sometimes the old religious leaders actually lose their flocks: new rabbis are elected and rabbis of the old generation move away to retire (Shokeid and Deshen 1977: Chap. 7). But in several studies of the religious life of first-generation Oriental immigrants, Moshe Shokeid and I have observed a series of assertive, creative activities that do constitute attempts to overcome the gulf between the old and the new. In the context of a religious pilgrimage, Shokeid describes the religious response of a group of Moroccan immigrants to a specific problem of reversal of status; and in a study on the emergence of mystical explanations for male barrenness he depicts the religious vitality that prompts people to interpret their new problems in religious terms (Deshen and Shokeid 1974: ch. 2, 4). In studies on memorial celebrations and synagogue ritual of Tunisian immigrants (*ibid:* ch. 3, 6, 7) and on publication activities of holy books (Deshen 1975), I have portrayed people's sensitivities to their new socioreligious creativity.

These religious responses, however, are a far cry from a real transmutation of tradition as represented by the religious movements of European Jewry, which evolved over several generations. Instead, they are altogether specific, serving to solve only the particular religious problems of the individuals and groups we describe. The rather tragic phenomenon of the first generation of traditional Oriental immigrants is transient because of the age factor. This is clearly visible. Oriental immigrants have established numerous synagogues throughout the country in which services were usually held twice daily. Over time, more and more synagogue communities find they cannot gather a quorum for weekday services because of the demise of old men, first-generation immigrants, who used to attend daily. Many of these synagogues now function only on the Sabbaths and during the festivals.

This brings us to the question of the religious character of second-generation Oriental immigrants. Very many younger Orientals attend synagogue services on the major festivals and at family festivities. Young people of Oriental origin are also prominent in religioethnic activities: Moroccans and Kurds in particular are active in revived pseudotraditional festivities peculiar to their traditions; Tunisians, Tripolitanians, and again Moroccans in pilgramages; Tunisians and Yemenites in the publication of traditional religious texts and journals. These activities express religious vitality, but, as in the case of parallel activities of the older generation, we must caution against attributing too much significance to them. They are not very frequent and attract comparatively few people. At the same time, adherence to religious practice among second-generation Oriental immigrants is manifestly decreasing.[35] Religion does not even play a dominant role in the

[35]This is also true for support on the part of Oriental immigrants for the religious parties. Etzioni-Halevy (1977, ch. 3) concludes, on the basis of survey materials, that 19 per cent of the Orientals aged over 50 support religious parties in contrast with 4 per cent and 7 per cent of Israeli-born and European-born, respectively, in that age category. In the category of those 20 to 34 years old, however, the percentage of support for religious parties drops to about 6 per cent among all subethnic categories.

maintenance of the subethnic identities of immigrant groups. To the limited extent that Oriental immigrants act to sustain subethnic identities, they more commonly use nonreligious vehicles, such as supporting local football teams (particularly among the Yemenite younger generation) and engaging in local ethnic politics.[36]

Orientals do not generally participate in the new Mafdal educational and residential trends: ecological mobility is not toward particularly religious neighborhoods, and Orientals do not send their children to the new religious educational institutions in very significant numbers. The proportion of Mafdal adherents of European background who send their children to be trained in the new system is much larger. Those of Oriental background more often tend to educate their children in the regular religious high schools whose overall demands are far less rigorous than those of the new high school yeshivot. While these differentials are also related to general socioeconomic factors, they cannot be reduced only to these. The differentials express an actual religiocultural variety and a real weakness of Oriental traditionalism in the Israeli situation.

This weakness can also be seen in the training of rabbis. The yeshivot, mostly founded by European scholars, foster the European variants of Jewish scholarship and religiosity. Oriental immigrants have established only very limited rabbinical training facilities. Consequently, the yeshivot produce many rabbis trained in the European tradition, and comparatively few rabbis in the Oriental tradition. Quite beside the dearth of Oriental-type training institutions, there is comparatively little demand among Oriental youth for advanced talmudic education. A fair number of students of Oriental background who are interested in rabbinical training, however, proceed to study in the more recently established yeshivot sponsored by Agudat Yisrael and Mafdal circles.[37] These students have become absorbed into the orthodox European yeshiva culture, sometimes to the extent of picking up the Yiddish language and even switching their particular ritual of prayer to the European ritual. In fact, they emerge from their studies more or less acculturated in European tradition. The opposite trend—European acculturation to Oriental religious traditions—does not exist. The present trend, while indicative of a potential avenue for the emergence of religious figures from among the Oriental immigrants, implies an adoption of European-style orthodox ways.

Parts of this evaluation of Oriental Judaism are supported by survey data.[38] Rakover, Yinon, and Arad (1971), in a study of religious observance among teenage girls attending religious high schools, found that girls of Oriental origin were less observant and less under the influence of their parents than were their European

[36]See Deshen (1974) for a discussion of the relationship between Israeli political ethnicity and religiocultural ethnicity, and Zenner (1967: 186) for a pertinent general evaluation. See Liebman (1977) for an approach to the phenomenon of Israeli football, also Klaus (1975).

[37]See Herman (1970: 187–193) for a sketch of a young Yemenite acculturated to Mafdal yeshiva circles.

[38]In view of the reservations expressed earlier concerning survey analyses in the area of religion, a word of explanation is in order. Our historical overview has led us to perceive Oriental Israeli Jews as having particular cultural problems; therefore the variable 'Orientals', despite its inclusiveness, does have salience, in contrast with some of the other variables that figure in these surveys.

counterparts. Herman (1970: 122–125), basing himself on a comparatively large general sample of Israeli youth, reached the same conclusion. Earlier, Bachi and Matras (in Matras 1965: 103–108) in a general sample of maternity cases compared the religious observances of women with the religious observances of their mothers. Again, significantly, greater intergenerational differences were found among the Oriental than among European women. Moreover, Matras found that among Oriental women, failure to observe religious practices was positively correlated to increasing education. This finding is typical of people in the throes of a general breakdown of tradition—modern education acting as a catalytic agent in that direction. Among European women, however, there emerged the obverse correlation: religious defection was found to be negatively correlated to increasing education in religious high schools.[39] This finding is, again, understandable in the context of the orthodox and neo-orthodox trends of European Israelis. In these trends, in contrast with traditional Judaism, religiosity is rooted not in natural ongoing practice, but in considered rationalized decision. Therefore, modern religious education, in this context buttresses rather than undermines observance. In the traditional Oriental context, on the other hand, modern education, even when religious, tends to undermine observance since its inherent nontraditional components clash with custom.

The data concerning correlations of education and religious observance have ramifications for a prognosis of future developments. Formal educational standards are steadily improving in Israel. It is, therefore, to be expected that observance among Orientals will progressively decrease whereas among Europens, exposed to more rigorous religious schooling, it will increase.

CONCLUSION

In contrast with many studies in the area of religion in Israel, I have not proceeded from overt religiopolitical issues to an examination of the political and ideological positions of the various disputants. The procedure in this essay has been of a cultural–anthropological nature. In reviewing the historical background, I uncovered the antecedents of some of the major contemporary religiocultural patterns. I then followed the historical courses of these patterns as they unfolded into the present, my aim being to uncover the ways in which people transmuted the various patterns according to which they had lived in the varying vicissitudes of their situations. My selection of patterns does not exhaust the detailed variety of Israeli religious groups. Subtle differences, subgroups, and variants exist within each of these major religious patterns.[40] But I am confident that the four patterns I have described constitute the major ones.

[39] It should, however, be noted that the findings of another survey (Arian 1973: 66–67) are less clear-cut on this point.

[40] For an elaboration of this variety see (in addition to the references in the text) on orthodoxy and neo-orthodoxy: Weiner (1969), Werblowsky (1960), and Friedman (1975); on secular nationalists Kurzweil (1953), Shafran (1973), and Jacobsen (1972); and on Oriental immigrants Zenner (1965b).

It is in the more detailed elaboration of the major patterns that the study of religion in Israel must proceed. The various sociopolitical organizations and groups whose cultural roots lie in these patterns vie with each other over religious issues. Their struggles, as mentioned at the outset, are the only aspect of Israeli Judaism that has attracted sustained scientific interest, and these have been reasonably well discussed The major tasks now confronting the sociology and anthropology of religion in Israel are to bring to light the subtle religious factors underlying these struggles, and thus to uncover the detailed variety of Israeli Judaism as a religious phenomenon.

REFERENCES

ANTONOVSKY, A. (1963). Political-Social Attitudes in Israel. *Amot*, 6: 11–22. In Hebrew.

ANTONOVSKY, A., and ARIAN, A. (1972). *Hopes and Fears of Israelis: Consensus in a New Society*. Jerusalem: Academic Press.

ARIAN, A. (1973). *The Choosing People: Voting Behavior in Israel*. Cleveland: Case Western Reserve University Press.

ARONOFF, M. (1973). The Politics of Religion in a New Israeli Town. *Eastern Anthropologist*, 26: 145–171.

BEN-EZER, E., ed. (1974). *Unease in Zion*. New York: Quadrangle Books.

BIRNBAUM, E. (1970). *The Politics of Compromise: State and Religion in Israel*. Cranbery, N.J.: Fairleigh Dickinson University Press.

COHEN, H. Y. (n.d.). *Zionist Activity in the Middle East*. Jerusalem: Zionist Organization. In Hebrew.

DECALO, S. (1974). Messianic Influences and Pragmatic Limitations in Israeli Foreign Policy. *International Problems*, 13: 373–382.

DESHEN, S. (1970). *Immigrant Voters in Israel: Parties and Congregations in a Local Election Campaign*. Manchester: Manchester University Press.

DESHEN, S. (1972). 'The Business of Ethnicity Is Finished!'? The Ethnic Factor in a Local Election Campaign, in A. Arian, ed., *The Elections in Israel 1969*. Jerusalem: Academic Press, pp. 278–304.

DESHEN, S. (1974). Political Ethnicity and Cultural Ethnicity in Israel during the 1960s, in A. Cohen, ed., *Urban Ethnicity*. Association of Social Anthropologists monograph 12. London: Tavistock, pp. 281–309.

DESHEN, S. (1975). Ritualization of Literacy: The Works of Tunisian Scholars in Israel. *American Ethnologist*, 2: 251–259.

DESHEN, S. (1976). Of Signs and Symbols: The Transformation of Designations in Israeli Electioneering. *Political Anthropology*, 1: 83–100.

DESHEN, S. and SHOKEID, M. (1974). *The Predicament of Homecoming: Cultural and Social Life of North African Immigrants in Israel*. Ithaca, N.Y.: Cornell University Press.

DITTES, J. E. (1973). Beyond William James, in C. Y. Glock and P. E. Hammond, eds., *Beyond the Classics? Essays in the Scientific Study of Religion*. New York: Harper & Row, pp. 291–354.

DON-YIHYE, E., and LIEBMAN, C. (1972). The Separation of Religion and State: Slogan and Content. *Molad*, 5 (n.s.): 71–89. In Hebrew.

EISENSTADT, S. N. (1967). *Israeli Society*. New York: Basic Books.

ELON, A. (1971). *The Israelis: Founders and Sons*. London: Widenfeld and Nicholson.

ELON, M. (1973). *Halakhic Problems in Israeli State Law*. Jerusalem: Hebrew University Institute of Contemporary Jewry. In Hebrew.

ETZIONI-HALEVY, E. (1977). *Political Culture in Israel*. New York: Praeger.

FISHMAN, A. (1957). *The Religious Kibbutz Movement: The Revival of the Jewish Religious Community*. Jerusalem: Zionist Organization.

FRIEDMAN, M. (1972). The Chief Rabbinate: An Insoluble Dilemma. *State and Government*, 1: 118–128. In Hebrew.

FRIEDMAN, M. (1975). Religious Zealotry in Israeli Society, in S. Poll and E. Krausz, eds., *On Ethnic and Religious Diversity in Israel*. Ramat Gan: Bar-Ilan University, pp. 91–111.

GOLDMAN, E. (1964). *Religious Issues in Israel's Political Life*. Jerusalem: Jewish Agency.

GUTMANN, E. (1972). Religion in Israeli Politics, in L. Landau, ed., *Man, State and Society in the Contemporary Middle East*. New York: Praeger, pp. 122–134.

HAR-EVEN, S. (1970). A Secular Talk. *Ma'ariv, Aug. 8. In Hebrew. Also in M. Samet, ed., Religion and State.* Jerusalem: Hebrew University Faculty of Social Sciences, pp. 100–103. In Hebrew.

HERMAN, S. N. (1970). *Israelis and Jews: The Continuity of an Identity.* New York: Random House.

HOROWITZ D. and KIMMERLING, B. (1974). Some Implications of Military Service and the Reserve System in Israel. *Archives Européennes de Sociologie,* 15: 262–276.

JACOBSEN, H. (1972). On the Social Structure of a Progressive Community in Israel. *Shalhevet,* 9: 4–6. In Hebrew.

KATZ, E., and GUREVITCH, M. (1973). *The Culture of Leisure in Israel: Patterns of Spending Time and Consuming Culture.* Tel Aviv: Am Oved. In Hebrew.

KATZ, J. (1960). Traditional Society and Modern Society. *Megamot,* 10: 304–311. In Hebrew.

KATZ, J. (1968). The Jewish National Movement: A Sociological Analysis. *Cahiérs d'histoire mondiale,* 11: 267–283.

KATZ, J. (1973). *Out of the Ghetto: The Social Background of Jewish Emancipation, 1770–1870.* Cambridge, Mass.: Harvard University Press.

KATZ J. (1977). The Uniqueness of Hungarian Jewry. *Forum* (Jerusalem). 2: 45–53.

KESHET, S. (1969). *An Arrow from Sylvy Keshet.* Jerusalem: Schocken. In Hebrew.

KLAUS, A. (1975). Corruption and Violence in Israeli Sport. *Crime and Social Deviance,* 3: 35–48. In Hebrew.

KRESSEL, G. M. (1974). *'From Each According to His Ability...': Stratification versus Equality in a Kibbutz.* Tel Aviv: Gome. In Hebrew.

KURZWEIL, B. (1953). The New 'Canaanites' in Israel. *Judaism,* 2: 3–15.

KURZWEIL, B. (1966). *Between Vision and the Absurd: Essays on our Twentieth-Century Literature.* Jerusalem: Schocken. In Hebrew.

LESLIE, S. C. (1971). *The Rift in Israel: Religious Authority and Secular Democracy.* London: Routledge & Kegan Paul.

LIEBMAN, C. (1975). Religion and Political Integration in Israel. *Jewish Journal of Sociology,* 17: 17–27.

LIEBMAN, C. (1977). Toward the Study of Popular Religion in Israel. *Megamot,* 23: 95–109. In Hebrew.

LILKER, S. (1973). *Kibbutz Judaism: A New Tradition in the Making.* Ph.D. diss., Hebrew Union College, Jewish Institute of Religion, New York.

MATRAS, J. (1965). *Social Change in Israel.* Chicago: Aldine.

MINISTRY OF RELIGIOUS AFFAIRS, ISRAEL (1974). *Report of Activities, 1973.* Jerusalem: Government Printer. In Hebrew.

MORGENSTERN, A. (1973). *The Israeli Chief Rabbinate: The Foundation and Organization.* Jerusalem: Shorashim. In Hebrew.

OCKS, D. (1973). A Particular Yeshiva Pattern, in H. Urmian, ed., *Education in Israel.* Jerusalem: Ministry of Education, pp. 311–316. In Hebrew.

PERES, Y. (1976). *Ethnic Relations in Israel.* Tel Aviv: Sifríat Hapoalim. In Hebrew.

PETUCHOWSKI, J. J. (1971). The Shape of Israeli Judaism: Realities and Hopes. *Judaism,* 20: 141–152.

RABINOWITZ, L. I. (1971). The New Trend in Halakha. *Tradition,* 11: 5–15.

RAKOVER, S., Y. YINON, AND R. ARAD. (1971). Religious Observance among Girls. *Megamot,* 17: 166–177. In Hebrew.

REICH, A. (1972). *Changes and Developments in the Passover Haggadot of the Kibbutz Movement: 1935–1971.* Ph.D. diss. University of Texas, Austin.

RIM, Y. AND KURZWEIL, Z. E. (1965). A Note on Attitudes to Risk-Taking of Observant and Non-Observant Jews. *Jewish Journal of Sociology,* 8: 238–245.

ROBERTSON, R. (1972). Religion, in P. Barker, ed., *A Sociological Portrait.* Penguin, pp. 151–162.

ROSNER, M. AND OVNAT, A. (n.d.). *Judaism and Zionism in the View of Kibbutz Youth.* Giv'at Haviva: The Institute for Research on Kibbutz Society. In Hebrew.

ROTENSTREICH, N. (1965). *The People and Its State.* Tel Aviv: Kibbutz Hameuhad. In Hebrew.

RUBINSTEIN, A. (1967). Law and Religion in Israel. *Israel Law Review,* 3: 380–414.

SAMET, M. S. (1969 and 1970). Orthodox Jewry in Modern Times. *Mahalkhim,* 1: 29–40; 2: 15–27. In Hebrew.

SHAFRAN, N. (1973). The Red Rock: A Retrospective View. *Keshet,* 59: 5–22. In Hebrew.

SHAROT S. (1974). Minority Situation and Religious Acculturation: A Comparative Analysis of Jewish Communities. *Comparative Studies in Society and History,* 16: 329–354.

SHELAH, L., HARLAP, H., AND WEISS, S. (1971). *The Social Structure of Israel.* Jerusalem: Hebrew University Institute of Contemporary Jewry.

SHOKEID, M., AND DESHEN, S. (1977). *The Generation of Transition: First-Generation North African Immigrants in Israel.* Jerusalem: Ben-Zvi Institute. In Hebrew.

SINGER, Z. (1967). Israel's Religious Establishment and Its Critics. *Midstream,* March: 50–56.

SKLARE, M. (1955). *Conservative Judaism: An American Religious Movement*. Glencoe, Ill., Free Press.
SPIRO, M. E. (1967). The Sabras and Zionism: A Study in Personality and Ideology. *Social Problems*, 5: 100–110.
WEINER, H. (1969). 9 ½ *Mystics: The Kabbala Today*. New York: Collier.
WELLER, L. (1974). *Sociology in Israel*. Westport, Conn.: Greenwood.
WELLER, I. AND TABORY, E. (1972). Religiosity of Nurses and Their Orientation to Patients. *Bar-Ilan University Annual*, 10: 97–110.
WERBLOWSKY, R. Y. Z. (1960). Biblical Studies as a Religious Problem. *Molad*, 18: 162–168. In Hebrew.
WILLNER, D. (1965). Politics and Change in Israel: The Case of Land Settlement. *Human Organization*, 24: 65–72.
YARON, Z. (1975). Religion in Israel. *American Jewish Yearbook*: 3–52.
ZENNER, W. P. (1965*a*). The Israel Sephardim and Religion. *Alliance Review*, 39: 26–29.
ZENNER, W. P. (1965*b*). Saints and Piecemeal Supernaturalism among the Jerusalem Sephardim. *Anthropological Quarterly*, 38: 201–217.
ZENNER, W. P. (1967). Sephardic Communal Organizations in Israel. *Middle East Journal*, 21, 2: 175–186.

Chapter 14
Reform and Conservative Judaism in Israel

Ephraim Tabory

Powerful forces are currently at work in Israeli society to modify Orthodox Judaism in the direction of greater conservatism.[1] On a state level, efforts are being made to apply the *halakhah* to many spheres of public life—to enforce Sabbath prohibitions against public entertainment, soccer games, and El Al flights.[2] The Orthodox *yeshivot* and the chief rabbis are also becoming increasingly militant in their demands. It is in this atmosphere that the Reform and Conservative denominations in Israel are seeking to become established Jewish movements on an equal footing with Orthodoxy.

There would appear to be a market for Reform and Conservative Judaism in Israel. While about 17 per cent of Israel's Jews classify themselves as "religious" (basically co-terminous with Orthodox),[3] it is estimated that 75 per cent of the

[1]On Judaism and Jewish practices in Israel, see Ervin Birnbaum, *The Politics of Compromise: State and Religion in Israel* (Rutherford, 1970); Samuel Clement Leslie, *The Rift in Israel: Religious Authority and Secular Democracy* (London, 1971); Norman L. Zucker, *The Coming Crises in Israel: Private Faith and Public Policy* (Cambridge, 1973); S. Zalman Abramov, *Perpetual Dilemma, Jewish Religion in the Jewish State* (Rutherford, 1976); and Zvi Yaron, "Religion in Israel," AJYB, Vol. 76, 1976, pp. 41–90.

[2]Fifty-six of the 83 items contained in the coalition agreement to the tenth Knesset (signed on August 4, 1981, by representatives of the Likud, National Religious, Agudat Israel, and Tami parties) deal, directly or indirectly, with religious matters.

[3]Yehuda Ben Meir and Peri Kedem, "Index of Religiosity of the Jewish Population of Israel," *Megamot* (Hebrew), February 1979, pp. 353–362.

population observe a "non-secular" life style.[4] Many among the latter group could presumably be attracted to the more liberal forms of religion offered by Reform and Conservative Judaism. In fact, however, these movements have met with only a limited response in Israel. Of the more than 6,000 synagogues in the country,[5] only 40 (with a total membership of about 2,000 families) are affiliated with either the Israel Movement for Progressive Judaism (Reform) or the Movement of Masorati Judaism (Conservative).[6] The purpose of this article is to describe the social and religious characteristics of these movements and to analyze their possible impact on the future of religious life in Israel.

ESTABLISHMENT OF REFORM AND CONSERVATIVE JUDAISM IN ISRAEL

An initial attempt to establish a non-Orthodox form of Judaism in Israel was made by Rabbi Max Elk, an immigrant from Germany. In 1935 he founded a liberal congregation, Beth El, in Haifa, where he also set up the Leo Baeck School in 1939.[7] The school maintains close ties with Reform Judaism (it came under the formal auspices of the World Union for Progressive Judaism in 1971) and is currently headed by an American expatriate Reform rabbi, Robert Samuels.

Beth El congregation existed for only a few years. The generally anti-Zionist attitude of early Reform Judaism[8] was a primary cause of its dissolution.[9] A pamphlet describing the Reform movement in Israel does not even mention its pre-state history.[10] In any event, it is clear that the Reform movement in Israel had its "modern" beginnings only in 1958, with the founding of the Harel synagogue in Jerusalem. There are now about 12 Reform congregations which hold regular Saturday services; all but four were founded before 1970.

The first Conservative congregation was also established by a liberal immigrant rabbi from Germany. David Wilhelm founded the Emet Ve'Emuna congregation in Jerusalem in 1937. The World Council of Synagogues (Conservative) sought to establish a presence in Jerusalem in the 1930's, by constructing what is today one of Jerusalem's most prestigious synagogues, Yeshurun. The religious

[4]See Sammy Smooha, *Israel, Pluralism and Conflict* (London, 1978), p. 73.

[5]Eliezer Don-Yehiya, *Religion in Israel* (Hebrew), (Jerusalem, 1975), p. 37.

[6]Mevakshe Derech ("Seekers of the Way"), a congregation established in Jerusalem in 1962, is an independent liberal synagogue that encompasses several dozen families. Its style of service is similar to that found in Reform synagogues, but the congregation is unaffiliated with any religious organization.

[7]Meir Elk, "First Steps in the History of Our Movement in Israel," *Shalhevet* (Hebrew), 1, 1969, pp. 9–12.

[8]See David Polish, *Renew Our Days: The Zionist Issue in Reform Judaism* (Jerusalem, 1976), for a discussion of the changes that have taken place in the attitude of Reform Judaism toward Zionism.

[9]Ze'ev Harari, "Chapters in the History of the Movement for Progressive Judaism in Israel," (Hebrew), seminar paper, Hebrew Union College, Jerusalem, 1974.

[10]Shlomo Cohen, *Not to Negate Have We Come, But Rather to Pave the Way* (Hebrew), (Ramat Gan, n.d.).

adherence of the congregants, however, led the synagogue to adopt an Orthodox pattern of worship. The Conservative movement in Israel is larger, though younger, than the Reform movement; about 30 Conservative congregations hold regular services, and all but three of these were founded after 1970.

The manner in which Reform and Conservative synagogues have been founded is indicative of the demand for such congregations in Israel. The driving force behind the creation of many of the Reform congregations has been either a movement rabbi (one rabbi was responsible for the establishment of four different congregations) or personnel from the national movement office. In contrast, Conservative synagogues have generally been founded by a nucleus of American expatriates who, desirous of establishing such congregations, approached the national movement for assistance.

Only a few congregations have their own facilities; most Reform and Conservative groups use rented halls and school buildings. This situation has enabled state-religious authorities to hinder the congregations. Some institutions have allegedly been threatened with removal of *kashrut* certification, if they allowed non-Orthodox congregations the use of their facilities.[11] The efforts of Reform Jews in Tel Aviv to obtain permission to build a synagogue were thwarted for years by the religious parties in the municipal coalition. In one instance, permission to perform a wedding was withheld from an Orthodox rabbi because the ceremony was to be held in the hall of a Conservative congregation.[12]

The Israeli government has no "official" policy with regard to the Reform and Conservative movements in Israel. Local religious officials and local councils either render assistance or seek to impede developments, depending on the personalities and coalition politics prevailing at given times and places. In some communities, congregations have been sold land for the construction of synagogues for mere nominal sums. Even the national ministry of religious affairs has granted money to congregations for educational purposes, although the sums involved have not been listed under the ministry's regular budget lines.[13]

The legal system in Israel entrusts issues of personal status to the religious courts of the various religious communities.[14] Reform and Conservative rabbis are *ipso facto* enjoined from being considered as designates of the state for these purposes. Likewise, at times they have been prevented from conducting funerals. The conversions they perform are not recognized. For the past several years, the

[11]A letter from the mayor of Rishon LeZion (dated January 16, 1977) to the founder of the Reform congregation in that town stated it was impossible to allocate a place of worship to the congregation because of the "danger of increased public and social tension."

[12]These examples, and others, are discussed in Abramov, *op. cit.*, p. 350 ff.

[13]Some persons involved in the Reform and Conservative movements are opposed to the acceptance of such sums. They feel that the receipt of any government aid prevents them from arguing that they are discriminated against. At the same time, the manner in which the funds are transferred does not enable the movement to argue convincingly that this is a form of governmental recognition, especially given the small amounts awarded.

[14]See Zerach Warhaftig *et al.*, (eds.), *Religion and State in Legislation* (Hebrew), (Jerusalem, 1973); Menahem Elon, *Religious Legislation* (Hebrew), (Tel Aviv, 1964); and Pinchas Shifman, "Religious Affiliation in Israeli Interreligious Law," *Israel Law Review*, January 1980, pp. 1–48.

Orthodox rabbinate has placed advertisements in the press prior to the high holy days stating that the prayers of persons who worship in Conservative synagogues are not valid, and that individuals cannot fulfill the commandment of *shofar* in such houses of worship.[15]

While some Reform and Conservative congregations have had difficulties in renting facilities, and their rabbis are not recognized by the state, it would be a mistake to attribute the limited progress of the movements to these factors. First, in every case facilities have eventually been found. Secondly, movement leaders are aware that they would not necessarily attract more members to their congregations even if Reform and Conservative rabbis were permitted to conduct wedding services. While it might be argued that the actions taken against the rabbis are an infringement of civil rights, their actual effect on the growth of the Reform and Conservative movements has been limited.

ORGANIZATIONAL STRUCTURE OF THE MOVEMENTS

The Reform and Conservative movements in Israel, like those in the United States, are better characterized as federations of synagogues than as satellite congregations of united organizations.

The Israel Movement for Progressive Judaism is formally composed of representatives of all congregations, as well as such affiliated bodies as the youth movement, Leo Baeck School, Hebrew Union College—Jewish Institute of Religion, and the Council of Progressive Rabbis in Israel. A national council makes the major policy decisions that affect the movement on a day to day basis. One of the main responsibilities of the Council of Progressive Rabbis is the preparation of a new Israeli Reform prayer book. The rabbinic body also occasionally deals with religious questions posed to it by members of the Reform kibbutz.

In the Conservative movement the main division is between the synagogue body, the United Synagogue of Israel, and the rabbinic group, the Rabbinical Assembly in Israel. Working together, the two organizations have established a Movement of Masorati (Traditional) Judaism in Israel. The name was carefully chosen because of its compatibility with the philosophy of Conservative Judaism and its potential appeal to the many Jews in Israel who characterize themselves, religiously, as *masorati*.[16]

The leaders of Reform and Conservative Judaism in Israel want their movements to be seen as indigenous to the country. At the same time, they are affiliated with counterpart movements abroad. In the case of Conservative Judaism, it is the World Council of Synagogues; in the case of Reform Judaism, it is the World Union for Progressive Judaism. The main branches of both of these world movements are in the United States.

[15]Some Reform leaders have been disheartened by the fact that they have not been included in the Orthodox rabbinate's denunciations. Apparently, the Orthodox do not take them all that seriously.

[16]Forty-one per cent of the respondents in Ben-Meir's and Kedem's study, *op. cit.*, stated that they were *masorati*.

The Reform and Conservative movement in Israel are quite dependent on financial support from abroad. Over half of the Reform movement's budget is covered by the World Union for Progressive Judaism, which also subsidizes the salaries of several Reform rabbis. In general, the Reform movements in Israel appears to be subject to considerable outside influence. Thus, the vice-president of the Israel executive of the World Union for Progressive Judaism holds *ex officio* membership in the national council of the Israel movement. Publicly at least, the holder of this position, rather than the actual chairman of the Israel Movement for Progressive Judaism, is often perceived to be the leader of Reform Judaism in Israel. The Conservative movement in Israel has had some unpleasant arguments with the United Synagogue of America over the question of financial support. The perceived lack of greater support from abroad has led Conservative leaders in Israel to adopt a more independent course.

DEMOGRAPHIC PROFILE OF THE MOVEMENTS

A survey of the members of Reform and Conservative congregations, conducted in 1978, provides data on their demographic composition. While there has been some fluctuation in membership in the interim period (more Conservative congregations have been founded), the basic picture has not changed.[17] For comparative purposes, data from the United States National Jewish Population Study will also be presented.[18]

An initial difference between the movements relates to the number of families that have joined them. There were about 2,049 family units in the two movements in 1978; 64 percent (1,308 units) belonged to Conservative synagogues and 36 percent (741 units) to Reform synagogues.

Table 1 presents the family life cycle (a composite picture of the age of the members, their marital status, and the age of their children) of Reform and Conservative Jews in Israel, as well as comparable data for Reform and Conservative denomination members in the United States.

The Conservative movement in Israel is composed of younger members, and more members with younger children, than is the Reform movement. The Reform movement has a larger percentage of members with children no longer at home.

[17]Inasmuch as neither of the movements maintained a national membership list from which respondents for the survey could be drawn, it was necessary to obtain lists from each of the congregations. These lists accounted for 815 family units in the Reform synagogues and 1,500 in the Conservative houses of worship. A sample of adults in these households was sent a questionnaire dealing with a variety of synagogue-related issues as well as demographic characteristics. The questionnaires were accompanied by requests for cooperation from the heads of the movements. A total of 977 questionnaires (517 in the Reform movement and 460 in the Conservative movement) were obtained. The response rate in both movements was 85 per cent.

[18]The National Jewish Population Study was commissioned by the Council of Jewish Federations and Welfare Funds. Data relevant to this study are found in Bernard Lazerwitz, "Past and Future Trends in the Size of American Jewish Denominations," *Journal of Reform Judaism*, Summer 1979, pp. 77–82, and in Bernard Lazerwitz and Michael I. Harrison, "American Jewish Denominations: A Social and Religious Profile," *American Sociological Review*, August 1979, pp. 656–666.

TABLE 1. Family Cycle of Members of Israeli Reform and Conservative Synagogues, by Percent

			NJPS[a]	
FAMILY CYCLE	REFORM	CONSERVATIVE	REFORM	CONSERVATIVE
Under 36 and Single	2	3	1	1
Under 36, Married, No Children	1	2	1	6
Married, One or More Children Aged 13 or Younger	18	37	42	36
Married, One or More Children Aged 14–18	12	13	15[b]	18[b]
Married, All Children Over 18 (or No Children)	41	30	35[c]	31[c]
Not Married, Aged 31–54, No Children at Home	2	2	1	1
Not Married, Aged 60 or Over, No Children at Home	22	12	3	5
One-Parent Families	1	1	2	2
NA	1	0	—	—
Total Per Cent	100	100	100	100
N	517	460	841	1,160

[a]Source: Bernard Lazerwitz, "Jewish Denominations, Synagogue Membership, and Attendance," mimeographed, Bar Ilan University, Ramat Gan, Israel. Data refer to synagogue members.
[b]Married couples with children 14 years and older.
[c]Married, 36 years or older, no children now at home.

The significance of these findings is evident when comparing the Israeli members with Reform and Conservative members in the United States. Lazerwitz and Harrison report that 57 percent of Reform and Conservative members in the United States are married and have children under 16 years old in their households.[19] Whereas the Conservative membership in Israel closely resembles the American group (50 percent of the Israeli members are married with children under 19 in the household), the Reform membership does not (only 30 percent of the Reform members in Israel are married with children under 19 in the household). Another difference between the Israeli and American data is that a greater percentage of persons in the Reform and Conservative movements in Israel are elderly, with no immediate family members in the household. The implications of this situation will be discussed below.

The continents of birth of the members, presented in Table 2, show that a smaller percentage of Conservative than Reform Jews are of European origin. The basic difference between the movements is the relatively large number of persons in the Conservative movement born in North America (Canada and the United States). Jews of Asian-African and Latin American origins are virtually unrepre-

[19]See Lazerwitz and Harrison, *op. cit.*, p. 659.

TABLE 2. Continent of Birth of Members of Israeli Reform and Conservative Synagogues, by Percent

CONTINENT	REFORM	CONSERVATIVE	ISRAEL JEWISH POPULATION[a]
Israel	11	14	12
East Europe	32	20	{40
West Europe	45	29	
Asia-Africa	2	2	46
North America	8	24	{2
Latin America	1	3	
Oceania	1	8	
Total Per Cent	100	100	100
N	512	455	3.1m

[a]Source: Israel Central Bureau of Statistics, *Statistical Abstract of Israel 1978*, Volume 29, Table ii/23. First-generation Israel-born are classified according to father's continent of birth.

sented in the two groups. Within Israeli society, Asian-Africans comprise about 46 percent of the Jewish population.[20]

Over ten per cent of the members in each of the movements are native-born Israelis. These persons are younger than the other members—their average age in each of the movements is 42. The average age of the non-Israeli-born in the Reform movement is 61, and in the Conservative, 55.

The data in Table 2 point up the fact that Reform and Conservative Judaism in Israel are basically ethnic movements. Ethnic here is taken to mean that the members have a relatively homogeneous cultural background.[21] This common background is further underscored by looking at the members' continents of emigration in Table 3. It should be noted that the North American presence in the Reform and Conservative movements is embedded in a broad "Anglo-Saxon" framework; 11 percent of the members are from English-speaking countries other than the United States and Canada. In all, one out of three members of the two movements is from an English-speaking country. These persons account for close to half of all Conservative members, but only for about 20 percent of the Reform members.[22]

Following the English-speaking countries, the country contributing the largest percentage of members is Germany. Thirty percent of the Reform members and ten per cent of the Conservative members immigrated directly from that country. It is possible that the differences between the movements, with regard to "Anglo-Saxon" members in the Conservative group and the Germans in the Reform group, is due less to the intrinsic attraction of the movements than to the nature of immigration to Israel. The German immigrants to Israel brought Reform Judaism

[20]Israel Central Bureau of Statistics (CBS), *Statistical Abstract of Israel*, 1978, Table ii/23

[21]See Shlomo Deshen, "Political Ethnicity and Cultural Ethnicity in Israel During the 1960's," in Ernest Krausz, (ed.), *Studies of Israeli Society: Migration, Ethnicity, and Community* (New Brunswick, 1980), pp. 117–163.

[22]*Cf.*, CBS, *op. cit.*, Table ii/23.

TABLE 3. Immigrant Members' Continent of Emigration, by Percent

CONTINENT	REFORM	CONSERVATIVE	ISRAEL JEWISH POPULATION[a]
East Europe	26	11	{38
West Europe	54	30	
Asia-Africa	1	2	54
North America	14	40	4
Latin America	3	5	{4
Oceania	2	12	
Total Per Cent	100	100	100
N	450	384	3.1 m

[a]Source: Israel Central Bureau of Statistics, *Immigration to Israel, 1948–1972, Part II, Composition by Period of Immigration*, Special Series No. 489, Table 2.

with them. In addition, the nature of Reform Judaism abroad would not lead one to expect a large immigration of Reform Jews to Israel. In fact, Orthodox and Conservative Jews are overrepresented among American *olim* to Israel.[23] For that reason the number of "Anglo-Saxons" in the Reform movement is not higher. Supporting this contention is the fact that the average Reform immigrant has been in Israel 31 years, whereas the average Conservative immigrant has been in the country for 19 years. Over half of the non-Israeli-born Reform members came to Israel before 1944, whereas the median year of immigration for the non-Israeli-born Conservative members is 1965.

The ethnic nature of the Reform and Conservative movements is particularly evident in the synagogues. In only three of the twelve Conservative congregations does the percentage of "Anglo-Saxons" fall below 50 percent; in only two of the ten Reform congregations does the "Anglo-Saxon" presence rise above 50 percent. Most members of German origin are found principally in one of the Conservative and three of the Reform synagogues.

Members of Reform synagogues in the United States are generally of higher social status than Conservative Jews, although the difference between them is diminishing.[24] This study measures such social status by education and occupation.[25]

The data in Table 4 show that the members of the Reform and Conservative movements have higher educational levels than the general Israeli public. The differences are considerably diminished when Asian/North African Jews are excluded from the Israeli data, but the contrast remains. The differences

[23]See Bernard Lazerwitz and Arnold Dashefsky, "Success and Failure in Ideological Migration: American Jews in Israel," paper presented at the annual meeting of the American Sociological Association, 1979.

[24]See Lazerwitz and Harrison, *op. cit.*

[25]No attempt was made to assess family income because of the problems involved in obtaining a valid response in a mail survey. In Israel's inflationary society, where monthly salaries are supplemented by "bonuses" and extra payments throughout the year, it is particularly difficult to measure income accurately.

TABLE 4. Members' Highest Level of Formal Education, by Percent

			NJPS[a]		
EDUCATION	REFORM	CONSER-VATIVE	REFORM	CONSER-VATIVE	ISRAEL JEWISH POPULATION[b]
High School or Less	43	26	23	40	82[c]
Partial College	16	20	24	25	5[d]
B.A. Degree	12	15	25	11	9 (B.A. Degree, Some Advanced Studies, Advanced Degree combined)
Some Advanced Studies	10	10	14	10	
Advanced Degree	14	27	14	14	
NA	5	2	—	—	4[e]
Total Per Cent	100	100	100	100	100
N	517	460	841	1,160	1.1 m

[a]Source: Bernard Lazerwitz, "Jewish Denominations, Synagogue Membership, and Attendance," mimeographed, Bar Ilan University, Ramat Gan, Israel. Data refer to synagogue members.
[b]Source: Israel Central Bureau of Statistics, *Statistical Abstract of Israel 1978*, Volume 29, Table xxii/3. Data are for Jewish population age 14 and over.
[c]Includes primary, heder, yeshiva, vocational school, and secondary schools. Corresponds to 81.3% of the Jewish population having 0–12 years of education (in *ibid.*, Table xii/2).
[d]Includes teacher training colleges and other post-secondary schools.
[e]Referred to as "other."

between Reform and Conservative Jews themselves are attributable to the specific countries of emigration of the members, and to their periods of immigration. Formal education probably received greater emphasis among the many "Anglo-Saxon" members in the Conservative movement than among the European members of the Reform movement. In addition, Reform members generally immigrated to Israel before the Conservative members, and conditions in Europe prior to their immigration were not conducive to formal education. The needs of Israel at the time also worked against their seeking higher education; there was a greater demand for laborers than for academicians. Thus, while many Reform Jews do have some higher education, their number is surpassed by the Conservative Jews.

With regard to education, there is a reversal of patterns between the movements in Israel and the United States. In the U.S., a significantly larger percentage of Conservative Jews than Reform Jews have no more than a high school education. There is a corresponding difference between those holding a B.A. degree. In Israel, the differences relate to the graduate level, and it is the Conservative Jews who have higher levels of education.

Table 5 presents the occupational distribution of three groups: Reform and Conservative Jews in Israel; Israel's general Jewish population; and members of Reform and Conservative synagogues in the United States. The occupations are ranked from those of highest social prestige to those of lowest.[26] There is a basic

[26]See Moshe Hartman, *Occupation as a Measure of Social Status in Israeli Society* (Hebrew), Part A., (Tel Aviv, 1975).

TABLE 5. Occupational Distribution of Heads of Households, by Percent

			NJPS[a]		
OCCUPATION	REFORM	CONSER-VATIVE	REFORM	CONSER-VATIVE	ISRAEL JEWISH POPULATION[d]
Professionals	51	71	39	30	21
Managers	8	6	20[b]	44[b]	5
Clerical	16	8	20	14	20
Sales	11	6	15	8	8
Services	1	1	6[c]	4c	11
Agriculture	3	1	—	—	5
Skilled Workers	10	7	—	—	24
Unskilled Workers	0	0	—	—	6
Total Per Cent	100	100	100	100	100
N	384	366	841	1,160	1.04 m

[a]Source: Bernard Lazerwitz and Michael I. Harrison, "Denominationalism: What Remains After Americanization," mimeographed, Bar Ilan University, Ramat Gan, Israel.
[b]Owners and managers.
[c]Blue Collar.
[d]Source: Israel Central Bureau of Statistics, *Statistical Abstract of Israel 1978*, Volume 29, Table xii/18. Data relate to population aged 14 and above who are employed or have actively sought employment.

difference in occupational distribution of Reform and Conservative Jews in Israel—a much larger percentage of Conservative Jews are professionals. This pattern, a reversal of that found in the United States, is apparently explained by the differential immigration of American Reform and Conservative Jews to Israel. Twenty-three percent of the professionals in the two movements are American-born, and 70 percent of the American-born in the Israeli Conservative movement are professionals.[27]

Having examined the general demographic characteristics of Reform and Conservative members in Israel, we now turn to their Jewish traits. The first question to be dealt with is the synagogue affiliation of the members prior to their immigration to Israel. Are they merely continuing an institutional affiliation initiated abroad? Sixty percent of the Reform members and 70 per cent of the Conservative members did attend some synagogue abroad on a regular basis prior to their immigration. The data in Table 6 refer to these persons.

Over 20 percent of the members in both movements regularly attended an Orthodox synagogue abroad. This denominational "switch" is somewhat surprising, since it refers to the members' own behavior and not to a comparison of intergenerational change. Several possible explanations for this finding may be offered. First, "Orthodox" congregations in one area of the United States may be similar to Conservative congregations in another.[28] Thus some members might

[27]The percentage of professionals among American-born Reform members (46 percent) is higher than that among non-American-born Reform Jews (37 percent). However, the small sample (n=41) of American-born in the Reform movement limits the generalizations to be inferred.

[28]See Daniel J. Elazar, *Community and Polity: The Organizational Dynamics of American Jewry* (Philadelphia, 1976), p. 110.

TABLE 6. Movement Affiliation of Synagogues Members Attended Abroad, by Percent

SYNAGOGUE ATTENDED ABROAD	REFORM	CONSERVATIVE
Orthodox	28	37
Conservative	19	42
Liberal	28	7
Reform	16	3
Other (+ More than 1)	9	11
Total Per Cent	100	100
N	319	327

have attended synagogues in the United States that were quite like Conservative congregations in Israel, despite the different nominal affiliation. Second, some members might have attended Orthodox congregations abroad out of choice, but were looking for an alternative to the religious services held in contemporary Israeli Orthodox congregations. Indeed, about one-third of the Reform and Conservative members in Israel attended a synagogue of a different denomination on a regular basis subsequent to their immigration; for over one-half of these persons, that synagogue was Orthodox. Additional analysis shows that 80 percent of those persons in each of the movements who attended an Orthodox congregation abroad at some time also regularly attended an Orthodox synagogue in Israel. This accounts for ten percent of the total Conservative membership, and six percent of all Reform respondents.

At least 50 percent of the members in each of the movements who attended a synagogue abroad on a regular basis did not attend a synagogue affiliated with their current denomination. Furthermore, the members generally come from similar synagogue movements abroad, or from ones which may be considered "more" religious. This finding about the members' own synagogue attendance is matched by data concerning the synagogues their fathers attended. About half of all Reform and Conservative members come from homes in which the father attended an Orthodox synagogue. The pattern of an institutional "decline" from Orthodox to Conservative to Reform appears to be quite characteristic of modern Jewry.[29]

Overall, the data suggest that previous synagogue attendance on a regular basis is a prerequisite for affiliation with Reform or Conservative Judaism in Israel. Still, about 30 percent of the Reform members, and about 20 percent of the Conservative members, did not attend services regularly.

Aside from previous synagogue affiliation, there is the question of the members' present religious behavior. Table 7 shows the distribution of ritual practices of Reform and Conservative Jews in Israel. Comparable data for the adult, urban Ashkenazic population are also presented.

Both in Israel and the United States, Conservative Jews perform more ritual practices than do Reform Jews. The most striking feature of the findings in Table

[29]See Morris Axelrod *et al.*, *A Community Survey for Long Range Planning: A Study of the Jewish Population of Greater Boston* (Boston, 1967).

TABLE 7. Religious Behavior of Members, by Percent

RELIGIOUS BEHAVIOR	REFORM	CONSERVATIVE	ISRAEL POP.[a]	NJPS[b]
Refrain from Eating Bread on Passover	82	89	78	
Fast All Day on Yom Kippur	74	84	56	51
Light Shabbat Candles in Home Each Shabbat	72	82	60	
Make Kiddush in Home Each Shabbat	41	65	34[c]	19
Eat Only Kosher in Home	41	65	33[d] (bracketed with next row)	22 (bracketed with next two rows)
Separate Dishes for Meat and Dairy in Home	23	49		
Eat Only Kosher Outside Home	23	36	32	
Refrain from All Travel on Shabbat	6	18	15	
N	517	460	784	—

[a]Data on the general Ashkenazic Israeli population were provided by Dr. Peri Kedem, and are based on special computer runs. Missing data are excluded from these calculations. For details on her study see Ben-Meir and Kedem (supra, footnote 3).
[b]Source: B. Lazerwitz, "Minority Jews Contrasted to Majority Jews," unpublished paper, 1979. Data refer to all American Jews surveyed in the National Jewish Population Study (NJPS).
[c]Includes 9%—"occasionally" and "usually."
[d]Question asked was whether there is separation of meat and dairy in the home.

7, however, is the high level of religious observance of Reform Jews in Israel relative to both the Ashkenazic population and the general Jewish population in the United States. The finding in Israel is all the more significant in that Orthodox persons are included in the Ashkenazic population data. Indeed, it is probable that Israeli Reform members comprise the most observant Reform Jewish body in the world.

A multiple classification analysis of the factors leading to affiliation with either a Reform or a Conservative synagogue was undertaken.[30] This analysis, which accounts for 26 percent of the variance observed, confirms the importance of ethnicity as a differentiating factor in the movements. (The beta value of the continents of emigration was .23.) Likewise, the type of synagogue attended abroad has a relatively strong impact (beta of .21) on the synagogue attended in Israel. Religious behavior and occupation have a moderate impact (beta values of .16 and .14, respectively). The age of the members has a barely moderate effect (beta of .12).

The differences between the Reform and Conservative movements in Israel may be highlighted by comparing the multiple classification analysis results with

[30]See Frank M. Andrews *et al.*, *Multiple Classification Analysis: A Report on a Computer Program for Multiple Regression Using Categorical Predictors* (Ann Arbor, 1973). The absence of interaction between variables was ascertained by using the AID III program of Osiris. See John A. Sonquist *et al.*, *Searching for Structure* (Ann Arbor, 1974).

those relating to Jewish denominational choice in the United States.[31] In the U.S., education and occupation (as well as income) are not significant factors differentiating the two movements (their beta values are below .07). In Israel, however, the Conservative movement is composed of persons of higher social status than those who join the Reform movement, although the beta values associated with these variables are only of moderate (or only approach moderate) strength. Since the members of Conservative synagogues are also relatively young, the Conservative movement has a distinct advantage over the Reform movement in attracting young, socially mobile Israelis. The Western, "American" nature of the Conservative movement also works to its advantage inasmuch as Anglo-Saxons enjoy the highest prestige of all immigrant groups in Israel.

A factor influencing affiliation with Reform and Conservative Judaism in the United States, at least in the formative years of the movements, was the rising social status of the members.[32] A social status higher than that of the Israeli population in general also characterizes the native Israeli members (the majority of whom are of Western background). They are five times as likely as the general population to have had at least a college education; a much larger percentage are in professional occupations (57 percent in the Reform movement, 61 percent in the Conservative movement, in contrast with 21 percent among the general Israeli population). How did these persons come to attend Reform or Conservative synagogues? Some married Anglo-Saxon expatriates (7 percent in the Reform group and 14 percent in the Conservative group), and their spouses may have been instrumental in their joining the Reform or Conservative movement. Some Israeli members (26 percent in the Reform group and 19 percent in the Conservative group) came into contact with non-Orthodox Judaism while on visits or extended stays abroad. Over 30 percent of the Israeli Reform members and 35 percent of their Conservative counterparts say that they first heard about the movements from their family or friends. In this connection (but not limited to it), the bar and bat mitzvah services held in these congregations are important in attracting native Israelis. Twenty-eight percent of the Israeli-born in the Reform movement and 35 percent in the Conservative movement say that attendance at such celebrations (including those of their own children) first led them to attend their current congregations. It should be noted that membership and periodic attendance are requirements for the conduct of bar and bat mitzvah celebrations in most of the synagogues. Many families apparently do not maintain their membership beyond the requisite year.

It is very rare to encounter a Reform or Conservative congregation that has more than half of its registered membership in attendance on any *shabbat*. Still, the difference between Israeli-born and other members in this regard is noteworthy. Table 8 indicates that Israeli-born members attend religious services much less frequently. In the course of discussions with them, some native Israelis stated that they joined one of the movements only because they wished to indicate their

[31]See Lazerwitz and Harrison, *op. cit.*

[32]Marshall Sklare, *Conservative Judaism: An American Religious Movement* (New York, 1972), pp. 26–28.

TABLE 8. Frequency of Synagogue Attendance of Israeli-born Members, by Percent

	REFORM		CONSERVATIVE	
SYNAGOGUE ATTENDANCE	ISRAELI-BORN	BORN ELSE-WHERE	ISRAELI-BORN	BORN ELSE-WHERE
Each Shabbat (or Almost Each Shabbat) and Holidays	38	49	24	38
Holidays, and Occasionally on Shabbat	24	23	26	30
On Holidays (Including High Holy Days)	6	6	14	13
On Just the High Holy Days	4	9	17	12
Rarely or Never	28	13	19	7
Total Per Cent	100	100	100	100
N	47	470	62	398

support of religious pluralism, rather than because they were specifically interested in Reform or Conservative Judaism *per se*.

An important indicator of the future of Reform and Conservative Judaism in Israel is the ability of the movements to attract the children of present members. Only about half of the grown children of current members prefer the denomination of their parents; 32 percent of the children of Reform members and 22 percent of the children of Conservative members have no denominational preference. Only a minority of children of Reform and Conservative members who no longer live at home attend synagogues of the same denomination as their parents (27 percent in the Reform movement and 42 percent in the Conservative movement). Inasmuch as the average number of children of the current members is small (1.9 in the Reform movement and 2.3 in the Conservative movement), they cannot be counted upon to maintain current membership levels in the future.

RESPONSES TO THE ISRAELI SETTING

The demographic data help clarify the charge occasionally made in Israeli Orthodox circles that the Reform and Conservative movements are "imported."[33] Of course, an ideological element is present in this accusation, as well as in the offshoot argument that the movements are geared to the Diaspora and thus religiously "non-authentic." Nevertheless, Reform and Conservative leaders are well aware that they have not succeeded in attracting large numbers of native Israelis. In the hope of doing so, they have sought to alter some behavioral patterns

[33]See David Telsner, *The Sinai Covenant and Cincinnati "Religion"* (Hebrew), (Jerusalem, 1978).

and to undertake specific activities of an "Israeli" nature. This section focuses on some of these activities and analyzes their implications for the movements themselves.[34]

An interesting linguistic issue has arisen in the Conservative movement because of the unavailability of a Conservative prayer book containing only Hebrew. Several congregations prefer using an Orthodox prayer book rather than a Conservative prayer book with an English translation. While the liturgical differences between the two prayer books are not great, some congregants wish to avoid too obvious a manifestation of a largely Anglo-Saxon membership.[35]

Several Hebrew-only Reform prayer books have been published in Israel, and they have been clearly affected by the country's traditional Orthodox environment. The Reform movement has decided to issue a uniform prayer book for adoption by all congregations, although it is an open question (given Reform's stress on autonomy in matters of prayer and ritual) how many will choose to make use of it. Interestingly, one compiler of the new Reform prayer book has commented that it will have to be "fat" like the Orthodox prayer book, so that Reform Judaism will not be perceived as merely non-Orthodox. "People generally treat Progressive Judaism as 'abridged Judaism'. The Orthodox pray from a 'fat' *siddur,* while we pray from a shortened 'thin' one," he stated.[36]

The movement has established a Reform kibbutz (Yahel, in the Negev, some 70 kilometers north of Eilat) to demonstrate Reform Judaism's rootedness in Israeli society and its break with its anti-Zionist past. Rabbi Alexander Schindler, president of the Union of American Hebrew Congregations, stated at Yahel's groundbreaking ceremony in November 1976: "We demonstrate Reform's full flowering in its return to Israel—the people and the land."[37] The cover of a brochure describing the kibbutz features the words "Israel Reform Judaism" and "Rooted in the Land," and shows a smiling *kova tembel* hatted girl holding a cluster of grapes. The text of the brochure reads in part: "With the establishment of the new Reform kibbutz this winter, Israel Reform Judaism becomes, literally, rooted in the soil....Israeli Reform Judaism is not only in the land. It is of the land...." The brochure also states: "Israeli Reform Judaism grows because it meets the spiritual needs of a growing number of Israelis who seek a satisfying alternative to empty secularism and rigid Orthodoxy. It inspires those Israelis who wish to experience the beauty of Judaism."

Publicity wise, the kibbutz has been a great asset to the Reform movement. However, the members of Yahel have felt that the Reform movement, and partic-

[34]Berger's "market" theory of religion, which analyzes the need of religious movements to adapt to local "market" conditions in order to "compete" with alternative movements, is relevant here. See Peter L. Berger, *The Sacred Canopy: Elements of a Sociological Theory of Religion* (New York, 1967).

[35]Plans to print a Hebrew-only version of the Conservative prayer book, using plates provided by the Rabbinic Assembly in the United States, have not materialized for technical reasons.

[36]See Moshe Chaim Weiler, "On the Eve of Rosh Hashana 5737" (Hebrew), *Telem,* 10, 1976, pp. 1–2.

[37]Jerusalem *Post,* November 19, 1976, p. 2.

ularly the rabbinic leadership, have been slow in prescribing behavioral norms suitable to their needs. (The kibbutz has decided to observe *shabbat* in all public spheres, but not to interfere with what the members do in their private lives. Nevertheless, members who turn air-conditioners and lights on and off in their rooms have begun doing so in the kitchen and dining-room as well.) A greater question relates to what a kibbutz as a Reform institution means. Inasmuch as prayer and rituals are dispensed with on a daily basis, what distinguishes the kibbutz as a Reform enterprise?

The kibbutz has encountered difficulty in recruiting a sufficient number of suitable members. The Reform movement in Israel does not yet have a large number of youth interested in a Reform kibbutz. With the permission of the leaders of the movement, therefore, the kibbutz has turned to other youth organizations in Israel to recruit youngsters who are in the *nachal* program (combining military training and work in a developing kibbutz) of the army. But the persons recruited to Yahel in this manner have almost no religious background and are not interested in a specifically Reform Jewish outlook. There are Americans willing to settle on the kibbutz, but Yahel's present members fear that the kibbutz (which in 1982 had only about 60 members, about half of whom were American) will become "hopelessly" American if they are permitted to do so. This is one of the reasons why the Reform movement has decided to establish another kibbutz in the same area—to absorb the Americans. At the same time, the new kibbutz will have to absorb those native Israelis who wish to join a Reform kibbutz, so that a balance can be maintained. This means that Yahel will have to do without new members for the next few years.

The Reform and Conservative movements in Israel hope to create a core of dedicated youth through the development of national youth organizations. These organizations are still in the formative stage; in 1981 they claimed a total membership of less than one thousand. In order to reach a wider audience, the Reform youth organization, Telem Noar has affiliated with the Boy Scouts of Israel (Tsofim), and been assigned several lodges. The challenge facing the organization is to turn these youth, who have little, if any, religious background, into Reform Jews. The Conservative youth groups, attached to local congregations, are composed primarily of the children of current synagogue members. Regional and national activities serve to integrate Conservative youth into a united organization, Noam. The Conservative movement, in response to the demands of the high-school age youth, is planning the establishment of a kibbutz, so that young people will be able to devote their army service to the *nachal* (soldier-pioneer) program.

No survey of the youth organizations has been undertaken, but the directors note that many of the current members are either Anglo-Saxon, or the children of Anglo-Saxons. The movements are clearly serving an important integrative function in Israeli society. It appears, though, that the Conservative movement will have the edge in retaining its young people as members. Many Conservative congregations are well attended by children, thus completing their socialization as Conservative Jews. This is in contrast to the situation in Reform synagogues.

A very significant development in the Reform movement has been the inauguration of a rabbinical studies program for native Israelis. At the time that this study was carried out, five students (all men) were registered. (One of them has since been ordained.) Two of the student rabbis came into initial contact with the movement through the Leo Baeck School in Haifa. Another two became aware of Reform Judaism while they were exchange high school pupils in the United States. The fifth student became active in the movement as a result of having attended a Reform high holy day service (which he had learned about through a newspaper advertisement). None of these persons come from an Orthodox background; their families are either secular or traditional. The father of one student had been a member of the liberal movement in Germany. Two are married to Americans. The high visibility of the student rabbis greatly strengthens the Reform movement's claim of being part and parcel of Israeli society.[38]

While the rabbinical students are being trained to administer to the needs of established congregations, they may be better able than expatriate American rabbis to attract native Israeli youth to the Reform movement. They are very much interested in ideological issues, and participate actively in debates during national conferences. Some of the student rabbis are involved in editing *Shalhevet*, the Reform movement's publication. Their religious leanings and views (still in the formative stage at this point, since they have come to the Reform movement with only limited Jewish knowledge) can be expected to have a significant impact on Reform Judaism in Israel as they assume greater leadership responsibilities in the coming years.

CONCLUSION

A key feature of both Reform and Conservative Judaism is that they facilitate the "privatization" of religion, the isolation of religious life from public practice. They thus enable Jews to take part in secular social life without undue restrictions. As Sklare and Greenblum note, the practices retained by Reform and Conservative Judaism in the United States tend to be those that are compatible with the American social environment.[39] Many American Jews who want to be part of the general society and yet retain a degree of Jewish identification affiliate with the non-Orthodox branches of Judaism.

Obviously, in Israel adherence to Orthodoxy is less of an impediment to active participation in the mainstream of society than it is in the United States. Israel is geared to the observance of Jewish holidays; *kashrut* is observed in government institutions and many other places as well. Thus, there is less social pressure pushing Jews in the direction of the more liberal Jewish denominations.

[38]Wide publicity, including press and television coverage, was given to the ordination of the first Israeli Reform rabbi in February 1980.

[39]Marshall Sklare and Joseph Greenblum, *Jewish Identity on the Suburban Frontier* (New York, 1967).

In the United States, Reform and Conservative Judaism function as a vehicle for ethnic as well as religious identification. Non-affiliation with a religious denomination in America appears to lead to (as well as to indicate) marginality in the Jewish ethnic community. Thus, even persons who are religiously lax are motivated to attend, or at least affiliate with, the Reform or Conservative denominations (or other institutionalized forms of Judaism) in order to retain and demonstrate an ethnic Jewish identity. In Israel, however, a full Jewish ethnic life is quite possible; there is little fear of "assimilation" and thus less of a need for affiliation with a synagogue. In addition, the use of Hebrew as the vernacular in Israel and the incorporation of Jewish symbols into Israel's "civic" religion[40] negate or, at least, modify the function that the Reform and Conservative movements might play in strengthening Jewish identity.

A recent development in Israel might be noted, inasmuch as it points to a possible direction that the Reform and Conservative movements might take in the future. In accordance with government regulations enabling such action, some parents of children attending a non-religious state school in Jerusalem petitioned for the replacement of part of the curriculum with a richer program of Jewish studies following a basically Conservative syllabus. Many of the parents initially involved in this project were Conservative Jews who had immigrated from the United States. Significantly, however, the program has met with strong approval from parents unconnected with any Jewish denomination and not of Anglo-Saxon background. Enrollment in the school has consistently increased over the past three years, and there have been attempts by parents to establish similar programs in two other locations.

The desire to establish such institutions suggests that the need for religious modification in Israel might manifest itself in ways other than through synagogue forms and ritual practices. Perhaps there is a role for Reform and Conservative Judaism in transmitting a Jewish heritage that is less coercive than that demanded in Orthodox state religious schools, while richer than that provided in non-religious state institutions. The pattern of many Americans to "return" to the synagogue when their children come of school age in order to socialize them into Judaism may, in Israel, be transformed into a desire for a richer Jewish program in the school system.

One last point remains to be discussed in the light of this study's findings. Both the Reform and Conservative movements in Israel are more "traditional" than their counterpart movements in the United States, in that their religious practices are less "deviant" from Orthodox practices. The range of practices found in the synagogues of both movements is no greater than that observed within either of the movements in the United States. Is there, then, a need for two separate non-Orthodox movements in Israel? This question was posed to Reform and Conservative leaders in the course of the interviews with them. Some replied that the Reform and Conservative movements in Israel should combine forces and

[40]See Charles Liebman and Eliezer Don-Yehiya, "Israel's Civil Religion," *The Jerusalem Quarterly*, Spring 1982, pp. 57–69.

develop an indigenous, innovative responses to Jewish life in a Jewish society unfettered by institutional affiliations carried over from the past. This feeling, though, is much more prevalent among the leaders of the Reform movement, which has proven less successful than Conservative Judaism. On the other hand, many if not most of the Conservative leaders believe there should be only one movement, but that it should be their own. They feel that any cooperation with the Reform movement will further antagonize the Orthodox establishment. Furthermore, many Conservative leaders emphasize the basic incompatibility of the movements with regard to the acceptance of *halakhah* as authoritative law. Some Conservative rabbis have gained a measure of official recognition (including the occasional right to conduct weddings) in the communities in which they serve, and this, too, strengthens their determination to retain their independence.

Chapter 15

From Religious Zionism to Zionist Religion

Gideon Aran

In the early 1950s, in a secluded spot among the citrus groves of the Israeli coastal plain, a dozen or so teenagers held regular meetings in the conspiratorial manner of a secret sect. There, in a fervent state of heightened emotional consciousness, they would reveal to each other their deepest, heretical thoughts and together weave plans for a glorious future. Youthful dreams soon became the basis for a tight-knit social core, built around a daring and ambitious set of ideas. The group called itself "the Embers" (in Hebrew, *Gahelet*). It appears that even then they sensed the symbolic significance of their activities. They soon left off merely talking about their shared spiritual *Angst* and sought ways to root their mission in practical contexts, and to set about the systematic fulfillment of their dreams. Eventually, from these beginnings, they wrought a revolution in religious Zionism. Their path led them first to a transformation of the "Merkaz Harav" yeshiva in Jerusalem, and to a more general transformation of religious Zionist youth as a whole. The result, ultimately, was the creation of a unique nationalist-religious culture that crystallized in an active political and institutional framework. Thirty years later, almost all the members of *Gahelet* are to be found among the top leaders of Gush Emunim. A direct line led from naive youthful adventure to decisive influence over the entire national-religious sector; indeed, over the very identity of Israeli society and its governing institutions.[1]

Gahelet was the forerunner of Gush Emunim, and therefore it will serve as the axis of our discussion. The story of Gush Emunim begins with *Gahelet* not only because of the personal and historical continuity between the two, but also because we find revealed in *Gahelet*, for the first time, some of the typical patterns and unique features that later would come to characterize the Gush. Thus, *Gahelet* is the precursor of Gush Emunim in the symbolic sense as well as in the institutional one: here one finds both the structural and the ideological foundations of Gush Emunim as a politico-religious phenomenon. The underlying problem of both *Gahelet* and Gush Emunim in historical terms is the tension between traditional religion and modern, secular society, in general, and between Jewish Orthodoxy and nationally sovereign Judaism (i.e., Zionism) in particular.

Thus, for example, one finds expressed in *Gahelet* the same mystification of the Israeli experience of exalted statehood and, flowing directly from that, the same tension between faithfulness to Halakhah and *mizvot* on the one hand and faith in the reality of redemption, on the other, as one finds later in Gush Emunim. Similarly, one can point to the tension between the entrenchment of an institution of Torah learning, on the one hand, and the explosive momentum of a public movement, on the other, which characterized both the early and later incarnations of *Gahelet*. Many other points of contact and indeed identity between the two phenomena also exist: more specifically, e.g., the nature of the relationship between Rabbi Zvi Yehuda Hacohen Kook and his students in which the line between leader and the led is very difficult to trace; or, again, a similar recourse to a kabbalistic dialectic system permitting the simultaneous acceptance and rejection of the Zionist political enterprise.

In *Gahelet* we find that first encounter between the thought of Rav Abraham Isaac Kook and the personality of his son R. Zvi Yehuda, on the one hand, as they came to be personified in the Merkaz Harav yeshiva, and that small, unique group of young people, on the other; unique in the quality of their religious and national sensitivity, struggling with the tension between the two, against the background of a profound crisis in religious Zionism.

Gahelet represents the beginning of the trend toward radicalization among national-religious youth in Israel, a process which heightened both their religiosity and their nationalism, and thus the tension inherent in their identity containing both dissonant elements. This heightened consciousness became the basis of their strength and pride, and in due course, of their demands for leadership in the national-religious sector and beyond it, in Israeli society in general. In this paper we will be concerned chiefly with the role of *Gahelet* in the rejuvenation of Merkaz Harav and in the creation of the Kookist school of thought, more than with its role in the transformation of the national-religious sector of Israeli society. In any event, the two processes are closely linked. They are both the cause and the result of the growing internal tensions rooted in two parallel trends: the "Orthodoxization" of Zionism, and the "zionization" of Orthodoxy.

Gahelet had its beginnings in the first four years of Israeli statehood, and it ended roughly two to three years after the 1956 Sinai Campaign. Thus, it overlaps to a great extent with the early years of the new state. Most observers of Gush Emunim place its origins in the aftermath of the 1967 war or of the Yom Kippur War of 1973.[2] In my view, the roots of Gush Emunim lie buried further back in the past, in the decade after 1948. *Gahelet* and Gush Emunim have their origins in the establishment of the state.[3] Thus while the events of 1967 and 1973 are necessary for any explanation of the rise of Gush Emunim, they are not sufficient.

Gahelet and Gush Emunim were not created by one climactic event, as fateful as it may have been. Rather, their emergence was conditioned by a given long-term reality. The link between Gush Emunim and the wars of 1948, 1967, and 1973 is analogous to the relationship between the Sabbatean movement and the events of 1648–49.[4] In addition, of course, such climactic events are themselves the products or focused, sharpened expressions of broader historical developments. Where Sabbateanism was born within a Jewish religious context, conditioned by the experience of Exile,[5] "Emunism" can be viewed as a religious response to the experience of Redemption. The political fulfillment of Zionism was the underlying cause of a great crisis in Jewish Orthodoxy, caught between tradition and modernity, religion and nationhood.

The Six-Day War reinforced the development of national-religious trends and channelled it in a certain direction. The Yom Kippur War lent added stature and recognition to an already existing mood and a previously articulated set of ideas. But fundamentally these factors were superimposed upon a bedrock of preexisting concepts and tendencies. In 1967, the important new factors were the resurgence of the "whole Land of Israel" concept, and a heightened conviction of the imminence of messianic redemption. In the wake of 1973, political activism became more central, expressing with growing force the desire to lead the nation as a whole, secularists included.

Beyond these elements, however, the one dominant focal point of this complex of ideas was the fact of Jewish sovereignty itself: the reality of the national experience—modern and, essentially, secular. The establishment of the state was itself a symbol for a broader phenomenon. Political sovereignty, concretized in a network of governing institutions resting on a modern, secular basis, spelled the end of any illusion that Jewish secularism could be dismissed as a passing phenomenon. *Gahelet* was not a product of a historic event, but rather a function of a historic era, one which seemed to herald the triumph of the secular spirit.

Thus, it is possible to view *Gahelet* as a reaction to political secularism born within a defeated and bewildered Orthodoxy. Withdrawing somewhat from their previous interest in their social and cultural surroundings, those who reacted in this way also tended toward self-segregation and, naturally enough, to an extremism of their own distinctive kind. That is, one can point to a congruence between the dynamics at work in the birth of Gush Emunim and the real or perceived inferiority of religion and marginality of the religious sector in Israel.

While the achievement of statehood took place under the banner of secular Zionism, it was also the case, however, that the advent of national independence could be understood as a fact of supreme religious significance. Religious Zionists saw the establishment of the State of Israel as an unmistakable sign of the beginnings of a messianic fulfillment, a necessary first step toward complete redemption. The ingathering of the exiles, the return of the people to its land and the setting up of a sovereign government were all, traditionally, indicators of the approach of the messianic era.[6] A certain amount of religious excitement accompanied these events. It was indeed a time of exaltation, even intoxication, during which the more Orthodox sector went out of its way to cooperate with the secular public in Israel, and was welcomed in a spirit of acceptance and good will. Politically, this was expressed in the presence of Agudat Israel in the first cabinet.

Thus, the national state was accorded a certain sanctified status. It was precisely this point which became the stumbling block for religious nationalists. The new situation posed a direct challenge to Orthodoxy, demanding that it realize to the full the opportunity presented. The spiritual exaltation of 1948, if anything, made the religious dilemma more severe than would have been the case had no religious significance been assigned to Jewish statehood. *Gahelet*, then, must be seen not only as a reaction to antagonistic forces from without, but also—perhaps primarily—as a response to internal tensions within Orthodoxy, which had to be addressed on its own terms. This aspect did nothing to mitigate the problem: if anything, it made it all the more difficult. Ultimately, and paradoxically, the understanding of Israeli independence as a religious fact would help to reinforce the tendency to withdraw from direct involvement with the state as such into a mode of life increasingly segregated and alienated from its environment.

In our discussion of "religion" and Judaism in confrontation with modern nationalism, we refer specifically to traditional religion, more or less identified here with the terms "Orthodoxy" or "neo-Orthodoxy." It is the gap or opposition between traditional Judaism and Zionism that is the starting point for our examination of *Gahelet* and, ultimately, Gush Emunim as well.

As both the proponents and detractors of Zionism among the Jews will at least implicitly attest, Zionism is the great challenge facing Judaism. What is at stake is not only one or another abstract philosophical position, but an actual (and often bitter) encounter between two camps. To a great extent, for many, Zionism is the "positive expression" of the decline of Judaism.[7] This is the root of the troubled relationship between the two, and this is the problem for which Gush Emunim purports to provide a radical solution. Thus, although Gush Emunim hoists aloft the slogan, "There is no Zionism without Judaism, and no Judaism without Zionism," there is no doubt that they are fully aware of the divisions and antagonisms between the two. They do not deny, for example, that for the most part traditional Orthodoxy remained outside the Zionist camp in its early years, both in the Diaspora and in the *yishuv*. Despite the fact that they sometimes engage in a celebration of the religious "forerunners of Zionism," blowing up their historical role out of all proportion, their awareness of the general traditionalist attitude toward early Zionism is implicit in their championing of the Kookist position as a unique expression of national-religious thought.

Moreover, the Kookists cannot escape the other side of the coin: namely, that the Zionist enterprise and its prime motive forces were essentially secular, and that it self-consciously proclaimed its rebellion against traditional Judaism. On the contrary, they assign to this rebellion a paramount spiritual value.[8] The lesson they derive from the emergence of Zionism, accordingly, is that the bond between the

Jew, his people, and his land does not rest on the piety that finds expression only in the routine of religious observance and study; but that this bond comes from a deeper, hidden source of religiosity. The Zionists possess a hidden spiritual "spark," and Zionism is itself an unconditionally religious quality of spirit, regardless of subjective intent.[9] It is no accident that the spokesmen for Gush Emunim explicitly celebrate the secularism of Zionism: the Kookist outlook is expressly built upon this paradox, and seeks to provide the explanation for it. In the process of giving Zionism religious sanction, it sanctifies it.

In highlighting the frictions between Judaism and Zionism, it is certainly not my intention to argue that there is no underlying affinity between the two, or that Judaism and Zionism are polar opposites. The contrary is the case. The link between Judaism and Zionism is built on strong, positive elements, so that ambivalence better describes their mutual relationship than does conflict. Zionism, for all that it constitutes a revolution in Judaism, also derives its strength from it. Zionism aspires to a revitalization of Jewish life. Nothing illustrates better Zionism's dependence on religion-laden values than the most basic of all Zionist concepts: the yearning of the Jews for Zion. Zionism celebrates, and is nourished by, symbols that are prominently situated in the matrix of tradition.

But here precisely is the point at which Zionism constitutes a threat to traditional religion. Orthodoxy in fact recognizes that Zionism encompasses an element of "return" to Judaism. This element is at once positive and encouraging, and negative and threatening, from the traditionalist point of view. The Orthodox response to Zionism is therefore fractured, at times pointing with pride to Zionism's need to identify with traditional values, which may be taken as an indication of the primacy of religion; while at other times, in pursuit of the same argument, Orthodoxy denies any substantive link with Zionism.

In fact, however, Zionism's reliance on traditional Judaism is very selective. In searching for a usable past, it has gone very far back—to symbols of Jewish life prior to the destruction of the Second Temple—skipping over the heritage of almost two thousand years of Diaspora existence, as expressed in the Orthodox Judaism of our day. Thus, beneath the tension between Zionism and Orthodox Judaism *per se*, one can discern a much older fissure in Judaism: that line dividing rabbinic, halakhic Judaism on the one hand from the Biblical, politically sovereign Judaism of ancient Israel on the other.

Only in a later stage in the realization of the Zionist idea, when some of its initial self-assurance was lost, did there emerge a tendency to reorient Zionism toward some Jewish Diaspora values. This, however, intensified rather than dispelled the tension with Orthodoxy. Zionism still poses a problem for Judaism, in that while it borrows traditional symbols, Zionism turns them "on their head." Orthodoxy understands this very well. Take, as a prime example, the transvaluation of messianism—a central feature of Zionism as it took shape historically. The reestablishment of the Jewish nation was predicated on removing supernatural elements from the national consciousness. Nationalism was inspired by traditional messianism, from which it derived both ideological force and emotional momentum. But first, a critical transformation had to take place, from a "miraculous" to a "realistic" messianic idea. This is what Zionism accomplished, and in fact one may say that this was its essential role in Jewish history.[10] The heritage of traditional Judaism had to undergo a process of secularization and modernization before it could be turned into a unifying and driving force for modern Jewish nationalism. The revolution this involved is summed up in the phrase, "modern, secular messianism." Thus, Zionism does indeed hark back to the traditional foundations of Judaism, but it removes them from their original context and formerly accepted understandings.

Secularization has at least two important connotations, which are not mutually exclusive.[11] The term refers, first of all, to the emancipation of the social-cultural sphere from the religious sphere. Society as such is vested with an autonomous existence, and, indeed, claims priority over the religious sphere. Religion remains but one among many sectors of society, within strictly defined boundaries. Secularization in this sense takes place both on the structural and the ideational level: the state, for example, separates itself from the religious establishment, while philosophy, ethical thought, art, and science similarly no longer are founded on a belief in God. This separation usually (though not necessarily) is bound up with a decline of the authority of religion, in its now-restricted purview. At the height of this process, religion appears in a pluralistic social context and becomes a purely "private" matter for each individual or sub-group choosing to define itself religiously in a "free market" situation.[12]

The other sense in which secularization may be understood refers to the transfer of religious values—symbols, especially—from their "natural" original context, where they fit into a belief in the supernatural, to a new social sphere where they serve other purposes entirely. The new content of such symbols is foreign to their traditional forms, altering their essential character and orienting them in this-worldly directions. The best illustration here is the transformation of the Judeo-Christian messianic theology into socialist, liberal, or nationalist ideologies. Once the religious symbolism is harnessed to a secular framework, the attendant emotional baggage and overall mentality are similarly removed and enlisted in causes whose aims directly or indirectly subvert those originally associated with these symbols.

Secularization in the first sense would seem to be a necessary precondition for secularization of the second kind, although it is the second which carries the graver implications for religion. This is particularly the case when a modern, secular society takes as its primary object the preservation and faithful realization of those traditional values which it has taken over and claimed for itself. This is what Zionism has done to traditional Judaism. But Zionism was only the second stage of a secularization process that began in the context of European Jewish emancipation and the Enlightenment.

What emerges from our discussion is that the tension between Judaism and Zionism encompasses several layers of conflict: the one between religion and society and that between tradition and modernity, in addition to the old-new ones, i.e., that between religion and nationality and that between religion and the state.

We are dealing with two phenomena which are, after all, close to one another and yet the distinction between them is crucial.

From the traditional religious point of view, Zionism is secular in that its basic drive is toward this-worldly sovereignty. Zionism wants the Jew to be the master of his fate—where traditional Judaism saw only God as the ultimate Master, necessarily imposing limitations on both the individual and society. The Zionist state makes its own laws, which Orthodoxy must to some extent view as competition with or rejection of divine law (i.e., Torah law). Zionism is based upon the *a priori* definition of man and the national collective as autonomous entities. The principles and causations of man's behavior are immanent rather than transcendent. This is the procrustean secular understanding that enabled Zionism to lead Judaism back into history and to bring the Jews to political independence.

But Orthodoxy is aware of the dualism inherent in Zionism: not only continuity for the sake of revolution, but a revolution for the sake of continuity, as it were. Zionism is, certainly, a reassertion of Jewishness. This good intention, however, is the source of the problem insofar as it sets up nationalism as a substitute Judaism. In this sense, in comparison with Reform Judaism, Zionism is judged to be the greater threat, because Reform resulted (so the traditionalist argument goes) in the alienation of individual Jews from the proper paths of Torah; while Zionism leads astray the national collective as such—a form of mass assimilation.[13]

This critical evaluation of Zionism stems from the kind of analytical virtuosity so characteristic of traditional Judaism. The Orthodox are sensitive to the nature of the threat to tradition constituted by the transplantation of religious elements to the secular realm:

> Our opposition to Zionism and to the state is not based on any objection to Jewish settlement in the Land of Israel, which is a *mizva*, and is certainly not founded on enmity towards the Jewish people, God forbid. Quite the contrary. It comes out of a desire to purify and sanctify these values which Zionism reduces and empties of significance, giving them meanings which are foreign (i.e., not Jewish).[14]

Here is a perceptive understanding of the nature of the secularization process that is inseparable from Zionism precisely where it champions the assertion of Jewish identity. Rather than offering a set of alternative, secular values, Zionism effects a transposition and hence a transformation of significant meanings derived from religious tradition. The result is a blurring of the distinction between traditional religion and secular nationalism—a dangerous development from the Orthodox point of view. Gush Emunim, on the other hand, has been able to put this blurring of the lines to good effect. Nevertheless, ironically, any future success on its part will contribute to the sharpening of the lines of division.

At this point it should be noted that tradition itself was altered in the course of its confrontation with modernization and secularization. At about the end of the eighteenth century, the encounter gave birth to a new social phenomenon: Orthodoxy.[15] While Orthodoxy represents itself as the sole legitimate heir of traditional Judaism, it is in fact only one stream among others—although it is arguably the closest to the original medieval rabbinic mold. Orthodoxy, in practice, is a defensive reaction against the other modern trends in Judaism which it views as contrary to tradition.

We have thus far referred to Orthodoxy in its broadest sense in speaking of traditionalist Jewry as a whole. In fact, however, it will be necessary to refine the concept and narrow it for the purposes of this discussion.

Beginning in the second half of the nineteenth century, one can discern two distinct trends emerging within Orthodoxy. Each of these two Orthodoxies subdivided still further along a range of positions, but the significant differences between the two major camps were the overriding ones, and indeed, the gap between the two continued to widen. Ultimately, each came to reject the other's position as unacceptable. On the one side, we find the neo-Orthodox, whose origins go back to the school of thought enunciated by Samson Raphael Hirsch ("Torah and worldliness") and among whose products we can point to the Zionists of Mizrahi and HaPoel Hamizrahi ("Torah and labor"). On the other side, we find the ultra-Orthodox, represented by a variety of subgroups (generically known in Hebrew as Haredim), both in Israel and in the Diaspora. These groups oppose any significant innovation in religious life or indeed in any sphere of their social activity. While the first camp attempts to come to grips with modernity and its secularity, internalizing some of its aspects to some degree, the second seeks to avoid this encounter as far as possible. Among the modern or neo-Orthodox are the religious Zionists; religious anti-Zionists are typically located in the ultra-Orthodox wing.

In theory there is little difference between the "neo" and the "ultra": both are firm in their commitment to the Orthodox tenet of *torah min hashamayim* (the Torah as divine law) and a complete acceptance of the binding nature of the *mizvot*. In practice, however, they differ considerably in terms of life style.

Gush Emunim occupies a position somewhere between these two extremes. Its direct lineage, of course, lies within neo-Orthodoxy; however, the Gush understands itself as an opposition to the mainstream of modern Orthodoxy and in some ways takes up positions that are close to those of the ultra-Orthodox camp.

It is noteworthy that those Orthodox elements who identified with Zionism in its early years favored an alignment with the Central and West European sections of the Zionist movement—which by and large were not actively involved in matters of religion and many of whose members might be called assimilated to a considerable degree—rather than with the East European Zionists, with whom they found it difficult to achieve a modicum of dialogue and cooperation. The tension between the religious Zionists and the (other) East Europeans in the movement stemmed from the fact that many of the latter were consciously and outspokenly antireligious, having themselves rebelled against the traditional life.

In addition to this, however, one must consider that the East European secularists presented greater problems for the Orthodox, because of the secularists' attitude to the question of the content of Zionism. Their predilection to think about the Zionist reassertion of Jewish nationhood as a matter of cultural consciousness implied a search for something that might replace religion. This sort of Zionism was aimed at providing a solution not only for the "Jewish Question," but also to the "question of Judaism." Those who saw Zionism's goal as the creation of a "new Jew" could hardly serve as proper partners for the Orthodox, who, rather, were more readily able to find a common language with those who attached little importance to the matter of *kultur.*[16] This paradoxical alliance reached its most ironic point when the Orthodox Zionists supported the Herzlian faction in the debate over Uganda (1903). Here were Orthodox Jews willing to relinquish, if only temporarily, the Holy Land.

One way or another, Orthodox Jews have had difficulties in coming to terms with Zionism. True, the regnant tendency among religious Zionists has been to deny that an inherent paradox exists in their position. Nevertheless, a number of leading figures among them, while fully committed to both their Orthodoxy and their Zionism, have acknowledged that some such tension exists.[17]

It should come as no surprise that the confrontation between Zionism and Judaism has been particularly acute in Israel itself. Here the basic problem has been complicated and exacerbated by the variety of points at which the two cultural visions meet and collide on a concrete level: in social relations, economics, and politics. We have only to look at the vexed relations that developed in pre-state days between the so-called old *yishuv* and the new *yishuv*.[18] On the one side, the Haredim of the older settlement had come to live in the Holy Land out of motivations which surely included the desire to escape from the challenge of the non-Jewish European environment (and the radically changing Jewish environment, at that), to seek a refuge of traditionalism and fortify themselves there against the tide of modernity. On the other side stood the pioneering settlers of the new *yishuv* who were fulfilling their vision of Zionism by building a country and a nation.

The land of Israel was not just the scene of contention between the two factions: it was, in itself, the bone of contention. It was the real and symbolic focus of the conflict, serving both the Zionists and the traditionalists as the linchpin of their ideology. Orthodox opposition to Zionism derived from Orthodox attachment to the land—and this, of course, predated the rise of Zionism and the reaction against it.

The developing relationship between Zionism and Orthodoxy was put to its definitive test when the State of Israel was established. The dilemma was institutionalized, and theoretical issues became practical questions. At stake was the matter of what constituted law for the people of Israel: would a sovereign Jewry be ruled by Torah law, as religious tradition demanded, or not?

Israel is, after all, a *Jewish* state. That is its official self-definition, that is the substance and essence of its public identity, and that is how the overwhelming majority of its citizens perceive it. Hence, Orthodoxy cannot treat it as if it were simply another state. Moreover, statehood restored to Judaism a public dimension, gave it properties of civil society, that had been all but lost under the blows of secularization, modernization, and emancipation.[19] The new state filled the vacuum that was created by the crumbling of the traditional religious structure in the Diaspora.

Yet it was in Israel that—after a somewhat euphoric but brief respite around the time of the War of Independence—the tensions that existed before Israeli statehood were intensified. This may be attributed to a variety of causes, from the sociodemographic to the symbolic. For one thing, only with statehood were conditions created that mandated the taking of binding decisions for the entire population of the country. Previously, there had not been—nor could there have been—binding obligations, as there had not existed any political sovereign entity encompassing the various subcommunities of the *yishuv*. Rather, these voluntary communities had pursued parallel but essentially autonomous paths, while cooperating to a greater or lesser degree out of practical necessity. Statehood, by its nature, limited the self-determination of each subgroup.

A second factor was mass immigration. This not only altered the scale on which the society operated, but also increased the heterogeneity of culture and social mentality in the population, necessarily arousing issues of national identity. For example, broad new sectors of the population now existed whose stance vis-à-vis religious tradition was basically positive.

Finally, with a new generation born into the reality of Israeli statehood, it was only natural that the previous, paramount goal of establishing a state would now be replaced by a questioning and rethinking of concepts and positions taken for granted in the past.

The duality of nation and religion has existed within Judaism from its very beginnings, and has accompanied it through history as a distinguishing feature. The tension between religion and the state is also one of its classic leitmotifs. Hence the fundamental opposition between the priest or prophet and the Israelite king. Exilic existence in many ways freed Judaism of these internal conflicts. The restoration of Jewish independence, naturally enough, has brought them once more to the fore. But this time, the problem is different, quite unprecedented in Jewish history, and therefore all the more difficult. The State of Israel confronts Orthodox Jewry with a reality never before encountered by Judaism—nor even imagined: the existence of a *Jewish secular* state. Traditional sources offer no guidance in the case of a sovereign Jewish polity that is also secular.

In theory, Orthodox Judaism has two archetypal options in responding to this situation. The one alternative is that usually associated with the ultra-Orthodox. The extreme Haredim reject the Zionist state out of hand and refuse to cooperate with it on any level. This is a well-defined religious position, with its own internal logic. The other available position, generally speaking that of religious Zionism, borders on the sanctification of the state. Israel, despite its secular character, is the bearer of such religious significance that any faithful Jew becomes obligated to take an active role in its life and share in the responsibilities of citizenship, almost on a par with the obligations imposed by the Torah.

Of course, in practice the majority of Orthodox Israelis refrain from taking either position to its logical conclusion, adopting mutually incompatible elements from both archetypal options, and this compounds the tensions within Orthodoxy. In the process, Israeli Orthodoxy has fallen in the esteem of the broader public, in its own esteem, and particularly in that of its younger generation.

Nonetheless, it must be emphasized that the two extreme positions are not abstract "ideal types," but really exist in the form of known groups in the Israeli population. They serve as points of orientation for the rest of the religious sector, who place themselves along a spectrum stretching between the two. One widespread "compromise" position is the one that affirms Jewish statehood as a positive development, not because the state is viewed as a religious end in itself, but because it is seen as a means to an end. The state, despite its secular character, creates the preconditions that allow for the observance of the *mizvot* that are obligatory only in Israel, helps in fostering a fully Jewish life style, and assures the safety, well-being, and pride of the Jews.

Some members of the religious Zionist camp recognize, however, that such compromises were bought at the price of a certain amount of self-deception. Moreover, the delicate balance thus achieved was not destined to last very long. Orthodox nationalists could only be satisfied on a very superficial level by promises and guarantees of narrow party interests which avoided making religious demands upon the general public. Critics charged that religious Zionism had made its peace with the secularity of the Jewish state—had indeed placed on it its stamp of approval—all for the sake of its own social and political welfare: in a word, it had "sold out." Such charges became characteristic of the Kookist camp, first in *Gahelet* and later in Gush Emunim, to which we now turn our direct attention.

As noted at the outset, *Gahelet* was the creation of a group of youngsters who were students at religious Zionist schools in Israel in the 1950s. The group, associated with the Orthodox Bnei Akiva youth movement, displayed an unusual degree of social and religious commitment and activism, and was deeply troubled by the predicament of religious Zionism. *Gahelet* was at once an expression of the Orthodox Zionist dilemma and an attempt to offer a solution to it. *Gahelet* emerged from the ranks of Orthodox Zionism and in opposition to it. Aside from anything else, it was an authentic religious response to the challenge of Zionism.

Gahelet began at Kfar Haroeh, a well-established agricultural settlement affiliated with Hapoel Hamizrachi that maintained an Orthodox boarding school. It was the only such school in the country at the time, headed and founded by Rabbi Moshe Zvi Neria, and destined to become the model for the network of Bnei Akiva-linked yeshiva high schools. Rabbi Neria was a chief spokesman and an outstanding personality of the religious Zionist movement. In 1951–52, the school was involved in the campaign to counter what the Orthodox camp saw as an "anti-religious war." Those years were characterized by a depressed spirit that followed hard upon the ecstatic first year of Israeli independence.

The entering class of 1951 included members of the "Eitanim" branch of Bnei Akiva, from the Tel Aviv area, who arrived at the school as an established social unit. Among them, however, were a number of exceptional individuals who, from the very first, kept their distance from the rest and formed a school "aristocracy."

Their group consciousness and ideological development took on a distinct form, based on purist aspirations. Their meetings were marked by intense and intimate outpourings of thought and feeling, and were generally conducted at night in secluded spots. There was much frank soul-searching and heated argument, informed by what they felt was the fatefulness—even holiness—of the hour at hand. They quickly became a closed, selective community with a highly developed sense of mutual responsibility.

These were youngsters aged thirteen to fifteen, and their youth certainly played a crucial role. *Gahelet* was, among other things, an adolescent rebellion against parents whose moderation and compromises were viewed with disdain. (Indeed, the sons, by and large, were to become more strictly Orthodox than their parents.) Their rebellion was also expressed in the challenge they threw down to their youth movement's leadership—both the group leaders with whom they had direct contact and the national leadership; a rebellion that began modestly from minor infractions but which ended in an open conflict over principles, that created a revolution in the movement. And one can also say that they rebelled against the authority of their teacher, Rabbi Neria, whom they held in the highest regard, but whom they quite consciously coopted and led in their own direction more than they allowed themselves to be guided by him. This blurring of the distinction between rabbi and followers was to be repeated later in the early growth of Gush Emunim.

Their age manifested itself in a number of other group traits, among which one can point to a naive romanticism. Thus, for example, there were group "confessions," often revolving around a newly discovered attraction for the opposite sex, something which resulted in their partnership with a girls' group called *Nogah*.[20] Their romanticism found expression also in their preference for picturesque settings full of magic and drama. Important in this regard, as well, was the conspiratorial air that they fostered, from the very beginning, which often had no instrumental purpose.

To all this we must add the exaggerated seriousness with which they viewed their every word and deed, which was a factor in the frequent internal quarrels and threatened splits. They were plagued by typical adolescent identity crises, but they also (again, typically for their age) displayed very little patience or tolerance for middle-of-the-road positions, moderation, or compromise. They demanded clear-cut definitions, total consistency. Their radicalism was inspired by a world-embracing idealism, breadth of vision, spontaneity and originality, exuberance and chutzpah—as well as ambition and self-confidence. There was undoubtedly an element of delicious excitement too, with all their youthful innocence. Hence their exclusivity and elitism, with regard to those outside the group, and their far from modest self-image among themselves, which was reinforced by the admiration of outsiders. They were treated as something special, regarded as somehow older than the others, and given greater latitude.

Gahelet's romanticism, rebelliousness, and radicalism are well-known qualities of youth culture and typify the classical youth movement. Thus, the group "confessions" of adolescent boys in a male-only educational setting; the long nights around the campfire; the compulsive searchings for a higher sense and order in the world and for the meaning of God—all of this also took place in the early days of the socialist Zionist youth movements, perhaps no less so among the more right-wing nationalists, in the style of "Young Germany" of the 20s.[21]

About a half-year after the inception of *Gahelet*, the group published its first newsletter, a primitive attempt in mimeograph. In it, they declared their intention to "kindle the flame of future generations, to look forward to the day on which every man in Israel will sit under his vine and fig tree in full observance of the Torah of Israel."[22] Among the other guiding principles mentioned in this first issue of *Gahelet*, one finds "love of all the Jewish people and mutual responsibility for all Jews"; "nationalism and patriotism"; "dedication to the nation and loyalty to the state"; "readiness to sacrifice for the sake of the nation." One also finds a strong sense of their confidence in being able to reach out and affect the general public and to lead it in the prescribed direction.

These very closely linked ideas may, in the Israeli context, be subsumed under the word *halutziut* (inadequately rendered in English as "pioneering spirit"), and it is this highly untypical juxtaposition of Torah and *halutziut* that *Gahelet* placed on its banner. In addition to its classical symbolic connotation, the name *Gahelet* was an acronym for "Nucleus of Torah-Learning Pioneers." Later on, they formulated very specific goals, among which was the founding of a new religious kibbutz in which to put their ideals into practice. The center of their kibbutz was to be the yeshiva, where the male member of the collective would spend the bulk of their time in study while the community's economy was looked after by the women.

The original group grew from a founding trio who gathered around them a dozen students, selected from the cream of their seventy classmates, and an additional five from the school at Pardes Hannah. At the end of the first year, the group numbered twenty members; by the end of the second year, it had doubled in size. When the class graduated after four years, *Gahelet* claimed a membership of close to one hundred.

Qualifications for membership were strict. The two main criteria were the social compatibility of the candidate with the group and his standards of religious observance. In the group's publications of the time it was argued that the two criteria were in fact integrally linked, as the distinction between the social and religious elements was difficult to establish. A candidate was accepted only by a two-thirds majority vote, and he then could take four days to reconsider his fateful step. No one remembers a single instance, however, in which an accepted candidate changed his mind.

In the first years, only graduates of yeshiva schools were accepted. Afterwards, when the group came to value quantity as well as quality, in line with the drive for wider influence (in the Bnei Akiva movement, first of all), it opened its ranks to the "better" members of the local youth groups.[23]

Heavier demands were made of members than of potential candidates. Peer pressure was exerted to maintain the most stringent standards, particularly in the realm of religious behavior. Laxity or infringements carried a heavy social cost, which could include warnings, public reprimand, even "excommunication." All this, of course, merely heightened the prestige and group consciousness of the members, and the lines drawn around the insiders became ever sharper. This accounts for the superiority and even the snobbery with which outsiders were treated. The cultivation of secrecy also helped tie the group together. Indeed, it was quite some time before wider youth movement circles became aware of what was happening.

Another method of social control and indoctrination was the introduction, unusual in the Israeli context, of regular exhortatory sermons. Such *musar* talks, to be sure, had a long tradition in the yeshiva framework, going back to Rabbi Israel Salanter in the late nineteenth century, and are still a part of ultra-Orthodox yeshiva life today. The use of this specific method for rekindling the commitment of the faithful points up the somewhat dissonant combination of a spontaneous, open-ended spiritual experience and a drive toward a strict, conformist regimen. The history of religions provides several examples of initial charismatic outbursts and mystical yearnings which are gradually harnessed into Orthodox patterns, reinforcing and sanctioning old norms and ritual obligations.

This "Orthodoxization" was expressed, as well, in the adoption of a style of speaking, writing, even dressing, that emphasized the didactic, the spiritual, the pious. "Modest dress," speech studded with expressions from the yeshiva world and scriptural allusions—all were characteristic of this behavior and were elevated in importance almost to the level of ritual observance itself. The calculated spirituality came across in the sermons, too, which were almost entirely devoted to "religion and ideology." This atmosphere was clearly felt by members and outsiders to be the special quality of the group, and had a most profound impact on the girls who became associated with it. As they themselves claim, they transformed their life style radically to conform to the standards set by the boys.

Aside from such psychosocial factors, it is worth noting that the setting at Kfar Haroeh lent itself particularly well to a process of separation from the outside world. The yeshiva was a "total" educational environment, socially and institutionally, which made for a heightened separation from parental homes and a concomitantly enhanced influence exercised by teachers and mentors. Even its ecological situation fostered separateness: the yeshiva was located relatively far from the community of Kfar Haroeh itself. It was, in effect, a "hothouse" that allowed the students in some sense to avoid confronting the Israeli reality of the time, and permitted them to construct a religious ideology that had no need to face "historical" tests. In later years, this sort of "monastic" setting would be recreated in the Gush Emunim West Bank settlements, where the purist standards of a sacred code could be maintained.

With the yeshiva boys as the dominant and guiding element, the emphasis of the group's ideas shifted from "Torah and labor" to "Torah," exclusively, with Torah-study as the ideal. Scrutiny of the day-to-day life of the religious kibbutzim revealed the disappointing fact that study was not as central a concern as *Gahelet* members believed it ought to be. Nor, as they found to their chagrin, was religious behavior strictly monitored—particularly in the area of socializing with women.

Returning during vacation periods to the mainly urban, local branches of the youth movement, *Gahelet* members took on roles of group leadership, acting as guides to those their own age. In this way, their experience began to communicate itself to a wider periphery. The impact of *Gahelet* on Bnei Akiva is reflected in the youth movement's bulletin, *Zeraim*, of those years.[24] *Gahelet* members were also sent as representatives to national conferences. Their crowning achievement was the decision taken by the movement, in conjunction with the army, to permit the graduating members to study at a yeshiva for a year before doing their military service.

This was a radical departure from previous Bnei Akiva policy, and in retrospect marked the beginning of a new radicalism. From here on, the emphasis shifts away from the values of kibbutz settlement and focuses on Torah education.[25] High school yeshivas of Bnei Akiva were now established, followed by the *"hesder"* yeshivas which attracted the best of religious high school graduates. The direction that many students took was toward becoming teachers, raising the status of the yeshiva faculty that previously had kept itself outside the more influential and authoritative circles of the rabbinate. In the process of "Orthodoxization," the movement developed a more positive self-image, a greater confidence in confronting the broader public, and what may be called "religious pride."

The success of *Gahelet* in transforming the values of the religious-Zionist youth movement can also be read in the fate of the "losing side": the religious kibbutz. Originally intended to expand and continue its development, *Gahelet* and the youth movement as a whole reached a point of downgrading the kibbutz as an ideal, if not actually rejecting it. Bnei Akiva, educating youngsters toward "Torah and labor," had been intended as the main reservoir of future religious kibbutz members. The new spirit in the movement, although not yet completely dominant, had already alienated many members from the original message.

The advances made by the *Gahelet* group and its sympathizers aroused a good deal of opposition at the time: local branches of the youth movement were divided ideologically and socially by the competing camps. There was palpable tension between the smaller group and the general membership. A more serious problem developed, however, between the radicals and the national leadership and its institutions. *Gahelet* had in fact anticipated opposition, and had therefore initially kept its activities in recruiting adherents secret. Its fears were well-justified: when the existence of the group became known, it was charged with creating a private organization, inimical to the unity and aims of the movement. Differences also arose over the character of the group's intentions for its post-graduation goals, as well as their timing. The conflict came to a head when the national leadership demanded the immediate dismantling of *Gahelet*.

In the end, the group was in fact split up, but by that time the influence of its ideas within the movement was an accomplished fact—felt even in the top echelons. The very man sent to oversee the dismantling of *Gahelet* was won over to its point of view and in fact joined it—or at least the faction that broke its ties with Bnei Akiva. That man was Haim Druckman, who later became one of the most influential educators of religious Zionist youth and a leader of Gush Emunim.

In their eleventh-grade year, the *Gahelet* group helped to initiate a twelfth-year study program at Kfar Haroeh, in the framework of a *beit midrash* (study center) established there. The following year they helped to found a new yeshiva at Kerem Beyavneh. The latter's importance as an innovation—one which grew directly out of the *Gahelet* experience—was that the aim was not merely to add another year of study prior to military service, but to establish an independent yeshiva to serve as the center of the new ideology.

Most of the group's members, however, including the original founders, chose to study at already established yeshivas, where they hoped to mold the character of the schools to their own way of thinking. In the main there were three yeshivas that attracted the *Gahelet* alumni: "Netiv Meir" and "Merkaz Harav" in Jerusalem, and "Hadarom" in Rehovot.[26] Kerem Beyavneh was the creation of those who remained, and was the first yeshiva founded by young Israelis.

At Kerem Beyavneh the *Gahelet* group continued to stick together, maintaining a distinct identity. It was during this period that a chain of events—perhaps coincidental, perhaps inevitable—led the Kerem Beyavneh group to meet with their former classmates in Jerusalem, and through them, to a personal encounter with R. Zvi Yehuda Hacohen Kook of Merkaz Harav. Long discussions took place about the relationship between the Jewish people, its land and the Torah. R. Zvi Yehuda's character and ideas left a profound impression on the group, and when (in the early spring of that year) the yeshiva at Kerem Beyavneh was left without a head, it was only natural that the students should gravitate toward Merkaz Harav.

A second meeting with R. Zvi Yehuda was arranged at Passover, during which the group asked him to provide instruction in the thought of his father, the late R. Abraham Isaac Hacohen Kook. This was the decisive juncture at which the link with "Merkaz Harav" took shape, and with it came the feeling among members of the group that they had finally found themselves an appropriate mentor.

Even the proudest "Kookist" will admit that, until the coming of the *Gahelet* group, the Merkaz Harav yeshiva was not widely regarded as an important center of Torah study. Even in religious Zionist circles it tended to be ignored or actually forgotten. R. Zvi Yehuda's own status, both inside and outside the yeshiva, was not particularly high. The truth of the matter is that even during the lifetime of Rav Kook himself, whose personality was certainly outstanding, both in the yeshiva and in society in general, the yeshiva itself did not achieve the kind of central importance which its founders had hoped for. It certainly did not achieve its original intention of serving as a bridge between the traditionalist "old *yishuv*" and the "new," Zionist settlers.

In the twenty years after Rav Kook's time, the yeshiva had lost track of the distinctive role it had intended to play in Zionism and in the secular world in general, and lapsed into the routine of a typical yeshiva. Its financial and its physical condition deteriorated, and it lacked connections with any public body or faction that might have supported it. It had very few students, of rather poor quality, and a staff of mediocre teachers.[27]

The *Gahelet* alumni generally maintain that they came "not to the yeshiva, but to the rabbi." This implies, of course, a negative judgment of the spirit which existed at "Merkaz" before their coming; but it equally reveals the personal and intimate quality of their encounter with its principal. Indeed, almost from the very first, the group took to spending long hours in study and discussion with R. Zvi Yehuda, developing warm and especially close ties with him. His preference for these students over the others was marked, and it soon became apparent that an "in" group existed. To borrow a hasidic term, they made R. Zvi Yehuda their "rebbe." He became their discovery: a hidden genius, previously unappreciated, now revealed in all his glory as an exceptional personality. They surrounded him with a myth of their own creation: he became a towering figure of irresistable magnetism. His was a charisma that owed more to the veneration of his followers than to his own qualities.

The "love at first sight" between *Gahelet* and R. Zvi Yehuda proved to be of lasting duration—not least because each side of the partnership had found in the other exactly what it had been looking for. They fulfilled each other's needs almost perfectly, and the relationship enjoyed a singular mutuality, even a completeness. To the young men, R. Zvi Yehuda was their teacher, their leader, their father; to him, they were disciples, sons, a public.

With their attachment to "Merkaz" and to R. Zvi Yehuda, the group had seemingly given up its original ideal, that of combining *halutziut* and Torah—although in time they would develop the argument that the path they had chosen indeed represented this combination, in its highest expression. However, for the moment, the group excused itself from the religious-Zionist challenge. This withdrawal from activity in the public arena to the sphere of traditional learning, nonetheless, did not solve for them the basic tension between Zionism and Orthodoxy. Instead, they brought that tension with them as they penetrated further into the world of Torah. The contradictions were expressed not only on an ideological level, but on the social-institutional level as well.

Although there is something to be said for a number of interesting similarities between the yeshiva world and a youth movement—the common elements of youth culture, elitism, strict devotion to the cause, etc.—the entry of *Gahelet* into a traditional yeshiva structure was fraught with incongruities and tensions.

The first effect on the group was the abandonment of those qualities which were specific to the youth movement: the social-political activism, the focus on the surrounding society. They entered the yeshiva environment wholeheartedly, concentrating solely on the study of Torah. They justified this, at the time, by arguing that the building of the yeshiva "from within" had to precede any attempt to affect the society outside the yeshiva. They were indeed aware of the nature of the turnabout they had made, if only from the attitude of the religious kibbutz movement, Bnei Akiva, and the religious Zionist party circles towards them. The youth movement and the kibbutzim were not quite sure what to do with *Gahelet* any more, while the party assumed that, as yeshiva boys, they no longer had a voice in political matters. Only they themselves still considered themselves to be "political." It was in this unique position, straddling the two worlds, that the group set out to develop its distinctive philosophy, based on the paradoxical belief that it was here, enclosed within the four walls of the house of study, that they would reach the full meaning of the political.

Not quite ten years after the start of their yeshiva career, some *Gahelet* members emerged from their study hall to organize a faction within the National Religious Party. Criticizing the party's policies in general, and the role played by its "Young Guard" in particular, they pulled together a number of young yeshiva men interested in a revival of the spirit of "Torah and labor." Their actual power was minimal, but they were convinced that "quality"—i.e., the fact that they were scholars—would weigh heavily in their favor. The faction was recruited from Merkaz Harav and elements drawn from Bnei Akiva and the religious kibbutz movement, and their first challenge were the party elections in the N.R.P. in 1963–64. They called the faction *Hug Emunim* ("circle" or faction of the faithful).

Their effort was stillborn, and this fact was no less significant than that of their embarking on the project in the first place. R. Zvi Yehuda forbade the leaders of the faction—R. Zephaniah Drori and R. Haim Druckman, in particular—to continue their political activities. "Either politics or Torah," he told them, stating what was the traditionalist view, though he thus negated some basic mystic-messianic principles of his father's philosophy. He did, in fact, soften his ultimatum, arguing that it was important to strive to influence the state and Israeli society, but that this did not include the formation of anything as formal as a party faction. The fledgling politicians heeded his instruction, and returned to their studies.

The forerunners of Gush Emunim, thwarted and disillusioned in their confrontation with their society and with Zionism in its secular, political terms, sought refuge in the religious tradition. Seeking a basis for the Zionist component of their identity, they turned to the religious component which their parents had to some extent compromised in creating the religious Zionist option. In identifying more with Zionism, they had distanced themselves somewhat from traditionalist values and style. Gush Emunim, on the other hand, having gone the route of distancing itself from practical Zionism as a way of rediscovering the world of tradition, would later find it necessary to "rediscover" Zionism. The path of *Gahelet* led—not inevitably, nor did members at the time foresee what lay ahead—to a heightened political consciousness.

With *Gahelet*, we have a small, even marginal, group withdrawing from the fray, paradoxically because of its zealous devotion to state and nation. It did not abandon its attachment to them, but the ambivalent nature of its attitude to them became more extreme. From within the Orthodox yeshiva world, they were both increasingly attracted and repelled by the political world outside. It took twenty-five years, but the alumni of *Gahelet* finally did break into the political arena, eager to capture it for religious Judaism via the fulfillment of Zionism. One may say that if *Gahelet* represented "Orthodoxization" for the sake of Zionism, Gush Emunim was "Zionization" for the sake of Orthodoxy.

Gahelet is a historic turning point for religious Zionism. A group that is zealously devoted to a set of traditional values, even if marginal or small, can have a disproportionate influence on the general public. This is particularly true with regard to the influence of such a group upon those sectors of society which themselves owe allegiance to those same values. The compromisers are in effect "held captive" by those on the extreme who demand consistency between theory and practice.

Against the background of the challenge of a secular modernity (in the guise of Zionism) poised to conquer Judaism, and of the seeming inability of the "national religious" option to meet it, *Gahelet* offered a new solution to the problem. It approached Judaism and Zionism as a unity, and embarked on a course of dual radicalization: a more extreme Orthodoxy together with a more extreme nationalism. Though involved in the state and its society, the members of *Gahelet* came to view them from an external vantage point. *Gahelet* admired the ultra-Orthodox, just as they admired the secularists, for what they saw as their self-sufficiency and the faithfulness to principles which endowed them with authority and legitimacy.

The solution offered by *Gahelet* embraced a nationalist-political experience clothed in mystical-messianic terms; it was a deep and authentic religious revival that used Zionism as its medium. In *Gahelet* we see the beginnings of the change from "religious Zionism" to "Zionist religion." This reversal is the essence of what I have called "Kookism." Kookism is a value and idea complex—an ideology, mentality, and life style—that originated in *Gahelet* and became in the course of time the characteristic feature of the radical activist sector of religious, land-settling Zionism. The roots of the phenomenon lie in the encounter between Rav Kook's theological system, mediated through the personality and educational endeavors of his son, and the individuals of a small "sect."

Gahelet, however, was not the inevitable product of any earlier developments, but rather an independent, original phenomenon. It may be surprising to learn that until they came to the old house on Rav Kook Street in Jerusalem, the youths of *Gahelet* were not familiar with the thought of Rav Kook. With R. Zvi Yehuda as their guide, this now became an overriding preoccupation. Today, the graduates of the group cite Rav Kook's thought as the source of their emergence—even if only through indirect and hidden influences of which, at the time, they were not aware. But in precise historical terms, it is clear that they were believers in search of a dogma. The matching of the spiritual doctrine and its cult was a case of "elective affinity."[28] Kookism led them to the mystical-messianic solution of the Zionism-Judaism dilemma, and at the same time brought them further into the traditionalist world. This, of course, heightened the tension which they experienced as nationalists and as Orthodox Jews in the State of Israel.

The meeting of the group's search for a solution and the thought of Rav Kook transformed the latter from a theology to an ideology. *Gahelet* benefited from the added depth—both spiritual and ideological—as well as the added strength afforded by the weight of tradition, when they attached themselves to Kook's ideas. Those ideas, on the other hand, benefited from the place of honor they received in an actual social-political framework, when in their original context they had exerted little real influence. At last translated into a platform for action, the mystical-messianic complex faced the challenge of historical reality. At first, Kookism was a rationalization for the group's set of ideas, an external or instrumental tool for the articulation of an independently developed consciousness. In due course, however, the ideology took on an independent existence, with a considerable potential of its own. It took the Zionism-Judaism dilemma out of its this-worldly context and placed it in the transcendental realm of Torah, kabbalistically interpreted.

Until the advent of *Gahelet*, in its Kookist phase, the mystical messianism of Rav Kook was understood as an individualistic and esoteric doctrine.[29] To the extent that it had achieved prior recognition, it was generally an object of bitter criticism, from the "right" (i.e., the ultra-Orthodox camp), or exploited and patronized by the "left" (secular Zionists) which romanticized it without understanding it.[30]

Rav Kook's great stature as a thinker notwithstanding, in his ambition to apply his conception to all sectors in the yishuv, to unite them finally under an all-embracing "sacred canopy"—containing the profane as well—his enterprise was a dismal failure. His messianic mysticism, appropriating Zionism within its folds, was never accepted by the secular camp. It was, at the same time, repulsed by large and important parts of the Orthodox community. Consequently, it was only natural that Rav Kook's most important public project—the establishment of the chief rabbinate, which meant the institutionalization of his theology—turned out to be, at the very least, less than successful. To this day, its authority is not quite accepted by the secular public while the Orthodox right wing (from Agudat Israel rightwards) totally denies it. Instead of serving to bridge the gap between the Orthodox and the non-Orthodox, it actually emphasizes the differences dividing them.31

Such was the fate of Rav Kook's tragic attempt to break through toward the Zionist pole of his ingenious synthesis. His more modest enterprise, the yeshiva which he founded, not only did not live up to the classical standards of an institution of halakhic learning, but also failed to play any role in the general social and political system. It took nearly thirty years before *Gahelet* discovered Rav Kook's legacy and revealed its enormous potential—even while altering it in the process.

Once the encounter occurred between *Gahelet* and the teachings of Rav Kook—between social experience and civil consciousness on the one hand and the religious idea and emotion on the other—each became linked to the other in a relationship which revealed new dimensions on both sides. Rav Kook's thought took on the aspect of a platform for political involvement and was harnessed to the aspirations of an active social force. In a parallel development, those aspirations took on spiritual depth and enjoyed a new legitimation for what had until then been merely dreams and feelings. In the process, both assumed an essentially new and different significance, which could not then have been appreciated, and cannot now be exaggerated. Its distinctive and lasting expression is Gush Emunim.

NOTES

This paper is a condensed and translated version of a chapter in a Ph.D. dissertation to be submitted to the Department of Sociology and Social Anthropology of the Hebrew University (1984). The broader study consists of description and analysis of Gush Emunim, its social dimensions and cultural significance. It is based primarily on three years of field research which included intensive participant observation, open in-depth interviews, and documentary analysis. Although Gush Emunim, as a social movement, is usually analyzed in terms of political sociology, extensive use is made here of the analytical perspective of the sociology of religion.

It is my contention that the activist public face of Gush Emunim, salient and important as it is, is basically a function of the religious nature of the group. Elucidation of this less obvious and more complex aspect is essential for an understanding of the way in which the movement presents itself in public life. The analysis of Gush Emunim as a religious movement sheds light on some basic features of Israeli society, in its relationship with the traditional Jewish heritage in particular, and on the problematics of the relationship between society and religion in general. The chapter from which excerpts are presented here is followed by a chapter analyzing the teachings and activity of Rabbi Abraham I. Kook (Rav Kook), and another devoted to his son and his Merkaz Harav yeshiva. Together, these three chapters form the framework in which we deal with the origins of Gush Emunim. This is followed by a study of the culture, values, and characteristic ideas of Gush Emunim, and finally by chapters dealing with its structure, dynamics, organizational, and political patterns.

The term "Zionist religion" has been used previously, though in a different sense, by Y. Eilam, "Mashber ha-ziyonut—mashber ha-yahadut," *Bitfutsot hagolah* (1975).

My thanks are due to the editors of *Studies in Contemporary Jewry* for their initiative and counsel, and particularly to Eli Lederhendler for his help in translation and editing.

1. *Gahelet* is practically unknown outside a very limited circle of those who were directly involved in it. It has been ignored in the literature, with the one exception of the forthcoming book (1985) by M. Bar-Lev, which deals with *Gahelet* in the context of the development of the Bnei Akiva movement.
2. See, e.g., J. Odea, "Gush Emunim: shorashim ve-du-mashma'uyot." *Bitfutsot hagolah* 1979/80, and A. Rubinstein, *Mi-Herzl ad gush emunim u-behazarah* (Tel-Aviv: 1980).
3. E. Goldman used a similar chronology, with reasons closely approximating my own. Though he did not pursue the subject historically or sociologically, as an educator and thinker with a close familiarity with the subject he raises very interesting points, from the perspective of religious Zionism and of the religious kibbutz movement in particular. See his "Meshihiyut pashtanit," *bitfutsot hagolah* 1979/80. Without citing it by name, Goldman alludes to the *Gahelet* phenomenon as an early manifestation of what later developed into Gush Emunim. His perceptive comments were necessarily brief, coming as a reaction to the first piece of research on Gush Emunim (Odea, see note 2 above). He did not go into details, nor did those who adopted his analysis in subsequent discussions. See e.g., E. Sprinzak, "Gush Emunim: model hakarhon shel ha-kizoniyut ha-politit," *Medinah, mimshal, ve-yahasim bein le'umiim* 17 (1981).
4. See Gershom Scholem, *Shabbetai Zvi ve-hatnu'ah ha-shabtait biyemei hayav* (Tel-Aviv: 1974), esp. chapter 1.
5. *Ibid.*
6. Gershom Scholem, "Le-havanat ha-ra'ayon ha-meshihi be-yisrael," in *Dvarim bago* (Tel-Aviv: 1975).
7. Such a view is expressed, for example, by B. Kurzweil, "Mahutah u-mekoroteha shel tnu'at ha-kna'anim," *Luah ha-aretz* (Tel-Aviv: 1953).

8. See, e.g., Hanan Porat, " 'Ayin be-'ayin yir'u be-shuv ha-shem ziyon," *Petahim* 1975.
9. *Ibid.*
10. See J. Katz, *Le'umiyut yehudit* (Jerusalem: 1979), esp. pp. 15–36.
11. For the distinction between the two senses of secularization and their application in Jewish history, see *ibid.*, pp. 72–85, 132–154.
12. For the definitive expression of this idea, see P. Berger, *The Sacred Canopy* (New York: 1969 [1967]); T. Parsons, *Social Structure and Personality* (New York: 1970).
13. The Lubavicher Rebbe, as quoted by Y. Eilam. "Mashber ha-ziyonut—mashber ha-yahadut," *Bitfutsot hagolah* 1975.
14. *Ibid.*, p. 46. Cf. I. Gitlin (of the extreme right-wing ultra-Orthodox camp) in his critical essay, *Yahadut ha-torah ve-ha-medinah* (Jerusalem: 1959), p. 26.
15. My brief and general discussion of Orthodoxy is based on the historical-typological description by M. Samet (mimeo., no date), "Ortodoksiah—tipologiah ve-historiah," and particularly on Eliezer Schweid's analysis in *Ortodoksiah ve-humanizm dati* (Jerusalem: 1977).
16. This motif is repeated to a certain degree in the Gush Emunim experience: the Gush also tends to prefer the non-ideologically secular over those non-Orthodox Israelis who have their own articulated approach to Jewish culture and identity.
17. Aside from the controversial views of Leibovitz (e.g., as presented in *Yahadut, am yehudi u-medinat yisrael* [Tel-Aviv: 1976]), for whom the tensions between religion and secular nationalism are central, we can cite a number of figures who have enjoyed a much greater acceptance, despite their unusual candor: Baruch Kurzweil (e.g., in his already-cited essay on the Canaanites—see above, note 7); Rabbi Adin Steinsaltz, who stated that Zionism is "the negation not only of the Diaspora but of Jewish tradition itself" (in *Petahim* 23 [1972]).
18. On the Orthodox community's attitude toward Zionism in the pre-state *yishuv*, see M. Friedman, *Hevrah va-dat* (Jerusalem: 1978) and "Yahasei datiim—hiloniim likrat hakamat ha-medinah," in A. Shapira (ed.), *Sugiyot be-toldot ha-ziyonut ve-ha-yishuv* (Tel-Aviv: 1982/83).
19. The terms are used by S. Avineri: *Ha-ra'ayon ha-ziyoni ligvanav* (Tel-Aviv: 1980), see esp. his "Epilogue."
20. Among the more first-hand accounts which I was able to gather (from interviews and the writings of the *Gahelet* members from those years), I found the testimony of a young woman who was close to one of the founding members of *Gahelet*, and who afterward joined the group with the rest of her group of girls, to be of particular importance. In the course of her own subsequent career, as a student of social psychology at the Hebrew University, she wrote a term paper on *Gahelet* as a case study of a "small group." A copy of the paper, written twenty years ago (and thus still close in time to the actual events) is in my possession.
21. See, e.g., W. Laqueur, *Young Germany* (London: 1962).
22. The wrinkled and yellowed pages of *Gahelet*'s bulletins of thirty years ago were of particular use to me in my research.
23. Among the first members of *Gahelet* who later played an influential role in Bnei Akiva, in the Merkaz Harav yeshiva, and finally in Gush Emunim (or the "Kookist" camp out of which it grew), all of them well-known rabbis today, we can cite the following: Zephaniah Drori, Yaakov Filber, Zalman Melamed, Ariel Fuchs, Shabbetai Zelikovich. All of them began their political careers at age fourteen. Other prominent personalities who associated themselves early on with the group are: Haim Druckman, the Bnei Akiva group leader who became a "follower" of the boys he ostensibly led; and Moshe Levinger, then affiliated with the "Ezra" group in Jerusalem. After his military service, he turned to Torah studies and fell under the spell of the group at Kfar Haroeh, still in

its formative stage. Later, at the Merkaz Harav, he formally joined the group. One might also mention Rabbi Waldman, who arrived from the United States at about that time and encountered the group during the founding of the yeshiva at Kerem Beyavneh.

24. See, e.g., *Zeraim* of 1954/55.
25. *Zeraim* no. 1, 1954/55. The Bnei Akiva bulletin at the time published a revealing cartoon, depicting a boxing arena: the defeated fighter, lying on the floor, bears the caption, "kibbutz"; his elated victor stands above him, arms aloft, bearing the label, "yeshiva." *Zeraim* no. 2, 1954/55.
26. Their choice was limited, as most of the yeshivas belonged to the ultra-Orthodox camp (the so-called black yeshivas), and were not quite what they had in mind in terms of developing the *Gahelet* point of view. It should be noted that in the early stages of choosing a school for the group as a whole, Merkaz Harav was considered but rejected. They felt that it was loosely organized and "not serious," giving the impression of being on the level of a European "heder"—and not for Israelis like themselves. Rav Zvi Yehuda sent two representatives to Tel-Aviv to speak with the group and attempt to convince them to study at his yeshiva, but they sent the two men back without as much as granting them an interview. Within a generation, these very youths became central figures at Merkaz Harav and took part in founding a "heder" for their own children, attached to the yeshiva.
27. At the time that *Gahelet* became part of Markaz Harav, there were some twenty other students there, who conducted their studies in a very traditional fashion. See M. Z. Nahorai, "Lihyot yehudi," *Amudim* (May 1976).
28. On the role of "elective affinity" in social processes, see Max Weber, in H. Gerth and C. Mills (eds.), *From Max Weber* (London: 1948), pp. 284–85. Cf. E. Fischoff, "The Protestant Ethic—History of a Controversy," in S. N. Eisenstadt (ed.), *The Protestant Ethic and Modernization* (New York: 1948); and P. Berger, "Charisma and Religious Innovation," *American Sociological Review* no. 28 (1963).
29. For a description in similar terms, see G. Scholem, *Major Trends in Jewish Mysticism* (New York: 1971 [1941]).
30. See M. Friedman, *Hevrah va-dat;* Rivka Shatz, "Reshit ha-masa neged ha-rav Kook," *Molad* 1973/74; David Kna'ani, *Ha-aliyah ha-shniyah ve-yahasah la-dat ve-lamasoret* (Tel-Aviv: 1976); Muki Tzur, *Le-lo kutonet pasim* (Tel-Aviv: 1976).
31. See Friedman, *Hevrah va-dat.*

Index

A

B

C

D

E

F

G

H

L

M

N

O

P

R